Pinochet's Economic Accomplices

Pinochet's Economic Accomplices

An Unequal Country by Force

Edited by Juan Pablo Bohoslavsky,
Karinna Fernández, and Sebastián Smart

LEXINGTON BOOKS
Lanham • Boulder • New York • London

Published by Lexington Books
An imprint of The Rowman & Littlefield Publishing Group, Inc.
4501 Forbes Boulevard, Suite 200, Lanham, Maryland 20706
www.rowman.com

6 Tinworth Street, London SE11 5AL, United Kingdom

This book was previously published in Spanish by LOM Ediciones under the title *Complicidad económica con la dictadura chilena. Un país desigual a la fuerza* in 2019.

British Library Cataloguing in Publication Information Available

Library of Congress Cataloging-in-Publication Data

Names: Bohoslavsky, Juan Pablo, editor. | Fernández Neira, Karinna, editor. | Smart, Sebastián, editor.
Title: Pinochet's economic accomplices : an unequal country by force / edited by Juan Pablo Bohoslavsky, Karinna Fernández, and Sebastián Smart.
Other titles: Complicidad económica con la dictadura chilena. English
Identifiers: LCCN 2020033146 (print) | LCCN 2020033147 (ebook) | ISBN 9781793616494 (cloth) | ISBN 9781793616500 (epub)
Subjects: LCSH: Chile—Economic conditions—1973-1988. | Chile—Economic policy. | Chile—History—1973-1988. | Chile—Politics and government—1973-1988.
Classification: LCC HC192 .C57813 2020 (print) | LCC HC192 (ebook) | DDC 330.983/065—dc23
LC record available at https://lccn.loc.gov/2020033146
LC ebook record available at https://lccn.loc.gov/2020033147

To Antonio Cassese,
who forty years ago began to write this book

Contents

Editors' Note

This book was originally published in Spanish by the Chilean publishing house LOM in January 2019. This English edition includes a foreword written by Juan Méndez, former UN Special Rapporteur on Torture, and several new developments related to the responsibility for economic complicity with the Pinochet's government.

One of the findings of this book is that the physiognomy of the Chilean economy imposed by the dictatorship by force, which benefited a few at the expense of the majority of the population, is still in place. This fact explains, to a great extent, why toward the end of 2019, millions of Chileans protested in the streets against the brutal levels of inequality and why the state reacted with cruel repression against them. Again, in May 2020, the most disadvantaged groups hit harder by the COVID-19-induced crisis are repressed in the streets when claiming that due to the economic impact they are suffering from hunger.

The political and economic power of the corporate accomplices of the dictatorship shaped the Chilean Constitution, created in 1980 during the Pinochet's government, as it has one of the most regressive declarations of economic, social, and cultural rights in the region, with practically no reference to social justice. This is why, in the context of the ongoing constitutional reform process in Chile, recognizing the highest legal status of economic, social, and human rights as well democratizing the generation and distribution of resources in the country to ensure their realization, is intrinsically linked to the accountability of the dictatorship's accomplices.

In his most recent book, Samuel Moyn argues that human rights are "not enough" to address social and economic inequality. We will not contest this idea here; we will just say that it very much depends on what we consider human rights law and its implications for the economic policies. As seen in this book, we believe a precondition for a truly transforming social and economic agenda in Chile is that the Pinochet's economic accomplices, in particular those still benefitting from the radical inequality in the country, are held accountable.

Foreword

From Economic Support of Dictatorship to It's Not 30 pesos, It Is 30 Years

Juan E. Méndez

As the English version of this book sees the light, the conventional wisdom about the "economic miracle" that Chile represents lies shattered under the weight of massive and sustained protests that question the very foundations of the economic model that was first imposed during the Pinochet dictatorship and left virtually untouched after the return of democracy thirty years ago. In particular, the mass mobilizations that have continued to grow in the final quarter of 2019 point out the fallacy of President Piñera's statement, in early October of that year, that Chile was an "oasis" of peace and consensus in a continent marked by instability and authoritarianism. Today, Chileans in large numbers are demanding a fair distribution of wealth and an end to radical inequality. In that sense, Chile has joined similar struggles in all of Latin America, in particular against economic policies premised on guaranteeing growth by rewarding—and even guaranteeing—concentration.

To be sure, that model had seemed successful in Chile and virtually nowhere else in the region. For about four decades, the Chilean economy had produced successful outcomes, if measured in purely macroeconomic terms. The country had seemed to find a niche within a global economy that allowed it sustained growth through exports of its traditional resources such as copper, but also of some agricultural and agro-industrial products. The accommodation of Chile to the needs and demands of the dominant economies of the world was made possible also because of a political consensus whereby center-left and center-right parties succeeded each other through free and fair elections without challenging the fundamentals of the economic model that was Pinochet's enduring legacy.

It would be unfair to present that consensus as leaving the structures of the dictatorship wholly untouched. In the three decades since the return of democracy, the Chilean political system did not only yield sustainable economic growth. In incremental steps, it also abolished undemocratic institutions such as the "senators for life" that guaranteed that *pinochetista* power would not be threatened by the majority's rule. In terms of social and economic justice, democracy did lift the quality of life for the poorest among Chileans. However, life for the working poor and middle classes continued all this time to be hard. The promise of prosperity for the majority of Chileans was marred by insufficient investment in public education and health, and by a privatized pension system that seemed to guarantee inequality not only in salaries and public benefits but also in the rewards for labors of a lifetime.

The Constitution left by Pinochet was amended (and improved upon, of course) several times in the democratic period. Significantly, however, even now that Constitution contains clauses that guarantee the inequality of distribution of wealth and rewards. That elevation of policy choices to constitutional hierarchy had made it virtually impossible for Chileans to improve their democracy through the political process, and hence the spectacular mobilizations that have shown to the world the weakness of the economic success story that had been Chile. Unsurprisingly, an important demand of the mobilization has been the overhaul of the Constitution. As of this writing, the government as well as the political opposition have come to recognize that need as a way out of the crisis. The other major demand made by the street demonstrators is to conduct that Constitutional reform not through agreements between the established political parties but through an elected Constituent Assembly, as a means to guarantee the broadest political participation in the choices that need to be made. The government and Congress have agreed to constitutional changes but the means through which they will be adopted remains a matter of debate.

An important point brought home by this book is that there has not been accountability for the role played by powerful economic sectors, in Chile but also from abroad, in the mass atrocities committed in the Pinochet era as the indispensable means by which that regressive reorganization of Chilean capitalism, still standing, was achieved. In the 1970s, the role of multinational economic powers in sustaining the dictatorship was known and condemned, at least by some human rights leaders. Chief among them was the late Italian jurist Antonio Cassese, to whom this volume is very deservedly dedicated. At that time, however, the human rights movement was developing an effective methodology to monitor, document, and obtain condemnation for the most serious violations of the rights to life, physical integrity, and fair trial. That methodology, popularized by Amnesty International and later by Human Rights Watch, had great influence in making transnational mechanisms of protection at the United Nations and at regional organs more effective in isolating the governments that insisted on committing mass atrocities. On the other hand, the means of enforcing economic, social, and cultural rights lagged far behind. As a result, the political authoritarianism and ruthless repression by the military government was exposed and condemned; but the accomplices of Pinochet in the international corporate world generally brushed off the criticism of their role in supporting atrocities. Perhaps for the same reason, when Chile recovered democracy, the country did confront the legacy of abuses in exemplary ways, even though in modalities that have been criticized for their "gradualism." Still, Chile today has done more than any other country (except Argentina) to explore and disclose the truth, to offer reparations to all victims and their families, and to investigate, prosecute, and punish war crimes and crimes against humanity.

This book offers reasons and arguments to understand the limitations and weaknesses of the unfinished transition to democracy in Chile. In that sense, it makes a significant contribution to the theories of transitions and more specifically to the field that has come to be known as "transitional justice." Many of the contributors have elsewhere published about transitional justice or have carefully analyzed the specific practices and policies adopted in several countries to address the legacies of mass atrocities left by dictatorship or armed conflict. It has long been a matter of debate whether such policies should focus on the immediate legacy of torture, extra-judicial killings, and forced disappearance of persons, and travesties of justice such as prolonged arbitrary detention, forced exile, and exclusion of persons from society based on ideological grounds. Since those violations took place in each country against the background of drastic policies of negative redistribution of wealth, some have argued that initiatives to redress only violations of civil and political rights are insufficient and in fact ignore the plight of countless—and unnamed—victims of discrimination based on social standing—in other words, the majorities of citizens that are counted as the "losers" in the regressive distribution of wealth and income. In any event, it has never been explained how violations of economic, social, and cultural rights could be redressed by means of truth-telling, criminal prosecutions, reparations schemes, and measures of non-repetition, which have been the preferred mechanisms adopted in most countries undergoing transitions to democracy. At the same time, as some of the authors in this volume have demonstrated, the actual transitional justice exercises in Latin America have never really ignored the social and economic background against which thousands of persons suffered torture, disappearance, or political murder. In fact, an effort has always been made to understand the economic and other structures that made possible—and even required—the tragedy of mass atrocity, and what has been correctly identified as facilitating those violations has in large measure referred to the struggle for control of economic policy and more specifically ownership of means of production and appropriation of the results of wealth creation.

Nowhere more clearly that in Chile has that connection between repression and economic rewards been established. That relationship has been present in virtually every military coup d'etat or civil/military dictatorship in the region, at least as one of the ultimate purposes for unleashing extreme repressive policies. Even as dictators and their sycophants alluded to "subversion" as a threat to national security that required extreme measures, it was always clear that their definition of subversion went well beyond the armed organizations that conducted violent actions, in some cases properly categorized as terrorism. The definition of "subversives" also included neighborhood activists, trade union leaders and rank-and-file members, students and academics, priests and ministers of religion who questioned the status quo, lawyers who defended those trapped in the repressive policies. In other words, subversives were all those who had to be neutralized if the transfer of wealth from the poor to the rich was to be achieved. Clearly, success of that aim was only possible through massive and systematic violations of human rights. In other countries, the military and their accomplices only partially succeeded in their fundamental purpose and as a result, when transition to democracy was possible the regressive model was at the very least under discussion. In Chile, the beneficiaries of that radical change were protected from accountability for their support of Pinochet because at the recovery of democracy the political system felt that political and economic stability demanded a continuation of those policies. As stated earlier, the democratic governments since 1989 did correct some injustices, particularly in the search for truth, justice, reparations, and measures of non-repetition for the many serious crimes committed during the Pinochet dictatorship. They also corrected some undemocratic aspects of the political architecture left by Pinochet. And even in the social and economic sphere, some measures have been taken to address extreme poverty. The prosperity that has been achieved—albeit with unfair distribution of wealth—has also made it possible for Chile to achieve through infrastructure programs. In social issues such as racial inequalities against indigenous peoples, lack of protection of the environment, gender discrimination including against LGBTI persons, denial of reproductive rights and restrictions in access by the poor to quality education, progress has been very slow even as the society itself has become tolerant and receptive to diversity. And most fundamentally, the entrenched economic model has continued to produce a scandalous gap in income and wealth between the majority of Chileans and those who still hold the reins of political as well as economic power.

And yet the majority of Chileans seem to have reached a point in which the inequality has become intolerable. It is time to correct the legacy of Pinochet in terms of the economic model he imposed and the continuity of which he attempted to guarantee for the future. At least, Chile seems to be on the verge of ensuring a deeper sense of democratic participation. It may be possible that Chileans, in free and participatory democratic debate, will decide what to keep of economic policy and what to drop. If that happens, the country's democracy will have leaped forward in quality and depth. This book could not be more topical or timely.

Washington, DC, December of 2019.

Chapter 1

Complicity in Context

It's the Economy, Stupid!

Juan Pablo Bohoslavsky

The 1973 military coup, the consolidation of the dictatorial government, and the atrocities that it committed had the purpose of creating the necessary conditions for the implementation of economic policies that would benefit a minority in the country and abroad, and, consequently, would be rejected by a large part of the population.[1] The rationality of the dictatorship was primarily economic. The strong redistributive bid that started all over the world in the 1970s, exacerbated by the implications of the Cold War for the region, became a reality in Chile.

This book, through its twenty-six chapters, reveals the role that economic actors played during Pinochet's dictatorship, presenting and explaining it from a systemic and interdisciplinary dimension. The book attempts to complete the historical narrative of the dictatorship, as entrepreneurs and businesses' involvement has been virtually absent from public debate concerning Chile's recent past.

The reader will develop an understanding of the fact that economic complicity, which inspired the writing of this book, goes far beyond the cases of corruption and illicit enrichment that were exposed in the Riggs Bank scandal.[2] As explained by the International Commission of Jurists in 2008, the issue at hand is the contributions that enable, exacerbate, or facilitate crime.[3] It is necessary to clarify that both private and state-owned companies can contribute to the perpetration of serious human rights violations, as explained by Fernández and Garcés in their chapter, in relation to the Arauco Fishing Company case and the LAN Chile pilots who complied with orders given by the Chilean secret police, the National Intelligence Directorate (DINA).[4]

This does not mean that every economic actor who has in some way contributed to the consolidation of the dictatorship must now face criminal sanction. There were a wide range of complicit conducts, including commanding the DINA to assassinate trade union leaders, the provision of company facilities and transportation for kidnapping and torture, financial assistance provided to the government with little questioning, information manipulation to ensure the impunity of criminals, and the development of scientific arguments to justify policies of exclusion and/or repression. The chapters by Bohoslavsky and Sferrazza and Bustos explain the legal consequences of each of these actions from the perspectives of international, comparative, and Chilean law.

While accountability is a cornerstone for the consolidation of peace, justice, and democracy, the debate must go beyond the strict framework of legal responsibility. Thus, in addition to broadening the scope of the narrative on the Pinochet dictatorship and providing guidelines for tackling the issue of responsibility of economic accomplices, this book also encourages reflection on how the search for truth, memory, reparations, and nonrecurrence could (and should) consider the role of businesses, entrepreneurs, and economic policies implemented by the government. At the same time, it suggests relating this new narrative concerning economic complicity with the current agenda for social justice. Do socioeconomic problems and constraints which explain the coup and the policies of the dictatorship still persist in democracy?

Why is the economic support that an authoritarian government receives crucial?

Authoritarian governments suffer from a structural deficit of legitimacy; therefore, their remaining in power is subject to the balanced use of two types of instruments: (a) strategically assigning economic resources, by trying to purchase loyalties and support from key sectors of the society; and (b) repressing of certain sectors of society or opportunistically granting civil freedoms to minimize criticism.[5] Buying people's trust and establishing an efficient repressive tool require financial resources.

It is not surprising then, that quantitative analyses indicate that the greater the financial assistance and direct foreign investment the longer these criminal regimes can remain in power.[6] These resources help authoritarian governments to consolidate themselves, that is, to deploy their strategy of buying people's trust and of repression in an effective manner.

How did this dynamic of rational choices and statistical assumptions operate during the Pinochet dictatorship?

First, as explained by Bohoslavsky and Rulli in their chapter, the Pinochet government obtained massive external financing, thanks to its immediate international geopolitical alignment in the fight against communism. This ensured a continuous and sufficient flow of funds even in a context of low growth, high unemployment, and fiscal deficit.

Overall, the instruments and channels through which financial resources were allocated strategically, that is, to gain the support of powerful sectors in

Chilean society, included new policies regarding taxation, budget, industry, forestry, mining, banking and finance, urban development, prisons, social security, foreign trade, and the privatization of state-owned enterprises. All of these sectoral policies are discussed in the chapters of this book. The common denominators of said policies were the economic benefits granted to Chilean elites as well as to national and transnational companies, who fostered inequality in the country, and played the role of accomplices to the regime.

Clearly, the military had its own ideological and political agenda for accessing and remaining in power: defeating communism, reestablishing social order, depoliticizing the masses, and increasing the budget for its sector. From this perspective, the military appears to have used the economic sector as a tool to remain in power.

However, a closer look at that dynamic—which includes, for example, the fact that some of Pinochet's executive officials were the representatives of the very sectors being benefited by the government—will show us how difficult it is to determine the origins of the causative chain: Was the government implementing policies that benefited certain economic sectors so that it could remain in power, or were these sectors supporting Pinochet (and they were doing it before the coup) so that he would implement these policies? The answer to this question can lead us to rethink who was the accomplice in this situation. Economic crimes that greatly benefited military personnel, civilians, and entrepreneurs were another efficient tool for allocating resources and purchasing loyalties. The latter became a reality, for example, in the explicit political support for the government shown by the business chambers or, at the very least, their silence in the face of the crimes against humanity that were being committed. The complicity of journalists, the media, think tanks, and academics can be explained as well not only by their clear ideological and political alignment but also by the material benefits they were receiving.

This micro dynamic had a macro correlate as explained by Ahumada & Solimano and Rodríguez Weber in their respective chapters. The radical and rapid transfer of national wealth (after the coup) in favor of the dominant groups and to the detriment of the working class, which brought on an abrupt increase of socioeconomic inequality, was the result of the imposition of neoliberal economic policies. Discontent was contained with extreme state violence against trade union representatives (see Winn and Vergara's chapter) and with a serious weakening of workers' collective bargaining power, which resulted (see Marzi's chapter) in a clear deterioration of their working conditions (including their salary).

This economic aspect of the Pinochet dictatorship's criminal plan, that is, the *virtuous link* between repression and concentration of wealth, is nothing new. Antonio Cassese, Special Rapporteur appointed in 1977 by the United

Nations (UN) Commission on Human Rights, with a specific mandate to assess the relationship between the financial assistance received by the Pinochet regime and human rights violations that the Chilean population was experiencing at the time, presented a detailed official report in 1978.[7] His main conclusion was that

> As foreign financial assistance largely serves to strengthen and to prop up the economic system adopted by the Chilean authorities, which in turn needs to be based on the repression of civil and political rights, the conclusion is warranted that the bulk of current economic assistance is instrumental in the consolidation and the perpetuation of the current repression of those rights.[8]

This sophisticated 260-page report was neglected for decades; that is why the main conclusions are reproduced in a separate chapter in this volume.

Moreover, while the magnitude and severity of the violent crimes committed by Pinochet's dictatorship are known, it is necessary to point out here that in a context of fiscal constraint and reduction in public expenditure, spending on defense and policing increased significantly—from 14.9 percent of public expenditure in 1969 to 23.3 percent in 1982, while social expenditure decreased.[9] Here again, the rationale behind the use of state resources can be observed: financially sustaining an effective bureaucratic-repressive tool to implement economic policies that generated social and political resistance.

Another factor that corroborates and confirms the link between financial support and the serious human rights violations committed by an authoritarian government was the policy that the James Carter government—in contrast with its predecessors—adopted toward Chile as of 1976: the United States (in addition to other European governments) reduced and eventually stopped military and financial assistance to Chile—a decision based explicitly on the country's human rights situation.[10] The reluctance to contribute financially to the Pinochet regime sought to weaken it and force it to grant civil and political freedoms.

PENDING ISSUE

The Chilean agenda of truth, memory, justice, reparations, and institutional reforms has focused its discursive, legal, political, and institutional resources almost exclusively on violent crimes, marginalizing the role and possible responsibility of the economic accomplices of the Pinochet dictatorship. The debate on the economic rationale that was present during the Pinochet dictatorship was limited almost exclusively to illicit enrichment, brought to light by the Riggs Bank scandal and its shady dealings with Pinochet and his family, and a few other state corruption cases.

This is not a phenomenon exclusive to Chile, but it is part of a general trend of international human rights law to lay responsibility mainly on heads of states and their agents. The responsibility of businesses and their owners who facilitate and/or benefit from authoritarian governments has, in the past, remained off the radar of transitional justice, as Roht-Arriaza explains in her chapter. Even though the Nuremberg trials dealt with the responsibility of businesspeople who contributed to the Nazi regime,[11] this responsibility did not reemerge in transitional contexts but sporadically and partially.

For various reasons, this sense of inertia is changing rapidly, as described by Payne, Pereira and Bernal-Bermúdez in their chapter. On an international level, the work of the UN Human Rights Council, which has crystallized corporations' international obligations regarding human rights, has brought forth a change to the legal paradigm in which only states must respect human rights. Over the past decade, an increasing number of Truth Commissions have incorporated the issue of economic complicity to their agendas. At a regional level, Argentina, Brazil, and Colombia are progressing in the implementation of transitional justice measures that explicitly cover economic accomplices. The international academic literature in this field is also growing exponentially. It is time to ask these questions in the Chilean context, as suggested in a letter sent to the Chilean government, in May 2015, by two independent experts of the UN (one of whom is the author of this book).[12]

Would the Chilean political and economic system fall apart if the accountability radar picked up on economic accomplices? Leigh Payne (one of the authors of this book), together with other experts, developed a quantitative study which arrived at two conclusions relevant to address this question.[13] The first one is that the scope of transitional justice measures (e.g., to extend them to civilian perpetrators) is proportional to the growth and economic development of the countries concerned. The second one is that the chances of implementing measures that are conducive to attain the objectives of transitional justice become greater over time. This data is encouraging in the Chilean context, even more so in light of the experiences of Argentina, Brazil, and Colombia, where despite moving forward with an agenda of accountability for economic complicity, the system has not fallen apart. In any case, the quantitative study previously mentioned, in addition to the legal (binding) nature of accountability of economic accomplices, should not prevent the laying out of an intelligent and realistic strategy in which gradualism can be a great ally.

Following on from this, it is also important to highlight that the Supreme Court of Chile sentenced on November 16, 2017, Francisco Luzoro Montenegro (businessman and former President of the Paine trade union of lorry owners) to twenty years in prison for the murders of farmers committed in the Paine commune in 1973, in conjunction with repressive state forces.[14] Also, in March 2018, the Appeals Court of Concepción prosecuted executives and members of staff of the CMPC paper company as accomplices in the Laja-San Rosendo case, which involves the murder of nineteen workers who were executed in 1973 as a result of the information, guidance, and logistic help provided to the Chilean police by the accused, who not only identified the targets but also aided with the executions and the cover-up afterward.[15]

Nevertheless, Chile could (and should) do more regarding this subject. In the first place, a commission for investigating economic complicity during the dictatorship could be established in parliament. This commission should be composed of representatives of government bodies, the civil society, networks of victims and business chambers, and its powers, as well as enough resources, should be ensured. The work of the Commission of Inquiry, which analyzed alleged irregularities in the privatization of state-owned companies before 1990, and was created in the Lower Chamber in 2004, is a relevant precedent in this area. The Human Rights Program of the Ministry of Justice and Human Rights, whose goal is promoting legal actions that help to determine the whereabouts and the circumstances of death or disappearance of the people who were forcefully disappeared, detained, or executed during the dictatorship, should provide legal counseling to the victims' families who decide to bring civil actions against complicit companies and businesspeople while demanding compensation and a truthful account of what happened (the subplot of collusion and crimes involved). In the cases where complicity was detrimental to the national treasury, it is the state who should seek the corresponding reparations.

Furthermore, in some cases, the Ministry of Justice and Human Rights can file criminal complaints against the accomplices, as has been recently established by the Chilean jurisprudence quoted in previous paragraphs. Civil and criminal investigations against accomplices, as well as those against the authors of violent crimes, mostly committed by the police or the military, should not be limited to examining, prosecuting, and judging individual violent acts of the past, but should also help to shed light on the social, political, and economic background of these crimes and their relation to the present.[16]

The companies involved in these processes should also carry out unambiguous and cooperative internal investigations with the goal of establishing accountability and, when necessary, providing material or symbolic reparations to victims. This was the course of action that some of the multinational companies that contributed to the Nazi regime adopted. Memorials, plaques, and museums can also be built and dedicated to remembering the role played by companies and businesspeople during the dictatorship. Along these lines, history and human rights study programs should include and examine these issues.

Last, institutional reforms to guarantee non-repetition can be implemented by, for example, removing (and invalidating for future cases) the benefits gained through complicity with authoritarian governments, as well as banning complicit businesspeople from holding public office.

The architecture of the political, economic, and social systems designed and imposed by the dictatorship can in many ways constitute a heavy burden on the Chilean society even today, as explained by Julio Pinto Vallejos in the final chapter, which clearly shows how the past, present, and future are inherently connected. Economic inequality in the present, with its political, social, economic, and cultural implications, is deeply rooted in the most violent period of the country's history and looms over its future.

AUTHORS AND CHAPTERS

The authors come from a wide range of disciplinary, methodological, geographical, and ideological backgrounds, which has guaranteed the comprehensive and diverse nature of this book. The majority of its chapters were presented and discussed at two workshops organized to enhance their synergy and a systemic approach. The first took place at the University of Oxford in May 2017 and the second at the University of Valparaíso in July of the same year.

In addition to this introduction, the book consists of six sections with a total of twenty-six chapters. The section entitled "Economic Complicity—Past and Present" opens with chapter 2 , written by Naomi Roht-Arriaza, who presents and analyzes the reasons why, in recent decades, the matter of economic complicity in authoritarian regimes did not deserve special attention in the field of transitional justice, as well as why this issue has become so important in the recent years. The importance of discussing economic complicity specifically in Chile is tremendous, according to the author, first because for many years the country was considered the *poster child* of how neoliberalism and authoritarianism, together, brought prosperity to the Chilean society. Second, due to the rampant corruption during the dictatorship that resulted in the barely studied link between systematic state looting and the profound deficits of state services during democracy. And third, because the failure to consider corporate complicity, as well as the way in which economic policies have contributed to the deterioration of human rights, led to a *tunnel vision* of what human rights are, marginalizing economic and social rights. The author also describes recent developments in Argentina and Brazil in the field of responsibility for economic complicity.

Chapter 3 is a reproduction of an article by the world-renowned Italian lawyer, Antonio Cassese, published in the *Texas International Law Journal* in 1978. It summarizes the comprehensive report presented by the UN Special Rapporteur from the same year, which studied the impact of foreign economic aid and assistance on human rights in Chile. It concludes that, on the one hand, most of this assistance helped to strengthen and keep in power a system that pursued a policy of systematic human rights violations; on the other hand, to obtain economic assistance, the government had to ensure a "healthy" economy, which implied a policy of wealth distribution to the detriment of the vast majority of the population. It was a cyclic relationship: economic assistance strengthened the regime and facilitated the perpetration of human rights violations, and in turn, the vicious economic model attracted investments, given the resulting high profitability.

In chapter 4, Karinna Fernández and Sebastián Smart critically analyze the contributions and challenges that Cassese's Report considered (see the previous chapter). On the one hand, they highlight the report's novel methodology as regards the understanding of the relationship between a country's economic and financial assistance and human rights violations, the interrelationship and interdependence of human rights, and the scope of the principle of noninterference in domestic affairs. On the other hand, it highlights Cassese's ability to critically describe the Chilean social and economic context and link this to the financial aid the country was receiving and the massive human rights violations that were being perpetrated. Finally, the chapter points out the pending issues regarding Cassese's contribution almost four decades ago. These include the proper assessment of the report, its contribution to the current debates, and the establishment of responsibilities.

In chapter 5, Elvira Domínguez Redondo and Magdalena Sepúlveda Carmona further explore what happened with the *Cassese Report* once it was officially published, looking for key points to understand the past and the possibilities that the future holds. This is analyzed in the context of the delayed and weak reaction of the UN human rights monitoring mechanisms, special procedures in particular, in the face of economic, social, and cultural rights violations and the complicity of companies. Notwithstanding the gradual progress in this subject, an (unjustified) dichotomy persists in human rights (civil and political on the one hand, economic, social, and cultural on the other) within the UN system. Some of the reasons why the *Cassese Report* was received with indifference remain, while others do not, and this allows for the chance to promote a more robust international agenda in Chile regarding economic, social, and cultural rights as well as corporate accountability.

In chapter 6, Leigh Payne, Gabriel Pereira, and Laura Bernal-Bermúdez present the results from their database, taking into account the transitional justice mechanisms incorporated from the Nazi crime trials onward, and all over the world, and demonstrate the existence of greater accountability for the economic accomplices than originally thought. This can be seen in the work of truth commissions and the legal proceedings that are presented throughout the text. Latin America has been playing a leading role in this process, where social and legal mobilization as well as institutional innovation and strategies have produced important, yet limited, outcomes. The political context helps counterweight powerful veto players in the business community. The chapter specifically applies its Archimedes' Lever Approach to the Paine case in Chile.

The section "Pinochet's Economy" begins with chapter 7, where José Miguel Ahumada and Andrés Solimano reflect on the neoliberal economic model imposed by the dictatorship and its legacy for democracy. Three phases of the Pinochet dictatorship are analyzed and categorized into different periods: the *capitalist restoration* (1973–1975), the *neoliberal-revolutionary* phase of the establishment of a new economic model (1975–1981) followed by the first major crisis of this model in 1982–1983, and the subsequent recovery based on greater financial regulations and promotion of exports (1984–1989). Finally, the authors evaluate the economic results (e.g., the concentration of wealth) and social effects (marked inequalities) of the Pinochet period, and its progress toward the establishment of a neoliberal market society, in which, after 1990, these traits become deeper and more widespread. They conclude that, although the democracy's political economy has been subordinated to the economic regime originally established during the Pinochet dictatorship, this feature of Chilean society is now challenged by several actors that did not benefit from this scheme.

In chapter 8, Juan Pablo Bohoslavsky and Mariana Rulli explain the financial assistance that the Pinochet regime received using a rational choice approach. They examine the Chilean economic policy and performance, focusing on the role of financial aid provided by multilateral, bilateral, and private lenders in terms of political, economic, fiscal, and budgetary support of the regime. Then, they present the United States' stance toward Pinochet's government, in particular, the financial policy during the Carter administration which was influenced by the administration's assessment of the human rights situation in Chile. The chapter concludes with legal considerations of the responsibility for economic complicity and presents the progress that has been recorded by the countries of the region.

In chapter 9, Sebastián Smart argues that the Chilean extractivist model, as it is known today, originated during the Pinochet dictatorship and, in essence, continues to this day. The chapter begins by analyzing the main characteristics of the extractivist model implemented during the dictatorship. It then proceeds to critically present the arguments put forward in the dictatorship (and that are still present in a democracy) to defend this model. Finally, the chapter describes how the economic actors who entered the mining business with Pinochet have become stronger over the past few decades, which explains the close link that still exists between extractivism, state capture, and concentrated appropriation of rent in that sector.

In chapter 10, Javier Rodríguez Weber specifically addresses the problem of economic inequality in Chile from a historical perspective, focusing in particular on the significant deterioration of income distribution that occurred under the Pinochet dictatorship. The growth of inequality was not caused by the free operation of supply and demand but by strict economic, social, and criminal policies (repression of the trade union movement), the most prominent being the legal and practical (violent) containment of work-related demands, the privatization (and commodification) of key services and companies in the economy with strong social implications (such as health and education), and a monetary, financial, and budgetary policy plan with regressive results, particularly during crises. Growing inequality in Chile caused, among several other damaging effects to society, a rise in unemployment and a drop in real wages. Equally, the decrease in social spending caused a slowdown in the improvements in education and health systems, which had characterized the period of 1940–1970. Those structural reforms, implemented during the Pinochet dictatorship, explain the strong resistance that the democratic governments and the trade union movement still face in their attempt to prevent Chile from being one of the most unequal countries in the world.

In chapter 11, Marcos González Hernando and Tomás Undurraga explain and reflect on the role that intellectuals played in Chile in terms of the promotion, legitimacy, and consolidation of the dictatorship, and how they used this to their advantage. The symbolic capital that a large number of experts and scientists (as well as the institutions that brought them together) deliberately provided to the Pinochet dictatorship, with self-interests in mind, had a decisive influence on the way in which its policies, and even its crimes, were understood and judged, an influence that is still prominent today. Since the 1973 democratic interruption, these intellectuals have justified the subsequent human rights violations and the imposition of a political-economic model of exclusion without the checks and balances of democratic procedures. They also took advantage of privileged information and access to public resources for private enrichment, and consolidated an academic context in which censorship and marginalization of other positions were acceptable. The analysis includes the role of lawyers, economists—in particular, the Chicago Boys—the media, university lecturers, political scientists, engineers, and private think tanks. The account is completed with the experience of a few research centers that resisted the attacks and offered a critical view of the government and their policies.

The section "A Game of Support, Corruption and Material Benefits" starts with chapter 12 in which Rodrigo Araya Gómez gives an account of the support that chambers of commerce provided to the Pinochet regime. The chapter begins by explaining that these chambers of commerce initially carried out several forceful measures against the Allende government to destabilize and eventually overthrow it. Once Pinochet came into power, the chambers' representatives publicly and explicitly endorsed him while demanding complete free enterprise. Representatives of these chambers were members of the regime's economic cabinet. Their support was self-serving: this economic sector benefited (to different extents depending on the sector and year) from the redistribution of national wealth and the repression of the opposition, both of which were a result of the new neoliberal economic policy of the Pinochet dictatorship. Therefore, it is not surprising that these chambers did not report the human rights violations that were being committed in the country. The government was subject to only restrained and limited criticism when the economic situation dramatically deteriorated. During the transition, the chambers accepted the need to engage in dialogue with other social actors. However, free enterprise and silence in the face of the atrocities of the recent past continued as union policies. In fact, in 1988 the chambers of commerce joined the "Yes" campaign during the run-up to the referendum.

In chapter 13, Carla Moscoso presents the role played by the media during the dictatorship. It begins by explaining that the private structure of the media in Latin American strongly depends on the economic and political elites. It then goes on to describe the historical progression of the media market in Chile, which was also dependent on and dominated by the national elite. The chapter ends by explaining how the dictatorial policy of persecution and commercialization of the media system resulted in the loss of pluralism and a market concentration that continues to this day. This strategy involved the complicity of the most important cultural industries, namely, the radio, television, and the written press. Through their information policies and articles concealing and/or exonerating human rights violations, they assured the hegemony of the military regime. They helped silence or cover up criticisms on the social cost of economic policies, while simultaneously glorifying consumer culture even above civil liberties and political freedoms. For the larger conspirators within the media, this agreement resulted in direct economic benefits and/or guarantees to compete in an increasingly deregulated market. Few media companies attempted to resist these attacks of censorship and persecution, and those who did suffered the consequences.

In chapter 14, Mariana Rulli describes the process and consequences (even today) of the privatization of the Chilean pension system in 1980, which was carried out without any room for social dialogue or political involvement of workers or trade unions. This reform directly benefited and strengthened a Chilean economic elite linked with the international financial groups that owned the pension fund administrators (Administradoras de Fondos de Pensiones—AFP). The only sector of the workforce that was not forced to adopt the new system was the armed forces. The transition from one system to the other implied a massive rise in fiscal expenditure for the state, which in addition to higher administrative costs for affiliates, limited and unequal coverage for the general population, a slowdown in the development of capital markets, enormous profits for AFPs and high market concentration in that sector constitute one of the most costly legacies passed on by the dictatorship, and account for a large part of the current economic and social inequality in the country.

In chapter 15, Sebastian Smart explains how and why the Pinochet dictatorship carried out a broad and unprecedented process of privatization of land and state companies operating in a large number of sectors of the economy and its economic and social consequences. Reversing the previous period of greater participation of the state in the economy, the Chilean state went from 596 state companies at the beginning of the dictatorship to only 49 in 1989. Between 1974 and 1975 the companies that had been intervened by the democratic government were restituted to their former owners, between 1976 and 1981 multiple companies directed by CORFO (Corporación de Fomento de la Producción in Spanish, Corporation of Production Promotion). were auctioned, and after the crisis of 1982 the so-called popular capitalism began, that is, the sale of share packages of the most important state companies to leverage the capital market, the privatization of banks and pension funds. This process of privatization generated a huge concentration of property and income, and an underfinanced state, all of which has contributed to the current inequality rates. The privatizations were plagued by irregularities, gross conflicts of interest, and acts of corruption that harmed the national treasury and benefited concentrated economic groups that were close to the government, the military, or public officers. The violent conquest of the state apparatus and the consequent opacity in the handling of public funds, the lack of freedom of the press, and the absence of state counter-powers made this massive privatization process possible.

In the section entitled "Repressive Rules and Procedures for Corporations," Daniela Marzi Muñoz presents chapter 16 on the legal changes that affected trade unions' rights. An aspect of these changes all shared was the deterioration of the collective rights of employees, thus weakening their bargaining power. The so-called "Plan Laboral," implemented in 1979, involved the decentralization of collective bargaining at the company level, the use of resources to ensure that strikes did not paralyze economic activity, the dissolution of trade unions (even within the same company), and the depoliticization of their bargaining field. The degradation of collective labor rights occurred alongside a deterioration in individual rights which regulated working conditions. The structure of this (anti-) trade unionist reform remains virtually intact, even after the reform of law No. 20,940 in 2016. This is reflected in the small number of trade unions in the country.

In chapter 17, Ángela Vergara and Peter Winn describe the depth, breadth, and the social, economic, and political implications of the deterioration of labor rights and trade union activity that the Pinochet regime violently imposed. The authors explain precisely how workers' collective and individual rights were undermined by the "Plan Laboral," both practically and legally. Practically by repressing workers and their representatives; legally by suppressing, loosening, or deregulating a wide range of labor rights related to trade union activity (e.g., strikes) and working conditions (such as redundancy pay and working hours, among others). This form of repression and labor policy correlates and is consistent with the imposition of a neoliberal economic model that resulted in the exclusion of the majority of the population and the enrichment of select few business groups. The deregulation of the labor market and the weakening of trade union activity were two of the most entrenched legacies in the transition from dictatorship to democracy.

Chapter 18, by Silvio Cuneo Nash, examines the impact of economic policies imposed during the dictatorship on current incarceration rates in Chile. Under the dictatorship, the dismantling of the welfare state marked the start of a process of poverty management through increased repression and imprisonment, justified through penal populism. Nash's premise, which can also be applied to other countries, is that the neoliberal model that proposes economic deregulation—resulting in disruption of basic social services, job insecurity, and segregation of the population—has generated a policy of criminal overregulation. He concludes that the imposition of policies of privatization, deregulation, and cuts was compensated for by a larger penal state, which has rooted itself even more securely in democracy. In short, the context of economic segregation and criminalization of poverty in Chile has been, and still is, one of the contributing factors in the exceptionally high rate of imprisonment in the country.

José Francisco Vergara-Perucich unravels and explains the repressive urban policy of the Pinochet government in chapter 19, with regard to the development of Santiago. The policy was based on the use of eviction, segregation, and violence as tools to increase profits for certain economic groups and ensure that exclusively the wealthiest people had access to the city's most valuable land. Taxation and public policies were introduced, by force when necessary, through the state's repressive regime, with the aim of social control by managing the transformation of the city. Through these measures and policies, repressive city planning became a feature of Santiago. Real estate, which was handed over to the market, generated (and continues to generate) huge income for the developers, at the expense of the violent displacement of thousands of impoverished residents to the surrounding areas, who, if they were lucky, got a ramshackle house and access to basic services. All of this further fuelled the socioeconomic segregation of the city, in which the democratic and solidarity components have had a marginal effect.

In chapter 20, Cristián Olmos Herrera explains how the national mining model imposed by the dictatorship still has deep (negative) social, cultural, and natural resources-related implications for local communities in northern Chile. The legal and institutional platform forged during the Pinochet administration and reinforced during democracy, which extensively commodifies the extraction of minerals and the use of water, has facilitated for the mining sector to put pressure on northern communities to exploit their water resources both above and underground. The case of the mining company Sociedad Química y Minera (SQM) in the Atacama Desert is presented in detail, a company that grew its business (and power) during the dictatorship but that was not weakened in democracy, and that for many years was administered by Pinochet's son-in-law.

In chapter 21, José Aylwin describes the counter-reform of the forestry industry brought about by the Pinochet government, and how it still adversely affects the rights of the Mapuche people, the environment, and the socioeconomic indicators of the regions involved. The author explains that the large forestry companies supported the coup, and subsequently the dictatorship, with the expectation that Allende's sectoral policy, geared to the state management of forestry resources, would be reversed. There were also many high-ranking public officials of the regime from the forestry industry. All this support resulted in a substantial expansion of the territories that they owned, many of which were traditionally inhabited by the Mapuche people, and generous financing through state subsidies and exemptions. Large forestry companies also benefited by being able to purchase privatized state businesses for a fraction of its market value. Some of these businesses became involved in criminal repression against their workers. While the Mapuche people's social protest against the persistence of this system in the forestry industry has grown in the past twenty years, and despite increasing support by regional and international organizations, crimes and repression against them have intensified.

In the section "Case Studies," Karinna Fernández and Magdalena Garcés Fuentes present the cases of Pesquera Arauco and Colonia Dignidad in chapter 22. The state-owned Pesquera Arauco provided their company's resources (such as facilities, vehicles, and manpower) to the DINA so they could carry out multiple crimes against humanity. As for the leaders of Colonia Dignidad, they did not only commit the crimes they are known for, such as sexually abusing the children they were allegedly caring for; they also made their facilities available to the DINA so they could torture, murder, and forcefully disappear victims. During the dictatorship, Colonia Dignidad benefited from the state's generously lax taxation and control. Directors from both businesses benefitted economically. Judicial investigations in both cases have progressed very slowly without satisfactory results for the victims and their families. They continue to move forward without a holistic methodology for the inclusion of corporate collusion in a broader narrative which explains the mechanics of civil–military relations as a whole.

In chapter 23, Nancy Guzmán describes the role of Agustín Edwards Eastman and his newspaper El Mercurio before and during the dictatorship. On the one hand, it explains his role as instigator and facilitator of the democratic breakdown, which was demonstrated, among other things, by the smear campaign El Mercurio launched against the government of Salvador Allende. Furthermore, the newspaper systematically and deliberately covered up the serious human rights violations being committed in the country. Through a strategy arranged and agreed on with the government, a large media manipulation campaign was launched to hide the crimes committed by the state from the general public, while accusing the persecuted opposition groups themselves. The chapter also discusses the funds El Mercurio received from the United States and foreign companies to promote an anticommunist agenda (the unclear objective for which the United States had earmarked the money) and the financial assistance the group received from Pinochet to ensure a smooth transition.

The section "Legal Elements of Economic Complicity" begins with chapter 24 by Juan Pablo Bohoslavsky. It analyzes the legal elements of responsibility for corporate complicity from an international and comparative law perspective. It begins by addressing the question of whether conduct that involves economic contributions to a regime that systematically commits serious human rights violations implies unlawful behavior. The answer is, in principle, affirmative. It goes on to study the complexities of the criteria for adjudicating civil liability for complicity: the causal link, the subjective element, and the damage. The criteria used to determine whether the supply of a commodity was legal or not depends on the foreseeable consequences of their use, rather than their intrinsic nature. Also, the chapter states that the possible civil actions for corporate complicity are not subject to statutes of limitations under international standards.

In chapter 25, Pietro Sferrazza Taibi and Francisco Bustos analyze whether economic conspirators can be held liable in a criminal or civil sense and, if so, under what laws. First, they examine the scope and severity of a crime with regard to responsibility, participation, and instigation, explaining how these criminal offenses (criminal conspiracy in particular) function within the complex web of actors and relationships involved in economic complicity during the Chilean dictatorship. Second, they describe how the Chilean legal system works regarding civil responsibility for complicity, demonstrating that, as in the case of criminal responsibility, because the crimes dealt with are crimes against humanity, statutes of limitations do not apply in this area.

In the final section, entitled "Conclusions and Prospects," Julio Pinto Vallejos presents in chapter 26 the genealogy of the business paradise: how the complicities of businesspeople during the dictatorship explain (and deepen) the present inequalities. The chapter presents three periods that describe the symbiosis between the business world and the Pinochet government. First, the chapter addresses the fears encouraged and exacerbated by the business community against the Popular Unity government and its redistribution policies. Then the author describes the maximized profits that the concentrated business amassed thanks to the neoliberal policies imposed by the Pinochet government. The growing commodification of rights (education, housing, social security, health care, rights of indigenous peoples, and so on) contributed to this inequality. Finally, the post-dictatorial legacies of that set of connivances that are still projected on Chile are analyzed. In the transition, the business community distanced itself from the excesses of the dictatorship but consolidated (and even expanded) the neoliberal policies and the inequality gap. The author warns that as a consequence of this economic model, individualism and materialism are deeply rooted in Chilean society, and he also wonders if this model is consistent with certain fundamental human values.

NOTES

1. See Naomi Klein, *The Shock Doctrine: The Rise of Disaster Capitalism* (Buenos Aires: Paidós Ediciones, 2008).

2. "Corte Suprema ordena decomiso de bienes de Pinochet por US$ 1,6 millones," *La Tercera*, August, 2018, available at https://www.latercera.com/nacional/noticia/corte-suprema-ordena-decomiso-bienes-pinochetus-16-millones/294647/.

3. International Commission of Jurists, *Corporate Complicity & Legal Accountability*, vol. I (Geneva: ICJ, 2008), 9- ss.

4. *The National Commission for Truth and Reconciliation Report*, T° 2 (Santiago, 1996), 722–27.

5. Bueno de Mesquita Bruce et al., *The Logic of Political Survival* (Massachusetts: MIT Press, 2003); Ronald Wintrobe, *The Political Economy of Dictatorship* (Cambridge: Cambridge University Press, 1998).

6. Juan Pablo Bohoslavsky and Abel Escriba-Folch, "Rational Choice and Financial Complicity with Human Rights Abuses: Policy and Legal Implications," in *Making Sovereign Financing & Human Rights Work*, eds Juan Pablo Bohoslavsky and Letnar Jernej (Oxford: Hart Publishing, 2014), 17–32.

7. Antonio Cassese, "Study of the Impact of Foreign Economic Aid and Assistance on Respect for Human Rights in Chile" (*Cassese Report*), vols. I–IV 1978, (E/CN.4/Sub.2/412).

8. Ibid., p. 24.

9. Thomas Sheetz, "Military Expenditure in Chile, Peru and Argentina," *Economic Development* 25, 1985. This data in absolute values points to a spending of 624.3 million dollars in 1969 and 1,263 million dollars in 1982 (both values in dollars in 1977).

10. Robert Bejesky and Juan P. Bohoslavsky, "Carter's Human Rights Policy towards Southern Cone Countries: A Contribution to the Current Debate on Financial Complicity," in Bohoslavsky & Cernic, op. cit., 302–22.

11. *United States v. Goering* (The Nuremberg Trial), 6 F.R.D. 69, 112 (Int'l Mil. Trib. 1946).

12. OL CHL 1/2015, 26 May 2015, available at: https://spdb.ohchr.org/hrdb/30th/public_-_OL_Chile_26.05.15_(1.2015).pdf.

13. Tricia Olsen, Leigh Payne and Andrew Reiter, "At What Cost? The Political Economy of Transitional Justice," *Taiwan Journal of Democracy*, vol. 6, no. 1 (2010): 165–84.

14. Role No. 1568-2017.

15. C.A. Concepción (March 15, 2018), Role No. Sección Criminal-Ant-174-2017.

16. Hannah Franzki, "Criminal Trials, Economic Dimensions of State Crime, and the Politics of Time in International Criminal Law. A German-Argentine Constellation" (Doctoral thesis, University of London, Birkbeck, December 2016), available at http://bbktheses.da.ulcc.ac.uk/304/.

Section 1

ECONOMIC COMPLICITY—PAST AND PRESENT

Chapter 2

The Belated Centrality of the Economic Dimension in Transitional Justice

A Case Study

Naomi Roht-Arriaza

INTRODUCTION

Chile was one of the pioneers in carrying out—and combining—measures of what has become known as "transitional justice." I define these as the suite of policies and practices that a society uses to confront past massive or systematic human rights violations. It was one of the first countries to use a truth commission to clarify and recognize the patterns, methods, and consequences of grave violations of basic rights. The slow development of public policies to support victims and their families and to prosecute those responsible, and the commitment to the reforms needed so that these events never happen again, also provides important lessons for the region and the world. However, when it comes to the issue of the complicity of economic and financial actors, the contribution of the private sector to the design and implementation of repression, how these actors benefited from repression, and the corruption and plunder of the country's resources by the schemes of the dictatorship, Chile has done very little.

The need to confront the economic aspects of dictatorships and armed conflicts is more and more evident, for backward-looking as well as forward-looking reasons, as a factor in explaining the limits of present-day democracies. In this initial exploration, I attempt to explain why the incorporation of economic aspects into the discussions on transitional justice has taken so long, and how this is quickly changing around the world.

In Chile, this discussion is important for three reasons. First, the Chilean experience under dictatorship is generally considered nationally and internationally as a combination of great economic success accompanied by unfortunate human rights "excesses," as though the economic policies were completely disconnected from the destruction of labor unions and peasant associations, and to the silencing of any criticism of the exploitation and export of the country's natural resources. For a long time, Chile was the poster child for arguments that "authoritarianism," with its "labor discipline," its privatization of pensions and services, and the reductions in the state budget could eventually create the conditions for a stable democracy. And that therefore the unfortunate violations of human rights were worth it. Especially in light of the 2019 demonstrations against this model in Chile, it is past time to dismantle this narrative.

Second, an important aspect of the Chilean case is the relationship between dictatorship and corruption. A corollary of the arguments on the supposed success of the dictatorship's economic policy was the insistence that General Pinochet and his circle were paragons of personal probity, torturers perhaps, but at least not thieves. This was part of the dictator's continuing political appeal. It was not until the Riggs Bank scandal, when in the course of a larger money-laundering investigation, the U.S. Congress uncovered some of the secret accounts in offshore tax havens, the tax evasion, and irregular arms deals of the Pinochet family. It was only then that the right-wing political parties had no choice but to distance themselves from the general as a political figure.[1] But the relationship between the systematic plunder of the state during the dictatorship and the problems confronting state services in democracy has been insufficiently studied.

Third, the silence surrounding the complicity of the private sector, the banks, the large landlords, and on the ways in which economic policies contributed to the human rights disaster, led to a warped and anemic view of human rights. During quite some time, the term *human rights* was a synonym of concern for enforced disappearances, or at most, with torture and extrajudicial executions. I am not arguing that these were not, and are not, fundamental rights, nor am I in any way minimizing the need and priority of the struggle to end these violations. But during democracy, with a series of new challenges, it was harder to expand the popular vision to economic and social rights, reconceptualize human rights in a broader and more integrated fashion, and connect multiple social issues with the idea of defense and promotion of human rights. In part, the insistence on the economic aspects of the dictatorship allows pulling together several threads that have been separate for too long.

This chapter situates these ideas within some general observations on the evolution of the treatment of economic themes and the role of finance capital and economic power within the global rights discourse. First, I consider why it took so long for this approach to take hold, and then I turn to an overview of how, little by little, this panorama has changed.

INITIAL TRANSITIONAL JUSTICE EFFORTS AND THE FOCUS ON BASIC PHYSICAL INTEGRITY RIGHTS

In its first decade or two, the transitional justice agenda focused largely on violations of basic physical integrity rights. Advocates pushed to overturn amnesties and statutes of limitations in cases involving forced disappearances, executions, and torture. The first generation of truth commissions likewise focused on bringing forth evidence of death squads and secret arrests and killings by security forces; only in the past ten years or so have a new generation of truth-seeking exercises gone beyond this same narrow band of violations and violators. Reparations, both through courts and through government administrative programs, were generally limited, where provided at all, to monetary compensation for wrongful death, disappearance, torture, or arbitrary detention or exile, and to health and education services for the survivors and families of victims of those violations. In the Chilean case, for example, neither the Rettig Commission nor the first round of reparations covered anything beyond deaths and forced disappearances; it was only later, with the 2004 Valech Commission report that survivors of torture or detention were included.

This focus on a narrow set of crimes attributed to security forces and government leaders goes back to the origins of transitional justice as a field. Although war crimes trials have existed for centuries, and Nuremberg and other post–World War II trials and reparations programs set some of the basic norms and standards for international justice, the field as we know it today largely originated with the end of the military regimes in Latin America, the fall of Eastern Europe's pro-Soviet regimes, and later the transition to majority rule in South Africa. As Paige Arthur has discussed,[2] the human rights movements' turn to dealing with the past in the wake of a change from dictatorship to elected governments reflected the politics of the moment. In particular, it reflected the failure of both right- and left-wing projects aimed at changing the economic or structural bases of society in "developing" countries. On the right, the theories of the economic take-off of Rostow and others, reflected in the Alliance for Progress, had been unsuccessful. On the left, the revolutionary project of social justice through renegotiating terms of trade and redistributing land and wealth, with its intellectual underpinnings in Marxism and dependency theory, was similarly unsuccessful, with limited exceptions.[3] Combined with this, in most countries of Latin America, by the time of the transition the Left had been defeated, often violently, and with the loss of several generations of social leaders. Its remnants were exhausted and, after the fall of the Berlin Wall in 1989, without a clear economic project. There was a turn from a politics of redistribution to what was seen as a more feasible politics of participation, democracy, and rule of law. This was true in South Africa and Eastern Europe as well. In this context, human rights became synonymous with basic physical integrity and civil rights.

Part of what drove the legal form that many early efforts at transitional justice assumed was the predominance of lawyers, rather than economists, in these early efforts. Lawyers particularly wanted to take advantage of increasingly robust international human rights mechanisms. The early fact-finding mission of the United Nations (UN) Human Rights Commission to Chile in 1975 was the first use of the commission's fact-finding powers outside the sui generis issues of South Africa and Palestine, and it strengthened the commission's ability to react to violations.[4] The Executive Secretary of the Inter-American Human Rights Commission's visit to Chile on October 12, 1973, and of the full Commission on August 2, 1974, combined with the entering into force of the American Convention (Pacto de San José) a few years later, increased the visibility and perceived legitimacy of the regional human rights system. The Torture Convention was being drafted during these years, and opened for signature in 1984.

But even as the international human rights machinery was gearing up and becoming more effective, it was marginalizing economic, social, and cultural (ESC) rights. The UN mechanisms required a showing of a consistent pattern of gross violations,[5] which were interpreted to mean violations of physical integrity and extreme discrimination. The American Convention does not contain ESC rights, and the subsequent Protocol of San Salvador makes very few such rights justiciable before the Inter-American Court.[6] By 1993, the Vienna Conference on Human Rights had declared all rights to be interdependent and indivisible, but this declaration was not followed up by consistent action. It was not until 2013 that individual complaints about violations of ESC rights could be brought to a UN treaty-based expert body.[7] Thus, the emphasis on the use of international judicial or quasi-judicial mechanisms came with an emphasis on some rights and not others.

Soft law[8] on transitional justice also skewed in favor of seeking truth and justice about government and insurgent or militia forces, but not necessarily about their private-sector backers or collaborators. When the UN then Human Rights Commission initially took up the subject of impunity, for example, it divided the subject into two studies: one on civil and political rights, with Louis Joinet as rapporteur; and one on ESC rights, with El Hadji Gisse as rapporteur. Mr. Gisse's report[9] recommended, among other things, criminalization of corruption-related crimes, debt relief for poor countries, and compensation in cases of ESC violations. While Joinet's report was followed up on and eventually updated,[10] there was no follow-up on Gisse's report, and eventually, the concerns he raised were transferred to other experts and taken out of the anti-impunity context, to become part of a development- and debt-related discourse.

One of the first efforts to connect economic policies and external financial support with human rights violations was a report about Chile. The then-expert sub-commission of experts of the UN Human Rights Commission charged Italian professor Antonio Cassese with a report, published in 1978, entitled "Study on the Impact of Foreign Aid and Assistance on Human Rights in Chile."[11] The report analyzes how the policy of suppressing labor rights was designed to attract foreign investment, that the lack of civil liberties affected the quality of public policy decisions, and that foreign aid, in design and implementation, supported the authorities' socioeconomic decisions and programs. The economic policy required the repression of basic human rights because its implementation was only possible in the absence of social protest.[12]

Part of the hesitation regarding opening up the discourse and practice of transitional justice to include a broader range of actors and violations was the emphasis on "transition." The paradigm was that of a relatively short period of changeover from one reality to another, accompanied by specific, manageable actions like a (short-term) truth commission or reparations program. Given the pacted or negotiated nature of most transitions and the long-standing and complex issues of structural inequality in Latin America (and South Africa), there was a sense that these larger issues would bog down any specific TJ initiatives, and that the moment in which past-focused initiatives could prosper would quickly pass. In practice, of course, most TJ initiatives have taken far longer than their proponents initially envisioned: reparations programs and trials continue some twenty to thirty years after the events at issue, as Cath Collins has detailed.[13] But concern for speed, manageability, and the politics of coalition dictated a narrow choice of objectives.

The weight of the Inter-American Court and its jurisprudence on ensuring rights and amnesties also affected the conceptualization of transitional strategies in the region. As a human rights body, the focus of the system was (and is) necessarily on states and state actors. Admittedly, from its earliest days, the Inter-American Court of Human Rights recognized that non-state actors could commit violations, but the focus was on the responsibility of the state to prevent the violations, and, if it failed, to investigate, prosecute, and provide redress.[14] The rules of international humanitarian law, which bind both state and non-state actors, were little used in Latin America because neither side was much interested in using them. States did not want these events characterized as "internal armed conflicts" because of the fear that their opponents would be considered legitimate belligerents, while human rights advocates thought that it was wrong to speak of a state of war in cases where a state repressed its (mostly) unarmed civilian population.[15]

The emphasis on state actors, especially political and military leaders and security forces, also derived from an insistence by advocates and family members of victims on the special role of the state as a guarantor of rights. Recognition of this special role counteracted the "theory of the two devils" under which both sides committed equivalent violations. It was politically as well as legally necessary to keep the focus on the state—which meant that other actors, especially economic actors, were largely ignored.

The limitations imposed by a focus on prosecutions also explain why the initial focus of transitional justice was not on economic actors. Criminal prosecutions, which generally require guilt beyond a reasonable doubt for a narrowly defined band of acts, do not deal well with shades of culpability. Passive acquiescence, moral complicity, acceptance of benefit, being a far link in a long causal chain may all be wrongs, but they are generally not criminal acts. Bystanders are not easily reached by the criminal law, which means that the focus turns to the small group of people who gave the orders (or refrained from suppressing the crimes) and who acted on them.[16] So to the extent advocates focused on criminal prosecution as the centerpiece and ultimate goal of their efforts, attention to broader patterns of complicity was abandoned.

Legal doctrines also tend to shield economic actors from criminal liability. The Rome Statute of the International Criminal Court only extends to natural, not corporate, persons. Its definition of aiding and abetting requires that the aider or abettor share the purpose of the principal in committing the crime. This is difficult to prove and a departure from earlier jurisprudence of international tribunals, which required merely that he (or she) know about the crime.[17] In most cases, economic actors were supremely indifferent to the specific purposes of the military, so long as the order was maintained, troublemakers were removed, and profit-making continued.

With respect to truth-telling, the imperative of breaking the silence dominated demands for truth commissions in Latin America, South Africa, and Eastern Europe. This claim for the "right to truth" was based on the security forces' refusal to recognise their involvement in forced disappearances, the use of death squads and "third forces", as well as the widespread use of informants and surveillance. While the Peruvian and Guatemalan official truth commission reports discussed structural factors to a greater or lesser extent as background conditions for violence, the focus was on the actions of armed groups.[18] Similarly, the South African Truth and Reconciliation Commission (TRC) recognized the structural nature of apartheid and held a thematic hearing on the role of business, but its mandate and focus were on those acts that were illegal at the time under South African law, including murder, torture, forced disappearance, and arbitrary detention.

The social networks involved in the fight against impunity and the fight for economic justice have also been separate until recently. The participants, funders, and institutional forums—national and international—have had few points of intersection, and both networks are small and under-resourced, which means little time has been available to work on issues, however worthy, that fall outside each group's stated mandate. Human rights, in part due to the visibility of networks of family members, victims, and advocates, came to be defined largely in terms of civil and political rights in the public space. Those activists, often from a younger generation, working on socioeconomic justice did not frame their demands in terms of rights. It is only quite recently, with the increased visibility of resource-related struggles around indigenous peoples, climate justice, and questionable "development" projects, that the human rights, environment, women's, and development communities have (partially) converged. One way to read the 2019 explosion of unrest in Chile is as a final coming together of many of these strands.

Finally, the governments that replaced repressive regimes or that followed peace deals, and their international supporters, were for the most part content to follow the economic orthodoxy of the time. Transitional justice was seen as important to reestablish the rule of law. But the rule of law prominently included respect for property rights and existing economic arrangements, and was part of a global paradigm that aligned liberal democracy with open markets and the free flow of capital. This was especially true in the 1990s, and in South Africa and Eastern Europe, but it was also the case in Latin America during the period of the Washington Consensus. Under these conditions, new governments were reluctant to antagonize the business community by inquiring into their role in support of repression, or demanding any kind of reparations or anything, for that matter, that might scare off foreign investment. The few initiatives along these lines were largely unsuccessful. South Africa's TRC proposed a one-time surcharge or "wealth tax" on South African business and industry,[19] but the government at the time rejected the idea.

IS THE PANORAMA CHANGING, AND IF SO, WHY?

Starting in the mid-2000s, the reluctance to tackle the economic dimensions of dealing with the past began to change slowly. In part, this is due to the continuing fragility of post-conflict/post-dictatorship countries, where economic and social marginalization drives continuing violence and dampens enthusiasm for democratic reform. The early hopes that trials and truth commissions focused on core crimes and civil and political rights violations would usher in robust, inclusive democracies have, not surprisingly, proven difficult to fulfill. Critics, including many from countries that have implemented one or more transitional justice measures, began to note that despite a wealth of transitional justice measures, the everyday lives of the majority had changed little or even gotten worse. At the same time, the elites who had, by all accounts, been complicit in the violations were enjoying most of the fruits of the new dispensation. Obviously, something was missing.

The critique of transitional justice as too "top-down," too elite-driven, and too responsive to donor rather than local priorities merged with a sense that transitions were not generally a neat, short-term, one-dimensional package but a messy, unpredictable, and longer-term affair. This critique, in turn, coincided with one that found that the emphasis on civil and political rights in transitional justice unnecessarily reflects the—unjustified—privilege those rights receive in Western rights discourse.

There is now greater recognition among academics and policymakers that justice is broader than just criminal justice, and a look at root causes of conflict is a key component of truth-seeking.[20] Moreover, the prevailing view today insists that socioeconomic rights must have their due in considering both the violations and their remedy, although how exactly to do so remains quite uncertain.

Broadening the transitional justice agenda to consider economic violence corresponds to a new attention to ESC rights as both justiciable and necessary, one that emerged with the end of the Cold War. Thus, courts in South Africa, the Philippines, Colombia, and elsewhere have found that such rights may be claimed in court.[21] As mentioned, the UN Optional Protocol on ESC Rights went into force in 2013. The UN Human Rights Council has paid increasing attention to ESC rights, appointing Special Rapporteurs or Representatives on food, water, environment, foreign debt, housing, extreme poverty, and other ESC issues.

Alongside the attention to these rights is a new focus on private actors, especially corporations and banks. The work of UN Special Rapporteur John Ruggie to create a framework[22] and Guidelines[23] on Business and Human Rights led to the formation of a Working Group on Corporate Responsibility at the Human Rights Council and to efforts to create national implementation plans. In June 2014, two resolutions moved forward the process of studying, and eventually drafting, a legally binding instrument on corporations and human rights. While most host countries of large multinational corporations predictably opposed the idea, and any such process would be long, contested, and uncertain, the issue is once more on the table after decades of failed efforts.[24] The Inter-American Commission of Human Rights has appointed a Special Rapporteur on ESC Rights and held thematic hearings on the extraterritorial obligations of states with respect to their businesses, with an emphasis on mining corporations.[25] Other thematic hearings have followed, along with an Advisory Opinion of the Inter-American Court of Human Rights on the environment, which has implications for extraterritorial obligations of states with respect to private business.[26]

Major private banks have signed on to the Equator Principles committing them to socially responsible finance, while multilateral development banks have put in place safeguards and created investigation mechanisms for complaints about their lending.[27] In several countries, national legislation requires attention to trade in conflict minerals; an example is the provision in the U.S. Dodd-Frank Act requiring disclosures about the sourcing of such minerals, or the "Kimberley process," which attempts to restrict the sale of "conflict diamonds."[28] Tort suits in the United States and elsewhere have attacked corporate aiding and abetting of core human rights violations.[29] Disclosure regimes, national and international, attempt to trace the use and abuse of corporate funds.[30]

The new attention to private actors is reflected in transitional justice initiatives. The biggest change has come in the findings, and mandate, of some recent truth commissions. The Sierra Leone Truth Commission, for example, placed "the central cause of the war" as "endemic greed, corruption, and nepotism that deprived the nation of its dignity and that reduced most people to a state of poverty."[31] The Commission traced how the actions of elites, including but not limited to the extraction and exploitation of diamonds, had set the stage and contributed to the conflict. Its recommendations were broad-ranging, including land reform, better service delivery, and combating corruption. However, most of the recommendations dealing with ESC rights were not made mandatory.[32] The Liberian Truth Commission also focused on economic root causes, denouncing an "entrenched political and social system founded on privilege, patronage … and endemic corruption which created limited access to education, and justice, economic and social opportunities," as well as recognizing the centrality of "historical disputes over land acquisition, distribution and accessibility."[33] The Kenyan Truth Commission's report has a chapter on Land and Conflict detailing injustices regarding land acquisition, forced eviction, and displacement by colonial authorities, post-independence political and economic elites, and multinational companies.[34] Its most controversial findings, which caused a government attempt to suppress this portion of the report, discussed the illegal expropriation of large tracts of land by powerful families, including that of the former president. The Truth and Dignity Commission of Tunisia investigated violations of ESC rights, especially labor rights. As part of its mandate, the Commission was to identify cases of electoral fraud and corruption, although that part of the mandate was curtailed by powerful private actors.[35]

In Latin America, the focus on the past has also broadened. Argentina and Brazil are until now the clearest examples. Brazil, after years of civil society pressure, in 2012 created a Truth Commission to investigate and clarify grave violations of human rights practiced between 1946 and 1988, indicating the circumstances and authorship. Its final report, presented in December 2014, has a chapter on the contribution of civilians, especially business leaders, to the coup of 1964, the subsequent anti-worker economic measures, and the repression. The report names the businesses and individuals who helped finance, provided locales and support, and helped create repressive bodies. Other chapters detail the participation of landowners and businesspeople in torture, forced disappearance, and arbitrary arrests of workers and peasants.[36] Its recommendation to create a follow-up body to investigate further has not happened, but may be revisited given the election of a new president in 2019.

Argentina also began to consider the role of the private sector in the dictatorship years. There have been a number of criminal cases against businessmen for their role in the disappearance of their workers. In 2014, the Congress approved a new Civil and Commercial Code that declares that there is no statute of limitations on civil (tort) actions alleging the commission of crimes against humanity, including economic complicity in those crimes. Congress also approved a proposal to create a National Truth Commission on Economic Complicity at a national level, and a similar proposal was approved in the province of Río Negro. The Central Bank and the National Insurance Commission created their human rights units to investigate the role of financial actors during the dictatorship, but these did not survive the Macri government. It remains to be seen if the incoming Fernández government will revive these or similar initiatives.

In addition to the work of truth commissions, there have been calls to extend criminal investigations to the financiers of repression and the buyers of conflict minerals, and several criminal cases have been filed around the world. Several factors contribute to the increased willingness to look beyond a narrow group of state agents as perpetrators. First, the very success in some (but not all) countries in overcoming the obstacles and bringing the military and security forces to trial has established that democracy can coexist with trials, that the sky will not fall, the military will not stage a new coup d'état, and the economy will not disintegrate if individuals are held to account. This confidence allows for thinking about establishing a more fulsome and complete story about what happened during the years of repression and armed conflict, one that includes the role of actors such as the church or the economic elite.

Second, the distance between groups focused on justice for the crimes of the past on the one hand and those involved in current struggles for justice on the other has decreased. Both groups now find that their issues are interrelated, and that the failure to confront inequality, corruption, and the increasing gap between rich and poor creates the conditions for continuing impunity, criminalization of social protest, and mistreatment and violence against protesters. Thus, for example, many of the disputes around control of natural resources, mining and oil exploration, protection of indigenous and rural communities, and the like bring together the human rights, environmental, and development communities in new ways. Recent demonstrations in the second half of 2019 around the world, including in Chile, have stressed how democracy has not ended the self-dealing of elites or the concentration of wealth in fewer and fewer hands, with dire effects on health, education, and livelihoods. This convergence, in turn, creates new civil society coalitions around a broader narrative of the past, one that explores the roots of today's struggles in a failure to adequately confront the past. It also reflects a generational passing of the torch, to a new generation unencumbered by the defeats of the past and conscious of the increasing inequality and impoverishment of many globalized societies.

NOTES

1. On the Riggs case, see National Security Archive, *The Secret Pinochet Portfolio: Former Dictator's Corruption Scandal Broadens* (March 15, 2005), available at http://nsarchive.gwu.edu/NSAEBB/NSAEBB149/index.htm.
2. Paige Arthur, "How 'Transitions' Reshaped Human Rights: A Conceptual History of Transitional Justice" (2009) 31 *Human Rights Quarterly*, 321.
3. See, in general, Jorge G. Castañeda, *La Utopia Desarmada* (Ariel, 1995).
4. Ingrid Nifosi, *The UN Special Procedures in the Field of Human Rights* (Intersentia, 2005), p. 16.
5. See the language of UNGA Resolutions 1235 and 1503.
6. The Inter-American Commission and Court have addressed economic, social, and cultural (ESC) issues, but largely through the lenses of discrimination, equal protection, protection of property, family life, or others. The San Salvador Protocol only allows cases involving education and labor rights to be taken to the Court. Organization of American States, *Additional Protocol to the American Convention on Human Rights in the Area of Economic, Social and Cultural Rights ("Protocol of San Salvador")*, November 16, 1999, OAS Treaty Series No. 69; 28 ILM 156 (1989). The commission also supervises the implementation of the American Declaration of the Rights and Duties of Man, which contains extensive provisions on ESC rights, but it has not often invoked those provisions.
7. The Optional Protocol of the UN International Covenant on Economic, Social and Cultural Rights, which provides for an individual complaint mechanism to the expert Committee on ESC Rights, entered into force in 2013, and to date has twenty-four state parties.
8. Soft law can be defined as a wide variety of influential but not legally binding norms, including Principles, resolutions of the UN General Assembly, Standard Minimum Rules, Guidelines, and other similar documents.
9. United Nations Sub-Commission on the Promotion and Protection of Human Rights, *Final Report on the Question of the Impunity of Perpetrators of Human Rights Violations (Economic, Social and Cultural Rights)*, 1997 (E/CN.4/Sub.2/1997/8).

10. UN Human Rights Council, *Report of Diane Orentlicher, Independent Expert to Update the Set of Principles to Combat Impunity—Updated Set of Principles for the Protection and Promotion of Human Rights through Action to Combat Impunity*, August 2, 2005, E/CN.4/2005/102/Add.1.

11. See discussion of the study elsewhere in this volume.

12. Commission on Human Rights, Sub-Commission on Prevention of Discrimination and Protection of Minorities, *Study on the Impact of Foreign Aid and Assistance on Human Rights in Chile.* E/CN.4/Sub.2/412 (Vol.II) Aug. 10, 1978, paras. 113 et seq. See also chapter 23 of this book.

13. See, for example, Cath Collins, *Post-Transitional Justice: Human Rights Trials in Chile and El Salvador* (University Park: Penn State University Press, 2010).

14. Velasquez Rodriguez Case, Judgment of July 29, 1988, Inter-Am.Ct.H.R. (Ser. C) No. 4 (1988); Barrios Altos Case, Judgment of November 30, 2001, Inter-Am Ct. H.R. (Ser. C) No. 87 (2001).

15. Chile was something of an exception. Courts found that whether or not there actually was a state of war, the military regime had declared that such a state existed in September 1973 and so was bound to respect the laws of war, including Common Article 3 of the Geneva Conventions. This theory was never unanimously accepted by the human rights groups.

16. L. Fletcher and H. Weinstein, "Violence and Social Repair: Rethinking the Contribution of Justice to Reconciliation" (2002) 24 *Human Rights Quarterly*, 573.

17. Rome Statute, Article 25(c). Some commentators have said that purpose can be secondary or nonexclusive. For example, Cassel, "Corporate Aiding and Abetting of Human Rights Violations: Confusion in the Courts" (2008) 6 *Northwest Journal of International Human Rights*, 315, writes that "one who knowingly sells gas to the gas chamber operator for the primary purpose of profit may be inferred to have a secondary purpose of killing people, so that he can keep selling more gas to kill more people." See also Doe v. Nestle, Case No. 10-56739, U.S. Ninth Circuit Court of Appeals, Sept. 4, 2014 ("Driven by the goal to reduce costs in any way possible, the defendants [chocolate producers] allegedly supported the use of child slavery, the cheapest form of labor available . . . the use of child slavery benefitted the defendants and furthered their operational goals in the Ivory Coast, and therefore, the allegations support the inference that the defendants acted with the purpose to facilitate child slavery.")

18. See, for example, Volume 8 of the Peruvian Truth and Reconciliation Commission final report ("Factors that made the violence possible"); Guatemalan Commission for Historical Clarification, Memory of Silence, Conclusions.

19. TRC Final Report, Vol. 6, Section 5. Former Archbishop Desmond Tutu revived the idea of a wealth tax in 2011.

20. Louise Arbour, "Economic and Social Justice for Societies in Transition," in *Annual Lecture* (New York University School of Law, 2006); Zinaida Miller, "Effects of Invisibility: In Search of the 'Economic' in Transitional Justice" (2008) 2 (3) *International Journal of Transitional Justice*, 266; Ismael Muvingi, "Sitting on Powder Kegs: Socioeconomic Rights in Transitional Societies" (2009) 3 (2) *International Journal of Transitional Justice*, 180; James Cavallaro and Sebastián Albuja, "The Lost Agenda: Economic Crimes and Truth Commissions in Latin

America and Beyond," in Kieran McEvoy and Lorna McGregor (eds), *Transitional Justice from Below, Grassroots Activism and the Struggle for Change* (Oxford and Portland, OR: Hart Publishing, 2008), p. 122.

21. Government of the Republic of South Africa & Others v. Grootboom & Others 2000 (11) BCLR 1169. (Constitutional Court); Oposa et al. v. Fulgencio S. Factoran, Jr. et al (G.R. No. 101083, Supreme Court of the Philippines), July 30, 1993. On Colombia, see Rodrigo Uprimny, "Should Courts Enforce Social Rights? The Experience of the Colombian Constitutional Court," (2017), available at https://cdn.dejusticia.org/wp-content/uploads/2017/04/fi_name_recurso_67.pdf.

22. His "respect, protect, remedy" framework can be found at www.reports-and-materials.org/Ruggie-report-7-Apr-2008.pdf. See chapter 9.

23. The Guidelines can be found at www.ohchr.org/Documents/Publications/GuidingPrinciplesBusinessHR_EN.pdf.

24. The 26th session of the UN Human Rights Council in Geneva considered two resolutions. The first, led by Ecuador and South Africa, directs the Council "to establish an open-ended intergovernmental working group with the mandate to elaborate an international legally binding instrument on Transnational Corporations and Other Business Enterprises with respect to human rights." The second, less controversial, requests that the UN Working Group prepare a report considering, among other things, the benefits and limitations of legally binding instruments. Negotiations have continued, with a "zero draft" in 2018 and a revised version in 2019, although to date capital-exporting countries have been wary of the exercise. For updates on the negotiations, see https://www.business-humanrights.org/en/binding-treaty. For a skeptical view on a binding treaty, see John Ruggie, "The Past as Prologue? A Moment of Truth for UN Business and Human Rights Treaty," July 8, 2014, available at www.ihrb.org/commentary/past-as-prologue.html.

25. The first of these hearings was in November 2013. See https://www.earthrights.org/blog/inter-american-commission-human-rights-consider-home-country-liability-extraterritorial-actions.

26. Inter-American Court of Human Rights, Advisory Opinion on Human Rights and the Environment, OC23-17, November 15, 2017, available at https://www.escr-net.org/sites/default/files/caselaw/iacthr_rt_to_a_healthy_env_judgment.pdf.

27. See, for example, safeguards on indigenous people and forced displacement. The World Bank has created an inspection panel and other banks use similar mechanisms to deal with complaints. This is not to suggest that such measures are sufficient or even effective, simply that they have assumed more salience in the past decade or so. For the Equator Principles, see www.equatorprinciples.org. See also chapter 9.

28. See, for example, Reuters, "Financial Regulation Hits Congo Mineral Trade," at www.reuters.com/article/2010/07/15/financial-regulation-congo-idAFN1545972220100715?pageNumber=1&virtualBrandChannel=0. The SEC issued regulations in December 2019 loosening the requirements. On the Kimberley Process, see www.kimberleyprocess.org.

29. The most prominent, although not the only, example are suits under the U.S. Alien Tort Statute and Torture Victim Protection Act, 28 U.S.C. 1350 (1991). These suits have been curtailed by the U.S. Supreme Court's decision in Kiobel v. Royal

Dutch Petroleum Co., 133 S. Ct. 1659 (2013), among other cases, but they have not been eliminated.

30. See, for example, the Extractive Industries Transparency Initiative, at www.eiti.org.

31. *Witness to Truth, Report of the Sierra Leone Truth and Reconciliation Commission* (2004), Vol. II, 27.

32. William Shabas, "The Sierra Leone Truth and Reconciliation Commission," in Roht-Arriaza and Mariezcurrena (eds), *Transitional Justice in the Twenty-First Century* (Cambridge University Press, 2005).

33. *Liberia Truth and Reconciliation Commission, Consolidated Final Report (2009)*, Vol. II, 16–17.

34. The Truth, Justice and Reconciliation Commission of Kenya, "The Final Report of the TJRC" (2013), available at www.tjrckenya.org/index.php?option=com_content&view=article&id=573&Itemid=238. An analysis of the controversy over land can be found in Christopher Gitari Ndungú, *Lessons to Be Learned: An Analysis of the Final Report of Kenya's Truth, Justice and Reconciliation Commission* (ICTJ, May 2014).

35. Government of Tunisia, Organic Law on Establishing and Organizing Transitional Justice 2014, art. 8, at http://www.ohchr.org/Documents/Countries/TN/TransitionalJusticeTunisia.pdf. In September 2017, corruption cases were in effect granted amnesty from prosecution. Human Rights Watch, New Reconciliation Law Threatens Tunisia's Democracy, October 2, 2017, available at https://www.hrw.org/news/2017/10/02/new-reconciliation-law-threatens-tunisias-democracy.

36. Final Report, National Truth Commission of Brazil, Vol. II, chs. 2, 3, and 8.

Chapter 3

Foreign Economic Assistance and Respect for Civil and Political Rights

Chile—a Case Study

Antonio Cassese

INTRODUCTION[1]

The question of whether foreign economic assistance to states grossly disregarding human rights has an impact on the enjoyment of civil and political rights in those states is undoubtedly very complex. The nexus between economic assistance and human rights is often indirect and subtle. In addition, there arises the thorny question of evidence: Upon what elements can one show the multifaceted yet elusive nexus between foreign economic aid and various forms of human rights that on the surface appear to have few economic implications?

Without attempting to address all problems that fall within the purview of the subject-matter, I have limited the discussion to five questions that appear crucial:

1) Have human rights violations within state discouraged governments, international agencies, or private institutions from sending economic assistance to that state?
2) Might a state's human rights violations attract foreign economic assistance in some situations?
3) Have restrictions on civil and political rights caused inefficiencies in or had an adverse consequence on the utilization of foreign economic aid?
4) Do the benefits of foreign economic assistance reach those persons who have been victims of human rights violations, particularly the families of persons arbitrarily detained or imprisoned?

5) To what extent has foreign economic assistance supported the recipient Statés social and economic policies which have an adverse impact on the enjoyment of civil and political rights?

CHILE: A CASE STUDY

This chapter will briefly address these five questions specifically in regard to Chile. The reasons for this choice stem from the fact that there is sufficient documentation available, both from the Chilean authorities and from the United Nations, to analyze the relationship between foreign economic assistance and civil and political rights in that nation.

This analysis assumes that the various pronouncements of the UN General Assembly regarding Chile's poor human rights record are indeed correct.

A. *Violations of Civil and Political Rights in Chile and the Withholding of Foreign Economic Assistance*

The first of five questions referred to above can be broached based on replies of various governments to information requests sent in 1977 by the Secretary-General on the United Nations[2] and by the Rapporteur on Chile of the Sub-Commission on Prevention of Discrimination and Protection of Minorities. Reference is made here only to the official comments of a few Western governments concerning their economic relations with Chile since the military *golpe de estado* of September 11, 1973.

In its reply to the Secretary-General's information request, the Federal Republic of Germany stated that as a consequence of the disregard for human rights in Chile, "The Federal Government has not provided Chile with any more development aid. In negotiations for the rescheduling of debts, harder terms have been imposed. University partnership have not been continued."[3]

The government of Italy, in response to the request for information of the Rapporteur on Chile, stated:

> Economic, financial, cultural and technical cooperation between Italy and Chile have been strongly influenced since September 1973 up to the present—not at the multilateral and bilateral level—by the attitude adopted by our country towards the military Government [*sic*] headed by General Pinochet. In keeping with the unequivocal positions it has taken at the political level, Italy has gradually broken off all forms of collaboration, so that it can now be said that official aid by Italy to the Chilean Government is virtually non-existent.

As to economic and financial cooperation within the competent multilateral organizations in regard to loans granted to Chile . . . Italy's position has always been negative; in particular, [in the World Bank] Italy voted against the grant of a loan to Chile in January 1974 and in May 1975 ($20 million for an agricultural reorganization programme), and it abstained from voting on the decision concerning three other loans to Chile in February ($33 million) and December 1976 ($25 million and $35 million).

In the Inter-American Development Bank . . . , the position adopted with regard to the grant of two loans to Chile . . . was as follows: abstention on an integrated technical assistance programme which also includes Bolivia and Peru, and a vote against the grant loan of $20 million exclusively to Chile.

With regard to multilateral technical operation . . . Italy has not failed to express reservations concerning programmes for Chile, in view of the non-observance by the Chilean Government of the resolutions adopted by various United Nations bodies which call for respect for human rights and the restoration of fundamental freedoms in that country.

As regards the consideration of economic and financial relations on a bilateral basis, irt must be pointed out that, during the period in question, Italy suspended the privileges enjoyed by Chile under the Insurance and Export Credit Law and that, consequently, no request concerning that country has been considered by the competent organizations.

A similar attitude has been adopted in regard to bilateral technical co-operation. In September 1973, various programmes were being executed in fields such as occupational training, university education and building, together with volunteer programmes, chiefly in education. Today, there is only one volunteer programme (nine persons), for occupational training of personnel of the Curanilahue coal mines, which has not been discontinued because of its distinctly social character.

This consistent over-all attitude . . . is also reflected in the refusal by our authorities to take part in multilateral talks held within the Club of Paris with a view to restructuring Chile's external debt.[4]

The government of the Netherlands responded to the information requests by declaring that it had taken "a number of concrete steps which it hopes will contribute to the restoration and safeguarding of human rights and fundamental freedoms in Chile. Financial assistance in the framework of development co-operation has been suspended. Ais is provided only in respect of certain small welfare projects, directly benefiting the poorest section of the population. This aid is channeled through non-governmental organizations . . . . In the field of trade, credit guarantees by government bodies for export transactions by Dutch companies have been discontinued as from 1973."[5] In a note to the United Nations on December 21, 1977, the Government of the Netherlands informed that since the golpe de Estado of 1973, but that "[t]hrough some non-governmental organizations funds are supplied for activities funds are supplied for activities which are directly benefiting the most distressed groups of the Chilean population."[6]

Norway, in a note to the United Nations dated November 25, 1977, stated that as a result of the suppression of democratic institutions in Chile.

Bilateral aid given to Chile from Norway has been suspended. Together with the governments of the other Nordic countries, the Norwegian government has voted against loans to Chile from the World Bank. At the twenty-third session of the Governing Council of UNDP, held in January 1977, the Norwegian representative and those of the other Nordic governments in a joint statement made clear that the land program of Chile did not enjoy their support because of the failure of Chilean authorities to concur with past UN resolutions to improve the human rights condition in Chile.[7]

The degradation of human rights in Chile since the 1973 coup d'etat has also severely strained relations between Chile and the United States. A recent study submitted to the Ad Hoc Working Group on the situation of human rights in Chile stated:

> Since 1974, Congressional critics of United States Chilean policy have legislated limitations on military and economic aid to Chile on the grounds of its human rights violations ... Thus far, when all military aid and most forms of bilateral economic aid have been denied to Chile by the United States Congress and it has become increasingly evident that very little aid would be available, the Chilean government has responded by renouncing any United States bilateral assistance. The complete rejection of this aid came in response to the State Department's decision to delay for 60 to 90 days $ 9.3 million from the $ 27.5 million economic assistance package for 1977, to express disapproval of human rights violations by the Chilean government of President Augusto Pinochet ... The Chilean junta issued a note in which formally spurned the proposed US $ 27.5 million economic aid package, [and] angrily react[ed] against the Carter Administration's attempt to use human rights as a factor in the considering foreign aid distribution.[8]

However, economic relations between Chile and the United States improved somewhat in 1978. According to press reports, on April 24, 1978, the Commodity Credit Corporation, a private corporation under the auspices of the Department of Agriculture, approved 38 million dollars in commercial export credits for farmers and ranchers in Chile. The Washington Star reported:

> State Department officials confirmed ... that approval of the credits was delayed for some time, but they denied that the credits reflect a departure from the administration's emphasis on human rights.
>
> Officials emphasized that the credits were for private parties rather than the Chilean government, and were intended primarily to aid American farmers.
>
> They also stated that the credits reflected approval of what was described as encouraging political developments within Chile´s military government [*sic*]. One State Department official cited the recent amnesty for many political prisoners in Chile and the government's decision to turn over to United States authorities to Michael Vernon Townley, the 35-year-old US citizen, who has been charged with conspiracy in the murder of the former Chilean Ambassador Orlando Letelier in 1976.[9]

Senator Edward Kennedy, however, felt that the credit would have been more appropriately used if allocated to the improvement of human rights in Chile. [10]

From the above, it is clear that most of the states that have commented on their economic relation with Chile after the coup d'etat, have either discontinued or significantly decreased their economic assistance to Chile as a direct consequence of its suppression of civil and political rights. Thus, the introduction of a repressive system in Chile has resulted, in much of the international community denying economic aid to Chile in the hope of using such pressure to force the present Chilean authorities to restore human rights.

Although the aforementioned change recently occurred in United States policy, this change has been justified primarily by emphasizing that the Chilean authorities are in the process of improving the human rights situation in that country. While I do not pass judgment on the U.S. assessment of the Chilean situation, one must recognize that even this new stand reveals a close link exists between foreign economic assistance and respect for human rights in Chile.

B. *Repression of Human Rights as a Means of Attracting Foreign Economic Assistance*

The relationship between foreign economic assistance and the economic policy of the present Chilean government on the one hand, and Chile's current repression of civil and political rights on the other, is quite visible. Gross violations of human rights, particularly trade union rights, have become an important factor in attracting foreign economic investment to Chile.

Chilean authorities regard attracting foreign investment as a "central economic principle."[11] Among the most important aspects of this effort to attract foreign capital are the offer of cheap labor and the strict enforcement of industrial discipline. Immediately after the military takeover, editors of the highly influential newspaper *El Mercurio* began to advocate "the perfecting of the labor market" suggesting, among other things, that "the cost of hiring labor should be reduced substantially in relation to the capital."[12] The elimination of virtually all trade union rights, including the right to elect trade union representatives freely, to bargain collectively, and to strike, have put Chilean workers in a situation of impotence, with few means of asserting their rights to decent living and working conditions. This distressing situation has been amply documented in reports of the International Labor Organization and the UN Commission on Human Rights, which have urged the Chilean government to "promulgate new trade union legislation as soon as possible and to repeal Legislative Decree No. 198, in order to ensure the normal functioning of trade union activities."[13]

Minister of Economy Sergio de Castro explained in a seminar on Chilean policy on foreign investment: "We think that foreign investors take their capital from one place to the other, looking for the highest profitability. This is why they have to periodically evaluate the variables for their companies' profits, such as wages levels and salaries, taxes and custom tariffs." Thus, Chilean authorities offer foreign investors the economic benefits derived from violating the rights of Chilean workers—rights that have been universally agreed upon at the United Nations. Foreign investors are openly invited to translate the transgression of these human rights into increased profitability.

C. *Effects of the Restrictions on Civil and Political Rights on the Utilization of Foreign Economic Assistance*

The serious violations of human rights that are still occurring in Chile have adverse consequences on the actual use of the foreign economic aid flowing onto Chile. Grave restrictions on freedom of expression, freedom of association, and trade union rights prevent most Chilean people from taking part in the decision-making process. The government can request and use foreign economic assistance without close scrutiny by the Chilean population. This lack of freedom of expression and the existence of a ruling group which makes all the basic decisions affecting the lives of the people permits neither a free exchange of ideas nor the introduction of improvements or corrections in the execution of economic policies, including in the utilization of foreign economic assistance.

The Permanent Committee of the Episcopal Conference of Chile, in a statement issued on March 25, 1977, has forcefully analyzed this situation. After stressing that "for many families, especially for those who are unemployed or earning a minimum wage, the extremely precarious and difficult conditions in which they are living become almost intolerable" and that "the peasants, the workers and settlers appear to be bearing an excessive and disproportionate burden," the Permanent Committee said:

Economic development depends on decisions taken at the national level and the right of participation defended by the Catholic social doctrine is also applicable to the economy. In the economic sphere it is easy to create a technocratic elite which aspires to make all decisions itself ... To maintain that economic problems have only one solution, without any alternative, is to establish the rule of science and the scientific elite over human responsibilities. It is also to assume that decisions made are based only on scientific reasons and that no part is played in them by reasons of dogma or group interest. But this is not the case: doctrinal positions and group interests often play a part in making decisions, though somewhat unconsciously.

In the name of human rights and the right of participation, the church asks that the various economic options should be the subject of open discussion, and that access to decisions and the possibility of exerting influence should not be reserved to a single scientific school or a few more privileged economic groups. Without a great national debate, the reasons given by the specialists lack their full credibility. There is usually more wisdom in the discussion of differing opinions than in a single opinion which is affirmed dogmatically and without contradiction.[14]

Workers feel this same need to participate in the decision-making process. In a letter sent on April 29, 1977, to the president of the Republic of Chile, a group of trade union leaders cited the "historical failure of private enterprise" and called for workers' participation in the development of a "new national investment plan."[15]

The views expressed in general terms by the Permanent Committee of the Episcopal Conference and by the trade union leaders also apply to the subject of this chapter. Since the junta allows no political parties or political groups in Chile, and strictly controls trade unions, only people in the ruling group participate in the decision concerning the type of economic assistance to be requested abroad; the choice of the states, international institutions, or private groups which may furnish economic assistance; the conditions under which such assistance can be accepted; and the social or economic areas targeted for foreign economic assistance. Fresh ideas and perspectives from excluded groups could correct the major defects in foreign assistance schemes which at present limit the beneficial influence foreign economic assistance could have.

D. *Foreign Economic Assistance and the Condition of Those Suffering from the Present Disregard of Civil and Political Rights in Chile:*

In its February 1, 1978 report the United Nations, the Ad Hoc Working Group on the situation of human rights in Chile, created established by the Commission on Human Rights, pointed out that Chilean authorities "continue to refuse to respect the liberty and security of persons believed to be opposed to the present regime. The system of intimidation through arrests, detentions, torture or ill-treatment and harassment continue to be used to repress those sectors of the Chilean population."[16] According to the Ad Hoc Working Group, "Persons detained by the security agencies continue to disappear, though at a rate significantly less than in the past."[17]

The fate of political detainees and relatives of missing persons or political detainees raises particularly serious problems. Their lot has been aptly described by the representative of Amnesty International. In a statement before the Commission on Human Rights on February 24, 1978, he pointed out:

> Often, the victims of arbitrary arrest and imprisonment were from the poorer sectors of society. They could be divided into four different groups. The first consisted of prisoners charged with political offenses, the greatest number of whom were in the three major prisons of Santiago, and their families. Where the prisoner has been the chief breadwinner, the family lived in the utmost need and poverty. The second category comprised political prisoners charged with and tried for a common law offense. That was a phenomenon particularly noticed in recent months and which Amnesty International had only recently begun to investigate, and it had not always been possible to ascertain beyond all reasonable doubt that there were political reasons behind the arrest. The third category was composed of former political prisoners and former detainees who had been held without trial under the provisions of the state of siege. On release they faced common problems and underwent extreme hardship. Finally, there were the families of missing persons, possibly the most tragic group, who suffered severe psychological disruption and often serious financial stress. It was estimated that over 10,000 persons had been affected.[18]

In 1978, the Ad Hoc Working Group received the report of a mission that visited Chile in 1977 under the auspices of the World Council of Churches. According to the Ad Hoc Working Group, this report stated that "the mental and physical health of the families, especially the children, of persons who have disappeared has been severely affected. The information provided to the Group in this report concerning 145 specific cases of children revealed somatic disorders, psychological problems, and retardation of development...2."[19]

It appears that medical doctors detained for political reasons often lose their right to work when released.[20] "In addition, the families of the "disappeared" frequently undergo hardship even in the field of education. No less serious is the fate of persons who oppose the government's social policy or who are regarded by the authorities as potential opponents.

Thus, trade union leaders and members often lose their jobs or encounter great difficulty in obtaining employment.[21] Up to now, relief agencies have aided relatives of missing persons, or political detainees and opponents.[22] These groups have also received financial and other forms of support from some governments and private institutions. It seems, however, that the financial means available to these people are not sufficient. Sources of foreign economic assistance do not design their programs to help the victims of political detention, and the Chilean government does not directly aid to this group.[23] The conclusion, therefore, seems warranted that at present foreign economic assistance provided to the Chilean authorities does not benefit those people who suffer directly or indirectly from deprivation of liberty for political reasons (i.e., detention, disappearance). These persons receive assistance from relief agencies operating in Chile through direct funding from foreign governments or private organizations.

E. *Socioeconomic Policies Adopted in Chile: Repression of Civil and Political Rights and Foreign Economic Assistance*

Chilean authorities seek the following social and economic goals: (a) enhancement of the role of private enterprise in the national economy; (b) opening of the Chilean market to imported products and reducing customs tariffs and duties; (c) removal of present price controls; and (d) drastic reduction of state expenditure, including the reduction of staff wages and salaries.[24] These socioeconomic policies have had certain consequences for the Chilean people, including (a) increase in unemployment; (b) reduced income of wage earners; (c) decreasing purchasing power of wage earners; (d) bankruptcies of small and medium-sized national enterprises; (e) serious deterioration of public services such as the health services; (f) food shortages for the poor; and (g) reduction of categories of persons economically eligible for admission to university education.[25]

Discontent and a profound sense of dissatisfaction are the byproducts of these policies. Some groups in Chile have voiced strong protests. Recall the important statement issued on March 25, 1977, by the Permanent Committee of the Episcopal Conference of Chile,[26] and the letter sent to the President of the Republic of Chile by Chilean trade union leaders.[27] Significantly, the government has not prevented the public expression of dissent or criticisms by prominent groups. In more democratic societies, however, when governmental authorities draw up and implement economic and social measures that disadvantage the interests and needs of the less privileged strata, usually trade unions oppose those measures through strikes, walk-outs, public protests, and so forth. Lack of freedom of assembly, association, and, in particular, trade union rights prevent this reaction in Chile. A close link apparently exists between the kind of policies carried out by the present authorities in the socioeconomic field and repression in the field of civil and political rights. In short, without suppression of or serious restrictions on civil and political rights, the military government could not impose and enforce its economic and social policies.[28]

Foreign economic assistance to a great extent serves to prop up the present governmental authorities in Chile.[29] The assistance, through design or implementation, supports the policy that the authorities choose and carry out in the field of socioeconomic relations. The economic policy fosters the repression of basic human rights because the implementation is only possible without dissent. It follows from the above considerations that foreign economic assistance, to the extent that it reinforces the present government in Chile and its socioeconomic strategy, contributes to consolidating and perpetuating the repressive system which to a great extent is "a counterpart of the socioeconomic policies of the Chilean authorities."[30]

CONCLUDING REMARKS

The present gross violations of human rights in Chile are related to economic assistance in two respects. First, and most apparently, the bulk of this assistance helps to strengthen and maintain power in a system that pursues a policy of large-scale violations of human rights. This applies to some forms of economic assistance concerned with development as well as to most forms of economic assistance that showed no concern either with human rights or development. The same holds true for many cases of assistance directly related to human rights (assistance given with the specific aim of improving the situation of the population in the fields of housing, sanitation, hospitals, health centers, and so forth).[31] Often the government uses this assistance to replace national resources, which are diverted to other ends, including that of financing the repressive system. In all these cases, economic assistance often appears instrumental in perpetuating or at least maintaining the current situation of gross violations of human rights.

The second aspect is no less important. To obtain the assistance which it seeks abroad, the government has to ensure a favorable presentation of the indices by which an economy is normally held to be "healthy." It must appear to be "creditworthy" (i.e., it must have, among other things, a favorable balance of payments, controlled or diminishing inflation, a reduction of public expenditure). This domestic policy does not take into account the human factor and, in fact, creditworthiness can only be obtained by a redistribution of income which is unfavorable to the vast majority of the population. Furthermore, to the extent that it is not only foreign economic assistance in the form of loans (bilateral or multilateral) but investment that the government wants to attract, the state of poverty or backwardness of the working sector of the population does not appear as a negative factor. Instead, it appears as a positive element that may lead foreign enterprises, attracted by cheap labor and the low cost of production in the country, to make the decision to invest. In this respect, a deterioration in the benefits that workers and their families receive in other than monetary form also plays a major role in investment decisions. The absence of social unrest and restrictions on trade unions are important added advantages of a regressive system to foreign investors.

If the two aspects of the relationship between economic assistance and the violation of human rights are considered, one can see that in the second aspect the causal relationship is inverted: Repression encourages investment. Thus, together, they make up a closed circle of "cause" and "effect." Economic assistance to a very great extent permits the perpetuation of violations of human rights, and such violations, in turn, bring about the necessary conditions to obtain economic assistance.

NOTES

1. This chapter is based on a revised version of a section of a report prepared by the author for the United Nations. It was published in the Spanish version and was originally published in 14 Tex. Int'l L. J. 251. Antonio Cassese was the Professor of International Organizations, Department of Political Science of the University of Florence; Postgraduate Director of the School of International Affairs; Member of the Italian Delegation in several United Nations agencies, including the Human Rights Commission and the General Assembly. [Editors note] Antonio Cassese was one of the most influential international jurists of recent decades. His work reflects his vocation to challenge the positivist tendency of his time, working not only on the basis of what the law is but also what it should be. In this line, Cassese recognized that his academic life also fluctuated on a dichotomy between contemplation and action. This situation resulted in more than seventeen books and essays, twenty-one collective works, and countless academic texts in areas such as International Human Law, International Humanitarian Law, International Criminal Law, Constitutional Law, Public International Law, Public Policies, among others. In addition to his academic work, Cassese ventured several times to the complex international diplomatic

and jurisdictional exercise, participating for example as an Italian diplomat in the modification of the Geneva Conventions (1974–1977), as director of the Steering Committee on Human Rights of the European Council (1987–1988), as a member and director of the European Council for the Prevention of Torture (1989–1993), as an international judge in the International Criminal Tribunal for the former Yugoslavia (1993–1997), and as a member of the United Nations Commission for Research for Darfur (2004–2005). This work is based on the revised version of a section of the report prepared by the author for the United Nations prepared in 1978. The original of this work was published in 1978 (and republished in 2015) as "Foreign Economic Assistance and Respect for Civil and Political Rights: Chile a Case Study," *Texas International Law Journal*, Vol. 50 number 4, pp. 645–66. We thank the Texas International Law Journal for granting permission to publish this work here.

2. G.A. Res 31/124, 31 U.N. GAOR, Supp. (No.39) 104-05, U.N. Doc. A/31/39 (1976).

3. The Sub-Commission on Prevention of discrimination and protection of human rights in Chile, Report of the Secretary-General, 32 U.N. GAOR (Agenda Item 12) 9, U.N. Doc. A/32/234 (1977) [hereinafter cited as Report of the Secretary-General].

4. Study of the Impact of Foreing Economic Aid and Assistance on Respect for Human Rights in Chile, 31 Sub-Comm´n on Prevention of Discrimination and Protection of Minorities (provisional agenda Item 13) para. 407, U.N. Doc. E/CN.4/ Sub.2/412 (1978) [hereinafter cited as Foreign Economic Aid Study].

5. Report to the Secretary-General, supra note 3, at 12–13.

6. Foreign Economic Aid Study, supra note 4, at para. 409.

7. Id. para. 410. In its reply of December 5, 1977 to a request for information sent by the Rapporteur on Chile, the government of Sweden stated the following: The Swedish government extends no aid to the present Chilean authorities. The Swedish policy in this regard is illustrated by the following facts: On August 31, 1973, the Agreement, called the Development.

8. Centre for International Policy, *Chile: An Analysis of Human Rights Violations and United States Security Assistance and Economic Programmes*, July 1978, pp. 1–2.

9. Washington Star, May 5, 1978, at A-5.

10.

> In a speech from the Senate floor, Senator Kennedy said: I am disturbed by the Administration's recent approval of $ 38 million in Commodity Credit Corporation credits for Chile. [I] t would have been much wiser for the United States to loan this much money on the basis of substantial human rights movement in Chile. I am now consulting with the Administration to ensure that this action will not be misunderstood, or repeated in the absence of further progress. Let us not lose this opportunity to make a critical difference in the lives of the Chilean people, and to demonstrate that the United States can be an effective force for human rights in Latin America.
>
> Congressional Record, Proceedings and Debates of the 95th Congress Session, vol. 124, No. 64 (May 4, 1978)

11. *El Mercurio* (Santiago), «Informe Económico», August 1976, p. 16.
12. *El Mercurio* (Santiago), 1973.
13. Report of the Ad Hoc Working Group to investigate the human rights situation in Chile, U.N. ESCOR Annex (Provisional Agenda Item 5) 66, U.N. Doc. E/CN.4/1266 (1978), para. 133 [hereafter cited as a Human Rights Study].
14. El Mercurio (Santiago), March 26, 1977.
15. Report of the Economic and Social Council: Protection of human rights in Chile, Note by the Secretary-General, 32 U.N. GAOR, LII Annexes (Agenda Item 12) 286, U.N. Doc. A/32/227 (1978), para. 133 [hereafter, cited as a Human Rights Study].
16. Human Rights Study, supra note 13, at 73.
17. Id.
18. 34 Comm'n on Human Rights (1456th mtg.) 4-5, U.N. Doc. E/CN.4/SR.1456 (1978) (remarks of Mr. Rodley).
19. Human Rights Report, supra note 16, at 111.
20. Foreign Economic Aid Study, supra note 4, para. 172.
21. Id. para. 238.
22. Relief has been provided by the Vicaria de la Solidaridad, the Fundacion de Ayuda Social de la Iglesia Cristiana (FASIC), and the Ayuda Cristiana Evangdlica (ACE), as well as by the Intergovernmental Committee for European Migration, the Office of the United Nations High Commissioner for Refugees and the International Committee of the Red Cross.
23. See Foreign Economic Aid Study, supra note 4, chs. III and IV.
24. Id. paras. 88–112.
25. Id. paras. 113–248.
26. See supra Part C.
27. See id.
28. It is necessary to point out that this view does not constitute a novelty. As early as 1970, Jorge Cauas, one of the main economic policy-makers in Chile, who was Minister of Finance to the military government and is now Ambassador to the United States, showed himself to be aware that only political repression can allow a free market system to survive in such a society as that of Chile. In 1970, he described the political measures that should accompany the implementation of his economic theories and of the monetary policy he advocated (control of the money supply through restriction of domestic credit, a single exchange rate and a balanced budget, etc.), warning that serious problems were to be faced in applying that policy, most of them deriving from the need for discipline to ensure that the measures would be respected. "The main pressure factors to be taken into account are the actions of organized groups of workers in connection with wage policy and the ambitious governmental programmes which must be financed by noninflationary means." He concluded that "in a democratic system . . . , there are obviously both conceptual and practical difficulties" in applying the proposed scheme, but these disappear as soon as it is agreed to use "other measures, in the form of the establishment of a centralized system, with the consequent loss of freedom." Cauas Lama, Politica Economia de Corto Plazo, in 2 BANCO CENTRAL DE CHILE: ESTUDIOS MONETARIOs 25, 41-42, 44-45 (1970).

29. See Foreign Economic Aid Study, supra note 4, chs. I and II.

30. It is necessary to underscore that this conclusion has already been reached by other persons who have dealt with the problems of Chile. In this connection, it is worth citing a statement made on April 29, 1976, before the Sub-Committee on International Organizations of the Committee on International Relations of the United States House of Representatives by Mr. Leonard C. Meeker, a prominent lawyer and former Legal Adviser to the U.S. Department of State. Although Mr. Meeker refers only to the economic assistance furnished to Chile by the United States, his conclusions can also apply to the assistance provided by other states. After surveying the various forms of economic assistance provided by the United States to Chile, he stressed that this assistance did not go to those who are most in need, and concluded, "Under present programs, U.S. Government assistance is simply shoring up and easing the problems of a brutally repressive regime." Chile: The Status of Human Rights.and its Relationship to U.S. Economic Assistance Programs: Hearings before the Sub-comm. on Int'l Organizations of the House Comm. on Int'l Relations. 94th Cong., 2d Sess. 7 (1976) (statement of Leonard C. Meeker). Replying to a question by U.S. Representative A.T. Moffet, Mr. Meeker said:

> The U.S. Government needs to make it clear in its statements to the Government of Chile that it is deeply offended by the treatment that that government is meting out to human beings, that it is a kind of treatment that we simply cannot condone. We will not support that government in its policies, and we will not give it the practical sinews to continue its repression through grants of foreign aid that go to the government to be dispensed by the government at its discretion.

Id. at 12.

On May 4, 1978, Senator Edward M. Kennedy, speaking on "Challenges to Human Rights in Chile," stated before the U.S. Senate that "The economic assistance tragically continues which, in so many instances, is being used to perpetuate in power those particular forces and those particular interests which we state are alien to our own traditions and our own basic and fundamental principles." 124 CONG. REC. S6,987 (daily ed. May 4, 1978) (remarks of Sen. Kennedy).

31. For details on this form of economic assistance, see Foreign Economic Aid Study, supra note 4, paras. 472, 476.

Chapter 4

Cassese's Great Contributions and Unresolved Complaints

Karinna Fernández and Sebastián Smart

INTRODUCTION

On February 27, 1975, the Commission on Human Rights established an Ad Hoc Working Group to confront the human rights situation in Chile. This came as a result of a series of documents, interviews, and international concern for grave violations taking place. The Group carried out their work between 1975 and 1979[1] as the United Nations' confidential reports were called into question as to their capacity to handle allegations of human rights violations.[2] This was the first extra-conventional mechanism created by the United Nations to study human rights violations in a given country. It marked a milestone of particular relevance in the international organization's history and its functions because it represented a positive break from the way it addressed human rights violations and would allow for the future creation of Working Groups in Argentina, Guatemala, Equatorial Guinea, Iraq, and Myanmar, among others.[3]

In 1976, the Ad Hoc Working Group published its first report, concluding that Chile was subject to extended repression where enforced disappearances and tortures were systematic, and resolved to investigate these incidents.[4] In subsequent reports, the Ad Hoc Working Group continuously brought the international community's attention to two particular situations: (a) the impact of foreign aid and economic assistance on human rights in Chile; and (b) the need to provide humanitarian, legal, and financial aid to those detained or imprisoned in Chile under the state of siege or other emergency legislation, as well as those forced to leave the country and their families. Responding to the first situation, it commissioned a study on the impact of foreign aid and economic assistance on human rights in Chile, naming Professor Antonio

Cassese as Rapporteur for the project (*Cassese Report*, or the Report).[5] For the second, it established a voluntary fund.[6]

It is important to remember that from the early hours of September 11, 1973, Chile's armed forces and security forces, with the collaboration of civilians, carried out a massive and systematic policy of intimidation, kidnappings, enforced disappearances, torture and, in many cases, assassinations of opponents of the dictatorship. At the end of the military regime on March 10, 1990, this huge human rights violation had resulted in the murder or enforced disappearance of at least 3,216 people, and the torture of 38,254 people, who had survived the ordeal.[7]

Considering this context, this chapter will critically analyze the main contributions and challenges of the *Cassese Report*, produced during the initial years of the dictatorship, and shed light on certain aspects that we consider still unresolved. In this regard, this chapter should be read as a critical complement to the *Cassese Report* and his chapter in this book entitled "Foreign Economic Assistance and Respect for Political and Civil Rights: Chile—Case Study." To achieve this, the first section will analyze the general contributions of the report. By this, we mean those contributions related to tackling the study of human rights in a global context, highlighting the avant-garde nature of the report and its ability to interrelate civil and political rights with economic, social, and cultural rights. Cassese emphasizes that the dictatorship was characterized not just by criminal repression but also by its massive violations of economic, social, and cultural rights. Both were essential and inseparable requirements for the unpunished enforcement of its economic and political model. Overcoming obstacles imposed by the dictatorship, Cassese was able to describe how foreign economic assistance—from loans granted by states, multilateral institutions, and private investments—played a fundamental role in the creation of this repressive context which is discussed in the second part of this chapter. The third section aims to analyze aspects exposed by Cassese that are still unresolved, despite them having been made public forty years ago, such as the privatization of public enterprises. Finally, this chapter reaches a critical conclusion discussing Cassese's allegations' lack of impact.

GENERAL CONTRIBUTIONS OF THE *CASSESE REPORT*

The Report's Avant-Garde Nature and Its Use of a Scientific Methodology

Cassese's Report is avant-garde in at least two ways due to (a) the lack of precedents in reports dedicated to researching the influence that financial cooperation and international economic assistance could have on human rights violations; and (b) the use of a scientific method to analyze human rights within the context of a country.

The report's novelty must be understood within the context of a change of focus for the United Nations. Since 1967, the international organization had established itself as competent in dealing with situations that revealed "persistent occurrence of gross and flagrant violations of human rights."[8]

The second novelty is methodological. The attempt to study human rights violations in a given area with regard to the global context required a method that enabled the understanding of the circumstances and the political, economic, and cultural interrelations that surrounded human rights violations. It was also important to consider the methodological limitations that a project such as this would have to overcome in being carried out in a dictatorial country where, first, obtaining direct sources of information would be almost impossible due to the absence or inaccuracy of official information, and second, which prevented Cassese from entering the country.

To avoid reaching incorrect conclusions, Cassese created a scientific methodology that detailed the origin of the proposed theories and the sources used.

Another of Cassese's great contributions is the extensive and logical argument he made in the report to account for the capacity the United Nations would have to study and analyze the political, social, and economic context of a member country without contravening the principle of nonintervention.[9] Cassese made an important effort to systematize the arguments in favor of the ability and responsibility of the international community to develop a study that understands the relationship between economic assistance and human rights violations, without contravening this principle. This effort would come to serve as a basis for arguments so that different UN entities could meet and demand changes in situations of serious and persistent human rights violations.

The main argument behind noninterference in states' internal affairs proposed by Cassese stems from previous cases in which a government loses their democratic character, as in the Chilean case that kidnapped, exiled, and assassinated members of its community. This occurrence cannot demand noninterference of the United Nations when the repressive context is known. It would be a "healthy intervention of the national community conscience in a situation where rights are being violated."[10]

Interrelation of Economic, Social, and Cultural Rights and Civil and Political Rights

The report is innovative too in terms of the defense of human rights' interrelationship and interdependence principles, a rare focal point at the time. While the Ad Hoc Working Group asked Cassese to disclose the impact of economic assistance on economic, social, and cultural rights, Cassese himself had already acknowledged it was precisely these rights that were more directly affected.[11] This does not mean that the scope or repercussions that economic assistance can have on civil and political rights were ignored. It simply recognized that this link is subtler and less direct than the relationship between international cooperation and economic, social, and cultural rights. The decision to study human rights as a whole, beyond the operation of the Ad Hoc Working Group, is due to Cassese's unified and interdependent vision of human rights.[12]

The argument behind the indivisibility of human rights is simple. Cassese stresses that degrading treatment cannot be limited only to matters of civil rights. In his words, this means, "the concept of dignity [. . .] and the prohibition of all treatment contrary to humanitarian principles, including any measure or action executed by a public authority, no matter the specific field to which the measure or action belongs."[13]

In terms of the Chilean case, Cassese recognized that the repressive and criminal policies of the dictatorship were the basis for the implementation of an economic model that had resulted in the following: (i) the privatization of the economy, public services, and the promotion of private enterprise; (ii) the opening of the market to imports and the reduction of tariffs and customs duties; (iii) the elimination of price controls; and (iv) the drastic reduction of state spending, including wage cuts. This led to a clear deterioration in the economic and social situation in the country,[14] resulting in an increase in unemployment, a reduction in employees' purchasing power, the bankruptcy of businesses, degradation of public services—particularly in the healthcare sector—malnutrition in the poorest sections of the population, and a reduction in the rate of university income, among others. Despite affecting the majority of the population, these economic, social, and cultural rights violations did not result in social mobilization because of the strong repression and suppression of political and civil rights in the country. Some examples of this suppression include the development of economic policy without dialogue between the government and the affected social actors, the prohibition of political parties, the reduction of the right to freedom of association and assembly (regarding trade unions in particular), and the repression of strikes, demonstrations, and public protests. The dictatorship argued that these measures were necessary to impose and implement economic and social policies of the time.[15]

The suppression of civil and political rights, as well as economic, social, and cultural rights, was a fundamental prerequisite for the implementation of the economic model directed by the dictatorship. Furthermore, as we will see, foreign economic assistance was crucial for the development of an economic policy with these characteristics as it strengthened and supported the Pinochet dictatorship and its socioeconomic strategy. It contributed to different ways that consolidated and perpetuated the repressive system that was, by far, the counterpart to the Chilean socioeconomic policy.[16]

SPECIFIC CONTRIBUTIONS TO THE CHILEAN CASE

Avoiding Methodological Obstacles

Whether due to ignorance of the effects or the aim of creating a good diplomatic image, Pinochet's dictatorship had cooperated with international organizations before the visit of the Ad Hoc Working Group to produce reports on human rights violations in the country. A good example of this is the permission granted to the Executive Secretary of the Inter-American Commission on Human Rights to visit Chile in October 1963 and the commission's subsequent visit *in loco* in August 1974, as well as the Sixth General Assembly of the Organization of American States (OAS) in June 1976.[17] The dictatorship even granted the Ad Hoc Working Group entry a short time before the drafting of the *Cassese Report*. However, Chile's UN representative stated that the planned report on the impact of foreign aid and economic assistance on human rights in Chile was an unjustifiable and unacceptable interference in the internal affairs of their country.[18]

Cassese acknowledged that this lack of collaboration greatly affected the report's methodology, highlighting that, "to carry out an exhaustive and completely satisfactory investigation on the consequences of foreign economic assistance on human rights in Chile, it would need to be based in solid and indisputable evidence. It is only possible to gather such evidence if you can verify *in situ* how foreign economic assistance is used in this country."[19]

Therefore, Cassese reluctantly accepted the use of secondary sources (the media in particular) to obtain official information of the regime, alongside conducting interviews with people who had lived in Chile for a long time. This led Cassese to draw up a "global" report, classified by the author as one more, "extensive than consistent in direct verification on the ground of the advantages or adverse consequences of certain foreign economic assistance on human rights."[20]

Details of the National Socioeconomic Situation and the "Need" for Foreign Economic Assistance

Despite these limitations, Cassese was able to develop a detailed analysis of the Chilean economic situation, even challenging arguments that until then had been used to defend Pinochet's economic decisions.

The dictatorship's success, or macroeconomic "miracle," is usually referred to in local public debate and contrasted with the import substitution model that came to prevail in the country. According to Cassese, there were three economic concerns in the dictatorship: (1) solve the chronic inflation problem, (2) reduce the balance of payment instability, and (3) encourage the reactivation of the Chilean economy.[21] The Rapporteur recognized that Chilean authorities achieved to a great extent two of the main economic goals that had been set.[22] However, Cassese argued that to achieve these objectives, the civil–military dictatorship incurred more and more external debt, significantly increasing the proportion of debt owed to private international entities.[23] As a result, Chilean interest rates increased considerably so that for each dollar of exports, the Chilean government had to pay 55 cents to repay debts.[24]

The issue of external debt established clear progress in the macroeconomic field; however, it was mainly employees and local businesses that were adversely affected. First, employees witnessed a decrease in their purchasing power; indeed, "[the] employees' share of national income decreased from 64% in 1972 (51% in 1969) to approximately 30% in 1975."[25] Second, the large opening to foreign capital, coupled with tariff rate reduction policies, strongly affected Chilean companies and resulted in several of them going bankrupt, thereby significantly increasing unemployment.[26] The combination of these factors led to an increase in extreme poverty and continuous economic, social, and cultural rights violations in the country.[27] The relationship between foreign economic aid and human rights violations became apparent.

To understand the relationship between economic assistance and human rights violations, Cassese makes an analytical distinction between three forms of cooperation: (a) loans or economic assistance granted by other states, (b) economic assistance granted by multilateral institutions such as the World Bank or the International Monetary Fund, and (c) private investment. This analytical exercise allowed him to achieve the main objective of his mandate as he was able to elaborate on how different forms of economic assistance brought about human rights violations. Cassese recognized that the "strong indirect influence resulting from the government's desire to attract foreign investors, and the likelihood it would be more successful in the future, meant this sphere was considerably important for the Chilean human rights situation."[28]

With regard to the states' bilateral economic assistance, it is important to note that after the coup, the majority of countries that granted certain forms of economic aid decided to suspend it as a result of concern expressed for the human rights situation.[29] Many of these countries decided to redirect such contributions through nongovernmental agencies, mainly to help relatives of missing detainees or victims of political violence.[30] However, certain states continued with their bilateral moneylending policies. The United States was one of the most significant countries due to its increase in spending. From providing US$ 4 million in economic assistance in 1974, this increased to US$ 139.1 million in 1975 which was largely used to finance external debt and equip the military. This sparked a huge debate in the U.S. Congress and, after that year, they voted to limit bilateral cooperation in consideration of the human rights violations taking place in Chile. At the Latin American level, Argentina and Brazil stand out for the loans and bilateral monetary aid they granted of which, similar to U.S. cooperation, a large percentage was intended for the building of Chilean military capacity.[31]

On the other hand, Cassese revealed that the economic assistance of intergovernmental organizations, such as the International Monetary Fund (IMF), increased dramatically in 1974, not just in absolute terms (as it doubled between 1973 and 1974) but also in proportion to the total assistance granted. However, this began to decline from 1975 onward. This considerable increase was due to the decrease of bilateral loans and the almost inexistent economic assistance under President Salvador Allende's government. To an extent, the IMF sought to support austerity measures, and the liberalization of import restrictions and other controls on economic activity. These measures arose under the dictatorship and aroused the IMF's interest in Chilean economic policies and therefore its financial support. These economic policies, as we have seen, led to negative impacts on human rights.

The second type of intergovernmental assistance was granted by development banks (such as the Inter-American Development Bank and the World Bank) and specialized UN agencies (such as the UN Development Programme—UNDP) which focused on social considerations and development. However, only a small proportion of this assistance was directed at concrete health, food, and housing projects. The majority focused on improving the economy in general which economic authorities at the time emphasized would "trickle down" and generate profits for the poor. As we have seen, this did not happen and prompted criticism from the organizations involved.

The growing concern of the states and organizations involved in bilateral cooperation over human rights violations resulted in decreasing economic assistance from 1975 onward. Therefore, the Pinochet dictatorship decided to encourage investment and private loans and make them more flexible as a way of maintaining economic standards while still committing criminal human rights violations. Cassese acknowledged that "foreign private funding has turned out to be a means of circumventing the human rights policies of some foreign official institutions."[32] For example, after the United States' decision in 1975 to limit bilateral cooperation to US$ 27.5 billion per year, loans from private banks increased by more than 500 percent compared to the previous year, reaching US$ 520 million that year and increasing to nearly US$ 1,000 million in 1978. Cassese recognized that "since the fundamental motivation of commercial sources to grant economic assistance is profitability, the consequences for this assistance on basic human rights, like education, health and employment, were not generally a matter of concern for these sources."[33] These private contributions on the other hand allowed the Chilean dictatorship to avoid renegotiating their foreign debt with the Paris Club, thereby evading the financial pressure exerted by the international community to compel them to respect human rights. However, as the then Finance Minister, Sergio de Castro, said, this meant paying more money.[34]

Cassese's detailed analysis demonstrated the ineffectiveness of foreign aid in contributing to the country's development, as well as its relationship with human rights violations. Certain economic aid sought to directly promote and strengthen the dictatorial Pinochet government's repressive and military capacity, as is the case of the United States before the Carter administration. Others could have had a real intention to aid the development of the country or even end human rights violations, such as the multilateral cooperation of the Inter-American Development Bank and the World Bank but had the opposite effect. This is mainly due to Pinochet's social and economic policies that aimed to benefit certain private groups rather than the vulnerable groups where economic assistance should have gone. In addition, a large part of these funds was used to pay the external debt. [35]

In summary, Cassese made a detailed analysis of contributions from states, and international and private organizations to the Chilean dictatorship. He also made a comparison with contributions made during the *Unidad Popular* years, presenting contrasts, and gave a detailed presentation of the contributions offered by international organizations with reference to their internal regulations. He provided relevant information that, in our view, could have led to investigations—both within and outside of the law—into the liabilities that these financial organizations could have incurred.

UNRESOLVED ASPECTS

The Report's Worth

Cassese developed a methodology to describe the relationship between economic contributions and assistance and human rights violations from an integrated approach of human rights. While we have highlighted several novel aspects of the report, the limited impact the report had both in Chile and on a global level should also be acknowledged.

This lack of influence is evident in at least two areas: (a) the report has hardly been quoted in national or international doctrine, and (b) it is still unknown in Chile and has not been used for truth commissions, nor public policy preparation during the transition process, despite including crucial aspects and records that scientifically demonstrate the fallacies boasted by those who argue that the economy was the greatest achievement of the dictatorship. The report showed, for example, how the economic policy caused the bankruptcy of many national companies by focusing on foreign investment.[36]

According to Philip Alston, "once Antonio Cassese lost his re-election campaign for the Sub-Committee, the impact of the study disappeared."[37] Juan Pablo Bohoslavsky argues that because Cassese was able to demonstrate the relationship between foreign aid and human rights violations, certain powerful groups have understandably tried to block the report and have therefore ensured its lack of impact. What is less understandable is why the academic world and NGOs have also lost track of this noteworthy report.[38]

The Contribution to the Current Debate

The novelty analyzed in previous sections with regard to the interdependence and interrelatedness of human rights has not been considered by governments that have handed over the management of education and health systems to private companies, that do not recognize the right to housing, or that have privatized the pension system. Ultimately, a system that empowers economic power groups to the detriment of others is highly vulnerable to human rights violations, thereby reinforcing inequality.

If the *Cassese Report* had been valued by governments transitioning to democracy, many current debates on education, health, work, and pensions (among others) would have progressed. Cassese is able to focus on economic, social, and cultural rights from the perspective of vulnerable groups, whereas the Chilean political class has only ever been able to understand this through pressure exerted by civil society groups which has become more obvious and demanding.

Cassese raised issues in 1978 that are the clarion calls of social movements in the country today. These include the reduction of funds intended for university budgets;[39] problems concerning the selection and trend toward privatizing school education;[40] problems concerning the privatization of health and drug development services;[41] employers' nonpayment of taxes and the right to a minimum wage; the dismantling of corporate and labor systems in rural areas;[42] and malnutrition as an infringement on the right to adequate food.[43]

We believe that Cassese's conclusions would strengthen the debate by creating a link between public policies developed during democracy and economic decisions pushed forward during the dictatorship. In this sense, Cassese details the social consequences of certain economic policies that were implemented during Pinochet's dictatorship. For example, he writes how the system of privatization promoted by the *Corporación de Fomento para el Desarrolla* (Production Development Corporation—CORFO) and the foreign investment statute (Decree-Law 600) would result in the reduction of human rights protection and harm the most vulnerable groups. In this regard, various chapters of this book demonstrate that, rather than being apprehensive of the economic system imposed by the dictatorship, the transition governments have strengthened and deepened an economic system that privileges a reduced number of people, concentrating the economic power to the detriment of the general population.

The Establishment of Criminal and Civil Accountability

In a context of grave human rights violations, Chile should be able to establish criminal and civil accountability for those who contributed to the financing of atrocities committed by the dictatorship. Cassese presents a detailed analysis of the financing granted by national economic groups, private international banks, bilateral loans, and international organizations. He confirms that they contributed to shaping the dictatorship's global economic policy,[44] supported dictatorial authority, gave essential backing to repressive policies intended to suppress human rights,[45] and collaborated to consolidate and perpetuate the dictatorship.[46] However, up until the time of writing this chapter, the criminal and civil accountability of the lenders involved had not been established.

While this requires a political will that so far has been nonexistent at the national level, we strongly believe that the international community should be able to demand criminal and civil accountability for international organizations that financed projects and programs during the dictatorship and that were lax in ensuring their contributions were put to good use. Were a request for information to be petitioned, it would be interesting to observe its potential use to pursue the responsibilities in the commission of grave human rights violations by agencies such as the World Bank, the IMF, or the UNDP, all of whom dramatically reduced or even canceled funding Allende's government but restored strong loans during the dictatorship,[47] proving that "they do not base their actions on criteria related to human rights."[48]

CONCLUSION

This chapter aimed to critically address the main contributions and unresolved issues of the *Cassese Report*. The novelty of this report is important with regard to the interconnection of human rights and Cassese's critical capacity, despite the lack of up-to-date, concrete information, to understand the state of human rights violations and prevailing economic conditions in

Chile from 1973 to 1978. This report demonstrates without doubt Cassese's ability to put forward arguments on the principle of noninterference (to which he devotes almost a full volume in the report) and his analytical capacity to demonstrate how different types of economic cooperation resulted in human rights violations. Despite such contributions, we have seen that the report did not have the anticipated impact due to close, structural conditions stemming principally from political and economic elites. In our opinion, this is a lost opportunity as Cassese proposed visions of future issues which are now the clarion call of social movements, particularly those to do with violations of economic, social, and cultural rights.

While we have recognized the important contributions of the *Cassese Report*, we also believe that it has certain flaws which can be explained by the aforementioned methodological difficulties or by the lack of development of certain concepts which today seem obvious. One of the main lapses in the *Cassese Report* is the lack of a detailed dimension of repression and its specific impact on certain sectors, such as education. In our opinion, the report does not succeed in clearly reflecting the terror that different societal groups experienced and, while it explains how financial assistance affected certain vulnerable groups, this cannot be completely cutoff from the reality of the horror experienced at the time.

The report uses a limited human rights language that gives an account of the development it underwent in the mid-1970s. It does not mention, for example, the protection of rights, access as a fundamental part of economic, social, and cultural rights, the prison system, the situation of indigenous peoples, or the relationship of human rights violations with themes of inequality or inequity. In turn, attention is drawn to the lack of fluidity in the report of information obtained *in situ* by on-site visits and the preparation carried out by the Inter-American System of Human Rights.

Furthermore, and as already alluded to in the previous section, there is no follow-up from the United Nations, nor the governments going through the transition. The report was forgotten, and an important opportunity was wasted to follow-up with, for example, the consequences of privatization and the prevention of human rights violations. We hope that this chapter motivates us to give weight and importance to the *Cassese Report* for it to attain the impact and follow-up it deserves.

NOTES

1. Commission Resolution 8, 1317th meeting of the Commission on Human Rights on February 24, 1975, with 22 votes for, 4 votes against, and 6 abstentions. UN Doc, E/5635; E/CN.4/1179.

2. Primarily the efficiency of the 1503 procedure.

3. The Commission on Human Rights' first extra-conventional mechanism had a geographical scope: the Ad Hoc Expert Group in Southern Africa in 1967. See M. Lama, 'Protección internacional de los derechos humano: los mecanismos extra-convencionales de las Naciones Unidas', *Revista de derecho PUCP*, vol. 52, pp. 539–53. The Ad Hoc Working Group's report resulted in the implementation of a Special Rapporteur (1979–1990) to look into the human rights situation in Chile, the first Special Rapporteur with a country mandate. See M. Limon and H. Power, *History of the United Nations Special Procedures Mechanism: Origins, Evolution and Reform* (Universal Rights Group, 2014), p. 6.

4. Commission on Human Rights, Study of reported violations of human rights in Chile, with particular, reference to torture and other cruel, inhuman or degrading treatment or punishment, 19 February 1976, E/CN.4/1213.

5. Sub-Commission on Prevention of Discrimination and Protection of Minorities, *Study of certain questions relating to the situation of human rights in Chile*, resolution 11 (XXX) of August 31, 1977.

6. Final Report from Working Group, paragraph 6.

7. Figures from the National Truth and Reconciliation Commission (1991); National Corporation for Reparation and Reconciliation (1996); Valech Commission (2005); Valech Commission II (2011).

8. Phrase used for the first time in 1967 in resolution 8 (XXIII) of the Commission on Human Rights.

9. Paragraph 7 of article 2 of the Charter of the United Nations.

10. United Nations Conference on International Organizations, San Francisco, UNCIO/Role 1/P, 14 May 1945, page 7.

11. Cassese Report, para. 45.

12. A clear example of this statement is his comment on the European Commission of Human Rights' refusal to deal with the *Francine van Volsem against Belgium case. See* European Commission of Human Rights, *Francine van Volsem against Belgium,* decision of May 9, 1990, No. 14641/89.

13. A. Cassese, *The Human Dimension of International Law – Selected Papers* (Oxford: Oxford University Press, 2008), p. 335.

14. Cassese acknowledges that the Chilean economic and social situation steadily worsened between 1973 and 1978, reaching its worst point in 1975. See paragraphs 106 to 112 of the Cassese Report.

15. See paragraph 440 of the Cassese Report.

16. See Cassese Report, paragraph 443.

17. P. Engstrom, 'Chile and the Inter-American Human Rights System: Past, Present and Future' in *Chile and the Inter American Human Rights System*, K. Fernández, C. Peña and S. Smart (eds) (London: University of London Press), p. 21. E/CN.4/Sub.2/SR.797, para. 32.

18. E/CN.4/Sub.2/SR.797, para. 32.

19. Cassese Report, para. 77.

20. Cassese Report, para. 85.

21. Cassese Report, para. 88.

22. Cassese Report, para. 113.
23. Cassese Report, paras. 115 and 118.
24. Cassese Report, para. 120.
25. Cassese Report, para. 124.
26. Cassese Report, paras. 140 and 150.
27. Cassese Report, para. 147 and ff.
28. Cassese Report para. 251.
29. This was the case for the majority of Western European countries and Japan, for example; see Cassese Report paras. 276 and 277. Socialist countries decided to cut not just financial aid, but also diplomatic ties, as was the case with the People's Republic of China.
30. See Cassese Report, para. 261–262 and 292–299.
31. Cassese Report para. 278.
32. Cassese Report para. 375.
33. Cassese Report para. 377.
34. Cassese Report paras. 379 and 380.
35. For more details on financial assistance, see Chapter 7 of "Desentrañando la asistencia financiera al régimen de Pinochet."
36. Cassese Report paras. 137, 139, and 140.
37. P. Alston, 'Forward' *Making Sovereign Financing & Human Rights Work*, in J. Bohoslavsky and Cernic (eds) (London: Bloomsbury, 2014), p. ix.
38. J. P. Bohoslavsky, 'Introduction: Compelling questions for decades', *Texas International Law Journal*, Vol. 50, No. 4, pp. 645–66.
39. Cassese Report, para. 241.
40. Cassese Report, paras. 226 and 234.
41. Cassese Report, paras. 200 and 201.
42. Cassese Report, para. 170.
43. Cassese Report, para. 181.
44. Cassese Report, para. 309.
45. Cassese Report, para. 442.
46. Cassese Report, para. 495.
47. For example, World Bank loans to Chile were almost nonexistent between 1971 and 1973, while in 1974 they climbed to USD 13.5 million and in 1977 to USD 60 million (see Cassese Report paras. 327 and ff.). For a complete picture of the contributions of different organizations, see Cassese Report, paras. 300 and ff. and para 512.
48. Cassese Report, para. 512.

Chapter 5

Contextualizing the *Cassese Report*

The Dictatorship That Changed the United Nations Human Rights System and Its Legacy in Monitoring Economic, Social, and Cultural Rights

Elvira Domínguez Redondo and
Magdalena Sepúlveda Carmona

INTRODUCTION: CHILEAN DICTATORSHIP AS PRECURSOR OF NEW INTERNATIONAL FACT-FINDING MECHANISMS

After the 1973 military coup in Chile, international nongovernmental organizations, including Amnesty International, were quick to denounce the brutality of the regime to the United Nations (UN). In contrast, the UN General Assembly limited its reaction to a general condemnation of any form of torture.[1] However, the UN was under pressure to take a more palpable stance on human rights issues due to the widespread rejection that the atrocities committed in Chile attracted, as well as other significant events including the human rights situation in Argentina and the death by torture of Steven Biko.[2] The organization embarked on a long process of standard setting culminating in instruments such as the 1984 Convention against Torture and Other Cruel, Inhuman or Degrading Treatment[3] or the 1992 Declaration on the Protection of All Persons from Enforced Disappearances.[4] In addition, the Commission on Human Rights—the main UN intergovernmental body responsible for the promotion and protection of human rights since 1946 and replaced by the Human Rights Council in 2006—created its first fact-finding procedures[5] to investigate and report about the situation of human rights violations in South Africa, in 1967,[6] and Chile, in 1975.[7] Similar mechanisms were established to monitor the human rights situations in other countries (the so-called geographical procedures) or to investigate a phenomenon of human rights violations worldwide (thematic procedures). Still, the creation of the first thematic mandates was linked to the situation of human rights in specific countries. This is the case of the Working Group on Enforced or Involuntary Disappearances (the first thematic procedure), whose establishment, in 1980,[8] was instigated by the international reaction to the widespread practice of disappearances in Argentina as well as by the conclusions of the 1978 report of the Working Group on Chile.[9] The focus on the issue of disappearances was inherently linked to the right to life and coincided with the attention that the international community was also paying to the human rights situations in Guatemala, Kampuchea, and Syria, resulting, in 1982, in the creation of the Special Rapporteur on summary and arbitrary executions.[10] Three years later, the creation of the mandate of the Special Rapporteur on Torture and Other Cruel, Inhuman, or Degrading Treatment, was also influenced by the debate, within the UN, on the situation of human rights in Chile.[11]

The reaction of the international community to the systematic violation of human rights in Chile during the military dictatorship not only drove advances in regulation and monitoring mechanisms, but it also determined a new direction of the UN agenda in the promotion and protection of human rights. Following twenty years of denying its competence to investigate human rights violations, the Commission on Human Rights had changed its position in 1967 to address the policies of *apartheid* and the situation in the occupied Arab territories. These initiatives were still limited to issues that were not regarded as pertaining to the domestic affairs of a state. Furthermore, the actions of the Commission were preceded by others approved by the General Assembly and the Security Council as situations that constituted a threat to international peace and security.[12] With the establishment of the Ad Hoc Group on Chile, the Commission opted to examine human rights situations that, until then, had been opposed as undue interference in the internal affairs of states, breaching the fundamental principle of international law enshrined in article 2.7 of the UN Charter. The precedent of Chile opened the door to the creation of other human rights monitoring mechanisms that have become known as "special procedures."

Special procedures are mechanisms entrusted to independent experts acting individually or within the framework of a working group consisting of five members. All experts in charge of special procedures have the common mandate of investigating and reporting on human rights situations in a specific territory (geographical mandates) or a category of human rights (thematic mandates). In January 2020, there were eighty independent experts in charge of fifty-five special procedures.[13] Of these, forty-three are thematic mandates focused on a wide range of human rights such as freedom of expression, toxic waste, violence against women, health, or the right to water and sanitation. Geographical mandates report on the human rights situation in Belarus, Cambodia, Central African Republic, Democratic People's Republic of Korea, Eritrea, Iran, Mali, Myanmar, Somalia, Sudan, Syria, and the occupied Palestinian territories. The creation of a special procedure depends on a political decision adopted by a majority of the governmental representatives of whom the Human Rights Council is composed. Hence, their establishment and operationalization are not subjected to the consent of any concerned state, which translates into the universal scope of their mandates. The experts in charge of special procedures have developed flexible working methods. The majority accepts complaints about human rights violations to which they can respond promptly through "urgent appeals," if the life or physical integrity of a person or group is in danger. They also handle individual complaints on an ordinary basis when they believe there is reliable information that indicates the possible violation of rights under their competence. With the consent of the relevant states, the experts conduct visits to investigate human rights situations on the ground. By January 2020, 127 states have issued open invitations to the rapporteurs to visit their territories.[14]

The progress that the international investigation of the human rights situation in Chile brought about under the auspices of the UN was groundbreaking but, at that time, largely limited to the sphere of civil and political rights, as can be seen from the mandates assigned to the first fact-finding bodies and the range of rights that were prioritized in codification efforts. Both the General Assembly and the Commission on Human Rights reacted very timidly to the violations of economic, social, and cultural rights (ESCR) and failed to address the complicity of business and other economic agents in human rights violations. A notable exception was the *Study on the impact of foreign economic aid and assistance on respect for human rights in Chile*, undertaken by the leading international jurist, Antonio Cassese. Despite being a solid, relevant, and pioneering study, it had little impact, highlighting the absence of political will to address the economic factors and the role of businesses in facilitating the abuses that characterized the Pinochet regime. The lack of attention to these factors and the contempt demonstrated toward the violations of ESCR have continued in democracy.

This chapter delves into topics developed in other sections of this book, with the objective of explaining the key reasons underpinning the low impact of the *Cassese Report*. Through the lenses of the intergovernmental decisions establishing the mandates and scope of competences of special procedures, the analysis that follows demonstrates the absence of political will to equate the importance granted to civil and political rights with that granted to ESCR. The progress to mitigate this imbalance since the time of publication of the *Cassese Report* has been quantitative rather than qualitative. While ESCR have gained prominence over the years, most advances remain insufficient, especially regarding the role of business in human rights abuses. As long as the political decisions adopted within the human rights monitoring system do not implement the indivisibility of all rights, it will be very difficult to achieve substantial progress in this field.

The chapter is divided into three parts. The first explains the geopolitical coordinates in which the *Cassese Report* was discussed. It reveals that some of the factors that resulted in undermining its importance have survived over the years. However, other substantial and institutional parameters have changed and can shed light on the opportunities that exist today to address the complicity of business and other enterprises in human rights violations. The second part of the chapter explains the late incorporation of ESCR among those investigated by special procedures and how different political and institutional decisions have been decisive to perpetuate, for years, their lower "rank." The final section outlines the main reports of special procedures on democratic Chile, concluding that mandate holders should adopt a more systematic approach to the incorporation of corporate responsibility for human rights in their analysis and reports.

GEOPOLITICAL COORDINATES OF THE *CASSESE REPORT*: ROLE OF THE SUB-COMMISSION ON THE PROMOTION AND PROTECTION OF HUMAN RIGHTS

Fernández and Smart's contribution highlights the role of the Working Group on Chile in the decision to appoint an expert to study the impact of foreign aid and economic assistance on respecting human rights in that country. It is possible to speculate that entrusting the study to an expert of the then Sub-Commission on Prevention of Discrimination and Protection of Minorities (hereinafter Sub-Commission) subtracted weight from the final outcome, because the Sub-Commission was a body composed of experts. However, the *Cassese Report* was also tabled before the General Assembly, the only plenary intergovernmental body of the UN.[15] Most of the few references that can be found to the study, in databases of the UN and others, are limited to that session of the General Assembly, which Antonio Cassese attended in person. He also offered to answer questions, although summary records of the session indicate that no governmental representative used such prerogative.[16]

However, the delegations of the German Democratic Republic and Belarus drew attention to the report, noting that their conclusions were parallel to those made by Rapporteur Khalifa in his study on the adverse consequences for the enjoyment of human rights of the assistance provided to the colonialist and racist regimes of southern Africa.[17] Using arguments similar to those defended by the Chilean government,[18] the Moroccan delegation expressed deep disagreement with the preparation of this report, which it considered the product of a political decision contrary to the prohibition of interference in the internal affairs of states, accusing the Rapporteur of having acted ultra vires.[19]

Finally, General Assembly resolution 33/175 of December 20, 1978, expressed its appreciation to the Special Rapporteur for his report. The *Cassese Report* found some echo in the 1979 report of the Working Group on Chile.[20] The Secretary-General's report on the international dimension of the right to development, published that same year, also refers to Cassese's findings and conclusions in the sections dedicated to official aid (paragraphs 260–72) and the role of transnational corporations in realizing the right to development (paragraph 286).[21] Apart from those examples, we must wait until recent reports of the current Independent Expert on the consequences of external debt and international financial obligations on the enjoyment of human rights, Juan Pablo Bohoslavsky, to find references to the *Cassese Report*.[22]

The disparity between the relevance of the pioneering and substantive content of the *Cassese Report*, and its impact inside and outside the UN, reflects an intrinsic difficulty of the international human rights system. On the one hand, only experts detached from eminently political processes have the necessary tools and independence to conduct critical background analyses of the scope of the *Cassese Report.* However, guaranteeing such independence means a departure from governments and state agendas that ultimately implement national policies and create international human rights mechanisms. The disappearance of the Sub-Commission, in 2006, demonstrates the vulnerability of those who try to operate while ignoring the politicization of the bodies on which they depend. The lack of systematic follow-up to the *Cassese Report* illustrates the lack of political will to effectively implement the proclaimed indivisibility of all human rights, a legacy that has been perpetuated to this day.

The Sub-Commission always paid greater attention to ESCR than the Commission. Several reports prepared by its members were significant for the advancement of the analytical content of these rights.[23] The issue of corporate responsibility and rights continued on the agenda of the Sub-Commission after the *Cassese Report,* although progress over the years was slow and the reception by countries and the Human Rights Commission was poor. Only in 2003 did the Sub-Commission adopt the "Draft norms on the responsibilities of transnational corporations and other business enterprises with regard to human rights."[24] This draft referred to the "obligations" that international human rights imposed on businesses. Without the scientific rigor of the *Cassese Report*, the rules were criticized for the ambiguity of their legal foundations and for suggesting obligations on business actors that went beyond the existing legal framework.[25] Many governments and the business community vehemently opposed them, considering that they had gone too far.[26] The Commission on Human Rights openly rejected them and, in 2005, requested the Secretary-General to designate a Special Representative of the Secretary-General on human rights and transnational corporations and other business enterprises.[27] The appointed Special Representative, John Ruggie, radically changed the approach to this topic and carried out a consultation process to facilitate consensus among the various stakeholders.[28] In 2011, he presented a completely new set of principles, the "Guiding Principles on Business and Human Rights for implementing the United Nations 'Protect, Respect and Remedy Framework'"[29] (Guiding Principles) which were immediately supported by the Human Rights Council.[30] The Guiding Principles constitute the main and most complete input prepared by the UN on business and human rights. However, they have not been without criticism. For some states and academics, they contain softened obligations that are expressed only in terms of responsibility (and not an obligation) to respect human rights. It has been argued that the attempt to take into account and reconcile the views of all parties involved led to a lack of consistent conceptual foundations.[31]

These welcome advances represent a late and incomplete answer to the diminished status enjoyed by ESCR within the UN human rights machinery, as demonstrated in the mandates of special procedures established by now extinct Commission on Human Rights. The procedures related to ESCR have encountered obstacles both to achieving the majority of votes necessary for their creation and enjoying the same position in the unwritten hierarchy of rights that has permeated the promotion and protection of human rights at domestic, regional, and international level.

LATE CREATION AND DIFFERENCE IN TREATMENT OF MANDATES RELATED TO ESCR

The first special geographic and thematic public procedures have existed since 1967 and 1980, respectively. It takes decades for the Commission to create the first mandates focused on ESCR. The change of direction is marked by the establishment, in 1997–1998, of the mandates on structural adjustment programs,[32] the effects of external debt on the enjoyment of human rights[33] (merged with the mandate on structural adjustment in 2000),[34] extreme poverty,[35] the right to development,[36] and the right to education.[37] With the exception of the right to education, these mandates did not directly refer to ESCR as contained in the Universal Declaration of Human Rights and the International Covenant on ESCR (ICESCR). Since 2000, there is a more proactive approach, illustrated by the creation of the mandates related to the right to food,[38] the right to housing as an integral element of the right to an adequate standard of living,[39] and the right of every person to enjoy the highest level of physical and mental health.[40] Almost a decade later, the mandates relating to the right to safe drinking water and sanitation (2008)[41] and to cultural rights (2009)[42] were added to the system of special procedures, as well as mandates linked to the enjoyment of a plurality of ESCR, such as those related to international solidarity (2005), the promotion of a democratic and equitable international order (2011), environment (2012), and the right to development (2016). As mentioned above, the first special procedure dedicated exclusively to the topic of business and human rights was established in 2005.[43] In 2011, the Special Representative was replaced by the Working Group on the issue of human rights and transnational corporations and other business enterprises (Working Group on Business and Human Rights).[44]

To date, mandates related to ESCR are significantly lower in number than those focusing on civil and political rights. However, the difference is not only in the number of mandates but also in two important elements: (a) the terminology chosen for naming the procedure, and (b) the nature and scope of the competences assigned to the mandate holder.

a) Name of the Mandate

The reticence toward mandates on ESCR is reflected in the introduction of different denominations for the mandate holders of these procedures. The plurality of denominations (Rapporteur/Representative /Special Envoy or Independent Expert) does not have an express relationship with the content of the mandates or with the institutional position of the experts. Rather, the decision to opt for one nomenclature or another responds to political motivations.[45] The name Rapporteur has the connotation of underlining the seriousness of the human rights situation covered by the mandate. Until procedures that monitor ESCR, as well as the rights groups in vulnerable positions, or the so-called "third-generation rights," appeared on the scene, only geographical procedures were designated by names other than Special Rapporteur or Working Group. Although a few mandates directly referred to ESCR were conferred on "Special Rapporteurs" (education, food, housing, and health), all other mandate holders have been originally designated as "Independent Experts" or "Special Representatives."[46]

The greater weight associated with Special Rapporteur has prompted mandate holders that were appointed with other denominations to promote the change of title. This is the case, for example, of the mandates of the Independent Experts on the rights to drinking water and sanitation,[47] extreme poverty,[48] cultural rights,[49] and environment.[50] In the negotiations of the resolutions that renamed these mandates from "independent experts" to "special rapporteurs," it was evident that the change sought to "raise" their status and reinforce the legitimacy of the tasks formerly performed. In fact, several mandate holders had assumed, since their establishment, investigative, and monitoring functions, including responding regularly to communications and sending urgent requests and allegation letters, despite the literal letter of their mandates, as explained below.

b) Nature of the Mandate

Another important disparity in treatment between the mandates relating to civil and political rights and those addressing ESCR lies in the nature of the mandate with which they were created. On many occasions, the competences assigned to the mandate holders related to ESCR have been directed to studies and/or draft declarations or guiding principles, not including the competence to "respond effectively" or "investigate" violations of human rights, as in the case of mandates related to civil and political rights. For example, the original mandate of the special procedure on education required to report on the progressive realization of the right to education and promote assistance to governments in the development of action plans to gradually achieve compulsory and free education for all. Very similar in content were the competences attributed to the rapporteurs on housing and health. However, the independent expert on drinking water and sanitation merely received competencies to prepare a compendium of best practices related to access to drinking water and sanitation and a study to specify the content of human rights obligations in relation to this topic. This last example is especially striking because the procedure was created in 2009, when almost all mandate holders were investigating violations of ESCR, including individual communications, regardless of the literal wording of their mandate. The Independent Expert in the field of cultural rights also received a mandate focused on conceptual analysis and advisory work.

Although decaffeinated, the original mandate of the Special Rapporteur on the right to food contained a reference to the need to "respond" to the information received on aspects of the realization of the right to food, which was manifested in this Rapporteur adopting, from its establishment, a similar approach to other special procedures on civil and political rights in their working methods, including the processing of individual cases. For its part, the mandate of the "Working Group on Business and Human Rights" also differs from the conventional content assigned to mandates addressing civil and political rights. It focuses on promoting the Guiding Principles, identifying good practices, studying the possibilities of increasing access to effective resources for those whose human rights are affected by the activities of companies, and establishing a dialogue with different partners. Despite incorporating the possibility of visiting countries, it does not directly refer to an obligation—or even the possibility—to investigate violations.[51]

SNAPSHOT OF THE PRESENT AND FUTURE OUTLOOK

Compared to its predecessor, the Human Rights Council has contributed to narrowing the gap between the efforts devoted to ESCR and those categorized as civil and political rights. However, the Chilean case reveals the limits of this progress. To date, special procedures have not addressed systematically and comprehensively the abuses attributed to the dictatorship and how they continue to influence the enjoyment of human rights in the country. Considering the higher than average attention paid to Chile by special procedures, this is an unsatisfactory outcome.

Since its transition to democracy in 1990, Chile has been visited by a relatively high number of special procedures, including the Special Rapporteur on the Rights of Indigenous Peoples (2003 and 2009), the Working Group on Mercenaries (2007); the Working Group on enforced or involuntary disappearances (2012), the Special Rapporteur on human rights and fundamental freedoms in the fight against terrorism (2013); the Working Group on the issue of discrimination against women in law and practice (2014); the Special Rapporteur on extreme poverty (2015);[52] the Special Rapporteur on the right to education (2016);[53] the Special Rapporteur on the rights to freedom of peaceful assembly and association (2016); and the Special Rapporteur on adequate housing (2017).[54] The reports of the visits reveal that the violations to ESCR have received comparable attention to civil and political rights violations in recent years. This seems to be in line with the reality of the country, since, despite a significant improvement in the enjoyment of civil and political rights, the situation of ESCR remains a pending task.

Mandate holders have been quite critical on the performance of the Chilean government regarding ESCR. They have also addressed the role that business and other economic actors play in the enjoyment of human rights, expressing concerns over the limited protection of trade union rights, labor rights, and the right to strike;[55] the low participation of women on the boards of directors and decision-making positions in public companies;[56] the interference of corporate interests in funding education.[57] Special procedures have proposed that the National Plan of Action on Business and Human Rights should be applied to real estate developers;[58] they have encouraged the business sector to assume social responsibility and contribute to national resources for education,[59] and have recommended that companies that operate the mining, forestry, and agricultural industries on land claimed by indigenous peoples, adopt human rights standards in accordance with the Guiding Principles on Business and Human Rights.[60] To date, the most extensive analysis—not yet comprehensive—of corporate responsibility in reports made after country missions to Chile does not come from ESCR mandates, but from the report of the Special Rapporteur on the rights of indigenous resulting from his 2009 visit.[61] However, the analysis is inherently limited to a group of the Chilean population. There is still a need to examine the abuses of companies in relation to the entire population.[62]

While they have not carried out visits on the ground, the special procedures that have paid greater attention to the issue of financial complicity on the enjoyment of human rights are the Independent Expert on the consequences of foreign debt[63] and the Special Rapporteur on the promotion of truth, justice, reparation, and guarantees of non-repetition.[64] In 2015, both mandate holders directly requested information from the Chilean government on the measures adopted by the state to carry out or promote research on financial aid and the granting of loans that the Chilean State would have received during the military dictatorship of Augusto Pinochet, analyzing how this aid would have contributed or prolonged the nonobservance of human rights or increased the likelihood of human rights violations that characterized the military dictatorship in Chile.[65] Unfortunately, to date, this request for information has been disregarded by the Chilean authorities. Hence, special procedures have not yet systematically examined the range of abuses committed by business and other enterprises during the dictatorship and how they may have contributed to perpetuating human rights violations in Chile.

If this is the situation four decades after the *Cassese Report*, it is not surprising that the UN system's responses to the civic–military dictatorship focused on civil and political rights violations and ignored ESCR and corporate abuse. The rigor and breadth of the *Cassese Report* should have instigated greater monitoring of key abuses committed by companies that helped consolidate the dictatorship. Maybe the report was too progressive for its time. It was prepared by a leading international jurist, who analyzed the issue independently and oblivious to political considerations. His report was submitted to the Sub-Commission on Human Rights, which was an expert body, and, although it was also discussed by the General Assembly, this occurred at a time when the political organs of the system were not prepared to consider these issues. They did not even consider those rights of an economic, social, and cultural nature as "real" rights at the time.[66]

The fact that ESCR have been treated as a second-class category of rights also explains the delay in considering the issue of business and human rights, where the superficial distinction between categories of rights is inoperable. The creation of the relevant Working Group and the Guiding Principles on business and human rights became a reality in the second decade of the twenty-first century. In 2014, the Human Rights Council set up an open-ended intergovernmental working group on transnational corporations and other business enterprises with respect to human rights and mandated to elaborate an international legally binding instrument to regulate, in international human rights law, the activities of transnational corporations and other business enterprises.[67] Despite the progress made in the negotiations, from the outcomes of its fifth session in October 2019, the adoption of a text in the near future remains uncertain.[68]

The lack of equal enjoyment of ESCR and the neglect in assessing the responsibility of businesses and other economic actors were among the legitimate claims underpinning the social unrest that erupted in Chile in October 2019.[69] In the current context, ignoring corporate abuse is unjustifiable. In Chile, inequality of wealth and income has not registered great improvements in the past decade[70] and, despite modest advances, the levels of poverty and extreme poverty are concerning and much higher than in the OECD average country.[71] Moreover, the discourse and judicial protection of human rights still seems reserved only to civil and political rights.[72] Thus, it is essential to promote ESCR more firmly and to address the present abuses committed by companies and remedy past ones.

The UN special procedures should give greater attention to corporate social responsibility. With the support of the government, as well as civil society organizations, including NGOs, academic institutions, and trade unions, a visit to Chile by the Working Group on Business and human rights would serve as a catalyst to address these long-neglected issues. Forty years after the *Cassese Report*, it is the responsibility of all stakeholders to undertake the analysis and adopt the necessary strategies to address the complicity of companies in the past and present human rights violations in Chile. If stakeholders, including human rights monitoring bodies, continue to overlook the responsibility of companies in the enjoyment of all human rights, the future of the Chilean democracy could be at risk.

NOTES

1. General Assembly (GA) Resolution (Res.) 3059 (XXVIII), November 2, 1973.
2. Nigel Rodley, *The Treatment of Prisoners under International Law* (Oxford University Press, 2nd Ed. 1999), 18–45.
3. GA Res. 39/46, December 10, 1984.
4. GA Res. 47/133, December 18, 1992.
5. Elvira Domínguez-Redondo, *Los procedimientos públicos especiales de la Comisión de Derechos Humanos de Naciones Unidas* (Trotta, 2005), 34–48.

6. Commission on Human Rights (CHR) Res. 2 (XXIII), March 6, 1967, and Res. 7 (XXIII), March 16, 1967.

7. CHR Res. 8 (XXI), February 27, 1975, and Res. 11 (XXXV), March 6, 1979.

8. CHR Res.20 (XXXVI), February 29, 1980.

9. UN doc. E/CN.4/1266 (February 1, 1978) and GA Res. 33/173, December 20, 1970. See also, Ian Guest, *Behind the Disappearances. Argentina's Dirty War against Human Rights and the United Nations* (University of Pennsylvania Press, 1990) and Daniel Prémont, "United Nations Procedures for the Protection of all Persons Subjected to Any Form of Detention or Imprisonment," *Santa Clara Law Review* 20(1) (1980): 603, 625.

10. Economic and Social Council (ECOSOC) Res. 1982/29, March 11, 1989.

11. CHR Res. 1985/33, March 13, 1985. See also Rodley (1999) (n. 2), 18–45 and 134–46; on the joint discussion regarding the issues of genocide torture and disappearances, see Naomi Roht-Arriaza (ed.), *Impunity and Human Rights in International Law and Practice* (Oxford University Press, 1995), 26–28.

12. For example, Security Council (SC) Res. 134 (1960), April 1, 1960; and 181 (1963), August 7, 1963. See also, R. B. Ballinger, "UN Action on Human Rights in South Africa," in *The International Protection of Human Rights*, ed. Luard (Tahes and Hudson, 1967), 248–85, *esp.* 257–66 and Nigel Rodley, "The United Nations and Human Rights in the Middle East," *Social Research* 38(1) (1971): 217–40.

13. See full list on the Website of the Office of the High Commissioner for Human Rights (OHCHR) at https://www.ohchr.org/en/hrbodies/sp/pages/welcome page.aspx.

14. Information available on the OHCHR Website at: https://spinternet.ohchr.org/_layouts/15/SpecialProceduresInternet/StandingInvitations.aspx.

15. See CHR Res. 12 (XXXIV), March 6, 1978 (UN doc. E/1978/34 (SUPP) -E/CN.4/1292, 1978, pp. 116–18) requesting the expert to also present his report to the General Assembly.

16. UN Doc. A/C.3/33/SR.60 (December 1, 1978), paragraph 105.

17. UN Doc. A/C.3/33/SR.64 (December 7, 1978), paragraphs 3 and 34.

18. UN Doc. E/1978/34 (SUPP) -E/CN.4/292, pp. 116–18, UN Doc. E/1978/34 (SUPP) -E/CN.4/1292, paragraph 43.

19. UN Doc. A/C.3/33/SR.69 (December 12, 1978), paragraph 35.

20. UN Doc. E/CN.4/1310 (February 1, 1979), paragraphs 7, 258, 259, and 314.

21. UN Doc. E/CN.4/1334 (January 2, 1979).

22. UN Doc. A/HRC/28/59 (December 22, 2014) paragraphs 2 and 11; UN Doc. A/69/273 (August 4, 2014) paragraph 17; and UN Doc. A/HRC/30/27 (September 4, 2015) communication CHL 1/2015.

23. For example, UN Doc. E/CN.4/Sub.2/1987/23 (July 7, 1987); and UN Doc. E/CN.4/Sub.2/1993/15 (June 22, 1993).

24. Res. 2003/16, UN Doc. E/CN.4/Sub.2 /2003/12/ Rev.2 (August 26, 2003).

25. UN Doc. E/CN.4/2005/91 (February 15, 2005).

26. Speech by John Ruggie, January 28, 2014, available at:https://sites.hks.harvard.edu/m-rcbg/CSRI/UNBusinessandHumanRightsTreaty.pdf.

27. UN Doc. E /CN.4/ RES/2005/69 (April 20, 2005).

28. Karim Buhmann, "Navigating from a 'Train Wreck' to Being 'Welcomed': Negotiation Strategies and Argumentative Patterns in the Development of the UN Framework," in *Human Rights Obligations of Business: Beyond the Corporate Responsibility to Respect*, eds. Surya Deva and David Bilchitz (Cambridge University Press, 2013), 29.
29. UN Doc. A/HRC/17/31 (March 21, 2011).
30. Human Rights Council (HRC), Res. 17/4, June 16, 2011.
31. Carlos López, "The 'Ruggie Process': From Legal Obligations to Corporate Social Responsibility?" in Surya and Bilchitz (n. 28): 58.
32. CHR, Res. 1997/103, April 3, 1997.
33. CHR, Res 1998/24, April 17, 1998.
34. CHR, Res. 2000/82, April 26, 2000.
35. CHR, Res. 1998/25, April 17, 1998.
36. CHR, Res. 1998/72, April 21, 1998.
37. CHR, Res. 1998/33, April 17, 1998.
38. CHR, Res. 2000/10, April 17, 2000.
39. Ibid.
40. CHR, Res. 2000/31, April 22, 2000.
41. HRC, Res. 7/22, March 28, 2008.
42. HRC, Res. 10/23, March 26, 2009.
43. CHR, Res. 2005/69 (n. 27).
44. CHR, Res. 17/4, July 6, 2011.
45. Helena Cook, "International Human Rights Mechanisms. The Role of the Special Procedures in the Protection of Human Rights. The Way Forward after Vienna," 50 *International Commission of Jurists. The Review* (1993): 31–55: 43, 44.
46. The exceptions refer to the right to development and that of business and human rights.
47. HRC, Res. 16/2, March 24, 2011.
48. HRC, Res. 17/13, June 17, 2011.
49. HRC, Res. 19/6, March 22, 2012.
50. HRC, Res. 28/11, March 28, 2015.
51. HRC, Res. 17/4 (n. 30) See also original mandate conferred to the predecessor of this special procedure, the Special Representative of the Secretary-General, contained in CHR, Res. 2005/69 (n. 27).
52. UN Doc. A/HRC/32/31/Add.1.
53. UN Doc. A/HRC/35/24/Add.1.
54. UN Doc. A/HRC/37/53/Add.1.
55. See, for example, UN Doc. A/HRC/32/36/Add.1 and UN Doc. A/HRC/32/31/Add.1.
56. UN Doc. A/HRC/29/40/Add.1.
57. Ibid.
58. UN Doc. A/HRC/37/53/Add.1.
59. UN Doc. A/HRC/35/24/Add.1.
60. UN Doc. A/HRC/32/31/Add.1.
61. UN Doc. A/HRC/12/34/Add.6.

62. See the contribution of José Aylwin.
63. UN Doc. A/HRC/28/59.
64. Ibid.
65. Letter of May 26, 2015, CHL 1/2005, available on the Special Procedures communication database, at https://spcommreports.ohchr.org/TMResultsBase/DownLoadPublicCommunicationFile?gId=15121.
66. Magdalena Sepúlveda, *The Nature of the Obligations under the International Covenant on Economic, Social and Cultural Rights* (Antwerp: Hart, Intersentia, 2002).
67. HRC, Res. 26/9 (June 26, 2014), para. 1.
68. UN Doc. A/HRC/43/XX.
69. See, for example, Luis Maldonado, Juan Carlos Castillo, Julio Iturra, Jorge Atria & Francisco Meneses, "La demanda por igualdad y los caminos que cuentan con amplio respaldo ciudadano," Centro de Investigación Periodística (CIPER), December 6, 2019, available at https://ciperchile.cl/2019/12/06/la-demanda-por-igualdad-y-los-caminos-que-cuentan-con-amplio-respaldo-ciudadano/.
70. See OECD Income Distribution Database, available at: http://www.oecd.org/social/income-distribution-database.htm. See also, United Nations Development Programme (UNDP), *Desiguales. Orígenes, cambios y desafíos de la brecha social en Chile* (Unequal. Origins, changes and challenges in Chile's social divide) (UNDP, June 2017) and Economic Commission for Latin America and the Caribbean, *Social Panorama of Latin America 2019* (ECLAC, December 2019).
71. See, for example, Government of Chile, Ministry of Social Development, *Informe de Desarrollo Social 2017* (Social Development Report, 2017), available at: http://www.ministeriodesarrollosocial.gob.cl/pdf/upload/IDS2017.pdf.
72. See, for example, UN Doc. E/C.12/CHL/CO/4 (July 7, 2015).

Chapter 6

Transitional Justice and Economic Actors

Latin America's Protagonism

Leigh A. Payne, Gabriel Pereira,
and Laura Bernal-Bermúdez

INTRODUCTION

In this chapter, we demonstrate that corporate accountability has been part of transitional justice processes of memory, truth, and justice. The role of economic actors in past human rights violations has been referred to as the "missing piece of the puzzle" of transitional justice.[1] The data gathered for our Corporate Accountability and Transitional Justice (CATJ)[2] database shows, in contrast, that corporate accountability has been part of transitional justice since its origins in the post-Holocaust accountability processes and continuing through subsequent truth commissions and judicial actions in every region of the world.[3] In addition, the data indicate that Latin America has played a leading role in the struggle for truth and justice for corporate complicity. Latin America shows that social mobilization behind truth initiatives and legal mobilization promoting judicial action has produced important, albeit limited, outcomes.

Our focus on the region leads us to develop a "justice from below" argument. We claim that in nearly all phases of the development of CATJ, Latin American countries have taken a lead in advancing the concept. We explain these outcomes in the region using an Archimedes' Lever analogy[4]: weak actors (victims of corporate abuses in the Global South) with the right tools (innovative institutional strategies) can lift the heavyweight of corporate accountability, even when weighed down by powerful veto players in the business community and even without the help of international forces. Weak actors will need to apply less force when the fulcrum is positioned closer to the weight of corporate accountability, that is, when the political context is favorable to corporate accountability. In this chapter, we develop that concept and apply it to the Chilean process.

In the first section of the chapter, we provide a brief comparative analysis of the accountability mechanisms implemented since the Nazi regime crimes. Then we analyze the evidence of Latin America's leading role in this area of transitional justice. In the following section, we introduce our Archimedes' Lever approach explaining corporate accountability from below with particular emphasis on Latin America's leadership. Then we apply our approach to explain the only judicial case with a verdict in Chile. We conclude the chapter highlighting the main aspects of this work and its implications for the fight for truth and justice in Latin America.

CORPORATE ACCOUNTABILITY AND TRANSITIONAL JUSTICE

The focus of transitional justice to achieve justice, memory, and reparations has traditionally concentrated almost exclusively on state, or state-like, actors. It is only in exceptional cases that these mechanisms have focused on civil actors.[5] A close look, however, shows that economic actors' complicity has been included in transitional justice mechanisms in every region of the world, by truth commissions investigating and reporting on their participation in human rights violations or in judicial actions holding them responsible for such participation. Nonetheless, it is evident that these actors have been included less intensely than state, or state-like, actors.[6]

Moreover, the very origin of transitional justice with post-Holocaust accountability efforts linked the genocide to business activity. The CATJ reveals more than 300 businesses named in Holocaust crimes against humanity cases at Nuremberg, in the Allies' Military Tribunals, and U.S. courts. These efforts at justice and truth regarding economic actors have also occurred in recent processes. Our survey of final truth commission reports reveals that over half identified businesses as complicit in grave violations of human rights during authoritarian and civil conflict periods (59 percent; or twenty-three out of thirty-nine final reports). All of these reports name specific economic actors implicated in particular types of grave human rights violations during authoritarian regimes and armed conflicts. The CATJ contains a list of 329 names of economic actors extracted from reports from twenty countries around the world.

Despite revealing the association of so many economic actors in past human rights violations, these truth commission findings have received little visibility. An important factor could explain the lack of attention to this aspect of truth commissions' findings: very few truth commissions (four) had an explicit mandate to investigate corporate complicity. Another factor limiting the impact of truth commission findings is the small number of reports (three) that included judicial investigations into corporate complicity in their recommendations. In other words, although our findings show that corporate complicity played an important part in truth commission investigations, the lack of visibility of these findings means that these processes have not fulfilled the promise to victims of establishing truth, advancing justice, paying reparations, or guaranteeing non-repetition in these types of violations.

Chile provides an example. Its two truth commissions (Rettig in 1990 and Valech I in 2003) recognized a degree of complicity by naming a total of sixteen economic actors for presumed responsibility for gross violations of human rights. The Rettig Commission identified fourteen economic actors associated with general participation in repression and specific acts of arbitrary detention, torture, and on-site detention centers. The following companies were named: Elecmetal; EmporChi; ENAEX; Cia de Telefonos; LANChile; Ferrocarrilles; ENTEL; Aerolite; Luchetti; Cia Sudamericana de Vapores; DINAC; Empresa Navieras; ENDESA; Loncoleche. The Valech I commission identified two economic actors—Iansa and Felco—for arbitrary detention and on-site detention centers. Yet, the truth commissions carried out these investigations without a mandate, few know about these findings by the truth commissions, and no recommendations in the truth commission reports involve follow-up judicial investigation, reparations, or regulations.

Besides truth commissions, corporate accountability has also occurred in courts, a key transitional justice mechanism. The attempt to hold business accountable around the world has involved innovative legal strategies in domestic, foreign, and international courts. Of the 104 judicial actions recorded in the CATJ, fifty-one (49 percent) were held in domestic courts, fifty (48 percent) in foreign courts, one in an international court, and in three cases we were unable to determine the type of court. Unlike judicial actions involving state actors, businesses have been held accountable in both criminal and civil courts alike. Foreign courts have seen more civil cases (thirty-seven) than criminal cases (thirteen), while in domestic courts criminal trials represent the majority of cases (forty-two).

Contrary to what some have suggested, and reinforcing our justice from below argument, higher levels of accountability have been achieved in the courts of the Global South. Fifteen judicial actions in domestic courts have ended in tentative or final judgments, while only four have had the same outcomes in foreign courts. Additionally, ongoing litigation processes are observed in the Global South while few foreign judicial actions remain pending.

Corporate judicial accountability innovates on standard transitional justice processes. As we discuss elsewhere,[7] civil actions, standard practice in business, and human rights accountability cases, have been incorporated into the transitional justice tool kit. Of the fifty-three cases brought to domestic courts of the Global South, eight (15 percent) are civil, while forty-two (79 percent) are criminal.[8] Criminal trials are, thus, more frequent, but civil actions have provided innovative ways to advance CATJ.

Of the forty-two criminal actions, eleven (27 percent) accuse economic actors of indirect human rights violations, that is, financing violence. The majority (thirty-one, or 73 percent) constitute claims of direct violations: aiding state security forces in arbitrarily detaining workers (two, or 5 percent), torture, and disappearance of those who were arbitrarily detained (twenty-eight, or 54 percent), and a case in Colombia (one, or 2 percent) in which the company actively participated in the forced displacement of communities to appropriate their lands.[9]

These previous paragraphs show that efforts at corporate accountability have been, and still are, part of the set of global transitional justice mechanisms. The existence of these efforts challenges the view that only state and state-like actors are held accountable in such mechanisms. Also, the data suggests that domestic litigation in the Global South is producing positive outcomes.

LATIN AMERICAN PROTAGONISM

With regard to the CATJ data on truth commissions and judicial action, there is no doubt that Latin America has been the world leader in incorporating corporate complicity into transitional justice approaches to past human rights violations. With regard to truth commissions, the region had the highest concentration of reports identifying businesses involved in gross violations of human rights: eleven of the twenty-three (48 percent) reports and ten of the twenty countries with such truth commission reports (50 percent). In addition, most of the economic actors named in those reports are found in the region: 232 or 71 percent. The two countries with the highest number of economic actors named in their reports are in the region: Brazil with 123 or 38 percent and Guatemala with 45 or 14 percent of the total number of 329 economic actors named as complicit in truth commission final reports.

As stated previously, Chile is one of the countries in which corporate complicity is included in truth commissions. The two truth commissions (Rettig in 1990 and Valech I in 2003) identified a total of seventeen economic actors with alleged responsibility for serious human rights violations. The Rettig Commission identified fifteen economic actors associated with participation in the repression and in particular with arbitrary detentions, torture, and detention centers in its facilities. For its part, the Valech I commission identified two economic actors—IANSA and Felco—linked to arbitrary detentions and detention centers at their facilities.

Similarly, in trials, the region has also led with fifty of the fifty-one judicial actions held in domestic courts. Although there are few outcomes of these trials, at the moment countries within the region are also the leaders in convictions. Latin American courts were involved in 75 percent (fifteen) of all the convictions and convictions pending appeal in the CATJ. Further evidence suggests that Latin America is the region in which current legal mobilization is occurring. It is the region with the highest number of pending cases: thirty, compared to one in Africa and five in MENA. This suggests a recent trend in the region to bring these cases, a speculation that requires further investigation.

Chile is not the country that has moved the farthest in judicial actions in the region. Argentina and Colombia hold that place. Nonetheless, it has advanced farther than the majority of countries in the region and the world. The CATJ registers seven judicial cases and one conviction (Juan Francisco Luzoro Montenegro case for the Paine massacre).

This brief overview of accountability initiatives developed in Latin America shows that this region is leading the accountability process to hold economic actors accountable for their participation in human rights violations in TJ contexts. Efforts to achieve truth and justice in this region are those that offer greater—although insufficient—results when compared with those implemented in other regions of the world.

THE PATHWAY TO CORPORATE ACCOUNTABILITY

Civil society mobilization is a key factor for advancing corporate accountability in transitional justice contexts. It is critical to our notion of Archimedes' Lever[10] to explain corporate accountability. Archimedes' said: "Give me a lever long enough and a fulcrum on which to place it, and I shall move the world." We adapt this notion to suggest that even relatively weak actors (victims of corporate complicity in the Global South) can lift the weight of accountability when they have the right tools in their hands. The force to lift the weight of accountability comes from civil society demand/mobilization and institutional innovators, comprising human rights lawyers whose institutional role is taking the cases to courts, prosecutors, and judges, who are willing to take on cases that seem unwinnable. They face the mighty weight of strong veto players (i.e., economic actors) who weigh heavily on corporate accountability preventing it from lifting up. Key to Archimedes' Lever is the placement of the fulcrum, in our model the political context. When the context is more favorable to corporate accountability, or closer to it, civil society and institutional innovators will require less force to lift it up from under the weight of veto players. Unpropitious political contexts and two structural impediments—international law and business veto power—require even more force on the side of civil society mobilization to advance corporate accountability.

Regarding structural obstacles, formal international institutional fora do not yet exist to promote accountability for international human rights violations carried out by businesses. International pressure was a key component of promoting justice for victims of violence during dictatorships and armed conflict. Unsettled international law regarding the binding and enforceable human rights obligations of business entities, the absence of international enforcement mechanisms to hold economic actors accountable, and the related lack of international pressure on states to deliver to victims of corporate complicity their rights to truth, justice, remedy, and guarantees of non-repetition. A second structural obstacle is the strong veto power of business. These veto players have blocked efforts at binding international instruments, but they also have proved formidable in domestic judicial cases. It is difficult to imagine that veto power will weaken on its own.

Accountability forces aiming to counterbalance the force of veto players and the lack of international pressure are active in the region. Human rights groups have been active in countries such as Argentina and Brazil. Also, initial mobilization pushing for business complicity is emerging in Chile and appears to be developing in other parts of the region, as we discuss later in this chapter.

In Argentina, one of the countries with the highest level of judicial actions, human rights groups have been active on different fronts. On March 24, every year Argentine society commemorates the coup, and massive demonstrations occur in the main cities of the country. Such events are the opportunity for human rights groups to raise their memory, justice, and truth demands and bring them to the public arena. In the past decade, human rights groups included their demands for justice and truth about corporate actors. Also, human rights groups have mobilized and lobbied for policy reforms. A bill creating a truth commission on economic complicity was passed in 2015 during the more favorable government of Cristina Fernández de Kirchner. With the change in government under Mauricio Macri, the bill has not been implemented, and the commission has not yet been created. Human rights groups have lobbied to demand its effective implementation without success. At the judicial level, strong mobilization has accompanied the course of criminal and civil actions against businesses. These groups monitor the development of these cases and have publicly denounced judicial setbacks and a legal and political maneuver to affect the course of such actions. Also, these groups have held different meetings to discuss legal strategies to tackle business complicity in the recent civil–military dictatorship. Again, the success of these endeavors was limited during the unpropitious Macri government when economic actors applied their substantial veto power.

In Brazil, mobilization around the National and São Paulo State Truth Commissions could be said to have acted as a catalyst to investigate the role that corporations played in the 1964 coup and subsequent dictatorship. An unprecedented alliance of human rights groups and unions collected evidence demonstrating the role of business on the set up of the coup and the implementation of state terrorism. That evidence was incorporated by both truth commissions. Those investigations and parallel civil society activities led to public acts to reveal complicity. In one such act, students mobilized to petition for the removal of a São Paulo street name associated with one of the businessmen connected to the coup and repression. A video of their activities,[11] as well as a film about the businessman, circulated widely on YouTube. The truth commission and civil society pressure for accountability are considered to be crucial to the opening up of the lawsuit against Volkswagen for its role in the dictatorship's repressive apparatus.[12] The union's network involved in the collection of evidence for the truth commission joined together in an alliance called the Fórum de Trabalhadores por Verdade, Justiça e Reparação. Unsatisfied with the National Truth's recommendations, this alliance published its recommendations demanding judicial accountability that, through civil society pressure, made its way into the final official report. The Fórum has developed strategies to make visible business complicity and to advance the Volkswagen case.

The Brazil truth commissions illustrate the ways in which the mobilization of key civil society actors can advance corporate accountability. Their efforts alone are not sufficient. They depend on commissioners and members of staff in the commission to translate that mobilization into corporate accountability results. In truth commissions, this involves taking testimony from victims, families, and communities. Civil society groups can pressure to be heard. Innovative staff members are those who retain these testimonies, conduct their research into corporate complicity, and retain those findings in the final report even after substantial editing and redaction processes. Where innovative commissioners support these processes, civil society forces will prove much more likely to have their truths about corporate complicity included in final reports. Latin America is no doubt a leader in truth commissions owing to the pressure by civil society groups and the responsiveness of truth commission staff.

Latin American institutional innovators have also used sophisticated legal strategies in judicial processes. Public prosecutors, judges, and human rights lawyers have put forward two types of innovations in criminal cases. First, the extension of the prosecutorial activity to individual actors beyond the "usual suspects," that is, state and state-like actors. The innovation lies in a nonconventional approach to judicial accountability in transitional justice contexts involving challenges related to evidence and legal-doctrine. Public prosecutors and private lawyers have deployed strategies to connect regular crimes connected with crimes against humanity.

Chile provides an example. Juan Francisco Luzoro Montenegro has been sentenced by the Supreme Court to twenty years in prison for the homicide and attempted homicide of peasants in the Paine community. In this case, the evidence shows that Luzoro Montenegro participated in the operations where peasants were illegally executed. In this case, the institutional innovators moved beyond the TJ standard approach to prosecuting state actors. They decided also to investigate economic actors involved in the crimes and to seek evidence to establish their legal responsibilities.

In Argentina, in the Vildoza case,[13] several military and civilians are accused of illegal appropriation of properties belonging to disappeared people. The accused allegedly sold these assets to individuals and companies connected to the military. At question is whether the defendants incurred the crime of money-laundering, a crime incorporated into the Argentine legal system only in 2000. Although the law could not be applied retroactively to events of the 1970s dictatorship, two legal innovations proved relevant. First, the event was linked to crimes against humanity, making a "causal link" between the appropriation of assets from the disappeared and the subsequent economic benefits of the theft. Second, the economic benefits of money-laundering linked to a crime against humanity continue to be accrued, rather than requiring a retroactive application of the law.

Legal innovations in civil claims also considered the imprescriptibility of crimes against humanity in labor claims. In Argentina, two companies have been accusing of failing to fulfill their legal duties as employers in two separate cases. The illegal detention and subsequent forced disappearance of workers from the SIDERCA and Techint companies, according to the plaintiffs, occurred in circumstances related to the workplace. The companies were sued by the victims' families for failing to protect the safety of their workers and thereby facilitating crimes against humanity. Although the cases are similar, judicial outcomes differed. In the case against SIDERCA, the court made a final ruling, not subject to appeal further, that statutes of limitation do not apply to labor claims even when connected to a crime against humanity. Although the second instance tribunal made the same ruling in the case against Techint, the Argentine Supreme Court of Justice overturned this decision in 2019. It established that the state is obligated to seek reparations for victims of crimes against humanity under administrative procedures and, moreover, that suspending statutes of limitation in crimes against humanity include labor claims. These innovations had the potential to overcome structural barriers to addressing victims' rights. In the Techint case, the political context—the composition of the Supreme Court and the increasing veto power of business in the Macri government—are factors that limited civil society and institutional innovators from advancing these claims.

Truth trials can be regarded as another innovation advanced by institutional innovators in the region. In Brazil, despite the validity of the amnesty law prohibiting the prosecution of perpetrators of crimes against humanity, public prosecutors have investigated the Volkswagen subsidiary in São Paulo for involvement in crimes against humanity. In this case, as a consequence of the pressure of the network of trade unions involved in the collection of evidence for the truth commission, prosecutors decided to investigate to gather as much information as possible regarding the company's responsibility in human rights violations of its workers. While prosecutors are aware of the constraints imposed by the amnesty law, they are still able to investigate and seek incriminating evidence. This prosecution thus operates as a kind of "truth trial," in which prosecutors working with organized labor groups have begun to reconstruct the truth behind Volkswagen's complicity in the dictatorship's crimes against humanity; in this case, arbitrary detention and torture. While the company may never face trial, by reaching the public domain in Brazil and Germany, the investigation is potentially damaging to the company's image and may lead to its cooperation in paying extrajudicial individual and collective reparations.

Civil society is critical to advancing these processes. They depend on institutional innovators for their success in having demands translated into truths and judicial action. Yet the political context is also relevant, in particular the degree to which economic actors attempt to veto these processes. The political context in each country determines the position of the fulcrum. The region in general and individual countries in particular have gone through crucial changes in the past two decades. A longer period thus warrants detailed analysis that goes beyond the scope of this chapter. Accountability developments in Chile, however, illustrate how our approach can help to understand current developments in the region. We turn to this brief analysis in the following section.

JUDICIAL ACCOUNTABILITY FROM BELOW IN CHILE: THE PAINE CASE

In our book,[14] we apply our Archimedes' Lever model to the Paine case in Chile, the only judicial action of corporate complicity from the Pinochet dictatorship with a verdict.[15] As we discuss there, the case featured six different economic actors accused of violent land displacement. Shortly after the September 11, 1973, coup and the installation of the Pinochet dictatorship, the military and landholders of this rural community, located 20 miles south of Santiago, kidnapped, tortured, assassinated, or disappeared an estimated 1,000 members of the community. They had been the beneficiaries of the agrarian reform program adopted by democratically elected presidents Eduardo Frei Montalva (1964–1970) and Salvador Allende (1970–1973), who was ousted in the coup. The violence in Paine is sometimes linked to the wealthy Kast family and other large landholders of the region who supported the coup and the subsequent dictatorship. Under the cover of impunity, they allegedly violently retaliated against the rural community.[16]

Of the six defendants in the case, only one—Juan Francisco Luzoro Montenegro—has been sentenced so far. In 2016, San Miguel Appeals Court judge Marianela Cifuentes Alarcón found Luzoro guilty of homicide and sentenced him to twenty years in prison and to pay compensation to the families of his victims.[17] Some critics of the first instance decision consider Luzoro an easy target. As an owner of a small transportation company, he did not symbolize the ideological struggle to reverse agrarian reform policies violently. He might have been the safest defendant to convict if the aim was to bring justice to victims without reopening the political polarization of the past. Of those we interviewed from Paine and in the Chilean human rights legal and NGO community, few believe that justice will be extended beyond this token guilty verdict to include the other—more emblematic—named defendants.

Even if the other cases do not progress, an unprecedented judgment was rendered. There is little doubt that the magistrate involved is an institutional innovator. In a confidential interview, we were told that only a couple of appeals court judges—including Cifuentes—are willing to take on human rights cases as extraordinary visiting ministers, similar to investigator-judges in first instance tribunals. The majority of the court would like to end trials for past human rights violations. Pressure against trials of state perpetrators means even less motivation to hear cases of non-state business actors involved in those violations. In this judicial context, Cifuentes' conviction of Luzoro is particularly daring and innovative. Our informant was confident that other appeals court judges would not have reached the same decision and that future cases of justice for victims of corporate complicity will also depend on which particular judge is assigned to the case.[18]

The Paine case illustrates the need for mobilization to educate the public—including judges—regarding the violent and illegal human rights violations communities faced because of the business-military alliance before and following the coup. In the Paine case, that mobilization has been particularly strong, particularly since 2000. Survivors and relatives of disappeared organized the *Agrupación de Familiares de Detenidos Desaparecidos de Paine*, with women playing a lead role. The human rights group has pursued a wide range of activities to achieve justice, memory, and truth. It extends its mobilization to those directly affected by the violence in Paine, but also to those who were indirectly affected. They attracted significant support,[19] leading to the production of a documentary film and a highly publicized memorial site that has made Paine an emblematic case of illegal violence recognized throughout Chile. The *Agrupación* has also played a crucial role in the judicial action. It participated in Luzoro's court hearings and held public events throughout the trial.[20] The group has also made public the alleged involvement of other civilians in the crimes, such as the Kast family.[21]

Sensitizing judges to the experiences of victims and the application of criminal law to non-state business actors to bring justice to victims do not necessarily involve novel legal practices. As judges recognize that their peers are taking on these cases, they may prove more willing to do so themselves. The nongovernmental organization *Londres thirty-eight* invited the Chilean legal community to a presentation and discussion of our findings on corporate accountability for past human rights violations in Latin America.[22] Although the judges who attended mainly comprised those sympathetic to human rights issues, the event may have reinforced their resolve to expand the understanding of perpetrators beyond state actors and the need to fill the victims' gap in corporate complicity. The NGO community thus attempted to fulfill victims' international human rights.

This case illustrates that, in some instances, the most powerful force applied is an innovative tool in the hands of legal professionals to accompany civil society mobilization. Even unpropitious climates can be overcome when the set of civil society and institutional innovation factors work effectively together to apply the requisite force.

CONCLUSION

We have shown in this chapter that transitional justice has included corporate accountability as part of its judicial processes and in particular in truth commissions. Yet, even transitional justice experts are unaware of these advances in promoting truth, justice, reparations, and guarantees of non-repetition for victims of economic actors' abuses in dictatorships and armed conflicts. This chapter thus attempts to contribute to fill this gap.

It also endeavors to point out that Latin America has played a critical role in leading those processes. The region figures prominently in the truth commissions that have named economic actors for their alleged involvement in crimes against humanity. It is also the region that has gone the farthest in seeking justice for victims in domestic courts.

That Latin America has played that role relates to the existence of factors that form part of our Archimedes' Lever approach to CATJ from below. Civil society mobilization in the region constitutes a set of weak actors who are nonetheless able to exert pressure to lift the weight of corporate accountability. Their success in doing so has depended on institutional innovators in truth commissions and legal bodies. These innovators' tools and strategies have added to that pressure to lift corporate accountability. They have faced sometimes formidable barriers, however. Most crucially for our model is the counterweight of veto players in the powerful business community who resist accountability. The fulcrum, or political context, is also relevant to our model. When the political situation is closer to corporate accountability, and veto players are weak, civil society groups and institutional innovators need to apply less pressure to lift the weight than in unfavorable conditions. Although these promising elements to advance corporate accountability—civil society demand and mobilization, institutional innovators, weak economic actors, and favorable political contexts—are unique to Latin America, we find that they are more likely to emerge in the region. Over time, and with greater knowledge, the lessons learned from Latin America could move across regional boundaries.

At present, these processes are expanding across national borders in the region. Chile, for example, represents a country that has begun these processes. It has not achieved the highest degree of accountability for corporate complicity during the Pinochet dictatorship, nor is it stuck at the lowest level. Although we could argue that economic actors in Chile have traditionally held strong veto power, issues of corruption have recently weakened them. In addition, in the country's recent mobilizations there is a link to the legacy of corporate veto power: "It's not 30 pesos; it's 30 years." This increased civil society demand for accountability may prompt institutional innovations to look for the tools to realize those demands and a higher reception in those institutions to hearing and responding to them.

NOTES

1. Juan Pablo Bohoslavsky and Veerle Opgenhaffen, "The Past and Present of Corporate Complicity : Financing the Argentinean Dictatorship," *Harvard Human Rights Journal* 23 (2010): 160.

2. The CATJ database includes cases where businesses have been named in nonjudicial and judicial transitional justice mechanisms (truth commissions, justice and peace process in Colombia and judicial actions) as being complicit with abuses committed in the course of an armed conflict or an authoritarian regime. The authors acknowledge the funders of the Project for their invaluable support: Open Society Foundation and the ESRC Knowledge Exchange Impact Acceleration Account. In

addition, several individuals provided assistance in finding and coding cases for the CATJ. This list includes Andhes Research Assistant Cynthia Cisneros; Oxford University researchers Kathryn Babineau and Julia Zulver; University of Minnesota Mondale School of Law students Mary Beale and Ami Hutchinson; and Dejusticia researcher Lina Arroyave, and Dejusticia interns: Paula Szy, Sarah Dorman and Lyndsi Allsop.

3. The CATJ includes information on all of the initiatives taken by truth commissions and in judicial action related to corporate accountability and transitional justice from the crimes of the Nazi regime to the present. Although the methodology for finding such initiatives has its limits, because of being based on internet searches, the results represent the existing developments in this area.

4. Leigh A. Payne, Gabriel Pereira, and Laura Bernal Bermúdez, *Transitional Justice and Corporate Accountability from Below: Deploying Archimedes' Lever* (Cambridge: Cambridge University Press, 2020).

5. Transitional justice (TJ), as defined by the United Nations, is the "the full range of processes and mechanisms associated with a society's attempt to come to terms with a legacy of large-scale past abuses to ensure accountability, serve justice, and achieve reconciliation" Secretary-General, "The Rule of Law and Transitional Justice in Conflict and Post-Conflict Societies" (New York, 2004), para. 8. The mechanisms most commonly associated with TJ are criminal prosecutions, truth commissions, and victim reparations.

6. We use a broad definition of economic actors to include businesses, business associations and other collective entities, business people, owners, and managers, individual actors engaged in economic activity, but not necessarily part of a business entity.

7. Payne, Pereira, and Bernal Bermúdez, ibidem.

8. Regarding the other three judicial actions, one is before a military court and the other two we could not identify the type of court involved.

9. We could not find information about the specific type of violation in which the remaining two economic actors were involved.

10. Payne, Pereira, and Bernal Bermúdez, ibidem.

11. See *Projeto Adeus Boilesen*, June 13, 2013. https://www.youtube.com/watch?v=SDM-PXdAS2w).

12. Anthony Boadle and Brian Winter, "Brazil Dictatorship Probe Urges Prosecuting Military, Companies," *Reuters*, December 10, 2014, https://www.reuters.com/article/us-brazil-rousseff-dicatorship/brazil-dictatorship-probe-urges-prosecuting-military-companies-idUSKBN0JO20L20141210.

13. Case N° 13.340/08 "Vildoza, Jorge Raúl y otros s/ Delito de Acción Pública."

14. Payne, Pereira, and Bernal Bermúdez, ibidem.

15. This section of the chapter is extracted from pages 263 to 266 of Chapter 5 of our forthcoming book (Payne, Pereira, and Bernal Bermúdez, ibidem).

16. Miguel Kast Rist, an economist trained at the University of Chicago, was Labor minister and head of the Central Bank in the Pinochet regime. Other members of the Kast family are very connected politically, such as Deputy José Antonio Kast

who ran for president in the 2017 elections. For further discussion of the Paine case, see Rebolledo Escobar (2015).

17. Special Investigative Magistrate Marianela Cifuentes, *Paine-Episodio Collipeumo*, Rol 4-2002(b), March 31, 2016, 19 and the resolutive section. This sentence was ratified by the San Miguel Appeals Court under case reference Rol 58-2016, 20 December 2016, and reviewed before the Supreme Court as Rol 1.568-2017, 16 November 2017.

18. Idem.

19. Juan René Maureira Moreno, "Enfrentar Con La Vida a La Muerte Historias y Memorias de La Violencia y El Terrorismo de Estado En Paine (1960–2008)" (Universidad de Chile, 2009).

20. Marga Lacabe, "Corte Niega Libertad a Empresario Implicado En Desapariciones En Paine," *Desaparecidos.Org*, January 16, 2008, http://desaparecidos.org/notas/2008/01/chile-corte-niega-libertad-a-e.html.

21. El Ciudadano, "Lorena Pizarro, Presidenta de La AFDD: 'Familia Kast Está Vinculada Al Terrorismo de Estado,'" *El Ciudadano*, September 9, 2017, http://www.elciudadano.cl/justicia/lorena-pizarro-presidenta-de-la-afdd-familia-kast-esta-vinculada-al-terrorismo-de-estado/09/09/.

22. Encuentro abierto: "Verdad y justicia sobre desaparición forzada: responsabilidades del Estado y terceros actores," Instituto de Estudios Judiciales, Santiago, July 21, 2017.

Section 2

"PINOCHET'S ECONOMY"

Chapter 7

The Chilean Economic Model and Its Subordinate Democracy

José Miguel Ahumada and Andrés Solimano

INTRODUCTION

In Karl Polanyi's seminal 1944 work *The Great Transformation*, the economic anthropologist asserts that to understand the international political crisis that led to the emergence of fascism and World War II, it is imperative to look at the political and economic origins of the market society. This constitutes a return to eighteenth-century England and the violent commodification process that took place, affecting land, work, and money.

Polanyi's argument stressed the fundamental fact that the European crisis of the 1930s was a consequence of how the dominant economic order had been established and not just the result of erroneous political decisions. It was a *structural* crisis, not simply a *conjunctural one.*

Polanyi's assertion helps in understanding the current situation in Chile as the political system is delegitimized, the economy is stagnating, and the pillars of the neoliberal economic order are questioned. After decades of a radical model under which the economy and social services were privatized and the political elite were ensnared by economic power, social countermovements have emerged to fight against the commodification of education (student protests began in the early-2000s), land (notably the historic fight of the *Mapuche* people and new movements against forestry, mining, and fishing extraction), and pensions (recent protests against private pension funds AFPs [Administradora de Fondos de Pensiones]), and so on.

In the same manner, as in Europe, current problems with the Chilean economy and society are structural, a result of the economic model brought into force in the 1970s and 1980s which has been strengthened in the return to democracy. In this new order, the troubling influence of the economic elites arising from privatizations in the 1970s and 1980s stands out. These elites not only control the bulk of national wealth but also have a decisive influence on the current running of Chile's democracy. Their influential methods include financing policies, lobbyist activities, and control over the media.[1]

This chapter analyzes the economy's development during the military dictatorship, dividing the period into three stages: (1) the "capitalist restoration" stage that followed the overthrow of President Allende (1973–1975), (2) the "revolutionary-neoliberal" stage that established a new economic model (1975–1981), and (3) the model's first major crisis in 1982–1983 and its later recovery due to greater financial regulation and the promotion of exports (1984–1989). The chapter concludes with a general analysis of the economic and social outcomes of the Pinochet period and their progress toward the establishment of a neoliberal market society, with features that were rolled out and consolidated, with certain transformations, after the dictatorship ended (1990–2015.)

THE CAPITALIST RESTORATION STAGE (SEPTEMBER 1973–1975)

The military coup came to a violent end on September 11, 1973, with the *vía chilena al socialismo.* The capitalist restoration years then followed but with a strategic ambivalence as to what economic course to follow. The sociopolitical bloc that supported the military dictatorship was a variety of industrial capitalists, financiers, expropriated landowners, some middle-class sectors, and former members of parliament and political leaders from both the center and the right who had, until September 11, held important roles in democracy. In this context (closed parliament, controlled press, suspension of political party activity), this bloc remained devoid of a political project and defined economic model. Different visions of society were proposed and fought over, ranging from the corporate doctrine of Franco's Spain, also a military dictatorship, to Chile's conversion to neoliberalism. Seemingly, the only common goal that kept them united was the need to "restore" the lost order.[2]

Restoring the existing order to its pre-1970 state (i.e., before Allende and his socialist transition project that had altered the capitalist order) involved, first, the need to reduce inflation and stabilize the economy. Price controls were eliminated, factories and fields were returned to their previous owners, and attempts were made to reduce the fiscal deficit. At a deeper level, the aim was to return power to the upper classes threatened by nationalization and occupations of workers that took place under Allende's government. With regard to property, 250 companies were returned to their previous owners immediately after the coup and, until 1978, 230 other companies were tendered or sold to individuals. Meanwhile, around 30 percent of previously expropriated land was returned to agricultural owners.[3] In conjunction with this, there was a cycle of reduction in public spending and fiscal deficit to reduce inflation. This required the elimination of previous industrial promotion measures and subsidies to a range of social sectors, as well as wage reductions and mass dismissal of civil servants.

Regarding production, a labor regime was established that was strongly pro-business, prohibiting or limiting trade union action and repressing left-wing political organizations that had been a part of the *Unidad Popular* (UP), adding to the Revolutionary Left Movement (MIR).[4] Likewise, in the economic sphere, progress was made through trade reform and the launch of drastic tariff reductions in parallel with exchange devaluations as the interest rate was liberalized to create a domestic capital market.

The liberalization agenda, of trade, production, and finance, gained strength in the second half of the 1970s. Initially, during 1974 and part of 1975, the economic ideas of the Chilean soldiers who had assumed power were traditionally national-developmentalist, rather than free market based. However, faced with the difficulties in lowering inflation and stabilizing the economy, Pinochet decided to establish an emerging monetarist technocracy (the "*Chicago Boys*"), led by Sergio de Castro who took on the role of Finance Minister in 1976. Their agenda of economic liberalization and dissolution of unions and civil society was very appealing to Pinochet, who sought to consolidate his authority in power. He found this power to be consistent with the work of the financial sector, where this technocracy was strongly rooted.[5]

The military dictatorship would no longer be a "restorative" government of disoriented political consensus, like that of the *Unidad Popular* government, but a "revolutionary" regime that would build, with its politico-military apparatus, a new social, economic, and political order as an alternative to the past fifty years of Chilean economic and social history. Their verdict was that the past half-century had led to a steady increase in the size and power of the state that was stunting economic growth and individual economic freedom. To eradicate the "evils of populism," statism and socialism, a new economic sphere needed to be built that was autonomous and independent of political power. Furthermore, it had to subject this power to new rules—that were both "impartial and impersonal"—of the market and respect for private property. This would create a market economy that would lead to a "market society," in which the political system (and even basic human rights) would be subject to the needs of the market economy. This model, inspired by the writings of Hayek (see *The Constitution of Liberty*) and Friedman (*Capitalism and Freedom*), began to gain popularity among government elites and decisively influenced the preparation of the 1980 Constitution.[6]

THE NEOLIBERAL ECONOMIC REVOLUTION

Shock measures, initiated in 1975, involved the radical reduction of public spending and mass layoffs, alongside an increase in indirect tax and VAT. In 1976, trade liberalization was intensified (homogeneous tariffs approached 10 percent) and progress was made on financial liberalization, eliminating various controls on existing capitals. In addition, the government sought to accelerate the privatization of businesses that had been nationalized by the previous government.

These privatizations did not lead to the spread of ownership, nor the emergence and strengthening of a new middle class. In contrast, they resulted in a growing concentration of ownership among few individuals which, in turn, contributed to the creation of a powerful economic elite that held wide-ranging control over assets, markets, and political influence. At this time, financial groups began an extensive process of appropriation of these companies (according to Dahse, from the end of the 1960s to 1978, the assets of the Cruzat-Larraín, Vial, Matte, and Angelini Groups increased by 52.4 percent).[7] This process of concentrating and centralizing capital meant that these hierarchical economic groups could extend and diversify their portfolios to different productive areas, thereby creating a complex web of leverage through finance capital which had increasing access to foreign capital.[8]

Radical financial and trade liberalization led to economic and financial contradictions and imbalances, such as the increase in foreign currency liabilities from banks and businesses and the absence of adequate regulation, which would lead to the 1982 crisis. Trade liberalization was more effective in increasing imports than exports. The latter were affected by the use of the exchange rate as a mechanism to control inflation through currency appreciation. The boom in imports, mainly of consumer goods, led to an increasing deficit in the balance of payments bank account which would reach 14 percent of GDP by 1981 (see Chart 7.1).

National industry, already lacking previous protections and subsidies, could not compete with imports cheapened by an appreciated exchange rate and tariff elimination. Their participation in the product was reduced from 28 percent of GDP in 1973 to 23 percent in 1979.[9] The industry tried to survive through several mechanisms including borrowing and so falling into debt, restructuring their productive bases or becoming a part of import marketing, and abandoning national production.

In this scenario, investment stagnated and could not exceed the levels it reached before the coup, while indebtedness accelerated. In 1975, private debt represented 14 percent of the total internal debt; in 1981 it reached 64 percent. The need for families and companies to resort to private indebtedness was a source of extraordinary profit for financial conglomerates through

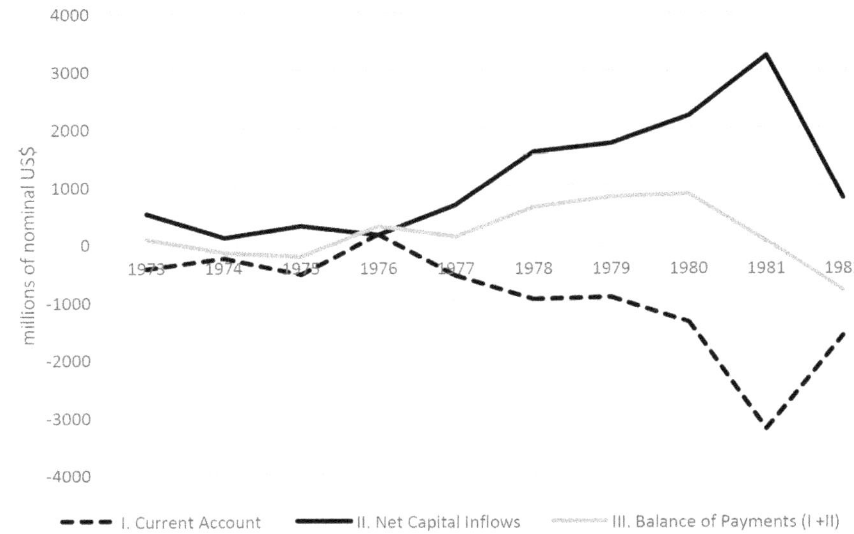

Graph 7.1 Chile: External Positioning (1973–1982) in Nominal US$ Deflated by External Price Index. *Source*: Own elaboration based on data from French-Davis (2010:70).

financial arbitration. It gave them exclusive access to an international financial system with high liquidity (due to the boom of money earned from oil); it gave them access to foreign loans in low-cost U.S dollars that were then mediated in Chile in the form of high-interest loans in pesos to the national industry (the difference between the interest rate in acquiring and selling loans increased their gross profits, as long as the peso was not devalued). This practice contributed to the increase in private external debt. The economic sectors that grew the most during this time were financial entities (banks, exchange houses, insurance companies financiers) and companies dedicated to marketing imports.[10] This boom of fictitious capital created a pillar of growth driven by finance ("financialization") and thereby created the instabilities that would then collapse in 1982.

Alongside the process of indebtedness and the formation of economic conglomerates was a new cycle of, "accumulation by dispossession" (Harvey, 2003). The so-called "seven modernizations" marked a decisive step toward the consolidation of the market society and crystallized the revolutionary character (of the right) of the civil–military dictatorship. As the first waves of privatizations focused on production activities and sought to dismantle the "State as producer and developer," the "modernization" measure aimed to privatize the "social functions of the State" such as education (through the municipalization of school education and funding cuts to public university education), health (through private health insurance companies under the ISAPRES [Instituciones de Salud Previsional model]), and pensions (through fund administration companies, establishing the AFP model). Furthermore, in 1979, a new Labor Code was approved that reduced union bargaining to an individual business level and encouraged the creation of multiple trade unions. In addition, a new state constitution was prepared and adopted in 1980 which enshrined the supremacy of private property over social rights, making it especially difficult to create public companies, as well as prolonging the validity of the authoritarian regime for several years.

From 1976, after the political shock of 1975, to 1981, the year before the financial crisis and severe repression and unemployment in 1982–1983, there was a period of economic recovery that accelerated the process of liberalization, deindustrialization, privatization, and economic concentration. However, the recovery of GDP growth also brought about internal and external financial fragility, accelerating international indebtedness. Moreover, by adjusting the exchange rate for anti-inflationary reasons, it rose the value of the peso, thereby affecting exports and raising the balance of payments bank account deficit. Chile's economy became very vulnerable to a cut in private external financing. As a result, GDP fell by 14 percent in 1982–1983, investment contracted by 35 percent, and unemployment rose by 20 percent.

FINANCIAL CRISIS, NEW POWER BLOC, AND A TURN IN EXPORTING (1982–1983, AND LATER YEARS)

The internal financial crisis of the early 1980s not only affected the economy but also threatened the political-economic bloc that had supported the dictatorship. Economic groups challenged the *Chicago Boy's* practices and the fixed exchange rate, which resulted in a confrontation via the media and, at the beginning of 1982, the dismissal of the Finance Minister, Sergio de Castro, the architect behind the fixed exchange rate. The bankruptcy of major financial groups, and their temporary nationalization by the state, severed the main link connecting the government to the business sector. As a result, criticism of the economic model began to emerge from their business associations.[11]

This unfavorable scenario for the regime does not stem only from the business associations. From 1983, many "national protest" days were organized by the Copper Workers Confederation, led by Rodolfo Seguel, and other social organizations. These protest days against the Pinochet regime entailed huge marches and night protests in working and middle-class areas that had been affected by unemployment, indebtedness, and a lack of democracy. A democratic opposition also began to form made up of left-wing, center, and moderate-right parties (such as *Alianza Democrática, Movimiento Democrático Popular*, and *Comité de Elecciones Libres* among others).

In 1983, Chile, like other Latin American countries, applied to the International Monetary Fund (IMF) and the World Bank for financial assistance to meet their foreign obligations. The IMF, as a part of their conditions, demanded the prioritization of external debt above the recovery of growth and employment, which involved reducing the current account deficit as quickly as possible.

How could a military government manage both the economic and political crises? A driving force for economic reactivation was the emerging export sector. The export sector and its dynamism became key for the government in its need to generate foreign currency. In 1983, this sector, with the support of the Confederation of Production and Commerce (CPC), developed a program to overcome the crisis called, "*Economic Recuperation: analysis and propositions.*" This program involved a new trade reform with a more pragmatic and less orthodox character, emphasizing the more active role of the state in promoting exports. (See table 7.1).

The export sector's development enabled economic recovery, making it easy for Pinochet to reclaim his leadership of the economic elite and ease the pressure for political openness and an election, with the help of repression.

The connection between capital and state from 1976 to 1981 is described as a nexus of financial conglomerates and the *Chicago Boys*, excluding business associations from the power bloc. However, the new period that instigated

Table 7.1 Second Commercial Reform (1983–1989)

Field	*Measure*	*Objective*
Exchange rate policies	Devaluation of currency by 80% (1982–1988)	Promotion of exports
Tariff policies	Tariff increase from 10% (1982) to 35% (1984) and then a reduction to 20% (1985) and 15% (1989)	Temporary protection for goods import substitution and SMEs
Price bands	Automatic modification of tariffs for key agricultural products (sugar, wheat, vegetable oil) according to variations in international prices (1983)	Protect traditional agriculture from imports
Export promotion policies	Simplified reinstatement (1985) Refund scheme (drawback scheme) for exporting goods (1985) (a) * Scheme for import of capital goods (1987) (b)	Export diversification

(a) Refund of tariff paid when consumables are imported for the exports of manufactured goods.
(b) Postponement of up to seven years for import tariff payments for capital goods.
Source: Own production

the 1982–1983 crisis had started to formally include unions in consultations on economic decisions, initiating a new alliance between private capital and the state based on the state subsidiary doctrine, which would be reproduced during democracy.[12]

The recovery of economic growth after the 1982–1983 crisis was led by the export sector and gave rise to a long expansive cycle between 1986 and 1997, marking a rapid recovery of GDP growth and enabled the reduction of external debt.

Contrary to what has been commonly stated, the export sector's dynamism (forestry, agriculture, fruit, and fishing) was not only the result of market forces accompanied by a competitive exchange rate policy, but also a consequence of the active role of the state which, since the 1960s, had aimed to promote exports, build infrastructure, and invest in human capital and key technology that enabled the modernization of these sectors. As Amsden said, "it was the government, and not the private sector, who held the long-term vision of making the agro-industrial sector the leading sector by heavily investing in it throughout the 1960s."[13]

The forestry sector received substantial public investments in human capital and infrastructure during the Frei and Allende government, while the military regime provided significant subsidies to cover the costs of planting and important loans to SMEs (Small and medium enterprises).[14] The fishing sector had the support of the Chile Foundation for importing and introducing salmon to the national territory, via strong investments in infrastructure and technological transfer. Finally, the agricultural sector modernized due to the agrarian reform previously implemented by Frei and Allende.[15]

In that sense, the "entrepreneurial moment" behind the Chilean export boom benefited both from the pro-export exchange rate policy that was advanced in 1983–1984, and from the support of the state that had been developing the infrastructure and technological forms to support the agro-industrial sector from the 1960s.

Toward the second half of the 1980s, and envisaging the possible end to the military regime, the third wave of privatization began, focusing this time on strategic public companies originally created by the Corporación de Fomento de la Producción in Spanish; Corporation of Production Promotion in English (CORFO). These were companies that would generate a high profit, such as electric companies (Chilectra), telecommunications companies (Entel), chemical companies (Soquimich), and steel companies (CAP). This privatization process has been frequently challenged, both for the enormous loss of the state's assets (as the companies were sold at prices considerably lower than their actual worth), and for the fact that they were sold to public sector officials, some of whom were related to General Pinochet (e.g., his son-in-law, Julio Ponce Lerou, acquired SQM).[16]

GENERAL ANALYSIS OF THE DICTATORSHIP'S SOCIOECONOMIC MODEL (1973–1989) AND POST-DICTATORSHIP FEATURES

Economic, social, and institutional results of the dictatorship's model can be analyzed from four angles: (a) the regime of economic and institutional rules, (b) macro-economic performance and economic growth, (c) levels of income and wealth inequality, and (d) conclusions: political economy of a neoliberal market society.

(a) Economic Regime

From the 1980s, privatization expanded to include education, health, and pensions in a market-profit-privatization model with a totalizing character. After the 1982–1983 crisis, the model introduced a degree of pragmatism into its economic policy. Financial regulations were introduced and the export sector was boosted, resulting in improvements in the balance of payments and the stimulation of economic growth. The Chilean development in exports was based on the comparative advantages of natural resources (copper, marine products, lithium, among others) and agro-industrial development (wine, fruit, and light manufacturing).

However, this development model was accompanied by a strong oligopolistic concentration of property (conglomerates) that dominated banking, telecommunications, energy, pensions, pharmacies, and other markets. The model is presented as neutral in its rules, but there is a marked "structural heterogeneity" where large companies coexist with a large number of SMEs, which require much more intensive work for a still-modest participation in production and the value they add to the economy. The restoration of democracy in 1990 and the confirmation of the model they inherited led to large foreign investments coming into the country, for copper in particular. Foreign investments now include banking, insurance, energy, telecommunications, and AFP property and are dominated by large multinational insurance companies (e.g., Metlife, Principal Financial Group, Grupo Sura, among others).[17]

(b) Economic Growth in 1973–1989 and 1990–2015

Today, Chile earns 24,000 dollars per capita, putting it in the range of a medium-high income country at the international level. It is also a member country of the OECD (Organisation for Economic Co-operation and Development). The growth process over the past four decades has been uneven and affected by different cycles of intensity. Recessions in the 1970s (1975) and 1980s (1982–3) were more intense than those of subsequent decades in

1999 (due to the Asian financial crisis) and 2009 (due to the global financial crisis).[18] As shown in table 7.2, the average annual growth of GDP per capita during the military regime (1.8 percent in 1973–1989) was inferior to the rate of growth in 1960–1969 (2.1 percent) and also 1990–2015 (3.5 percent).

Furthermore, two phases of recovery and growth have been identified in 1976–1981 and 1986–1989. Strong cycles and financial instabilities have made it difficult to achieve a sustainable process of capital accumulation despite a regime of privatization, deregulation, and labor control that was expected to ensure high profits. Moreover, during this period, the manufacturing sector decreased their GDP participation, initiating a process of "premature deindustrialization." On the other hand, inflation control was carried out at a slow pace and stabilization policies had considerable costs (e.g., like the 1975 shock) and the exchange rate rose in 1979–1982.

Economic growth accelerated in the 1990s after the restoration of democracy, and the average growth of GDP per capita in 1990–2015 (3.5 percent) was almost double that of the average in 1973–1989 (see table 7.3). This growth has been based on a high degree of external openness (the coefficient of exports plus imports with respect to GDP reached 63.7 percent of GDP in 1990–2015) and a labor and regulatory scheme that was pro-business. However, besides the concentration of ownership in a highly privatized economy, this growth is also based on the exploitation of nonrenewable natural resources and a very unequal society.

Therefore, trade liberalization has not strengthened a reindustrialization process, nor intensive value-added exports as it predicted (the so-called "second phase export"). At the end of the 1990s, the boom that had begun in the mid-1980s came to an end. Exports stagnated at a low value, while foreign investment in copper ended.[19] In this stage of stagnation, Chile was then hit by the Asian financial crisis which led to the loss of five years' worth of growth and productive dynamism (1998–2003).

This stagnation came to an end, not because of internal sources (from, e.g., a new corporate moment), but the increase in demand for copper (from China in particular) and its impact on price. The regime of ownership, labor, and specialization patterns had remained intact which explains the continuation of high inequality (apart from a faint reduction in the past few years) and the premature deindustrialization that affects the country.[20]

There is a recent trend toward economic stagnation or at least a slow-growing economy. From 2014 to 2017, the annual GDP per capita was around 1 percent.

Will we witness chronic stagnation (*secular stagnation*)? Is there a growing trend toward an excess of savings over investment? Why are there few investments in the private sector despite labor and regulation policies that are pro-business? These questions are part of an ongoing investigation.

Table 7.2 Chile: Economic Indicators in 1960–1989

	1960–1969	*1970–1973*	*1974–1981*	*1982–1985*	*1986–1989*	*1973–1989*
PPP Growth Rate	2.1	−0.4	2.4	−1.2	5.7	1.8
Gini	0.48	0.46	0.51	0.55	0.57	0.54
Manufacturing (as % of GDP)	23.7	25.3	23	20	18.7	21.5
Foreign Trade (as % of GDP)	27.5	25.9	46	47.3	60	48.6

Source: Own preparation based on data from World Development Indicators.

Table 7.3 Chile: Economic Indicators in 1990–2015

	1990–1997	*1998–2003*	*2004–2011*	*2012–2015*	*1990–2015*
PPP Growth Rate	6	1.4	3.2	2.2	3.5
Gini	0.55	0.55	0.51	0.51	0.53
Manufacturing (as % of GDP)	19.2	17.7	13.1	11.8	15.8
Foreign Trade (as % of GDP)	57.7	61	72	65	63.7

Source: Own preparation based on data from World Development Indicators.

(c) Income and Wealth Inequality

The dictatorship not only stimulated an export-extractivist kind of growth but also in its process of concentrating capital ("accumulation by dispossession") and dismantling unions, it provoked a radical increase in inequality. Income equality went from historic lows under the *Unidad Popular* government to record highs during the dictatorship.

The share of wages in total spending fell radically from 52 percent in 1972 to 30.8 percent in 1988 (see Graph 7.2). Meanwhile, the Gini coefficient of the income distribution rose from 0.46 in 1970–1973 to 0.54 in 1973–1989 and reduced the proportion of wages as national income.[21] On the other hand, the Gini coefficient of wealth distribution (distribution of real and financial assets) is significantly higher (more unequal) and rose to 0.70 (2010–2015) according to the Household Survey run by the *Banco Central de Chile*.

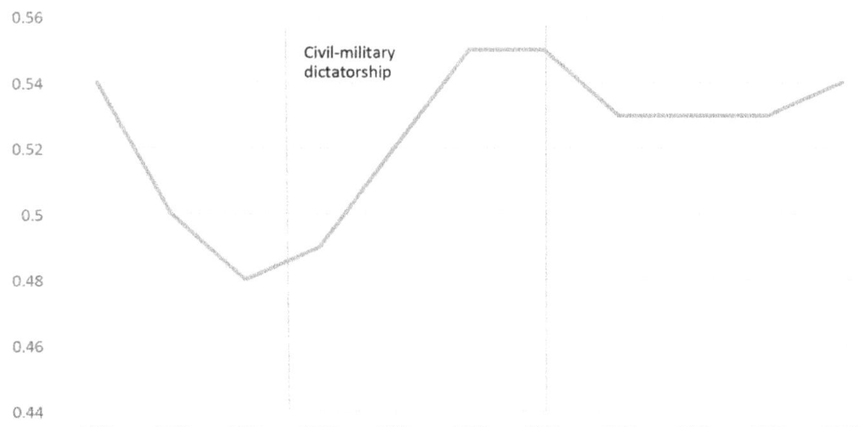

Graph 7.2 Inequality and Dictatorship: Gini (Personal Income). *Source*: Own preparation based on date from Rodríguez Weber òp cit.

Furthermore, the Gini on financial assets is higher than the Gini on total net wealth.[22]

There are a variety of causes behind the persistence of inequality in Chile: (a) the process of accumulation by dispossession and the concentration and oligopolization of the production structure, both accentuated under the military and post-dictatorship, (b) the weakness and fragmentation of trade unions and the lack of labor rights for workers, (c) the privatization of education and tiered nature of access by socioeconomic status, (d) the limited progress in the tax system, and (e) the capacity for saving (the accumulation of assets) is larger among higher-income groups which skew the asset possession in favor of these groups.[23]

(d) Conclusions: A Democracy Contingent on the Economic Regime

The dictatorship established a key project: a strong authoritarian state was going to reorganize the Chilean society to build a "free economy" anchored in a new political constitution in 1980. This Constitution established a political system of "protected democracy" or "semi-sovereign democracy"[24] through a series of mechanisms.[25]

Institutions such as the Constitutional Court, the autonomy of the Central Bank, the binominal electoral system, and the supermajorities to modify fundamental areas of the economic system were developed due to fear in the face of the democratic advance of the twentieth century.[26] Therefore, the dictatorship laid the foundation for a market society and a political regime that restricts deliberation and assures that ownership, pro-business labor regime, and the general pattern of specialization will not be subject to public scrutiny.[27] In other words, democracy is dependent on the needs of the neoliberal economic model.

It is these constitutional elements (in a low-intensity democracy) that established the fundamental pillars of the political and economic system present over the past twenty-five years in Chile. Today, this societal neoliberal project is being challenged by workers (although weakened and fragmented), students, environmentalists, and the middle classes who are in debt and excluded from powerful and influential spheres. The tension between an unequal economy and an effective democracy again leads to national public debate.

This chapter has systematized the economic stages of the dictatorship, from its cycle of financialization and centralization of capital during the 1970s, through its collapse in the 1982 crisis, and finally to its exporting phase during the 1980s. Both cycles were the result of a strong coalition between economic groups and the state. Its results, which are still part of the foundations of the domestic economic regime, have provoked fierce social inequality, job insecurity, and an extractive pattern of international insertion. These elements are precisely those that are being challenged today by social mobilization, opening the door for a new democratizing cycle that would surmount, at long last, the economic legacy of the military dictatorship.

NOTES

1. See A. Solimano, *Elites económicas, crisis y el capitalismo del siglo XXI* (Fondo de Cultura Económica, 2015) and for the Chilean case, see J. M. Ahumada & F. Sossdorf 'Transformación productiva y equidad en Chile' in F. Carmona *Ensayos para un modelo de desarrollo sostenible* (ICAL, 2017).
2. See P. Vergara, *Auge y caída del neoliberalismo en Chile* (Flacso, 1985). It should not be forgotten that the Chilean military coup was part of a wave of dictatorships in the Southern Cone, which suggests the cause of political destabilization was not just national, but the result of a general stagnation of the import substitution regime that had built up in the region. See G. O´Donnell, *El Estado Burocrático Autoritario* (Belgrano, 1982).
3. See P. Meller, *Un siglo de economía política chilena* (1890–1990) (Editorial Andrés Bello, 1998).
4. A. Cassese, "Study of the impact of foreign economic aid and assistance on respect for human rights in Chile," Commission on Human Rights, UN, E/CN.4/Sub.2/412 (vol. 1).
5. The strong connection between the Chicago Boys and the financial sector (especially with the Cruzát-Larraín, BHC, Edwards groups) has been widely studied. See, for example, E. Silva, *State and Capital in Chile* (Westview Press, 1996).
6. See A. Solimano, *Capitalismo a la chilena* (Catalonia, 2012).
7. F. Dahse, *El mapa de la extrema riqueza* (Editorial Aconcagua, 1979).
8. See R. Lagos, "Chile, la burguesía emergente" (1982), IFDA dossier 29.
9. See F. Fajnzylber, *La industrialización trunca de América Latina* (Nueva Imagen, 1985).
10. See R. Ffrench-Davis, *Economic reforms in Chile* (Palgrave, 2010), 17.
11. In fact, in 1983, the then-President of CPC, Jorge Fontaine, said: "Firstly, I have to say that the famous 'Chicago model' has failed, and there could have been no other outcome." Cited in G. Arriagada, *Los empresarios y la política* (editorial Lom, 2004), 149.
12. Unions began to participate in the formulation of exchange rate policies and interest rates. In 1984, Pinochet created the Economic and Social Council (CES) where the government and unions together agreed to economic policy measures and, in turn, the unions could propose their policies (see Arriagada, op. cit.).
13. A. Amsden, *Escape from Empire* (MIT Press 2007), 84.
14. See José Aylwin's chapter.

15. See Ahumada & Sossdorf, óp. cit, J. Collins & J. Lear, *Chile's Free Market Miracle: A Second Look* (Food First Books, 1995), M. Kurtz, "State developmentalism without a developmental state" (2001), *Latin American Politics and Society*, Vol. 43(2).

16. José Yuraszeck was a CORFO officer (Managing Director of Chilectra). See M. Monckeberg, *El saqueo de los grupos económicos al estado de Chile* (Editorial debolsillo, 2015).

17. See A. Solimano, *Pensiones a la chilena* (Editorial Catalonia, 2017).

18. See A. Solimano & D. Calderon, "The copper sector, fiscal rules and stabilization funds in Chile" (2017), *WIDER Working Paper* 2017/53.

19. G. Moguillansky, *La inversión en Chile: ¿el fin del ciclo expansivo?* (Fondo de Cultura Económica-CEPAL, 1999).

20. See Ahumada & Sossdorf, óp. cit. and Solimano, óp cit.

21. See : G. Alarco Tosini, "Participación salarial y crecimiento económico en América Latina, 1950–2011" (2014), *Revista de Cepal*, No. 113, 47.

22. See A. Solimano, *Global Capitalism in Disarray* (Oxford University Press, 2017).

23. See Solimano, óp. cit. y J. Rodríguez Weber, *Desarrollo y desigualdad en Chie, 1850–2009* (Dibam, 2017).

24. See C. Huneeus, *La Democracia semisoberana* (Editorial Taurus, 2014) and *El régimen de Pinochet* (Editorial Taurus, 2016).

25. Outside of the constitutional field, at the end of the 1980s, the dictatorship established a set of formal links with business associations, including them in economic decisions and including them in policies. Therefore, it not only obtained the support of trade unions, but it developed a network of influence over the executive power, which would be a determining factor in transition politics (see G. Arrigada, óp. cit.; E. Silva, óp. cit.).

26. What has been called the "constitutionalism of fear" in R. Cristi & P. Ruiz Tagle, *El constitucionalismo del miedo* (Editorial Lom, 2014).

27. It is interesting to note the tension that underlies democracy and the market society. To reproduce the market society, there was a need to politically ensure the merchandising character of principle production factors (land, labor, capital, money, expertise, etc.) and to provide the necessary certainties for capital generation to begin the accumulation cycle (via, among other methods, the technocratic control of areas central to economic decisions, such as the Central Bank, labor discipline, and adopting new laws, without public debate or clear economic decisions on, for example, the budget or fiscal policies). This collided with the democratic principles of public debate and the imposition of nonmarket criteria on the aforementioned spheres (such as social policies that assist in decommercializing the labor force, capital controls to gain autonomy over financial flows, or environmental regulations on land ownership.) This latent tension has been thoroughly analyzed in political economy by J.S Mill, K. Marx, D. Ricardo, J.A. Schumpeter and F. Hayek, among others. See W. Streeck, *How Will Capitalism End?* (Verso, 2016).

Chapter 8

Unraveling the Financial Assistance to the Pinochet's Regime

Juan Pablo Bohoslavsky and Mariana Rulli

INTRODUCTION[1]

Loans granted to regimes that carry out gross violations of human rights can contribute to their consolidation, thus extending their duration and increasing the likelihood of those very crimes being committed.[2] This conclusion applies to the official (multilateral or bilateral) and private lending.[3]

This presumption is based on a statistical analysis of 158 different cases of authoritarian governments in 91 countries, which shows that both foreign direct investment and net capital transfers tend to prolong the duration of autocratic regimes.[4] Clearly, these resources are crucial for a criminal state to work efficiently and for it to be able to buy loyalties in key sectors of society.

The rational choice framework presented in the introduction of this book, in which probable causalities as well as quantitative analyses are offered, must be contrasted with investigations that crystalize the causative links between the financial assistance received and human rights violations committed by authoritarian regimes. Therefore, the goal of this chapter is to apply this method to analyze the case of funding during the Pinochet's regime: Did he receive money? By whom, when, how much, and for what? What were the consequences of those loans in political, economic, fiscal, and budgetary terms? And what human rights implications did they have?

Not only will we consider the micro-behaviors (those that may develop between hit squads, the people who financed them and the victims)[5] but also the broader view related to the structures, processes and dynamics of Pinochet's dictatorship. This methodology contributes to a better understanding of whether the financial assistance that was provided to the Chilean regime allowed it to consolidate its position and remain in power, and in turn carry out a campaign of human rights violations, while achieving a balance between the purchase of loyalties and repression, as explained in this book's introduction.

This chapter is divided into three sections, in addition to this introduction. Section 2 studies Chilean policy and economic performance, particularly the role played by financial assistance offered by multilateral, bilateral, and private lenders in terms of political, economic, fiscal, and budgetary support of the regime. Section 3 presents the shifting stance of the United States regarding Pinochet's government. Carter administration's financial policy in particular was influenced by the situation of human rights in Chile, which shows the close connection that exists between human rights and funding. Section 4 includes the conclusions of the chapter and presents a prospective view on the subject of accountability for economic complicity in the region and in Chile.

THE FAR-REACHING IMPLICATIONS OF FINANCIAL ASSISTANCE: A ROBUST CRIMINAL STATE

Pinochet's government forcibly implemented a profound reorganization of the Chilean society, its goal being a drastic transformation of the economic model of capital accumulation. This process was not exclusive to Chile. During the 1960s and 1970s, several countries in the region experienced coups and dictatorship governments with distinct social and political characteristics. Most of these military regimes were supported and legitimized by large sectors of society, as a reaction to the political involvement of the popular sector, which was perceived as a threat to their interests and international alignment.[6]

There were two key elements in the political and social process during the Chilean dictatorship. First, the survival of bureaucratic-authoritarian states depends not only on the strength of the ruling classes and military forces in the country but also on the support they receive from international financial institutions. Without this support, authoritarian regimes would have been unsuccessful in maintaining political and economic stability.[7]

Second, the economic and social conditions in which bureaucratic-authoritarian states come into power explain the brutality and depth of the anti-popular policies implemented and the massive and systematic human rights violations perpetrated. As the economic crisis and social conflict become more widespread, the ruling classes and the military increasingly feel that their interests are being threatened, and therefore, they provide stronger support for the implementation of drastic policies to counter those threats. At the same time, even when economic policies are unable to achieve the investment rates needed for economic growth, or at least to overcome the crisis, the high level of cohesion between the ruling classes, the military, and their international allies compensates for the expected economic failure, as seen in Chile in 1973 and Argentina in 1976.

Accordingly, Pinochet's military government simultaneously carried out a double process: on the one hand, he generated a profound transformation of the economy through liberalization, sweeping privatization of state assets, and economic openness, and on the other hand, he altered the political playing field by promoting the concentration of power, the centralization of the state, and ideological control to demobilize popular sectors, which was essential for the implementation of the aforementioned economic reforms.[8]

During the first years of Pinochet's government, the size and sphere of influence of the state were drastically reduced not only in terms of its regulatory capacity and economic functions but also in its role of allocating and redistributing resources in society. Pinochet's first and most important economic policies were the privatization of strategic state-owned companies and lands belonging to the Agrarian Reform Corporation, the elimination of price controls on several goods, the opening of markets by removing trade barriers, the implementation of monetary policies such as the devaluation of the peso and restrictions on credit expansion, and fiscal policies such as cuts to social public spending and raises in military expenditure, in addition to a regressive tax reform and wage freezes. At the same time, the government was attempting to curb inflation, deal with payment imbalance, and rekindle economic activity with the appropriate incentives.

The monetary approach to the balance of payments, in a context of diminishing savings and investment rates and an excess of imports entailed a greater need for foreign currency,[9] and strategies for attracting foreign investment were crucial in Chilean economic policy since the coup of 1973.[10]

Concrete figures back this theory. In 1973, Chilean medium- and long-term public external debt added up to US$ 2,862 million, in 1975 it was US$ 3,597 million, in 1979 it was US$ 4,108 million and in 1983, US$ 7,843 million.[11] Private external debt also steadily increased during the dictatorship: US$ 399 million in 1973, US$ 670 million in 1975, US$ 2,166 million in 1979 and US$ 6,501 million in 1983.[12] The proportion of private and official creditors also changed: While in 1974 only 19 percent of Chilean foreign debt came from private lenders, in 1981 it reached 80 percent. Chilean debt with banks grew over 57 percent between 1977 and 1981, as opposed to most developing countries which saw a 28 percent rise on average. Chilean dependence on foreign aid was significant, and it became one of the most deeply indebted countries in private international capital markets, going from the eleventh place in 1976 to sixth in 1979.

In the words of the *Cassese Report*[13] mandated by the United Nations (UN),

> the goal of attracting foreign loans, credits and investment capital has played a key role in the formulation of Chilean economic and other policies since the military take-over in 1973. With what is reported to be Latin America's highest per capita debt and its second-highest ratio of debt servicing payments' to export receipts in 1976, Chile's need for external financial support has been a constant and central policy preoccupation.[14]

A concrete representation of the impact of sovereign financing on the regime's budget and its fiscal policies can be observed in the evolution and allocation of public spending, a trend that reveals which sectors were benefited or harmed (by violating human rights of all kinds[15]) by Pinochet's regime. Against a backdrop of fiscal restraint and reduction of public spending, police and military spending skyrocketed, going from 14.9 percent of the total public spending in 1969 to 23.3 percent in 1982,[16] while social spending dropped. Military expenditure includes salaries, maintenance of detention centers, logistical assistance, intelligence and counter-intelligence, the purchase of weapons, and military equipment, etc.

A disaggregated view of public spending shows more precisely the way defense and Carabineros (Chilean police) expenses were prioritized over other sectors.[17] Operational expenses, which include remunerations and the purchase of goods and services, increased in those areas.[18] Remunerations are the largest component within operational expenses in the budget of four sectors: general services, defense, health, and education. In the first place, between 1969 and 1979 the fastest growing sectors were defense and general services (which includes police as a sub-sector). These saw a 98.9 percent rise while education and health experienced a moderate 30.8 percent increase.

Second, during 1974, defense was the only sector that experienced any growth in remunerations. Moreover, operational expenses for the purchase of goods and services were earmarked for defense and general services, and were the ones that grew the fastest: in 1969, US$2,603 million were spent on defense, in 1975 US$9,033 million and in 1979 US$5,302 million, while in education, US$1,890 million were spent in 1969, US$2,221 million in 1974, and $2,078 million in 1979.[19]

On the other hand, there were around 15,000 fewer workers in public projects, while the number of employees in the defense sector and Carabineros rose from 76,960 to 110,180 between 1970 and 1978.[20]

A further disaggregation of public spending based on allocation reveals the same trend of prioritizing the military and police sectors. Three big areas can be observed: general administration, social services, and economic services. The area that grew the most between 1969 and 1979 is general administration, which includes the expenses of public, financial, judicial, and diplomatic administration, as well as police services and defense throughout the country.

Defense saw the largest budgetary rise, in 1974 it accounted for 13 percent of total public spending, and it remained on those levels over the next years, followed by police services, which saw a 99.4 percent increase between 1969 and 1979, and financial administration, which grew by 64.3 percent in the same period. By contrast, over the same period social services spending experienced a mere 7.4 percent increase, while economic services spending was cut by 24.6 percent.[21]

Given the context of fiscal restraint and contraction in public spending in the country, financial aid played a key role in sustaining a budgetary policy that prioritized strategic repressive sectors. It also spared Pinochet's government from having to request funds from the Paris Club, which would surely have questioned its human rights record, while demanding additional commitment to a policy of austerity and fiscal consolidation. This would have proven politically fatal to a government that was already implementing austerity measures and faced increasingly high levels of poverty.[22]

Despite the fact that the impact of private financing in terms of human rights is less clear, it remains an important factor to consider for a comprehensive analysis. Since 1975, the private sector captured the growing influx of foreign capital; however, a significant amount of those funds were transferred to the state, in the form of direct taxes: US$ 2.4 million were raised in 1973, US$ 10.6 million in 1974, and US$ 20.9 million in 1975. A similar trend can be observed in the case of indirect taxation: US$ 5.6 million were levied in 1973, US$ 10.9 million in 1974, and US$ 13.8 million in 1975.[23]

At the same time, and also from a spending perspective, financial openness became an additional tool for transferring public resources toward economic groups that were in privileged and key positions in the capital market, to the detriment of small Chilean businesses.[24] An analysis of the "transfers" category within public spending shows that between 1969 and 1979 subsidies to private activity saw the largest increase, and this in turn generated additional income through taxation. Loans also facilitated government subsidies for important companies, which secured political support from key sectors of the economy and society, consolidating its political position.

THE STANCE OF THE UNITED STATES AND THE CRYSTALLIZATION OF THE LINK BETWEEN FUNDING AND HUMAN RIGHTS

Shortly after the military take-over of 1973, Pinochet's government started receiving financial aid from several countries, most prominently the United States.[25] This fact reveals the United States' initial support to Pinochet's regime and other Latin American countries, which was geopolitically motivated by the fight against communism.

However, as of 1976, Carter's administration reduced and eventually suspended financial and military aid due to the well-known human rights situation in the country.[26] The amount of bilateral financial aid received illustrates this policy change: in 1974, United States offered loans for US$ 302.1 million, the same as in 1975, but in 1976 this number dropped to US$ 16 million.[27] Moreover, the Federal Republic of Germany, the Netherlands, Italy, and Norway also suspended most of their bilateral aid to Chile, thus condemning the human rights violations being perpetrated by Pinochet's regime.[28]

In the case of multilateral financial institutions, economic aid rose significantly after the coup of 1973, both in absolute terms and in proportion to the total amount of aid provided. The *Cassese Report* identifies two approaches to financial assistance, according to their objectives. On the one hand, IMF's assistance was destined for and tied to the implementation of liberal economic policies. On the other hand, financial assistance, granted by the World Bank, the Inter-American Development Bank, and several UN agencies, was allocated based on social criteria and promoted specific development goals.

Nonetheless, this last type of assistance represented only a fraction of the financial assistance offered,[29] and apparently had no meaningful positive impact on the rights of Chileans; first, due to the negative social impact of the austerity policies already mentioned, second, because foreign aid was mostly used to service the external debt and replace Chilean investment funds for public services which were eventually put to other uses. Driven by its foreign policy on the subject of human rights, the Carter administration pressured multilateral lenders, as of 1976, to restrict financial aid offered to the Chilean government (although the IMF appears to have shifted its stance toward Chile not because of human rights but on a purely economic basis).[30]

From 1976 onwards, official creditors were replaced by private multinational banks, which started lending enormous sums, disregarding the potential impact that those loans may have on civil and political rights. The U.S. government even explicitly warned that any bank lending money to Chile would be acting against U.S. foreign policy, which considered human rights to be a crucial factor when it came to deciding whether to financially support a regime.[31] The question remains as to whether today this would entail a certain degree of accountability for the state and head offices based on the principle of extraterritorial obligations ("Maastricht Principles") in the field of human rights.

According to the *Cassese Report*, the aforementioned official policies, which were supported by most of the international community and were respectful of human rights, were rendered ineffective by the financial practices carried out by a reduced number of banks.[32] The president of the *House Banking Committee* of the United States warned six of the main multilateral development banks who were granting loans to Chile, that their actions appeared inconsistent with the rules for preventing banking practices that interfered with the public interest, and therefore he was expecting a public explanation.[33] Banking leaders, however, responded that financial institutions should not be prevented from carrying out "normal business," regardless of the nature of the government they were dealing with.[34]

This reluctance shown by private lenders resulted in an unusual occurrence in the United States. In 1978, Senator Edward Kennedy introduced the *Foreign Bank Loans Disclosure Act*,[35] which demanded that banks disclose any loans they had granted to known criminal regimes. It also generated a debate within the U.S. Senate on the capability of Latin American dictatorships to remain in power. In that context, Senator Church commented that "*massive funding such as (what Hanover Trust provided to Chile's Pinochet) may be what enabled five Latin American governments . . . to continue their anti-democratic practices and violations of human rights.*"[36]

Although Carter's foreign policy appears to have contributed somewhat to the improvement of the human rights situation during Pinochet's regime,[37] some of its measures were unsuccessful. Specifically, the U.S. government failed in its attempt to influence North American banks, as previously explained. Furthermore, said the government was unsuccessful in trying to internationalize sanctions against the ruling dictatorships of the Southern Cone region. This can be seen, for example, in the fact that Chilean and Argentinian military governments turned to Israel and Western European countries when the United States imposed arms embargoes.[38]

Nevertheless, the measures implemented by the United States and other countries, as well as the *Cassese Report*, reflect an understanding that there was a relationship between foreign financial aid and the ability of the Chilean dictatorship not only to strengthen its political position but also to effectively carry out its criminal campaign.

CONCLUSIONS, DEBATES, DEVELOPMENTS IN THE REGION AND PROSPECTS

An analysis of the causal link between large-scale financial assistance and human rights violations must take into account the macroeconomic, fiscal, and budgetary consequences of the loans granted. A holistic approach, such as the one adopted by the *Cassese Report*, which demands the study of financial complicity, should be emphasized.[39] An interdisciplinary analysis offers the opportunity to address, identify, and understand the relationship between the ruling class, the military, foreign governments, financial institutions, and the victims of human rights violations. The success and failure of Latin American dictatorships, both in terms of political stability and economic results, depended tremendously on the financial support they received, and Chile was no exception.

The *Cassese Report* on Chile and financial aid is categorical: "*foreign economic assistance largely serves to strengthen and underpin the economic system adopted by the Chilean authorities, which in turn needs to rely on the suppression of civil and political rights. The findings confirm that the mass of the current economic assistance is instrumental in the consolidation and perpetuation of the ongoing crackdown on those rights.*"[40]

The measures enforced by the United States and other governments to block financial aid to the Chilean regime are also relevant to identify accountability for corporate complicity in the Chilean case. Those governments recognized in some way that financial assistance could facilitate the commission of gross violations, and that the limitations they were implementing derived from the highest level of international law.

As a result, what the Carter administration's did more than thirty years ago, as well as the efforts by Senator Edward Kennedy and other legislators of the United States all contribute to the current debate on the impact of money in terms of facilitating crimes and how the law should respond to this question. A closer look at the norms that the U.S. government was abiding by to deny assistance to Latin American dictatorships puts them undoubtedly under the category of *jus cogens*.[41]

Accountability for complicity, including the financial type, should be based on the foreseeable effect of the use of commodities rather than on their intrinsic qualities. To offer a concrete example: money can either improve or worsen a situation, and in the case of the United States, after repeatedly blocking financial help to the Chilean government, it gradually began shifting its stance, precisely because the Chilean authorities were in the process of improving the country's human rights situation. As stated in the *Cassese Report*, "*even this new stand reveals that a close link is instituted between foreign economic assistance and respect for human rights in Chile.*"[42]

The issue of the legal implications of the causal link between financial decisions and human rights violations has again become a feature of recent debates on an international level.[43] The *Thun Group of Banks*[44] published in January 2017 their second discussion paper,[45] warning that banks cannot be held responsible for the adverse effects on human rights that their clients' operations may have, because the said impact is not a part of those banks' operations. The answer provided by the UN Working Group on Business and Human Rights was categorical: "*If a banks proceeds with financing, absent rigorous due diligence and safeguards, then its decision to lend may contribute to adverse human rights impacts, since it could have mitigated or prevented harm through its due diligence processes and the terms of its loan.*"[46] On a similar note, in June 2017, the UN High Commissioner for Human Rights issued a document providing clarification on the meaning of human rights related due diligence for banks;[47] also, the UN Independent Expert on foreign debt and human rights (one of the coauthors of this chapter) addressed a letter to the Thun Group in October 2017, explaining why human rights due diligence in contexts marked by the existence of criminal regimes is particularly important for banks.[48]

Financial institutions may assist criminal regimes not only by granting loans but also by facilitating the commission of economic crimes for dictators. Thus, it is important to remember that since 1998 and until 2005 Riggs Bank was under investigation for its complicity with the Chilean military government, for the reception, hiding, and laundering of public funds stolen by Pinochet since the beginning of the dictatorship.[49] Moreover, Riggs Bank helped Pinochet and his family to avoid an asset freeze ordered by a Spanish judge.[50] This case also illustrates the legal relevance of financial intermediaries against the backdrop of mass human rights violation campaigns.

States that commit explicit human rights violations not only practice torture and violate the right to life, but can also impose economic models that undermine economic, social, and cultural rights. As explained by Antonio Cassese in a scientific paper published in 1979,[51] the connections between different human rights violations are usually part of a regime's strategy for survival.[52] Foreign investors may benefit from a regime's lack of respect for human rights such as freedom of association and the creation of unions, or the fragility of some countries' social, security, and health regulations. When companies make decisions based on profits (which are more likely to be higher when human rights are curtailed), economic assistance can contribute to the perpetuation of human rights abuses, and these abuses might, in turn, bring about the necessary conditions to attract and obtain additional economic assistance or new investments. Furthermore, in the case of a transition from an authoritarian regime to a democracy, practices entailing pernicious consequences for development may constitute a legacy of the regime, whose economic structures will influence the prospects of democratic consolidation.

The way in which financial assistance can contribute to the commission of massive human rights violations, and what legal consequences the lenders that provided funding for the authors of those crimes should face, are the kind of questions being asked by Colombian prosecutors who in 2014 submitted a financial report to the Court of Justice and Peace (Tribunal de Justicia y Paz), which gives an account of the systematic funding granted by banana plantation owners, cattle ranchers, and other businesspeople to paramilitary groups in Colombia.[53]

Along these lines, the victims of Argentina's last dictatorship filed in 2009 a civil lawsuit in Buenos Aires against several foreign banks that had funded the military junta after 1976.[54] "*I want to know who gave money to a military junta that was governing a bankrupt country but could afford to pay the salary of my parents' killers and buy the instruments used to torture them*," stated one of the victims that filed that claim.[55]

The time has come for that same question to be raised and responded in the Chilean context, as was demanded to the Chilean state in 2015 by two UN independent experts (one of whom is a coauthor of this chapter), with no answer whatsoever to this day.[56]

NOTES

1. This chapter expands and updates previous research by the authors, published in Anuario de Derecho Público (Universidad Diego Portales, 2011), 340–76. The opinions and conclusions in this chapter are solely those of the authors and do not reflect in any way those of the institutions with which they are affiliated.
2. See Juan Pablo Bohoslavsky, *Report on Financial Complicity*, UN Human Rights Council, UN Doc. A/HRC/28/59, December 22, 2014.
3. However, loans granted by private entities appear to be more harmful, due to them being subject to a less rigorous degree of accountability than that of official lenders or international financial institutions.
4. Juan P. Bohoslavsky and Abel Escriba-Folch, "Rational Choice and Financial Complicity with Human Rights Abuses: Policy and Legal Implications," in *Making Sovereign Financing & Human Rights Work*, eds Juan P. Bohoslavsky and Jernej Cernic (Oxford: Hart Publishing, 2014), 17–32.
5. See for example the case of businessman Ricardo Claro (Asper Limitada) who funded DINA through the payment of the salaries of some of its employees, Javier Rebolledo, *La danza de los cuervos. El destino final de los detenidos desaparecidos* (Ceibo, 2014).
6. Guillermo O'Donnell, "Reflections on the Patterns of Change in the Bureaucratic-Authoritarian State," *Latin American Research Review* 13 (1978), p. 6.
7. See the studies regarding Argentina, Brazil and Uruguay in Juan P. Bohoslavsky and Marcelo Torelly, "Cumplicidade Financeira Durante a Ditadura no Brasil: Implicações Atuais," *Revista Anistia Política e Justiça de Transição* (2012): 70–117; Juan P. Bohoslavsky, "Los prestamistas de la muerte," in *El negocio del terrorismo de Estado. Los cómplices económicos de la dictadura uruguaya*, ed. Juan P. Bohoslavsky (Montevideo: Penguim Random House 2016), 101–21; Juan P. Bohoslavsky and Veerle Opgenhaffen, "The Past and Present of Corporate Complicity: Financing the Argentinean Dictatorship," *Harvard Human Rights Journal* 23 (2010), pp. 157–203.
8. Vergara, Pilar, "Las transformaciones de las funciones económicas del Estado en Chile Bajo el régimen militar," *Colección de Estudios CIEPLAN 5*, Estudio Nº 53 (1981), pp. 117–54.

9. See Ricardo Ffrench-Davis, "El Experimento Monetarista en Chile: Una Síntesis Crítica," *Desarrollo Económico* 23 (1983), pp. 163–96; José De Gregorio, "Lo interno de la deuda externa. El caso chileno," *Nueva Sociedad* 84 (1986), p. 28.

10. The Decree-Law No. 600 (Foreign Investment Statute) of 1974, strongly protected foreign investors to attract them toward the country, guaranteeing them access to the exchange market, remittances for the entirety of their profits and capital, reinvestment of their operations' profits in Chile, in any activity, their inclusion under the norms applied for national investments, and fiscal invariability.

11. Central Bank of Chile, "Indicadores Económicos y Sociales de Chile 1960–2000," (Santiago, 2001).

12. Central Bank of Chile, "Deuda externa de Chile," (Santiago, 1984).

13. Cassese, Antonio, "Study of the Impact of Foreign Economic Aid and Assistance on Respect for Human Rights in Chile," (E/CN.4/Sub.2/412), (*Cassese Report*). See chapter 3.

14. Op. cit., vol. III, p. 8.

15. Here, we mean both the human rights abuses that arise directly from the financing of the repressive apparatus as well as the violations of economic, social, and cultural rights that stem from the allocation of budget items that should be destined to social spending to financing repressive mechanisms.

16. Thomas Sheetz, "Gastos Militares en Chile, Perú y la Argentina," *Desarrollo Económico* 25 (1985), pp. 316–17. These data meant in absolute terms an expenditure of US$ 624.3 million in 1969 and by 1982 an expenditure of US$ 1263 million (both based on the value of the dollar of 1977).

17. At the beginning of the dictatorship, both police forces (Carabineros and the Investigative Police) were removed from the Ministry of Interior and assigned to the Ministry of Defense, and institutional regulations were implemented to guarantee Carabineros a greater autonomy, which officially made them the fourth branch of the military, a situation that persisted until 2011.

18. See Jorge Marshall, "El Gasto Público en Chile 1969–1979," *Colección Estudios CIEPLAN 5*, Estudio N° 51 (1981).

19. (Millions of pesos from 1978), Marshall, op.cit.

20. Vergara, op. cit., p. 132.

21. Marshall, op. cit., p. 74.

22. See the report submitted to the United States Congress in 1978 by the Institute for Policy Studies, S 3631-Foreign Loans Disclosure Act of 1978, 124 Cong Rec 37677 1978.

23. Central Bank of Chile, op. cit. note 8, p. 86.

24. Vergara, op. cit., p. 138.

25. Cassese, op. cit., Vol. III, p. 5.

26. Robert Bejesky and Juan P. Bohoslavsky, "Carter's Human Rights Policy Towards Southern Cone Countries: A Contribution to the Current Debate on Financial Complicity," Bohoslavsky & Cernic, op. cit. note 4, pp. 302–22.

27. Cassese, op. cit., Vol. III, p. 10.

28. *Center for International Policy*, "Chile: An Analysis of Human Rights Violations and United States Security Assistance and Economic Programmes," (July 1–2, 1978).

29. In the case of multilateral assistance for the purpose of development, in 1974 it represented 13.4 percent, 15 percent in 1975 and 18.7 percent in 1976. Bilateral aid with the same purpose reached 26.8 percent in 1974, 16.9 percent in 1975 and 17.8 percent in 1976. For more details, see Cassese, op. cit., vol. IV, pp. 14–16.

30. Cassese op. cit., para. 253, 257, 300, 301–7, 407, 418, 468–70.

31. "Rights Policy Not Helped by Loans to Chile From Banks," *The Washington Post* (April 13, 1978).

32. Cassese, op. cit., Vol. III, p. 29.

33. "Several US Banks Accused of Undercutting Policy on Chile," *The Washington Post* (April 12, 1978).

34. For example, in his trip to Argentina in 1978, David Rockefeller—the president of Chase Manhattan Bank at the time—publicly criticized President Carter's human rights policy, underscoring that he should not be allowed to *interfere with normal relations between nations.* In 1978, the president of Lloyds Bank in London answered to the criticisms for the granting of loans to the Chilean dictatorship, admitting that this was a repressive regime, but pointing out that lending money to the country was not prohibited. "Lloyds Bounces Chile Protest," *The Guardian* (March 31, 1978).

35. S 3631-Foreign Loans Disclosure Act of 1978, 124 Cong. Rec. 37 678 1978.

36. Ibid.

37. Roberta Cohen, "Human Rights Diplomacy: The Carter Administration and the Southern Cone," *Human Rights Quarterly* 4 (1982), p. 212.

38. Cohen, op. cit., p. 233. (Ibid., 233).

39. See the report in note No. 2.

40. Cassese, op. cit., Vols. I–IV, 1978, p. 24.

41. In reference to the Argentinian case: "Arms Trade in the Western Hemisphere: Hearing before the Subcommittee on Inter-American Affairs of the Committee on International Relations," 95th Cong. (1978) (declarations by Patricia M Derian, Secretary of Human Rights and Humanitarian Issues during Carter's administration).

42. Cassese, op. cit., Vol. III, p. 89.

43. See in detail in *United Nations Environment Programme Finance Initiative*, "Banks and Human Rights: A Legal Analysis," (Geneva, 2015), available at http://www.unepfi.org/fileadmin/documents/BanksandHumanRights.pdf.

44. This informal group was created to discuss the implications of the UN Guiding Principles on Business and Human Rights for the banking sector. Currently, its members are UBS, Credit Suisse, Barclays, BBVA, BNP Paribas, Deutsche Bank, ING, RBS, Standard Chartered, UniCredit, and JP Morgan.

45. Available at http://www.menschenrechte.uzh.ch/en/publikationen/thun-group-of-banks.html.

46. Available at http://www.ohchr.org/Documents/Issues/TransCorporations/WG_BHR_letter_Thun_Group.pdf.

47. Available at http://www.ohchr.org/Documents/Issues/Business/InterpretationGuidingPrinciples.pdf.

48. Available at http://www.ohchr.org/Documents/Issues/Development/IEDebt/LetterThunGroup.pdf.

49. See the ruling issued by Judge Baltasar Garzón Real, Tribunal de Investigación No. 5 (Madrid), Case No. 28079-27-2-1996-0007036-78300 (2/25/05); Terence O'Hara, "Allbrittons, Riggs to Pay Victims of Pinochet," *The Washington Post* (February 26, 2005), p. A01.

50. Ibid.

51. See chapter 3.

52. Antonio Cassese, "Foreign Economic Assistance and Respect for Civil and Political Rights: Chile – a Case Study," *Texas International Law Journal* 14 (1979), 2, p. 251.

53. "El primer informe de la financiación paramilitar en el Urabá," *El Espectador* (February 6, 2017), available at http://www.elespectador.com/noticias/judicial/el-primer-informe-de-la-financiacion-paramilitar-en-el-uraba-articulo-678630.

54. The case is *Ibañez Manuel Leandro y otros casos/Diligencia Preliminar Contra Instituciones Financieras No Determinadas*, No. 95.019/2009, Justicia Nacional en lo Civil. See the *amicus curiae* presented on March 26, 2010, for that same case by the University of Essex and the Centro de Estudios Legales y Sociales, available at https://www.business-humanrights.org/ See also note No. 7.

55. "Los prestamistas de la muerte," *Página 12* (March 16, 2009).

56. OL CHL 1/2015, May 26, 2015, available at https://spdb.ohchr.org/hrdb/30th/public_-_OL_Chile_26.05.15_(1.2015).pdf.

Chapter 9

Extractivism as a Policy

From Its Dictatorial Origins to Its Democratic Continuity

Sebastián Smart

INTRODUCTION

Chile was the first Latin American country to introduce a neoliberal model of governance for natural resources.[1] This chapter shows how this model did not only generate an important mechanism for the attraction of foreign capital for extractive activities[2] but also brought forth significant social and environmental issues.[3] Despite this, and its strong link to current human rights violations in Latin America, academics have often ignored the responsibility of both those who generated this extractive model, and those who reaped its benefits and supported the civilian–military dictatorship lead by Augusto Pinochet from 1973 to 1990.

This chapter deals with the current impact of extractive policies on the Chilean economy and their effects on human rights and delves into the historical process that gave rise to the model of intensive exploitation of natural resources and their export as raw materials. To unravel those links, a *process-tracing* method is used. This method provides a tool for investigating and discovering the historical causes and the main shifts in policies, programs, and projects that have resulted in the current state of extractivism in Chile. By placing our focus on determining the degree of responsibility and complicity of key economic players in the creation and implementation of the extractivist model in Chile during the dictatorship, the chapter explains not only how the aforementioned model was created but also who was affected by it, and who was its biggest beneficiary.

To answer these questions, the main argument regarding economic complicity in the extractive model generated during the dictatorship will be divided into three sections. In the first one, an analysis will be provided on the prominent characteristics of the extractive model imposed by the dictatorial government. The second section will include a brief critical description of the leading arguments wielded by the dictatorship and democratically elected governments to defend extractivism; a defense which, as will be shown in the third section, should be analyzed taking into account the close interdependence between extractivism, state capture, and rent-seeking. The chapter concludes by stating that the institutional framework generated during the dictatorship and bolstered during the following democratically elected governments has consolidated a neoliberal economic and political model that benefits an elite (which is closely linked to Pinochet's figure) and harms mostly those social groups whose access to power has been limited.

EXTRACTIVISM IN CHILE

Chile is an extractivist country, mainly in terms of its mining industry, but also with regard to agriculture, forestry, and fishing.[4] Within the mining sector, copper has become the most extracted mineral in Chile and the whole Andean region. In 2011, copper mining in the region accounted for 45.2 percent of the total global extraction of the said material, which meant that 7,293.5 thousand tons of copper were extracted.[5] In the same year, 32.4 percent of the total global extraction was carried out in Chilean territory,[6] prolonging a trend that has seen Chile as the number one copper-extracting country in the world since 1982.[7] However, copper is not the only mineral extracted at a large scale in the country. Chile is ranked third worldwide in molybdenum extraction (38.7 tons in 2013), fifth in silver extraction (1,217 tons in 2013), and fifteenth in gold extraction (48.57 tons in 2013).[8] As for nonmetal mining, Chile is number two worldwide in lithium extraction (65,620 tons in 2012), which represents 37 percent of the world's total.[9]

So, the first question that should be answered is how this extractive model was economically and politically created.

Against a backdrop of strong repression and constant human rights violations, a model of concentration of capital was implemented and consolidated in the country. As a result, the system in place was one where repression and accumulation of wealth became inseparable, where the neoliberal model could not be understood unless the dictatorship's repression was taken into account, and the level of concentration of wealth could not be dissociated from its violent origins. Economically, this model was based on strong privatization policies[10] and an openness to foreign capital markets, under the strict supervision of the Chicago Boys,[11] who had sponsored it. By adopting the neoliberal ideas of the Chicago school of economics, the Chilean dictatorship set its sights, from 1975 onward, on imposing market dynamics as the cornerstone of society, thus creating a true market society.[12]

However, it was not until the beginning of the 1980s, and as a reaction to the financial crisis and the pressure of the exporting elites and industrial unions, that Pinochet's government started placing a special emphasis on extractivism,[13] a model that, according to Horacio Machado,[14] was based on three fundamental pillars: (a) Total legal security regarding mining concessions; (b) Large fiscal and commercial benefits; and (c) Extremely flexible environmental legislation and regulations.

A. *Legal Security Regarding the Ownership of Common Goods*

At the start of the 1980s, and as a reaction to a generalized feeling of threat experienced by the ruling classes, the idea of legislating in favor of full legal security regarding the ownership of natural resources in the country gained increasing support. Thus, the privatizing principles were created and afterward given official status in the Political Constitution of 1980, the 1981 Water Code, the 1982 Electricity Act and the Mining Code of 1983. Year after year there were attempts to consolidate the constitutional and legal model that aimed to privatize Chile's common goods, by offering full legal protection to investors and generating as a result the necessary conditions to establish a privatizing link between water, electricity, and mining in the country.

One of the key elements to soothe the ruling classes after the financial crisis was the implementation of the law of full concession. It was a model of mineral ownership that granted security of tenure to those that applied for exploratory and exploitation concessions, disregarding even the established rights regarding ownership of the land, enshrined by the previous legislations.[15] Despite the fact that the Constitution of 1980 establishes the right of eminent domain of the state over mineral reserves, at the same time it implements a system of private concessions and provides them with a constitutional framework that grants them preeminence over other property rights. Article 19 N 24 of the Constitution states that concessions can be granted to exploit any mineral substance, except for some which are reserved for the state.[16]

The man in charge of drafting the full concession law was José Piñera, who served as the minister of mining for the dictatorship between December of 1980 and December of 1984, and who shared the liberal principles taught by the Chicago Boys. The first constitutional reform to introduce the concept of full concession is the Organic Constitutional Law on Mining Concessions N 18,097, which was later ratified in the Mining Code of 1983, granting every person the right to sample and dig in lands of any domain in search for mineral substances, except in those within the limits of another mining concession.[17] And even though Piñera underscored that this framework eliminated the uncertainty which characterized the leading mining model at the time, and that it would be useful for channeling national and foreign private capital,[18] he did not consider the over-saturation of areas under concession rights, and the clear impact it would have on the territory, such as the overlapping of mining rights and ancestral indigenous territories.[19]

B. *Fiscal and Commercial Benefits Which Lasted between Twenty-five and Thirty Years*

Fiscal benefits were mostly related to invariable taxation, and their main trait was the low taxes paid by foreign investors carrying out mining operations in the country. Several studies have shown that during the 1990s, the fiscal situation of Chilean mining companies was marked by tax evasion. Furthermore, the state-owned mining company CODELCO (Corporación Nacional del Cobre in Spanish; National Corporation of Copper in English) paid, for example, 28.7 percent of its revenue in taxes between 1990 and 2001, while private-owned companies paid only 5.3 percent on average.[20] Similarly, in his compared case study of twenty-four mining countries, James Otto concludes that Chile ranks among the top five countries whose fiscal regulations are the least effective and most profitable for private investors.[21]

From the aforementioned data, another question arises: How were these fiscal and commercial benefits generated?

The Decree-Law N 600 of 1974 represented the first effort to lure foreign investment, albeit limited by its article N 1, section 4, which stated: "Foreign investment will not be accepted in those areas assigned by law to national investment." This meant that private investment was not allowed in the large sector of copper mining, which had been nationalized by the Constitutional Reform of 1971.[22] However, the Decree-Law N 1,748 of 1977 eliminates the figure of "areas assigned to national investment" by accepting credits associated with foreign investment in its article N 2, letter d. Afterward, in its article N 7, it derogates the obligation for export revenue to return to the country. In the words of Julián Alcagaya,

> Maybe in 1974, when the original Decree-Law N°600 was passed there was still a shred of nationalism within the high command of the military, but come 1977, the strategic leadership of the dictatorship, and their civilian advisers trained at the University of Chicago, were aiming directly towards submission to an international capital which was successfully putting pressure to be granted privileges in mining and other productive Chilean sectors.[23]

The DL N 600 was created by Pinochet's regime to attract foreign investment. But it was the Minister of Finance Hernán Büchi—who also shared the neoliberal principles introduced by the Chicago Boys—who, to bring confidence to foreign investors, increased the duration of franchise tenures, because in those years "*to invest in Chile was the same as to invest in Rwanda, one had to be crazy*," as recalled by a former staff member of the Foreign Investment Committee.[24]

C. *An Inexistent Socio-Environmental Legislation*

Toward the end of the dictatorship, the role of the Chilean State in environmental regulation matters was completely nonexistent. However, not only there was a lack of environmental legislation but also the normative framework generated during the dictatorship attempted to foster economic activity with no regard whatsoever for the socioeconomic impact it may have produced.[25] As an example, guarantee funds for environmental impact were suspended, there were important legal loopholes regarding mining environmental liability, pollution standards were lower than those of the World Health Organization (WHO), and control mechanisms were fragmented.[26] This resulted in unchecked mining practices, uncontrolled exploitation of marine resources, aquaculture that was exempt of any environmental regulation,[27] native forests being destroyed and replaced by monoculture planting of foreign species,[28] and deregulation and privatization in terms of water and air pollution.

DEFENSE OF EXTRACTIVISM DURING THE DICTATORSHIP AND DEMOCRATIC GOVERNMENTS

This openly neoliberal model was successful in terms of attracting foreign capital for extractivist exploitation in the country. In fact, Chile emerged during the decades of 1980 and 1990 as the model country for the rest of the world when it came to attracting resources for extractivist exploitation,[29] and in consequence, the model was mirrored by other countries in the region.[30] It is to be underscored then, that the liberalization and openness of extractivism in the country was conducive to the goal of attracting foreign direct investment, giving rise to a model of accumulation centered on the intensive export of natural resources. This model of capital accumulation in developing countries by central powers and newly developed nations, which was established during the dictatorship, was widely consolidated and strengthened during the democratic recovery that followed.[31]

Accordingly, it does not seem strange to observe, for example, that from 1994 onward copper extraction became more intensive in the private sphere than that in the state-owned CODELCO, a trend which has its roots in the dictatorship, but has had its effects during the following democratic governments

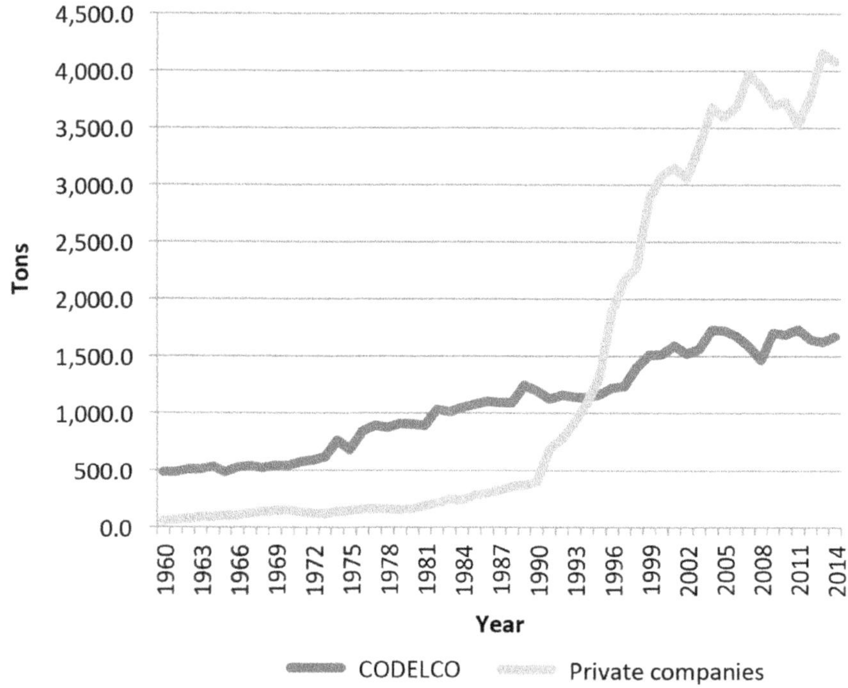

Figure 9.1 Chile's Copper Mine Production (Tons/Year). *Source*: Created by the author based on statistics by COCHILCO (Chile's Ministry of Mining) http://www.cochilco.cl/estadisticas/produccion.asp

as well, and which there appears to be no real political intention to change so far (figure 9.1). If in 1970 copper was regarded as Chile's salary, mainly because the state-owned companies concentrated 78 percent of its extraction, in 2014 the figure is the complete opposite, as the state controls merely 29 percent of the total copper extraction in the country.

The question that arises is this: Why has this model of accumulation of common goods by foreign capitals been defended so vehemently? The main arguments to defend the extractivist model are based, on the one hand, on considering it a tool for job creation, and on the other, on seeing it as a means to reduce poverty, through a redistribution of the wealth generated by copper mining. In other words, the founding premise of this reasoning is considering this model as a necessary means to generate real social inclusion. These arguments can be disputed. The first myth is that mining creates employment. If we observe the macroeconomic data we can see that even when mining represents approximately 13 percent of the country's GDP and nearly 53 percent of Chile's total exports, it employs only 1.5 percent of the nation's total

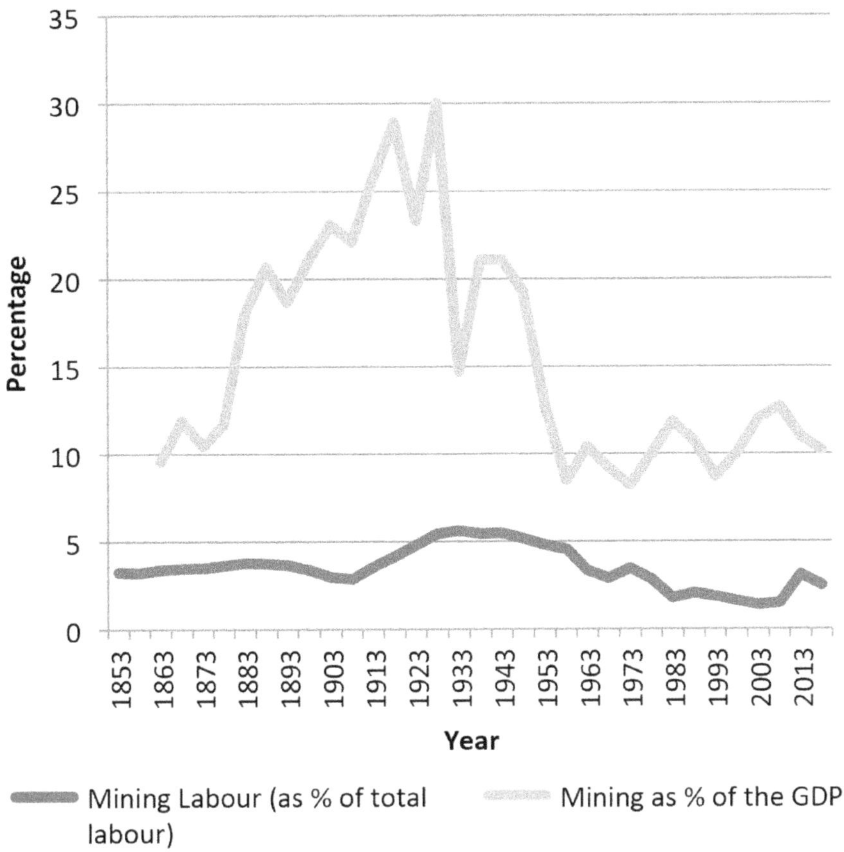

Figure 9.2 Mining as Workforce/Percentage of Total GDP (1853–2008). *Source*: Created by the author based on statistics by COCHILCO (Chile's Ministry of Mining) http://www.cochilco.cl/estadisticas/produccion.asp`

workforce. Historically, at least since 1853, the mining industry has not been able to create employment for more than 5 percent of the country's workforce (figure 9.2). This is due to mining being not a major source of employment, but one of the major capital extractions.

Moreover, given the already analyzed low amount of taxes that companies paid, the downturn experienced by CODELCO as a wealth generator in the country, and the intensity of common goods exports in Chile, it would be inaccurate to say that the mining industry is a source of wealth redistribution or a factor against poverty. *Mining is no longer Chile's salary.*

THE BENEFITS OF THE EXTRACTIVE MODEL (IN THE PAST, AND TODAY)

Considering that the so-called economic "miracle"[32] generated by the Chilean political and economic system during the dictatorship has not really been one, and that different authors have successfully offered proof of the detrimental social and environmental consequences of extractivist neoliberalism in the country,[33] the staunch defense of this extractive model carried out by democratically elected governments in Chile becomes difficult to understand.

Nevertheless, it should be remembered that the country's dominating political model has been openly labeled as top-down (presidential), and that it mostly benefits the Chilean economic and political elites.[34] Furthermore, the link between economic and political power born during the dictatorship has remained strong after democracy's return.[35] It follows that this link is the one which may explain, in general terms, the defense of extractivism by democratic governments. This thesis becomes even more apparent, as will be outlined below, with the process of disclosure of cases involving illegal contributions to politicians that starts in 2015 in the country, and that leads to the crumbling of public trust in the national political system.[36]

Everything Stays in the Family

Historically, extractivism has been presented as a source of job creation and public income. However, as could be observed in the previous section, this argument can be refuted by the macroeconomic data on Chilean extractivism. Despite the negative consequences of extractivism both in terms of pollution and human rights violations,[37] this model has remained virtually intact over the past twenty-five years, mostly benefitting groups with either family, friendship, or political ties to Augusto Pinochet. These groups include individuals who have actively participated in the design and implementation of the current extractive system, and who have used the said system to their advantage.

Perhaps one of the most representative examples of those beneficiaries is the figure of Julio Ponce Lerou, who was the director of the Sociedad Química y Minera de Chile (Soquimich or SQM)[38] and who currently holds the third place in the list of the wealthiest individuals in the country, with a net worth of 3.1 billion dollars.[39] Soquimich is a privately owned mining company, a world leader in the production of saltpeter, iodine, potassium, and lithium, all extracted in Chile. Julio Ponce was Pinochet's son-in-law, and he was also the executive director of the Corporación Nacional Forestal (CONAF) starting in 1974, and an executive in the Corporación de Fomento a la Producción (CORFO) starting in 1979. During his time in CONAF, he was denounced for auctioning hundreds of thousands of hectares confiscated during the Agrarian Reform and during that process, appropriating several estates.[40] In 1983, Ponce Lerou was forced to resign from his position as director of CORFO after claims against him of "illicit enrichment;" he rose to prominence as a powerful figure in lithium extraction that very year.[41] As María Olivia Monckenberg points out, according to the Commission of the Chamber of Deputies that investigated the alleged irregularities in privatizations during Pinochet's administration, Julio Ponce Lerou was one of the big winners of the extractivist model imposed by the dictatorship. She mentions that

> Soquimich is the largest producer of lithium carbonate in the world. It owns over a million hectares of mining property. Julio Ponce Lerou gained control of the company because of his personal situation and the contacts he established with economists and high-ranking military officials. Thus, he went from a simple forest engineer to the owner of a significant and now publicly known fortune. In order to achieve this, a few individuals were of key importance, such as the former minister Hernan Büchi or Juan Hurtado, both of whom shared the board of directors of Soquimich with him.[42]

Besides his involvement in the irregular financing of politics, as will be shown further down the chapter, the power of Ponce Lerou is also represented by the amount of land he owns. In fact, Soquimich owns the second-highest amount of land-based mining concessions, behind CODELCO.[43] This is a worrying situation, as the land acquired in the form of concessions for mining exploration and extraction has become a truly speculative real estate market, as noted by a former director of Sernageomin.[44]

It should be remembered that mining property is of a higher hierarchy than private property regarding land rights, which results in concessions being granted at the expense of communities that have historically inhabited those lands. Therefore, one of the consequences of the model of full concession established at the beginning of the 1980s in the country has been the emergence and spread of mining speculators, who manage to acquire concessions only to trade them with large mining or electricity companies, who are the ones that eventually set up extractive activities in those territories.

One of the owners of the largest amount of mining concessions in the country is María Teresa Cañas Pinochet, Augusto Pinochet's niece. She was the president of the Instituto de Investigaciónes Geológicas (currently Sernageomin) under Pinochet's administration and kept her position until the administration's end in 1990. After the end of the dictatorship, she and her husband, Jorge Iván de la Barra Valle—who acted as vice president of the Central Bank during the dictatorship—created the society "María Teresa Cañas y Compañía Limitada." Currently, Cañas, de la Barra and two of their children, Jorge and Andrea de la Barra, are listed among the largest owners of mining concessions in the country, a position that has earned the nickname "paper miners."[45] The use, and abuse, of mining speculation, plays a key role in the territorial impregnability of large extractive projects. To illustrate this point, concessions granted to Cañas Pinochet would be later used in the Hydroaysén project, headed by Colbún, which belongs to Matte group.[46]

As a result, the relationship between those groups close to Pinochet and the main economic groups in the country becomes clear to see, especially when the strong link between these groups and extractivism is considered. First, it should be highlighted that a large part of their power owes to the way they benefitted from the period of widespread privatizations known as "popular capitalism," which from 1985 onward attempted to diversify private ownership, but led to a greater economic concentration, according to Hugo Fazio.[47] Those privatizations allowed for the concentration of extractive projects in Chile in the hands of a few economic groups, most notably Luksic, Matte, and Angelini.[48] In extractive terms, Luksic group stands out nowadays for their power in the mining industry, mainly represented by Antofagasta Minerals, and in oil distribution through ENEX; Matte group's power lies in their ownership of the Compañía Manufacturera de Papeles y Cartón (CMPC), the wood pulp company Arauco, and the Isla Riesco mining company. Notwithstanding the fact that these companies were consolidated as economic groups after the end of the dictatorship, it was the privatizing trend of the dictatorship that allowed them to access the position of power and economic concentration that they hold today (see table 9.1).

Table 9.1 Degree of Market Concentration by the 250 Largest Companies in Chile (Four Main Groups)

	Companies		*Net Worth (December 1978)*	
Control	*N°*	*%*	*US$ million*	*%*
Cruzat Larraín Group	37	14.8	930.88	24.72
Vial Group	25	10	477.3	12.61
Matte Group	12	4.8	325.31	8.59
Luksic Group	8	3.2	139.06*	3.67

* Does not include MADECO (US$ 22.35 million)

Source: Table created by author based on data from Fernando Dahse, *El Mapa de La Extrema Riqueza: Los Grupos Económicos Y El Proceso de Concentración* (Editorial Aconcagua 1979), p. 147.

CONCLUSION: THE CONTINUITY OF A CO-OPTED SYSTEM

From the study of the authoritarian origins of extractivism, we can infer several conclusions. First, an analysis of the main legislative alterations and amendments in terms of extraction in Chile shows us a common thread in the way extractivism has been regulated in the country. This legislation stems politically from authoritarian governments and economically from a privileged class that has implemented and strongly defended the neoliberal ideas coming from the Chicago school of economics. And I say defended, as the interest of political and economic elites in extractivism has become apparent, reaching a point where there have been acts labeled as illicit financing of politics or tax evasion by both civil and common law.[49]

Second, one of the hypotheses that could explain the lack of political strength to modify the course of Chile's extractive model is the interrelation and mutual interdependence of the political and economic powers in the country, a relationship that Hugo Fazio has labeled as "fraudulent mechanisms for making a fortune."[50] As an example, there have been three major scandals regarding irregular financing of politics in Chile's recent history, the PENTA, Soquimich, and Corpesca cases, all of which are closely linked with Chile's extractivism. Another case that should be added to that list is the well-known Bank of Chile scandal, in which Andrónico Luksic, the head of the largest Chilean economic group, and strongly connected to mining, granted an irregular loan to Natalia Compagnon, the daughter-in-law of Michelle Bachelet.[51] The cases of irregular financing of politics and the connections between extractivism, power, politics, and shady deals are becoming more public and well-known in Chile, and this offers a tool, initially at least, to elaborate theories to understand the successful defense of the neoliberal extractivist model which has been the base of Chile's economy over the past forty years. In other words, the framework generated by the dictatorship and consolidated during democracy—due to its strong link to the country's elites—has produced an array of institutions marked by conflicts of interests and state capture by economic groups.

Last, this extractive model has been created to benefit the ruling classes that have remained in power at the expense of local, indigenous, and rural communities, which have had their rights continuously violated and have seen the environment around them progressively deteriorate. The appropriation of land by speculators has contributed to the rapid spread of socio-environmental conflicts at a local level. This can be observed when considering the relation between the number of minerals extracted, foreign direct investment in mining, the percentage of land under concession, and the socio-environmental conflicts that have emerged at a regional level in the country. In conclusion, these conflicts have come as an answer to the aggressive form of extraction that has been growing throughout the country over the past forty years and which has its origins in the civic–military dictatorship led by Pinochet.

NOTES

1. David Carruthers, "Environmental Politics in Chile: Legacies of Dictatorship and Democracy," *Third World Quarterly* 22 (2001), 343.
2. Gavin Bridge, "Mapping the Bonanza: Geographies of Mining Investment in an Era of Neoliberal Reform," *The Professional Geographer* 56 (2004), 406.
3. INDH, *Mapa de Conflictos Socioambientales En Chile 2015*, eds Silvana Lauzan and Dhayana Guzman (INDH, 2015).
4. *Central Bank of Chile*, "Cuentas Nacionales de Chile Evolucion de La Actividad Economica En El Año 2014: Evolución de La Actividad Económica En El Año 2014" (2014).
5. *CEPAL and UNASUR*, "Recursos Naturales En UNASUR: Situación Y Tendencias Para Una Agenda de Desarrollo Regional" (ECLAC, 2013).
6. *Comisión Chilena del Cobre*, "Estadísticas – Producción Minera," (2015), available at <http://www.cochilco.cl/estadisticas/produccion.asp> (last access on June 11, 2016).
7. CEPAL and UNASUR, op. cit. note No. 6.
8. *Comisión Chilena del Cobre*, "Metales Preciosos – Mercado Del Oro Y La Plata," (2014).
9. *Comisión Chilena del Cobre*, "Mercado Internacional Del Litio," (2013).
10. *Chamber of Deputies of Chile*, "Informe de La Comisión Investigadora Encargada de Analizar Presuntas Irregularidades En Las Privatizaciones de Empresas Del Estado Con anterioridad Al Año 1990," (2006).
11. Patricio Silva, "Technocrats and Politics in Chile: From the Chicago Boys to the CIEPLAN Monks," *Journal of Latin American Studies* 23 (1991), 385.
12. Karl Polanyi, "La Gran Transformación: Crítica Del Liberalismo Económico," (La Piqueta, 1993).
13. Ben Ross Schneider, "Business Politics and the State in Twentieth Century Latin America," (Cambridge University Press, 2004).
14. Horacio Machado, "Auge Minero Y Dominación Neocolonial En América Latina. Ecología Política de Las Transformaciones Socioterritoriales Neoliberales," *XXVII Congreso de la Asociación Latinoamericana de Sociología. Asociación Latinoamericana de Sociología* (2009).
15. See Nancy Yañez and Raúl Molina, "La Gran Minería Y Los Derechos Indígenas En El Norte de Chile," (LOM, 2008), 110.
16. Liquid or gaseous hydrocarbons, lithium, species located in maritime waters subject to national jurisdiction, and those areas declared of importance for national security. (Ley Orgánica Constitucional sobre concesiones mineras de 1981, article 3, section 4).
17. Article 14, section 1, Mining Code.
18. José Piñera, "La Ley Minera," *La Minería y el Desarrollo de Chile* (CEP, 1984).

19. Sebastian Smart, "Resistance against Mining Extractivism in Chile," *Critical Planning Journal* 24 (2017).
20. Rodrigo Pizarro, "La Consagración Del Royalty En Chile," *Regalías Mineras, Serie Minería y desarrollo* 2, 7 (2004); Yañez and Molina, op. cit., p. 114.
21. James Otto, "Royalties Mineros: Un Estudio Global de Su Impacto En Los Inversionistas, El Gobierno Y La Sociedad Civil," (Ediciones Universidad Católica de Chile, 2007).
22. Julián Alcayaga, "Manual Del Defensor Del Cobre," (Ediciones Tierra Mía, 2005).
23. Ibid., p. 61.
24. Marcela Ramos, "Los Enormes Beneficios Tributarios a Los Que Acceden Las Empresas Mineras En Chile," *CIPER Chile* (Santiago, June 19, 2011), available at <http://ciperchile.cl/2011/07/19/los-enormes-beneficios-tributarios-a-los-que-acceden-las-empresas-mineras-en-chile/> (last access on December 8, 2019).
25. See Carruthers, op. cit. Despite the pressure of some environmentalist groups, and a few rulings in local courts which tended toward the protection of the environment, this had a marginal effect.
26. Machado Araoz, op. cit., p. 5.
27. Miguel a Altieri and Alejandro Rojas, "Ecological Impacts of Chile's Neoliberal Policies, With Special Emphasis on Agroecosystems," *Environment, Development and Sustainability* 1, 55 (1999).
28. Roger Alex Clapp, "Waiting for the Forest Law : Resource-Led Development and Environmental Politics in Chile," *Latin American Research Review* 33, 3 (1998).
29. Bridge, op. cit.
30. Bolivia (1985–1991), Peru (1991), Ecuador (1991), Mexico (1992), Argentina (1993), Brazil (1996), Guatemala (1997), Honduras (1998), and Colombia (2001), see Machado Araoz, op. cit.
31. Alex Latta and Beatriz Cid Aguayo, "Testing the Limits: Neoliberal Ecologies from Pinochet to Bachelet," *Latin American Perspectives* 39 (2012), 163; Sally Babidge, "'Socios': The Contested Morality Of 'Partnerships' in Indigenous Community-Mining Company Relations, Northern Chile," *Journal of Latin American and Caribbean Anthropology* 18 (2013), 274.
32. See, for example, Arnold Harberger, "Up for Debate: Reform Without Liberty: Chile's Ambiguous Legacy," an interview available at: http://www.pbs.org/wgbh/commandingheights/shared/minitextlo/ufd_reformliberty_full.html (last access on May 31, 2017).
33. See Bresnahan; Carruthers; Babidge, op. cit.
34. Gabriel Salazar, "Construcción de Estado En Chile (1800–1837) Democracia de Los 'pueblos'. Militarismo Ciudadano. Golpismo Oligárquico," (Penguin Random House, Fifth edition, 2005).
35. Tomás Moulian, "Limitaciones de la transición a la democracia en Chile," *Proposiciones* 25, 25–33.
36. Ricardo Gamboa and Carolina Segovia, "Chile 2015: Falla Política, Desconfianza Y Reforma," *Revista de Ciencia Política* 36, 123 (2016).

37. Ximena Cuadra Montoya, "Nuevas estrategias de los movimientos indígenas contra el extractivismo en Chile," *CIDOB d'Afers Internacionals* 10, 141–163.

38. He was replaced as director by his brother, Eugenio Ponce Lerou, in 2016, after the corruption and illegal funding scandals that shook the country.

39. See Forbes magazine (2017), available at https://www.forbes.com/profile/julio-ponce-lerou/ (último acceso 22 de Marzo de 2017).

40. *Chamber of Deputies of Chile*, "Informe de La Comisión Investigadora Encargada de Analizar Presuntas Irregularidades En Las Privatizaciones de Empresas Del Estado Conanterioridad Al Año 1990," (2006), 178.

41. Alberto Arellano and Juan Pablo Figueroa, "El Día En Que El Estado Le Entregó El Control Del Salar de Atacama a Ponce Lerou," (CIPER Chile, 2015), available at <http://ciperchile.cl/2015/06/26/el-dia-en-que-el-estado-le-entrego-el-control-del-salar-de-atacama-a-ponce-lerou/> (last access on December 8, 2019).

42. Chamber of Deputies of Chile, op. cit., p. 133.

43. Soquimich holds 9.07% of exploratory mining concessions in the country, which represents 1.237.800 hectares of land. See Marcela Ramos, "Mineros de Papel: Quiénes Son Los 20 Mayores Dueños de Concesiones Mineras," *CIPER Chile* (Santiago, May 16, 2011), available at <http://ciperchile.cl/2011/05/16/mineros-de-papel-quienes-son-los-20-mayores-duenos-de-conceciones-mineras/> (last access December 8, 2019).

44. See "Sistema de concesiones en Chile: el acceso a la propiedad minera," *Minería Chilena* (Santiago, June 10, 2014) available at http://www.mch.cl/reportajes/sistema-de-concesiones-en-chile-el-acceso-la-propiedad-minera/# (last access December 8, 2019).

45. Ibid.

46. Claudia Urquieta, "El Blindaje Minero de Hidroaysén Que Lidera La Sobrina de Pinochet," (El Mostrador, 2008), available at <http://www.elmostrador.cl/noticias/pais/2008/09/24/el-blindaje-minero-de-hidroaysen-que-lidera-la-sobrina-de-pinochet/> (last access December 8, 2019).

47. Hugo Fazio, "Mapa Actual de La Extrema Riqueza En Chile" (LOM Ediciones, 1997).

48. José Miguel Sánchez and Ricardo Paredes, "Grupos Económicos Y Desarrollo: El Caso de Chile" (1994), 14–15.

49. See, for example, lawsuit for tax crimes in the trial *SQM en 8vo Juzgado de Garantía de Santiago, Rol 6474-2015*; criminal lawsuit in the trial *PENTA en 8vo Juzgado de Garantía de Santiago, Rol 6873-2014*. Moreover, at an international level it is worth mentioning that in April of 2017, the United States District Court for the Southern District of New York declared admissible the class action filed by a group of minority shareholders of SQM due to irregular payments made by SQM to Chilean politicians.

50. Hugo Fazio, "Los Mecanismos Fraudulentos de Hacer Fortuna: Mapa de La Extrema Riqueza 2015" (LOM, 2016).

51. See, for example, Gamboa and Segovia, op. cit.; and Patricio Silva, "A Poor but Honest Country: Corruption and Probity in Chile," *Journal of Developing Societies* 32 (2016), 178.

Chapter 10

Promoting and Ensuring Inequality

The Distributive Consequences of the Dictatorship

Javier Rodríguez Weber

INTRODUCTION

At the end of the 1980s, when the dictatorship was reaching its conclusion, Chile was among the most unequal countries in the world. This situation has been only partially reversed during this democratic period. Currently, the country is ranked as one of the twenty most unequal nations in the world, with the worst income distribution rates among those with a very high human development indicator.[1] In the present, Chile is not as unequal as in 1990, although its inequality rate is higher than during Eduardo Frei Montalva's presidency, during the 1960s.

This situation comes as a result of the deterioration of income distribution that occurred during the dictatorship. Effectively, after a thirty-year period, where democratic progress and the expansion of the middle-class brought about a process of reduction of inequality, the seventies represented a steep fall in distribution rates that brought about consequences that are still felt today.[2]

What role did the political context play in this process? Until recent years, most academic literature regarding economics had explained the changes in inequality rates—in Chile and other parts of the world—as a consequence of the changes in supply and demand. However, given the characteristics of Pinochet's political regime, offering an explanation based solely on the impersonal market mechanism appears particularly inadequate.

The present chapter will offer a description and an analysis of the economic and political instruments which fostered a radical distribution of income during the dictatorial period, and the factors that have hampered the reversal of this process in the following years, some of which were born from the structural reforms implemented by the Pinochet's regime. The chapter is divided into seven sections. The following one succinctly presents the main theoretical concepts that will guide the analysis. In "the state and inequality in Chile in the twentieth century," a summary of the historical evolution of income distribution is provided, with the aim to contextualize the dictatorial period. Both of the following sections represent the central part of the chapter. They provide an analysis of the economic and political mechanisms, both circumstantial and structural, which not only entailed a rapid deterioration in income distribution but also operated as an "anchor" for inequality during the democratic period.

POLITICAL ECONOMY OF INEQUALITY

It is to be expected that when an informed reader discovers that inequality increased rapidly in Germany during the thirties, they wonder about the Nazi regime's influence over this trend. The same line of reasoning could be applied to Chile under Pinochet, yet for some time most of the literature regarding inequality in the country provided explanations based exclusively on market mechanisms.[3] These works tended to focus on the influence of education as the leading explanation for the differences in workers' remuneration, and consequently for the levels of income inequality. In that way, the importance of political system changes—processes of democratization, coups d'état, quality of the democratic system, and so on—is overlooked. Moreover, the theoretical arguments and empirical evidence regarding the relevance of policies and institutions in the regulation of factor markets, particularly those which affect the differences in salary between workers with different qualifications, are overlooked as well. In the case of Chile, this literature normalizes the current situation, separating it from its origins in an exceptional political and institutional context.

This approach is a part of the orthodoxy that until recently was predominant in specialized literature. It represents what could be called a market-centered approach, which proposes that the distribution level is a result of the behavior of the forces within the market. If inequality rises, it is only due to the effect of demand and supply of factors of production. Income distribution among the working class is considered the most important factor of inequality—a conclusion that stems from the bias derived from household surveys—which is explained as the relation between the supply and demand for different types of jobs. Technical innovations, the process of globalization, and the expansion of education all contribute to generate changes in the supply and demand of skilled or unskilled labor, which affects the remuneration received by different types of workers, thus widening or reducing the income gap between them.[4] However, recent studies framed in an institutionalist approach to social sciences, and particularly to economics, have underscored how inadequate that approach has resulted to be.[5]

There exist two main channels through which political action and the institutional framework can affect income distribution. The most widely studied one is secondary distribution, which refers to redistribution through the tax system and public spending in services or transfers. Most approaches analyzing secondary distribution adopt the premise, shared by "market-centered" approaches, that there is already a primary distribution at work, which derives from the market's influence over the factors of production. This is the outcome that could be affected by political action, through the alternatives available to the state in terms of income and spending.

However, no market operates in an institutional vacuum. In other words, there is no such thing as primary distribution derived from the offer and demand of factors. Agents involved in the production process—mainly businesspeople, workers, and the state, both in its role as direct producer and as regulator—carry out a range of political actions which operate "inside" of primary distribution. This occurs because their behavior in the market is inseparable from the actions of other agents, as well as from the formal and informal institutional framework that regulates them.

By regulating both ownership rights and the terms of trade, institutions can influence the pricing of goods and services, even if this appears to be a result of offer and demand. The rules regarding property rights over assets, or labor relations, regulate a crucial part of the market's actions, and consequently contribute to determine, in conjunction with offer and demand, the income that "arises" from it.

Because the market does not exist outside of an institutional framework, the agents that exchange goods in the factor markets—such as capitalists and workers, landowners and lessors, or lenders and borrowers—are not only buyers and sellers. Relations of power and subordination exist between them and are expressed, among other things, in their capacity to influence the prices of the goods they are exchanging. By way of example, a highly unionized labor market will—probably—result in higher wages compared to another one where union involvement is repressed by the state.[6]

Power relations between the participants of the distributive conflict are mediated by institutions and policies which, by regulating the relations of the exchange, influence the pricing of factors. Thus, the state is the other actor in this conflict, and therefore its behavior—and its omissions—constitute another factor to consider when analyzing the elements of primary distribution. Moreover, the state has the capacity to create formal institutions—such as labor legislation, or property rights—as well as to directly take part in the conflict that opposes economic and social actors, be it by repressing strike or pressuring businesspeople into granting higher pay rises than they would want to. By interacting with market mechanisms, the state can reinforce, slow down, or reverse the distributive outcome of supply and demand.

THE STATE AND INEQUALITY IN CHILE IN THE TWENTIETH CENTURY

Distributive dynamics can be promoted as a driving force by the market, by institutional change, political action, or the redistributive conflict; however, they are never the result of the behavior of one of these factors exclusively. The remaining ones are always present. Nevertheless, a look at Chile's long-term history reveals an underlying trend: politics' role has become increasingly more preeminent as the analysis approaches the present day. If market behavior set the pace for inequality rates during the nineteenth century, from 1940 onward it has been the state which has acted as the driving force behind income distribution, although its actions have yielded different results.

Between 1940 and 1970, the state promoted a series of policies that fostered the growth of wages and the total payroll and led to a reduction in inequality rates (see figure 10.1). This took place against the backdrop of an important political turn to the left that affected every political and social sector, empowered wage-earners, and weakened the power of the ruling class.[7] As a result, besides isolated rejections—which became stronger during the fifties—a new common narrative was accepted, according to which the state had the right to intervene in the factor market by way of modifications to the formal and informal institutional frameworks, to encourage a fairer income distribution. The expansion of middle sectors and new labor market legislation were the main avenues used during the new political context to contribute to the reduction of inequality.

During the years of import substitution industrialization, structural changes, as well as the expansion of private and public services, generated an increased demand for white-collar workers. The employees—thus called to differentiate them from "laborers" —were middle-income workers that replaced the less productive and lower-paid job positions, mainly in farming but also in the service sector, and who rose as the determining political actor of the period. Therefore, the change in the occupational structure became a mechanism for upward social mobility that increased the middle sectors' wage share and contributed to the reduction of inequality.

This impact was underpinned by the income policy adopted during the forties, which targeted that very sector. Its cornerstone was the minimum wage, labeled as "vital employee salary." It was implemented during the thirties and

Figure 10.1 Income Distribution in Chile between 1935 and 2009. Gini index. *Source and comments*: Created by the author. The different styles of line represent the different methods used to make the estimates. The 1935–1970 period was estimated through a procedure of social tables. The information about the remaining years was obtained through employment, unemployment, and income and expenses survey, conducted by the Universidad de Chile.

was systematically raised above inflation rates throughout the next decade. Thus, not only did it encourage pay rises for the lower-income sector among employees, but also laborers. From the fifties onward, concern regarding inflation led to the abandonment of this policy of adjustment of employees' real income; however, the minimum wage continued to expand to include industrial and rural workers.

The consequences of the agrarian reform implemented during the seventies on income distribution are harder to ascertain, as there was no time to observe its effects. In any case, it contributed to a context of permanent mobilization in the rural sector which, in conjunction with other factors—such as the already mentioned minimum wage—constituted a fundamental part of a "spirit of the times" which encouraged the reduction of inequality, not only regarding income but also wealth.[8]

The approach changed drastically following the institutional breakdown of 1973. After the coup, the state remained as a key player in terms of determining how inequality evolved, although now it did so in a regressive sense. The dictatorship reversed those policies which during previous decades had tended to reduce inequality. This behavior is evidenced in how the union movements and political parties that had promoted them were repressed. The rules that regulated the labor market were modified again, first through terror and then thanks to a labor reform that aimed to crystallize in the legal sphere the system of labor relations and power asymmetries imposed by means of repression. Furthermore, the dictatorial context worsened the regressive effects of the 1975 and 1982 economic crises. The wage-earners, particularly the most vulnerable ones, were the ones to bear the burden of the majority of the damage caused by the crises, while the political system denied them the chance of pressing for policies with more balanced distributive effects. Last, the dictatorship promoted an asset redistribution which entailed public goods being transferred to private owners, resulting in a higher concentration of wealth. This process was carried out in a context of lack of transparency which made the enrichment of public officers belonging to the regime possible.

Thus, both short-term economic policies, such as those attempting to combat macroeconomic imbalances, and structural reforms, devised to implement a new economic and social model capable of enduring in a democratic context, presented a regressive bias as their common denominator. It proves hard to imagine that such transformations would have been possible in a democratic context, not only due to the regulations that this very system would have enforced but also because the political trend of the decades before 1973 reveals that the Chilean people's preferences were contrary to what was to be imposed from that year onward. The rest of this chapter will provide a more detailed analysis of the aforementioned distributive mechanisms that turned Chile into a highly and consistently unequal country.

MACROECONOMIC IMBALANCES AND REGRESSIVE REDISTRIBUTION IN A REPRESSIVE CONTEXT

The line of economic policy followed by the dictatorship was already present in *El Ladrillo* (The Brick). This document was written before the coup by a group of economists who would come to be known as the *Chicago Boys*, and was delivered to the military shortly after they seized the government. El Ladrillo offered a highly critical diagnosis of the development model implemented in the previous decades, by questioning the role of the state in directing production and income redistribution. This document stated that this represented the origin of an increasingly large cluster of inefficiencies and imbalances which fed, and were fed by, the distributive conflict and by rent-seeking. The Boys proposed a deep change in the objectives and instruments of the economic policy. The market needed to return to its central role in resource allocation and price setting, and the state was to assume a secondary role in this dynamic. Thanks to the coup, and following a period if internal discussion regarding the country's economic orientation, the authors of El Ladrillo were able to carry out their proposals.[9]

However, it must be acknowledged that the existing situation, when the *Chicago Boys* took over the economic leadership, was extremely complicated. During 1972 and 1973, the Gross Domestic Product per capita had dropped 2.9 percent and 7.2 percent, respectively. That final year, the total deficit had reached the incredible number of 30.5 percent of the GDP and prices had soared to 606 percent.[10] Therefore, it is understandable that their main worry was to control the short-term situation. To achieve that, they adopted measures that combined radical cuts to public spending with liberalization of prices and a contractionary monetary policy.

Nevertheless, inflation continued to grow at a three-figure rate until 1976. As a result, the main consequence of the monetary policy and public spending cuts was not price stability, but a deep economic depression: In 1975 the GDP plummeted 14 percent. Unemployment skyrocketed, while prices continued to grow at highly elevated rates, which severely affected the real salary. Thus, it is not surprising that after the 1975 crisis the Gini coefficient revealed a change in the levels of inequality that would become permanent (see table 10.1 and figure 10.1). Furthermore, over all those years of crises and drops in salary, not a single strike was declared, which would have been hard to imagine in a democratic context. In other words, repression made it politically viable to have the working class bear the load of the crisis.

Table 10.1 Real Wages, Unemployment, and Inequality (1974–1978)

Variation of Real Wage	*Variation of Industry Real Wage*		*Variation of Public Real Wage*				
Total	*Employee*	*Laborer*	*Employee*	*Laborer*	*Unemployment*	*Inflation*	*Gini*
−21%	−18%	−9%	−14%	8%	9%	369%	0.453
−5%	−17%	−14%	−16%	−7%	16%	343%	0.476
5%	8%	12%	0%	−5%	19%	198%	0.530
9%	12%	16%	17%	18%	18%	84%	0.529
6%	8%	8%	2%	−1%	17%	37%	0.526

Sources: Created by the author based on E. Jadresic, "Salarios en el largo plazo: Chile 1960–1989," *Colección de Estudios CIEPLAN* 29, No. 1, (1990) 9–34; Meller, op. cit.

Toward the end of the 1970s, the situation seemed to be improving. Inflation was slowing down, and the GDP per capita was higher than in 1974 levels. Even the real salary was higher in 1979 than in 1973. The foreign exchange backlog,[11] in combination with economic and financial liberalization, enabled a boom in the consumption of imported goods. Despite the fact that this represented an important current account deficit, it was not considered dangerous as long as it was compensated with a substantial influx of capital. As a consequence of this, the foreign debt tripled in four years. However, the *Chicago Boys* trusted the market and that the influx of capital would continue. They were shaken out of their dream in November 1981, when they were forced to intervene in the Banco de Talca and the Banco Español, which were severely crippled by their growing debt. The following year brought the worst crisis that the economy had endured since 1930. The government was forced to abandon the fixed exchange rate—which had become impossible to maintain—and devaluation increased the weight of the debts in dollars by 50 percent, adding to the wave of bankruptcies and unpaid debt. The severity of the situation forced the *Chicago Boys* to implement a "preferential" exchange rate for dollar debtors. This represented a subsidy that benefitted the middle- and high-income sectors—who owed dollars—the cost of which, added to the purchase of uncollectable debt, was higher than the total deficit.

The subsidy for creditors and debtors of dollars benefitted the high and upper-middle-income sectors; therefore, its redistributive effect was regressive. Nevertheless, this was not the most impactful measure of inequality among the ones that were adopted to combat the crisis. More profound were the effects of contractionary measures on unemployment and real wages. This occurred because wage cuts were the chosen instrument to lower aggregate demand, as well as the trade deficit. As a result, the current account surplus which was needed to service the growing foreign debt was achieved.

Economic growth during the sixties entailed an expansion of employment rates which kept unemployment at bay. Between 1960 and 1972, average unemployment rates in the Gran Santiago region reached 5.3 percent. As we have already mentioned, this indicator skyrocketed during the crises, amounting to 17 percent in 1976, and 22 percent in 1982 and 1983. For those who were able to keep their jobs, the crises did not only involve a reduction of their income, but also a wider gap between theirs and their employers'. Thus, laborers' average income went from representing 20 percent of their employers' remuneration between 1972 and 1974, to less than 10 percent at the end of the dictatorship (see figure 10.2). By that time, the GDP had grown only 18 percent in relation to 1972—which equaled a 1 percent yearly rate—but poverty indicators had doubled, and included 40 percent of all households. The

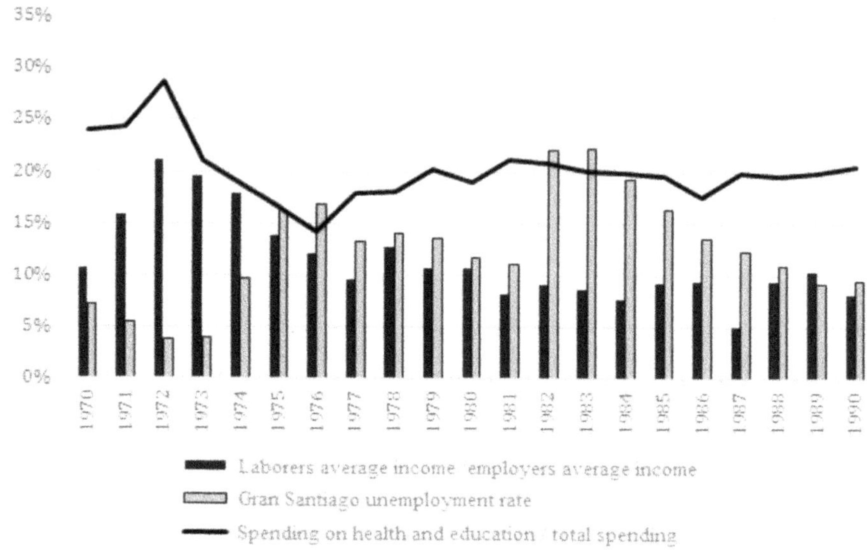

Figure 10.2 Labor Market and Social Public Spending between 1970 and 1990. *Source*: Figure made by author based on Central Bank of Chile; J. Díaz et al., *La República en cifras*. Ediciones UC, 2016.

minimum wage, which in the previous period had worked as a crucial tool to improve the poorest sectors' income and to reduce inequality, had plummeted. Its real value represented 42 percent of the one it had in 1970, the last year of the Christian Democratic government.[12] In consequence, while social spending and wages fell, unemployment soared, and inequality, which had remained stable between 1976 and 1981, returned to its upward movement (see figures 10.1 and 10.2).

Cuts to social public spending were not able to stop the upward trend that the main social indicators had been showing since the end of the nineteenth century. Thus, and despite the economic conditions that have been described, the century-long process of expansion of education and reductions in child mortality rates continued during the dictatorship. However, a tipping point was reached after the period of 1940–1970. During those decades, Chile did not only improve its indicators in the education and health sectors, but it did so at a faster pace than the United States, the United Kingdom, France, and Germany. This allowed the nation to narrow the gap with those countries in terms of human development. From 1970 onward, until the end of the century, Chile continued to close in on the leading countries, yet the rate at which it did so became slower.[13]

STRUCTURAL REFORMS AS AN ANCHOR FOR INEQUALITY

However, the measures adopted to face the crises were not the only ones that presented a regressive bias. A similar issue occurred with the economic and institutional reforms implemented by the dictatorship. Although short-term measures were the ones that brought forth the rise in inequality, the reforms implemented by the government set the foundations for inequality to remain at those levels for decades, even after the return to democracy. What happened with the labor reform and with privatizations exemplifies this.

Since its origins, the dictatorial government resorted to repression to enforce workers' discipline and their employers' authority inside their companies. The Labor Plan of 1979 was geared toward the use of the legal system to solidify the asymmetries of power between businesspeople and workers which had been imposed through terror. As a result, thanks to the Plan, the dictatorship was able to bequeath to the ensuing democratic governments a system of labor relations which in addition to loosening the hiring and firing processes, weakened unions and consolidated the business group's power.[14]

On the other hand, privatizations entailed a transfer of public property to private hands which led to high levels of concentration of wealth and served as the source of income and power for the elite. This process took place in two moments or waves. The first one occurred during the sixties and affected a large part of the companies that had been nationalized, although some, which were considered "strategic" by the military, were not included in this process. Because most buyers had obtained credits to acquire them, these companies began their activity highly indebted, which weakened them in the face of any change in the financial circumstances. When this came to pass, in 1982, a large number of them went bankrupt and was re-nationalized.[15]

The past years of the dictatorship included the second and most significant wave of privatizations. This affected not only the companies which had been nationalized as a consequence of the 1982 crisis, but also public services companies which had traditionally remained in the hands of the state, and had not been privatized thus far because of the regime's refusal. Although purchases on credit were not allowed, the process of alienation was extremely murky. Those who benefitted from it were able to acquire an enormous amount of public wealth at lower prices than what the market would have determined.

Many of them were officers of the regime, or their associates, which meant that they possessed privileged information.[16] Clearly, the government's goal was that the companies went to private hands, not that this process of privatization resulted in benefits for the state and the Chilean society.

In any case, the privatizing zeal was not limited to a change in asset ownership. It also covered several services linked to the state's secondary functions, such as health, education, or pensions. Therefore, several human needs whose satisfaction until that point had been considered the responsibility of the society as a whole were treated as merchandize. As of that moment, and with the exception of the poorest sectors, Chilean citizens lost the right to receive an education or to be treated in case of illness. Neither did they have to contribute, in the form of taxes, to the provision of those rights to the rest of their compatriots. Now, each individual had to resort to the market and received—in the best-case scenario—a service or pension according to how much they had paid. The most relevant aspect of this, from an inequality point of view, is that the commodification of these aspects of the social life opened the possibility to make a profit from them. Before the privatization process, the provision of these services required a large number of resources, but it did so by way of taxes, contributions to social security, or public spending; thus the room for profiteering from them was much smaller. Thereafter, the ISAPRES (Instituciones de Salud Previsional) or AFP (Administradora de Fondos de Pensiones) would rank among the most profitable companies in Chile and their owners and managers among the wealthiest and most powerful in the country.

Overall, these structural reforms in combination with others—such as the exporting reorientation—have paved the way for the rise of a new elite of extremely wealthy businesspeople, which are the owners and managers of conglomerates that control large sectors of the economic and social spheres. Their counterpart is a state which has been curtailed in its regulatory capacities, and barely existent and weakened unions. Thus, the enormous power of the elite who became wealthier during the dictatorship is one of the reasons—albeit not the only one—why during the democratic recovery the reforms which would have reversed, entirely or at least significantly, the sharp increase of inequality that took place during the dictatorial period were not implemented.

CONCLUSIONS

The new literature regarding the subject of inequality has returned to the study of its classic causal mechanisms: the relations of power and the conflict between social actors. Even to explain a market outcome such as the primary distribution of income—meaning before taxes and transfers—it is necessary to consider the institutional framework which regulates the interaction between the agents taking part in the exchange—the state being the most important one—and the relations of power, which are always asymmetrical, between them. The aforementioned relation gives rise to the distributive conflict between the agents, and whether explicit or latent, it is always present and can reach such intensity that it can become violent.

The high levels of inequality in Chile today have their roots in a highly repressive political context and are the result of a radical transformation of the economic system. In the new institutional framework established by the dictatorship, those who made political decisions did so in a way that entailed a regressive distribution of both the economic benefits and damages that stemmed from circumstantial situations and structural transformations.

While the short-term measures, implemented against the backdrop of an economic crisis, led to a leap forward in inequality levels which made Chile one of the countries with the worst income redistribution in the world by the end of the eighties; the structural reforms enforced by the dictatorship generated the necessary conditions for these inequality levels to remain as high during the democratic period as they were before. Although income redistribution has improved since the return to democracy, it has done so insufficiently. The development is extremely slow and the country today is still more unequal than it was during the sixties. Moreover, the reforms enabled a group of businesspeople to become extremely rich and, through the creation of conglomerates and groups, control large sectors of the economy. As the "political money" scandals have revealed in the past few years, their economic power results in an enormous political influence. In fact, the de facto and de jure power that these actors which held a privileged position during the dictatorship have maintained once it came to an end, constitutes a hardly insignificant element when it comes to explaining the democratic governments' inability to fulfill their repeated promise of fighting inequality.

NOTES

1. UNDP, *Informe sobre desarrollo humano 2016. Desarrollo humano para todas las personas* (United Nations Publications, 2016).

2. J Rodríguez Weber, *Desarrollo y Desigualdad en Chile (1850–2009) Historia de su economía política* (DIBAM-Centro de Investigaciones Diego Barros Arana, 2017); J. Rodríguez Weber, "Impulsando la desigualdad «de mercado»: el vínculo elite-Estado en Chile en el siglo XX," *Revista Perfiles Económicos* 1, No. 1 (2016), 11–41.

3. H. Beyer et al., "Trade liberalization and wage inequality," *Journal of Development Economics* 59, No. 1 (1999), 103–23; C. Sapelli, *Chile ¿más equitativo? Una mirada distinta a la distribución del ingreso, la movilidad social y la pobreza en Chile* (Ediciones UC, 2011).

4. This reasoning could be extended to other factors of production, particularly natural resources.

5. Anthony B. Atkinson, *Desigualdad: ¿qué Podemos Hacer?* (México D.F.: Fondo de Cultura Económica, 2016); Thomas Piketty, *El Capital En El Siglo XXI* (México D.F.: Fondo De Cultura Economica, 2015); Angus Deaton, *El Gran Escape:*

Salud, Riqueza y los Orígenes De La Desigualdad (México D.F.: Fondo de Cultura Económica, 2015).

6. See for more information on this subject, the chapters by Daniela Marzi Muñoz and by Ángela Vergara and Peter Winn.

7. J. Rodríguez Weber, "La erosión del poder de la élite en Chile entre 1913 y 1970. Una aproximación desde los ingresos del 1%," *Revista de Historia Economica – Journal of Iberian and Latin American Economic History* 35, No. 1 (2017), 49–80.

8. J. Rodríguez Weber, "Economía política de la distribución del ingreso rural en Chile durante la decadencia de la Hacienda, 1935–1971," *Revista Uruguaya de Historia Económica* 3, No. 3 (2013), 33–62.

9. M. Gárate Chateau, *La revolución capitalista de Chile* (Ediciones Universidad Alberto Hurtado, 2012).

10. J. Díaz et al., *La República en cifras* (Ediciones UC, 2016); P Meller, *Un Siglo de economía política chilena (1890–1990)* (Editorial Andrés Bello, 1996).

11. As monetary contraction could not contain inflation, the government adopted a fixed exchange rate policy in hopes of aligning the local inflation with the international one. However, the process of convergence of inflation rates was too slow and resulted in a deterioration of the real exchange rate. Patricio Meller, op. cit., p. 202.

12. F. Coloma and P. Rojas, "Evolución del mercado laboral en Chile: Reformas y resultados," in *La transformación económica en Chile*, edited by Larraín et al. (Centro de Estudios Públicos, 2000).

13. J. Rodríguez Weber, *Desarrollo y Desigualdad en Chile (1850–2009) Historia de su economía política* (DIBAM-Centro de Investigaciones Diego Barros Arana, 2017).

14. This was seen as a virtue by Fernando Coloma y Patricio Rojas, "Evolución del mercado laboral en Chile: reformas y resultados."

15. This resulted in what was called the "strange" sector of the economy, or what some ironically labeled "the Chicago's way to socialism." Nationalizations were so widespread that the concentration of means of production in the hands of the state was similar or even higher than what it had been during Allende's government. See B. Stallings, "Las reformas estructurales y el desempeño socioeconómico," in *Reformas, crecimiento y políticas sociales en Chile desde 1973*, edited by R. Ffrench-davis y B. Stallings (CEPAL—LOM ediciones, 2001).

16. Gárate Chateau, op. cit.; Meller, op. cit.; M. O. Mönckeberg, *El saqueo de los grupos económicos al Estado chileno* (Ediciones B, 2001).

Chapter 11

Experts and Intellectual Complicity in the Chilean Dictatorship

Marcos González Hernando and Tomás Undurraga

INTRODUCTION[1]

This book investigates the role civil society actors played during the Pinochet dictatorship as "economic accomplices." That is, it focuses on those who, from outside the armed forces, promoted, sustained, or benefited from the 1973 coup and the subsequent dictatorial regime.[2] A premise of the book, a fact that scholars in the field have long highlighted, is that the Chilean dictatorship was not exclusively military and required the constant collaboration of civilians, that is, it had a civic-military character.[3] Although state terrorism was executed by the security and armed forces, there were a number of private individuals, institutions, and companies that supported the dictatorship, providing it with goods, services, staff, and ideas.

With that in mind, this chapter focuses on a particular type of complicity, one that does not necessarily involve economic resources, which we call "intellectual complicity."[4] This type of complicity is attributable to civilians who, occupying privileged positions in what we call the "intellectual infrastructure" (e.g., universities, think tanks, the media), supported the military regime by promoting its ideas and policies. We will focus on the social sciences of the day—especially law, economics, and political science. The above renders our object of study different from other types of collaborators with the dictatorship: the "accomplices" of whom we speak did not, in general, directly participate in human rights violations, though some may have facilitated or justified them. In addition, they did not always profit as a direct result of the regime's—although many did, as we will see with the case of economists and engineers who jumped from the political and intellectual fields to the business world, benefiting from privileged information and opaque privatizations.[5] Instead, we study what "complicity" means from the standpoint of intellectuals and experts, with an emphasis on those working at institutions that produced and disseminated expert knowledge.[6]

In what follows, we clarify further what we mean by "intellectual accomplices." Subsequently, we examine the role of such accomplices in the justification of the military regime, with an eye on their actions and their effects on the "intellectual infrastructure." This chapter is an analytical exercise: it distinguishes between a defense of the dictatorship itself and a defense of the "free market" the dictatorship installed and promoted, all the while acknowledging the historical overlap of these justifications. Trying to identify every intellectual accomplice of the military regime is an ambitious enterprise; we limit ourselves to some of the most emblematic figures.

SOME PRELIMINARY DEFINITIONS

What do we understand by "intellectual" and by "complicity"? Among the many ways of defining "intellectual," we rely on the theses of Boltanski and Chiapello regarding the centrality of justification in contemporary capitalism.[7] According to them, capitalism requires constantly renewing its justifications, integrating the critiques that it receives. During the dictatorship, this pedagogical and justifying task was carried out by a variety of different media organizations, think tanks, universities, and business associations, conforming in the process what Thrift calls "cultural circuits of capitalism."[8] This endeavor was crucial for a nondemocratic government in a country whose political parties had a long history and which had seen slow but growing incorporation of the middle and lower classes into politics since the 1920s.[9]

This analysis stresses the centrality of ideas for justifying the dictatorship's reforms. Chilean capitalist modernization is generally interpreted as a "revolution from above," led by technocratically oriented civilians in positions of power within the military regime. Although this interpretation is correct, it must be complemented with an acknowledgment of the legitimizing role of experts and intellectuals from outside the state.[10] As Gárate indicates, every political transformation, especially one of a revolutionary nature such as Chile's, needs to be communicated broadly to attain approval from the public—or at the very least from political and professional elites.[11] Moreover, the intellectual authority of many of the experts involved—derived from their possession of academic degrees from international elite universities in a national context that precedes the expansion of higher education—granted them a significant share of prestige and power.

The concept of "complicity" is thornier. Avoiding the strictly legal discussion, "accomplice" has two relevant meanings: (i) a participant or associate in a crime or fault attributable to two or more persons and (ii) a person who, without being the author of a crime or a *fault*, cooperates in its execution with previous or simultaneous acts. Therefore, in relation to "intellectual complicity," accomplices do not necessarily need to collaborate directly with the regime's crimes against humanity (or even provide explicit legitimation) to be considered as such. Tacit consent is sometimes enough. On the other hand, the mere agreement with monetarism and the structural reforms that were imposed between 1973 and 1990—even acknowledging the inevitability of their social costs—is not in itself sufficient to call someone "complicit" if he or she condemns the nondemocratic imposition of such political-economic model and other crimes of the dictatorship.[12] So, on our preliminary definition, actors who agreed with the regime's reforms do not count as accomplices if and only if they explicitly rejected their dictatorial imposition. By contrast, those who supported the same policies while either explicitly embracing their dictatorial imposition or remaining silent on this question count, in the first instance, as accomplices.

However, accusations of complicity in dictatorial regimes are often problematic in practice. In the sociological literature, France under Nazi occupation is perhaps the historical context in which the problem of intellectual "responsibility" under authoritarian governments has been thought most carefully.[13] In that case, the National Socialist government in Paris and Pétain's in the south pursued and committed atrocities against the opposition, occupying printing presses, universities, radio stations, and the arts vetoing any critical demonstration against the regime and projecting the careers of hitherto marginal fascist intellectuals, all while pretending that the public discussion was proceeding normally. There are significant parallels between this case and Chile's, especially in relation to the impossibility of operating through public channels without the regime's acquiescence. But there are also important differences: the hierarchical model of capitalism devised during the Chilean dictatorship continues to be vigorously defended, which contrasts with the ideology of Vichy's France. The latter dictatorship was defeated militarily, while the Chilean *junta* negotiated its departure. However, an interesting similarity can be found in the forms of complicity by "omission" undertaken by participants in the public debate at a time when the intellectual infrastructure was under occupation and subject to censorship.

Extending the concept of complicity this far, however, runs the risk of diluting it, including too many actors and ignoring how complex it is to intervene critically in authoritarian contexts. To clarify, it is worth asking what are the specific behaviors by which someone could be considered an intellectual accomplice in the Chilean case. Thinking of "intellectual complicity" as the justification and promotion of ideas and actions of the military regime, we will evaluate it in relation to five possible responsibilities or *faults*, defined in relation to their opposition to democratic principles and the respect for human rights: (i) the democratic break of 1973; (ii) human rights violations; (iii) the imposition of a hierarchical political-economic model that undermined workers' rights without the counterweight of democratic procedures; (iv) the use of privileged information and access to public resources for private enrichment; and (v) the institutional promotion of an intellectual position, carried out as state policy, whose aim or result was to censor and marginalize other views.

The justification of each of the aforementioned behaviors is in theory independent of the others since it is possible that one fault is condemned while others are supported. However, in the Chilean experience, these faults are often difficult to separate in practice. In general, participation in one of them involved at least an attitude of leniency toward one or more of the others. Analyzing the various behaviors mentioned above will allow us to identify what type of actors participated more actively in the justification of each of these faults, locating historically the parameters with which policy decisions in the dictatorship were justified. This in turn will help us examine how those decades-old complicities are discussed in Chile today.

In line with Eyal, we analyze expertise as "a network linking together agents, devices, concepts, and institutional and spatial arrangements."[14] The complicity of civilians who intellectually supported the dictatorship, therefore, includes networks, practices, and spaces of knowledge production that were not necessarily centrally organized or coordinated. But from one platform or another, people and institutions empowered with expertise endorsed the ideas of the military regime, thus becoming their intellectual accomplices.

Likewise, it should not be assumed that those involved as accomplices always remained in the same position. The civic-military dictatorship was not homogeneous: it had several moments and multiple internal disputes—between civilians and the military, between more traditional economists and neoliberals, between lawyers and economists, between those who wanted to impose gradual reforms and those who preferred a more abrupt approach, as well as between those who took differing positions on the 1982–1983 crisis.[15] The same can be said about the dictatorship's privatization wave: rather than being the result of a coherent and premeditated program, it was marked by improvisations and experiments, with advances and resistances.[16]

PROMOTION OF THE COUP, JUSTIFICATION OF THE DICTATORSHIP, AND IMPOSITION OF STRUCTURAL REFORMS

Those who least problematically can be called intellectual accomplices are those who, before the coup d'état, called for the breakdown of the democratic order (the first fault) to reconstruct the moral and material basis of a "fractured nation"—for example, the owners of large economic groups (Luksic,

Matte, Edwards) and their political allies. Once the regime was installed, several civilians encouraged a new legal order and type of society, participating in the design and development of reforms to restore and expand the power of economic elites. Informed to a greater or lesser extent of the extent of state terrorism, many of them justified political repression in a context in which the opposition was prosecuted without trial. The diagnosis that civilians and military coup leaders had was that the pathologies of Chilean society could not be cured within the current democratic system. The reforms were imposed as a shock treatment,[17] where physical violence prepared the ground to avoid resistance. Pinochet himself mentions in speeches that the military junta had an "eminently creative," "libertarian," and "progressive" mission.[18]

A significant contribution to Pinochet's dictatorship was made by lawyers who advised the military in the formulation of Law Decrees. Jaime Guzmán is perhaps the most influential figure in drafting laws and advising Pinochet directly. His complicity is not only with the democratic break (the first *fault*) and the dictatorial imposition of radical reforms (the third), but also with the justification of human rights violations (the second), arguing that Chile was in a "civil war" "against terrorism and international communism."[19] Miguel Schweitzer, Hugo Rosende, and Juan de Dios Carmona were also legal advisors to the regime's Political Advisory Committee (ASEP), in its early years.[20] But it was especially through the drafting of the 1980 Constitution—approved through a fraudulent plebiscite—that the proponents of dictatorship laid the foundations of the country's political and economic model.[21] The process of designing that constitution was not rushed. Only nine days after the coup, General Gustavo Leigh brought together four Constitutional Law professors to rethink the 1925 Constitution and lay the foundations for a new institutional framework—the "Ortúzar Commission," which met regularly over four years. Jaime Guzmán, Sergio Diez, Jorge Ovalle, and Enrique Ortúzar were the first members of that commission, who were later joined by Enrique Evans, Alejandro Silva, Gustavo Lorca, and Alicia Romo.

A particular responsibility could also be attributed (especially concerning the fifth *fault*, censorship) to the authorities of the most influential universities in the country, the "designated chancellors" and their advisors. Many of them had a military background—though there were also quite a few lawyers and other civilians. These intellectual accomplices intervened in universities, closed academic departments, and persecuted opposition students, teachers, and officials. In the Law Faculty of the Universidad de Chile, for example, Dean Hugo Rosende was an advisor to the Ministry of the Interior and argued in front of the Supreme Court for the expulsion of Jaime Castillo Velasco and Eugenio Velasco, his colleague as Chair of Civil Law. Ambrosio Rodríguez played a similar role in the School of Journalism at the same university, where professors were expelled for "teaching Marxism."[22]

Inside and outside universities, a group of monetarist economists from the Pontificia Universidad Católica (PUC)—the *Chicago Boys*[23]—took key positions in Pinochet's government. They wrote the political and economic program called "the Brick," that guided the regime's reforms, which were implemented without democratic opposition (third *fault*). The antecedents of this program can be traced to Alessandri's campaign in 1970, which was prepared by PUC economists and members of business associations (e.g., SOFOFA (Sociedad de Fomento Fabril)). The alliance between corporatism and monetarism would give the *Chicago Boys* access to key positions in the regime. In the absence of an economic program and given the failure to stabilize the economy in the immediate years after the coup, the Chicago Boys entered the frontline of government in April 1975. Christian Democrat Jorge Cauas ("super-minister" of economic coordination), the navy officer Roberto Kelly (leading the Office of National Planning, ODEPLAN (Oficina de Planificación Nacional)), Sergio de Castro (Ministry of Economy), Álvaro Bardón and Pablo Barahona (Central Bank), Juan Carlos Méndez (Ministry of Finance), and Miguel Kast (later part of ODEPLAN) would lead the implementation of these reforms. The network of economists linked to the dictatorship is long, and not all were dogmatically monetarists, though the most orthodox line eventually prevailed.

Another group of accomplices (associated with the fourth *fault,* either as justifiers or beneficiaries), mainly economists and engineers, orchestrated privatizations, benefiting from privileged information and contacts to acquire state-owned companies, thus facilitating the emergence of new fortunes. The Pinochet regime implemented two large privatization waves. In the first wave (1975–1978), more than 200 state-owned companies were sold to private companies; many of them were reprivatized after have been expropriated during Allende's Unidad Popular. During the second wave (1985–1988), the banks that were nationalized after the 1982 sovereign debt crisis, their associated companies—the "strange area"[24]—and twenty-seven public companies historically owned by the state were privatized. These included CTC and Entel (telecommunications), Endesa (energy), CAP (Compañía de Acero del Pacífico) (steel), LAN-Chile (Línea Aérea Nacional) (air transport), CHILECTRA (Compañía Chilena de Electricidad) (electricity distribution), IANSA (Industria Azucarera Nacional Sociedad Anónima) (sugar production), and SOQUIMICH (nonmetallic mining). The companies that remained under the exclusive ownership of the state were only CODELCO (Corporación Nacional del Cobre de Chile) (copper), ENAP (Empresa Nacional del Petróleo) (oil), and Banco Estado.

To assess the responsibility of civilians in these privatizations, what María OliviaMönckeberg[25] calls the "looting of the state by economic groups," she distinguishes between those who were "decisive" and those who "facilitated" the process. Although the historical case to be made against each actor mentioned below is complex and the evidence in favor of the charge varies case by case, it is nonetheless commonly acknowledged that among those who played a "decisive" role in nontransparent and noncompetitive privatizations are as follows: Pablo Baraona (minister of economy, 1976–1978, and 1988–1989, then rector of Universidad Finis Terrae); Hernán Büchi (minister of finance, 1985–1989, then businessman and chairman of the Council of Universidad del Desarrollo); Carlos Cáceres (minister of finance, 1983–1984, and of the interior 1988–1990, then president of Chiletabacos and the think tank Libertad y Desarrollo); Sergio de Castro (minister of finance, 1976–1982, real estate investor and member of the Universidad Finis Terrae's Council); Jorge Cauas (minister of finance, 1974–1976, then director of banks and insurers); Juan Hurtado (director in public companies, as well as in the financial, mining, insurance, and real estate sector); Bruno Philippi (secretary of energy, 1974–1980, entrepreneur in the energy sector and member of the Universidad Andrés Bello Council); José Piñera (minister of labor and pensions, 1979–1980, and mining, 1981–1982, then international consultant on private pension system);[26] Julio Ponce Lerou (head of CORFO, then president of SOQUIMICH); Alvaro Saieh (dean of the Faculty of Economics and pro-rector at the Universidad de Chile, director of financial, retail, media and co-owner of Universidad Andrés Bello); Ernesto Silva (head of ENAP 1982–1983, then director of energy and insurance companies and rector of the Universidad del Desarrollo); José Yuraszeck (deputy director of ODEPLAN, architect of privatizations, real estate investor, director of energy, wine, and sports companies and linked to Libertad y Desarrollo).

Among the civilians who "facilitated" privatizations through their role in the state and benefited from their access to the companies involved, Mönckeberg highlights: Guillermo Arthur (minister of labor 1982–1983, then president of the Association of Private Pension Funds, AFPs); Álvaro Bardón (president of the Central Bank 1977–1981, financial consultant, and member of the Council of Universidad Finis Terrae); Jaime Bauzá (head of ENDESA, then director of the National Cement Industry); Marcos Büchi (head of CHILECTRA (Compañía Chilena de Electricidad), CHILGENER, and of insurance companies); Martín Costabal (minister of finance, 1989–1990, then head of AFPs and director of IANSA); Sergio de la Cuadra (minister of finance, 1982–1984, then director of SOQUIMICH); Carlos Alberto Délano (advisor, Ministry of Health, then director of Isapres—private health insurance—AFPs and Banco Penta); Álvaro Donoso (director of ODEPLAN, later Provida and Corpbanca); Hernán Felipe Errázuriz (minister of mining, 1982, and foreign relations, 1988–1990, then director of CHILECTRA); Juan Antonio Guzmán (minister of education 1987–1989, then manager of CHILGENER and rector of Universidad Andrés Bello); Teresa Infante (minister of labor 1989–1990, then director of AFPs); Luis Larraín (minister of ODEPLAN 1989–1990;

then director of AFPs and Libertad y Desarrollo); Joaquín Lavín (dean of economics at the Universidad de Concepción, president of Petrox, columnist for *El Mercurio*; then mayor and director of the Universidad del Desarrollo); Sergio Melnick (dean of economics of the Universidad de Chile, minister of ODEPLAN; then director of Banco Edwards); Juan Carlos Méndez (director of the State Budget, then in charge of IANSA and Forestal Terranova); Jovino Novoa (deputy secretary-general of government, 1979–1983, editor of *El Mercurio*, director of AFP Provida, then senator and president of the UDI party); Miguel Ángel Poduje (minister of housing, 1984–1989, then director of Provida, Copesa and Universidad Andrés Bello); Jorge Selume (dean of economics at the Universidad de Chile and director of Budget during the regime, then manager of Corpbanca and director of Universidad Andrés Bello); Máximo Silva (minister of labor, 1982–1983, then director of Banmédica, Clínica Santa María, and Banco de Chile).

As shown by this list, the links between civil collaborators, the state, private companies, and the intellectual infrastructure (universities, think tanks, and the media) are sweeping and comprehensive. The "complicity" of these actors not only pertained economic resources but also had an intellectual dimension, both in the explicit justification of the regime's policies and in the formation of institutions dedicated to perpetuating them. In that vein, one of the main organizations linked to the business sector is the *Centro de Estudios Públicos* (CEP), founded in 1980. Originally sponsored by the Matte Group, this was the main center from which the business class promoted its interests. CEP's original mission was "to be a training ground for managers and leaders, and a hotbed for ideas and information on public affairs."[27] Through conferences and seminars on the morality of the "free man," property rights, and the problems of statism, CEP became the most influential think tank in the private sector. After 1990, CEP became a space where business associations and governments discussed reforms and public policies. Although its original focus was to advocate the virtues of the free market, it gradually expanded its thematic plurality and intellectual diversity, although liberal economists maintained a preponderant position.

Here, we should also mention the civilians who, through press and television, celebrated Pinochet's successes and the ideas propagated by the regime, overlooking human rights violations, political repression, and the social costs of the economic reforms. Those who expressed these attitudes are complicit with, at least, the third and fifth *faults*—the dictatorial imposition of a political-economic model in a context of censorship. The case of Agustín Edwards Eastman is emblematic: his newspapers railed against Allende's government, promoting the coup and the military regime, justified the privatization of public firms, and misinformed the public about the crimes committed by state security agents.[28] During the dictatorship, *El Mercurio* and *La Segunda* supported the *Chicago Boys*, and were central to the ideological installation of the free market as a great social articulator, a "growth engine."[29] Among the main defenders of the regime in the media were the lawyers Ambrosio Rodríguez (advisor of the Ministry of Interior), and Pablo Rodríguez Grez (former Patria y Libertad and Dean of Law of Universidad del Desarrollo), journalists Julio López Blanco (TVN), and Claudio Sánchez (Canall 13), Jorge Fontaine (CEP), Hermogenes Pérez de Arce (*El Mercurio*), Joaquín Lavín (*La Segunda, El Mercurio*) Alberto Cardemil (deputy secretary of the interior and spokesperson for the regime, 1984–1989), Sergio Diez (Chilean Ambassador to the UN), Francisco Javier Cuadra (secretary-general of government, 1984–1987, then rector of Universidad Diego Portales), Orlando Poblete (advisor to the Presidency 1979–1987, then rector of Universidad de los Andes), and the priest Raúl Hasbún (Canal 13).[30]

Finally, another notorious group of accomplices was the Juventud por la Patria ("youth for the homeland"), mainly members of the youth divisions of right-wing parties and *gremialistas* linked to Jaime Guzmán. An emblematic meeting of these youth groups took place on Chacarillas hill in July 1977, when Pinochet announced the political institutionalization of the regime and its plan to redefine democracy, setting limits on popular sovereignty. Among this group were Carlos Bombal, Luis Cordero, Patricio Cordero, Cristián Larroulet, Juan Antonio Coloma, Andrés Chadwick, Juan Antonio Guzmán, Patricio Melero, Jovino Novoa, and Pablo Longueira, many of them then formed the Independent Democratic Union party (UDI) and became parliamentarians during the democracy that followed.

IMPLICATIONS OF INTELLECTUAL COMPLICITY FOR THE INTELLECTUAL INFRASTRUCTURE

So far we have mentioned civil actors who more or less directly justified the military regime and its economic plans, actively participating or benefiting from censorship of the opposition. In this section, we examine the more lasting effects of this complicity on the "intellectual infrastructure," which we believe underwent sweeping transformations. The first reason for this was that many in the regime thought that the radicalization of these types of institutions, especially universities, contributed to the democratic breakdown of 1973. Second, because the dictatorship derived part of its legitimacy from the reputation of its "expert" civil collaborators, it was necessary to present them as rigorous, convincing, and supported by reputable institutions. In that sense, a paradox had to be maintained: to pretend that there was a public debate and public policies guided by reason and populated by persuasive figures, in a context in which their ideological or intellectual rivals were censored, or worse.

That paradox is reminiscent of the two parallels we mentioned with Vichy France. First, it was difficult to avoid being complicit if one sought political influence. The media and university departments with significant presence on the left were purged or closed, and most of the reflection of that political sector was carried out in hiding or exile. Only from 1981 onward did the opposition slowly gain renewed visibility in the press. Second, and the obverse of this dynamic, intellectual positions that had been marginal before 1973 became central. This is clear in the case of two social science disciplines that—unlike sociology, anthropology, and others that were more severely persecuted—were central hotbeds of cadres and sources of legitimacy for the regime: economics and political science.

In relation to economics, it should be noted that starting in the 1950s—with the founding of the Economic Commission for Latin America and the Caribbean (ECLAC) —Santiago became an important node of economic thought in Latin America, and even the world. From the network of experts that emerged in this period—which included international figures such as Raúl Prebisch and Fernando Henrique Cardoso—arose the Latin American developmentalism school, which argued for the promotion of national industries. Experts influenced by those ideas—such as Sergio Molina and Pedro Vuskovic under Frei Montalva and Allende—had become central in politics and academia. Indeed, in the late years before the coup, the main opposition to ECLAC's ideas came from the left. The one exception to this was the Institute of Economics at the PUC, which from 1955 onward began to develop close links to the University of Chicago and the monetarist theory taught there. After the coup, experts trained in Chicago and PUC implemented the dictatorship's neoliberal reforms, justified their social and economic costs, and colonized the economics departments of other universities, homogenizing the teaching of the discipline under the influence of Friedman and Harberger. In a "cleansing operation," they replaced professors influenced by ECLAC's thinking. Joaquín Lavín guided this offensive at the Universidad de Concepción and Álvaro Saieh at the Universidad de Chile.

In parallel to these sorts of constraints on research and teaching imposed at traditional universities, the number of private institutions of higher education, especially after the 1980 educational reform, grew rapidly. Many of the actors mentioned earlier were part of the academic boards and directories of these new universities,[31] in which the teaching of economics had a strong monetarist bent. Since these very universities led the most important expansion of the higher education provision in Chilean history, their effects on the country's contemporary intellectual infrastructure are difficult to exaggerate.

Conversely, Chilean political science, which was a young discipline with diffuse boundaries, was quickly colonized by military officers appointed to the main universities. Perhaps because of this military presence, it was less surprising when academics became directly involved in human rights violations. The 2001 case brought forth by Felipe Agüero against Emilio Meneses—who was a custodian of detainees at the National Stadium and later a professor at the Institute of Political Science of PUC—is a notable example of that.[32] Over time that military presence and the dictatorial context marred the teaching and research carried out under its rubric, privileging geopolitics and the study of processes of democratization—although limited by the ideological counterweights that were considered necessary. In the words of a scholar of the field, "more than a simple denial of democracy, we are here faced with a neoconservative modulation of it."[33] The obsession with "governability" in political science curricula at the time, and especially in the 1990s, demonstrates this trend further.

The dictatorship also saw the birth of numerous think tanks. The Chilean case is peculiar: the majority called themselves "research centers" or NGOs, and mostly came from the center-left, either based on international institutions, splitting off from universities, or dependent on the Catholic Church. Their emergence speaks to the confluence of three factors: a floating population of unmoored intellectuals and experts produced as a result of purges in universities and the media, the support of international networks, and the fact that, although political parties were outlawed, the social sciences were not since the regime sought to derive legitimacy from them. Think tanks grew on the margins of politics, shielded by a discourse that sought to appear technically rigorous and politically neutral. Since this was one of the few ways to criticize the government publicly, these organizations provided a substitute for genuine political debate, facilitating the rearticulation of center-left thinking and networks, as well as providing a platform for elite public policy debate that later included the CEP and the right.

Puryear points out that think tanks helped the intellectual renewal of the center-left, which was paramount to the continuity of free-market policies after 1990.[34] Centers such as the Facultad Latinoaméricana de Ciencias Sociales (FLACSO), the Corporación de Estudios para Latinoamérica (CIEPLAN), the Centro de Estudios del Desarrollo (CED), and Fundación Sur were crucial to forging the Concertación, the center-left party coalition that ruled Chile between 1990 and 2010. The group of experts led by the 1990 Aylwin Government, the "CIEPLAN monks," evoked in many respects their technocratic predecessors on the right.[35] Economists became central in political parties, increasing their presence in positions of power and—as a growing number of them were educated abroad—the economic approach of the Concertación became similar to mainstream economics in the United States.[36] Thus, although it would be problematic to accuse these expert cadres with complicity to the dictatorship—they, after all, in many accounts of events, precipitated its end—they also show that the colonization of the Chilean intellectual infrastructure by the accomplices of the regime had lasting effects.

THE LEGACY OF INTELLECTUAL COMPLICITY

After the return to democracy, the networks of intellectual accomplices became crystallized in institutions and "cultural circuits" that last to this day. Therefore, much of the Chilean intellectual infrastructure's development was formed or, some might say truncated, by the dictatorship. Many of the alleged accomplices we have referred to helped to establish the rules of the intellectual field that would later continue to expand after the return to democracy. That heritage may explain why many of these accomplices proudly define themselves as fashioners of the country. Furthermore, at least two of the five *faults* are still openly justified today—(i) the end by the force of the Allende government and (iii) imposition of a political-economic model with non-democratic procedures. Only the *faults* (ii) violation of human rights—and to a lesser extent (iv) private enrichment from access to networks of power and privileged information and (v) censorship of positions contrary to the regime—are today publicly and privately repudiated by most political actors. After all, unlike Vichy, in Chile, the end of the regime was much less extensive and abrupt, and its intellectual accomplices are still well represented among the ruling elites who shape public debate.

NOTES

1. We thank the editors for their comments, as well as the valuable suggestions by Carlos Huneeus, Camila Cociña, Manuel Gárate, Rodrigo Cordero, and the participants of the workshops on this book carried out in Oxford and Valparaíso in 2017. This research received support from the Chilean Conicyt PIA Anillo de Ciencias Sociales SOC 180039, FONDECYT de Iniciación No. 11180611, and Conicyt + PCI + Max Planck Institute for the study of societies + MPG190012.

2. Gárate, M. 2012. *La revolución capitalista en Chile*. Chile: Ediciones UAH; Undurraga, T. 2014. *Divergencias: Trayectorias del neoliberalismo en Argentina y Chile*. Chile: Ediciones UDP.

3. Valdés, J.G. 1995. *Pinochet's economists: The Chicago School in Chile*. UK: Cambridge University Press; Rebolledo, J. 2012. *A la Sombra de los cuervos: Los cómplices civiles de la dictadura*. Chile: Ceibo Ediciones; Huneeus, C. 2001. *El régimen de Pinochet*. Chile: Sudamericana.

4. Two concepts that are semantically close to "complicity" but which we avoid using, are "intellectual collaboration" and—with clearer legal implications—and "intellectual authorship" (see Pietro and Francisco in this book). We employ

"complicity" instead because unlike the other two, it does not presume either direct cooperation or coordination.

5. Cámara de Diputados de Chile. 2004. *Informe oficial de la comisión privatizaciones*. Chile: Cámara de Diputados.

6. Rubio Azpiazola, P. 2014. *Los civiles de Pinochet. La derecha en el régimen militar chileno*. Chile: Dibam.

7. Boltanski, L. and Chiapello, E. 2006. *The new spirit of capitalism*. UK: Verso.

8. Thrift, N. 2005. *Knowing capitalism*. UK: Sage. According to Thrift, capitalism has become an increasingly theoretical enterprise supported by its own "cultural circuits," which produce theories that justify its purposes, recasting itself as creative and fun.

9. Undurraga, T. 2013. Instrucción, indulgencia y justificación. Los circuitos culturales del capitalismo chileno. In Ossandón, J. and Tironi, E. eds *Adaptación. La empresa chilena después de Friedman*. Ediciones UDP.

10. Another crucial factor in the Chilean capitalist revolution is the role of socio-scientific knowledge and new management tools for firms and the State. See Ramos, C. 2013. Conocimiento científico-social, gubernmentalidad y gestión de Empresas en Chile. In Ossandón, J. and Tironi, E. eds *Adaptación. La empresa chilena después de Friedman*. Chile: Ediciones UDP. pp. 167–98.

11. Gárate, M. 2013. La pedagogía monetarista: Difusión y debate de las nuevas ideas económicas en la revista *Hoy*, 1975–1979. In Ossandón, J. and Tironi, E. eds *Adaptación. La empresa chilena después de Friedman*. Chile: Ediciones UDP. pp. 109–33.

12. For instance, many Chilean Christian Democrats supported the regime's economic reforms, but not its human rights violations.

13. Ingrao, Christian. 2013. *Believe and Destroy: Intellectuals in the SS War Machine*. UK: Polity; Sapiro, G. 2011. *La responsabilité de l'écrivain: Littérature, droit et morale en France (XIXe-XXIe siècle)*. France: Seuil.

14. Eyal, G. 2013. For a sociology of expertise: The social origins of the autism epidemic. *American Journal of Sociology*. 118(4), pp. 863–907.

15. Huneeus, 2001; Valdivia, V. 2003. *El golpe después del golpe. Leigh vs. Pinochet*. Chile: LOM; Vergara, P. 1984. *Auge y caída del neoliberalismo en Chile. Un estudio sobre la evolución ideológica del régimen militar*. FLACSO, Documento de Trabajo 216.

16. Farías, I. 2014. Improvising a market, making a model: social housing policy in Chile. *Economy and Society*, DOI: 10.1080/03085147.2014.881596.

17. Klein, N. 2008. *The Shock Doctrine: The Rise of Disaster Capitalism*. UK: Penguin.

18. Pinochet, A. 1977. Discurso en Cerro Chacarillas. In *Nueva institucionalidad en Chile: Discursos de S.E. el Presidente de la República General de Ejército D. Augusto Pinochet Ugarte*. Chile: s.n. pp. 12–15 (our translation).

19. Guzmán, J. 1992. *Escritos Personales*. Chile: Editorial JGE; Cristi, R. 2000. *El pensamiento político de Jaime Guzmán: Autoridad y libertad*. Chile: LOM.

20. Cavallo, A., Sepúlveda, O. and Salazar, M. 1997. *La historia oculta de la transición*. Chile: Grijalbo.

21. Fuentes, C. 2013. *El fraude: Crónica sobre el plebiscito de la Constitución de 1980*. Chile: Hueders.

22. Montecino, S. y Acuña, M. 2013. Asedio al mundo académico. *Anales de la Universidad de Chile, Edición Especial a Cuarenta Años del Golpe de Estado*, pp. 149–92.

23. Rosende, F. ed. 2008. *La Escuela de Chicago. Una mirada histórica a 50 años del convenio Chicago/Universidad Católica*. Chile: Editorial Universidad Católica de Chile.

24. The "strange area" were 43 companies that were reprivatized after being bought by the state after the 1982 economic crash, which included two of the country's largest banks (de Chile and de Santiago), pension funds (Provida y Santa María), and companies linked to those financial actors (COPEC, Forestal Arauco, and Industria Forestal S.A.).

25. Mönckeberg, M. O. 2001. *El saqueo de los grupos económicos al Estado de Chile*. Chile: Ediciones B.

26. José Piñera was behind the labour plan which reduced workers' right and designed the individual capitalization pension system administered by private funds (AFPs).

27. Montero, 1993.

28. Herrero, V. 2014. *Agustín Edwards Eastman: Una biografía desclasificada del dueño de El Mercurio*. Chile: Debate.

29. Lavín, J. 1987. *Chile: Revolución Silenciosa*. Chile: Zigzag.

30. See Guzmán in this book.

31. Mönckeberg, M.O. 2005. *La privatización de las universidades*. Chile: La Copa Rota.

32. Verdugo, P. 2004. *De la tortura no se habla: Agüero versus Meneses*. Chile: Catalonia.

33. Ravecca, P. 2014. La política de la ciencia política en Chile y Uruguay. *Séptimo Congreso Latinoamericano de Ciencia Política, Bogotá, Septiembre 2014*. Accessed on August 25, 2015 https://www.academia.edu/7832767/La_pol%C3%ADtica_de_la_ciencia_pol%C3%ADtica._Ciencia_poder_contexto_versión_completa_y_oficial_incluye_el_cap%C3%ADtulo_teórico_ (our translation).

34. Puryear, J. 1994. *Thinking Politics: Intellectuals and Democracy in Chile*. USA: John Hopkins University Press.

35. Silva, P. 2012. Tecnócratas y política en Chile: de los Chicago Boys and los monjes de Cieplan. In Ariztía, T. ed. *Produciendo lo social: Usos de las ciencias sociales en el Chile reciente*. Chile: Ediciones UDP. pp. 73–100.

36. Ossandón, J. 2011. Economistas en la elite: entre tecnopolítica y tecnociencia. In Joignant, A. y Güell, P. eds *Notables, tecnócratas y mandarines: elementos de sociología de las elites en Chile (1990–2010)*. Chile: Ediciones UDP.

Section 3

A GAME OF SUPPORT, CORRUPTION AND MATERIAL BENEFITS

Chapter 12

The Support of the Chambers of Commerce to the Dictatorship

Rodrigo Araya Gómez

INTRODUCTION

The objective of this chapter is to analyze the support of the large business organizations to the dictatorship, in order to answer the question about the factors that determined this relation, raising as a working hypothesis, the unity of purpose between the military authorities and entrepreneurs in favor of the construction of a new model of society that is based on the values of military discipline and free economic initiative. For that purpose, a general overview of a historical nature will be presented, stressing on the conjunctures that will determine changes or inflections in business policy, albeit with a clear horizon, based on the defense of the dictatorship's work.

The chambers of commerce, from the beginning of the civil–military dictatorship, had a position of clear support for the authorities of the new state, a position derived from the opposition by these organizations toward the Popular Unity government.[1] Indeed, the employers' unions opposed the structural change policy promoted by the socialist president Salvador Allende, since they considered that the transformation of the Chilean economy into a socialist model threatened personal liberties, such as economic liberties, putting at risk the existence of private companies. Thus, the business community as a whole allied itself with the opposition to confront the government, seeking first its destabilization and then its anticipated termination through a strategy of harassment and demolition, expressed in calls for lock-out, strikes, and protests of its foundations.

The commerce unions, led by the Commerce and Production Corporation (CPC), the Society for Manufacturing Development (SOFOFA), and the National Agriculture Society (SNA), developed a polarizing strategy, which placed the Popular Unity as the antagonist or enemy of democracy, calling on the military to intervene to put an end to the crisis that the country was going through. As noted by the president of the CPC, Jorge Fontaine, in a speech on September 4, 1973:

> When a free and democratic country is bravely and decisively put under debate in order to avoid the domination of Marxism-Leninism, it is evident that all union actions are fused and intertwined with political action . . . currently. The unions' concern is not to gain certain improvements . . . but rather to fight for freedom, for the right to work . . . and for the right to produce and distribute goods and services under a regime that respects the right and individuality . . . . Having established order from above (by the resignation of the president or the incorporation of the Armed Forces into the total management of the administration . . . it is possible to join wills in this great struggle for development, national unity and the future of the homeland.[2]

In short, the commerce position was successful in contributing to the fall of Popular Unity, establishing a relation between the new military and business powers, which would last during the seventeen years of the dictatorship. Therefore, through the following pages, we will analyze the community of interests that was forged between the business community and the dictatorship, a relationship that marked the political orientation of the unions and allowed them to develop a position of power that they continue to hold today.

FROM "NATIONAL RECONSTRUCTION" AT THE TIME OF *LADRILLAZO* (THE "BRICK")

The chambers of commerce gave their unanimous recognition to the new rulers, putting themselves at their disposal and collaborating in the so-called "National Reconstruction Process." The business leaders shared the diagnosis of the military, of a country destroyed in their coexistence and the economy, which required urgent measures to overcome the state of crisis. Thus, on October 2, 1973, the Chilean Chamber of Construction (CChC) stated the following: "We hope that the Military Junta will remain in the government for as long as necessary to banish (evil) that found fertile ground . . . paid with a democracy distorted by demagogy."[3] Jorge Fontaine, in the account of his management as president of the CPC, along with thanking the intervention of the Armed Forces for defending the country from "external and internal aggression" critically forced upon the economic policies of the democratic period that "during many years, the Chilean businessman has lived in the bureaucratic tangle, has permanently been the victim of politicking and a suffocating statism, saying that 'the new economic measures would force entrepreneurs to adapt to' a bold process of expansion of the economy, like the one that now begins, where you have to compete efficiently, work harder, dispense with influences that are beyond national interests, modernize companies, effectively integrate workers into the common task."[4]

Therefore, the criticism of the overthrown socialist government was combined with a general questioning about the developmental economic model for having suffocated the private initiative and, along with it, a general criticism of the democratic system was also raised for having ultimately produced the conditions for the questioning of property rights, one of the limits for the business sectors of political action in a rule of law.[5]

The marked anti-Marxism of the trade organizations along with the communication policy of the dictatorship served to feedback the rejection of the overthrown Popular Unity and justifies the repression that affected their supporters. This environment gave place for the development of revenge measures taken by businessmen, who in some cases meant the participation in various degrees in crimes against employees or workers who had supported the Popular Unity,[6] or the indiscriminate dismissal of workers from companies that had belonged to the Social Property Area and now returned to its former owners.[7] In that sense, the issue of human rights violations was not a problem for business leaders, convinced of the need for the new authoritarian regime and "traumatized" by the experience of the Popular Unity, which led them to support the new authorities, especially when the first measures of the economic team tended to accept the demands of the business sectors.

The new economic team, which integrated people linked to developmentalist thinking, such as Raúl Sáez, and others linked to liberal currents and business connections, such as Fernando Léniz, executed a gradual plan for liberalization of the economy, which involved among other measures the end of price controls, which resulted in the exponential increase in inflation. Despite these problems, business organizations supported measures to normalize economic activity, such as the return of the companies confiscated by the previous government to their owners and the privatization plan that involved selling a large number of state-owned companies, a measure that implied the dismantling of the Social Property Area built by the Popular Unity[8] and also resulted in the development of new economic groups or the consolidation of existing ones, due to the purchase of old nationalized companies at low prices.[9]

Within the team of economic advisors of the Military Junta, a group of economists graduated from the Catholic University and with postgraduate studies at the University of Chicago, an institution where they were impregnated with the principles of neoliberalism supported by professors such as Arnold Haberger and Milton Friedman.[10] This group, known as the "Chicago Boys" soon reached positions of power within the dictatorial government thanks to the support they received from General Pinochet and the poor results of the gradualist policy, criticized by the "Chicago Boys,"[11] who defended a policy of "shock" that radically changed the statist orientation of economic policy.

In spite of the differences within the government on the evolution degree of the changes in economic policy, a liberal vision of the economy prevailed, in which the market had a leading role as a resource allocator and the private company was a key actor as an economic agent, to the detriment of the state. Entrepreneurs identified themselves with the new economic policy approach, although it was generating certain quarrels in business sectors, which observed a lack of dialogue and participation with the economic authorities in the implementation of the measures. However, the commitment to the dictatorship remained intact, because it was accepted that making "sacrifices" was needed so that the Chilean economy could take off definitively, a progress that could only be made within the framework of a Social Market Economy, the name given by adherents of the regime to the liberal economic model that was starting to be applied.[12]

In April 1975, amid uncertain economic scenario due to the effects of the crisis resulting from the rise in the price of oil and the lack of control of inflation, the "Chicago Boys" managed to gain control of the Ministry of Finance and Economy by shifting the supporters of the gradualist line from the direction of economic policy, with the figure of economist Sergio de Castro as a key player in the turn of economic policy toward neoliberalism. Thus, the application of the Economic Recovery Plan, better known as *el ladrillazo* or "shock" policy, was imposed because it drastically reduced public spending intending to directly combat the fiscal deficit and reduce the inflation rate.[13] These measures had the immediate effect of a fall in GDP, employment, and industrial growth rates, causing a severe recession in economic activity.

Despite this adverse scenario, for most entrepreneurs, the commitment to the dictatorship meant that the top business leaders carried out a task to convince their bases on the future advantages of the new economic policy, which was putting an end to protectionist policies in favor of the national industry and favoring the indiscriminate arrival of imported products due to the reduction of customs tariffs. According to a speech by Domingo Arteaga, president of SOFOFA, a complete identification between the "Chicago Boys" speech and the national leadership of SOFOFA would arise, since the highest president of the industrialists said that "an industrial structure was forced that did not always correspond to the real needs of the country . . . seeking national well-being and self-sufficiency, we fell into mediocrity and dependence."[14] Therefore, the entire economic policy applied by the National-Developmentalist State was condemned in its entirety, granting a historical legitimacy to the dictatorship, since they were making the necessary changes to solve the structural problems of the country, omitting any reference to the authoritarian context that allowed the transformations to be carried out without opposition of the social actors, and less from the persecuted leftist parties.[15] In that sense, for business leaders, complaints about human rights violations committed by the dictatorship were irrelevant, even they were reported before international scenes such as the United Nations.

Now, as the most negative effects of *el ladrillazo* allowed positive economic indices, the government, and the official press began to speak of the Chilean "miracle," a fact that validated—according to the Chicago Boys—the correctness of the monetarist measures. By virtue of these favorable indices, business leaders reaffirmed their option for the neoliberal model and for the dictatorship as a political regime that justly guaranteed the continuity of neoliberalism.[16]

Adherence to the dictatorship will be expressed in support of business organizations to the consultation convened on January 4, 1978, whereby Pinochet sought to respond with a demonstration of force to the UN's condemnation for systematic violations of human rights. Thus, in a meeting chaired by the president of the CPC Manuel Valdés, the leaders of the main business associations discussed ways to support the Military Junta in the face of UN's condemnation, and Valdés stated: "what each citizen has to ask himself . . . is that the only alternative left to lead the country within the framework of respect, order and tranquillity towards its institutional future is the frank and determined support of our current Government."[17] In another statement, the Central Chamber of Commerce affirmed:

> Its astonishment and stupor towards the attitude of some countries that, having made the defence of Human Rights the main flag of their international policy, lend themselves to co-sponsor an unfair vote against Chile, together with communist countries that hold millions of human beings under the most cruel and brutal repression.[18]

In other words, this organization, under the prism of an anti-communist discourse, rejected the "vote against Chile," linking the dictatorship's action with a national position, discarding in the background any state policy of violation of human rights. Thus, the business community raised a political position, despite the unionist discourse, which pointed to the apoliticism of business organizations, a discourse that was in tune with the antiparty ideology of the dictatorship.

To the extent that the effects of the economic *boom* were felt, supporters of the dictatorship granted it a legitimizing aim for effectiveness, that is, of reaffirmation of Pinochet's power through the success of economic management, compared to the problems that had affected the previous governments.

Moreover, the dictatorship promoted a series of transformations in the field of work, by imposing the Labour Plan in June 1979, a set of rules that liberalized labor relations, taking historical rights away from workers and establishing a dominant position for the employer, change that favored the interests of business associations.[19] Therefore, these new labor standards won the support of business organizations because, as noted by the secretary-general of the SNA, Juan Eduardo Correa, "we are very glad that the negotiation by sectors or by productive branches has finally been ruled out, because the only serious negotiations are those between a union and the employer because they face the same realities."[20] In other words, the leader of agricultural entrepreneurs praised the legal change because it clearly strengthened the position of the employer before the union action, reduced exclusively to the scope of the company.

Thus, in a favorable economic and legal context for entrepreneurs, the dictator accelerated the plans for the entry of a new constitution, based on the work carried out by the State Council and the so-called Ortúzar Commission. Thus, toward the end of July 1980, the draft Constitution was presented to public opinion, which was to be ratified or rejected via plebiscite on September 11 of the same year.

That plebiscite became an electoral milestone for the dictatorship's party bloc, including business organizations, which joined unanimously to support the YES option. Imbued with the optimism of the economic team, the directors of the business organizations joined through a series of statements to the plebiscitary campaign, because despite the unrestricted application of the neoliberal model generated objections in certain productive sectors, those supported Pinochet's continuity, as can be seen in the CPC statement: "Support for the government's effort to build the institutional future of the country . . . and continue advancing in economic, social development and integration of the Chileans."[21] For its part, SOFOFA stated that the new Constitution offered an «authentic democracy.[22]

Other organizations, such as the SNA and the Association of Metallurgical Industries, announced their support for the Pinochet himself and the plebiscite, although another organization, such as the CChC, defended the economic progress of recent years, also stating that in the case of a hypothetical triumph of option NO, the economic situation would be in deep chaos because the problems of shortage, the paralysis of investments, total anarchy would return in a few days;[23] resorted to the strategy of fear, of fear of the return of Popular Unity, a discourse based on a strong anti-communism, which had characterized the dictatorship's ideology and acted as a factor of historical legitimacy, as Carlos Huneeus said.[24]

The business community assumed a clear political position in defense of the dictatorship, linking it to the continuity of the neoliberal model, a fact that should be guaranteed with the approval of the new constitution, a fundamental rule that would protect property rights and economic freedom, values that they should inform the political system of protected and authoritarian democracy, a concept that sought to justify the authoritarian project. In this sense, Guillermo Campero stated that:

> For those union leaderships there seem to be three decisive factors [of support]: the defense of the property that is enshrined in the Constitution, the security guaranteed by the regime, also nominated by some as freedom, and the presence of the Armed Forces (or General Pinochet in other cases) that play a role, almost immanent, of endorsement or "spirit of government" that protects the principles beyond all struggle.[25]

Campero then argues that the business community shared the political ideology of the dictatorship, since this was the only one that guaranteed the absolute protection of the property rights and based on it its continuity as a social class, which would have been endangered during the Popular Unity government. This fear would have influenced the business policy to some extent in terms of denying human rights violations or actively participating in repressive acts, more serious situations that were not subject to debate or public questioning at that time.[26]

The 1980 Constitution was approved with 67 percent of the votes, under conditions that violated the minimum guarantees of pluralism and political freedoms, a situation that was not questioned by business organizations, interested in the protection of property rights that, in their opinion, could only be secured by General Pinochet and his supporters. The triumph of the YES according to its supporters would open an auspicious scenario of economic growth, to which the business leaders and economic groups that had consolidated in previous years, such as those led by Javier Vial and Manuel Cruzat and Fernando Larraín, joined. However, in a short time, the economic scenario changed abruptly, due to the outbreak of a serious international crisis in the early 1980s, which called into question the benefits of the neoliberal economic model, forcing business associations to adapt to the crisis scenario.

BUSINESS COMMUNITY AND THE ECONOMIC CRISIS OF THE EARLY 1980S

The national boards of business organizations, imbued with the optimism of the regime regarding the strength of the Chilean economic "miracle" did not glimpse the arrival of the crisis from abroad, despite a series of warning signs, as was the case with the bankruptcy of the CRAV, in May

1981, an emblematic company of the Ross group, one of which had grown thanks to financial speculation favored by the free flow of foreign capital. Subsequently, the economic indices began to show the loss of dynamism of the economy and the growing external indebtedness; these factors, together with a rise in interest rates and the continuity of high unemployment rates—over 15 percent—set up an adverse scenario, which was reflected in the multiplicity of bankruptcy applications in the industry and debt problems of agricultural producers.[27]

Despite these problems, the CPC, SOFOFA, and CChC relied on government statements that pointed to a complex economic situation of a transitory nature, supporting the permanence of Finance Minister Sergio de Castro, considered the architect of the neoliberal model and top defender of the automatic price adjustment policy. Thus, the president of SOFOFA, Bruno Casanova, said that industrialists adapted to the new productive conditions based on the confidence they felt in the continuity of economic policies.[28]

However, the crisis continued uncontrollably, while the "Chicago Boys" relied on automatic adjustment to deal with economic problems. Amid these problems, the unions linked to small and medium enterprises resumed their criticisms of the unrestricted application of the neoliberal model, making some expressions of protest that were quickly repressed by the dictatorship, as happened to the leader of the southern wheat producers, Carlos Podlech, expelled from the country in December 1982 after trying to form a multi-union with the participation of unions recognized as opposed to the government. However, the claims against the "Chicago Boys" began to take effect, when industrial sectors linked to SOFOFA demanded a radical change in economic policy that protected national producers, pressures that caused the fall of Minister De Castro in April of 1982.

In that context, the opposition to the dictatorship, led by trade unions, showed signs of growing activity in the face of the severity of the crisis, so that the Copper Workers Confederation convened a national protest day on May 11, 1983, which had an unexpected success, putting the block in power in check, because after ten years it showed clear cracks and the team of the "Chicago Boys" was replaced by more pragmatic economists who did not reject a major role of the state as an economic agent, especially to help the productive sectors most affected by the crisis. The opposition, in turn, managed to organize and raise through the protests a serious challenge to the stability of the regime, while the assumptions of the successful Chilean model were questioned by a civil society that demanded the return of democracy and an urgent improvement in their living conditions.[29]

In this context, it is possible to distinguish the positions assumed by the unions linked to small and medium enterprises and those linked to large businesses such as the CPC, SOFOFA, and SNA. In the first group, some sectors participated in the protest actions of the opposition as was the case of transporters and small merchants, organizations participating in the Assembly of Civility created in March 1986, to coordinate a unitary effort of the social opposition to end the dictatorship. In the second group, according to Campero[30] and Rolando Álvarez,[31] there will be an important change in business leadership by seeking a way to adapt to the future democratic regime, which allows them to retain their power as a political actor, guarantee of defense of the neoliberal model, one of the main works of the military regime, according to them.

Business Community and the Struggle for the Projection of Neoliberalism

The leaders of the CPC, SOFOFA, and SNA faced the challenge of the reactivation of the political-social opposition, with an unrestricted defense of Pinochet and his work, that is, the neoliberal economic model. Thus, business leaders underestimated the scope of the protests, questioning their effectiveness as a productive strike, as occurred during the strike call on July 2 and 3, 1986, when CPC president Jorge Fontaine said that "the percentage of absenteeism in the industrial sector has been low. Even yesterday it was lower than Wednesday . . . we are quite close to normal, despite the abnormality of a city in which the means of transport are stoned or burned."[32] Therefore, according to Fontaine, the protests did not attract the majority support of the population, so that street agitation responded to the action of minority groups.

However, in other cases, the magnitude of the opposition action generated concern in the business community, as expressed by the president of SOFOFA, Ernesto Ayala, when analyzing the effects of the protest on August 11 and 12, 1983, who expressed "his concern for the days of street violence that are destroying the capital, livelihoods, and life of small businessmen"[33] in a way that the revival policies acquired an urgent nature to avoid the multiplication of protests. In another statement, the Central Chamber of Commerce criticized the calls for protests because they would affect the right to work: "the environment caused by chaos and terror that produce this kind of demonstrations, restricts this desire for work, since employers are forced to close their businesses early and consumers refrain from buying."[34] That is, the fear of the leaders pointed to the normal development of their activities, omitting any reference to the authoritarian political context that justified them, a fact that led business organizations to defend hard-handed policies, such as the existence of permanent "constitutional states of exception," as can be seen from the opinion of the president of CChC, Germán Molina, who, referring to the establishment of the state of siege on November 6, 1984, indicated: "the

President of the Republic had no alternative against the terrorist escalation recorded in recent days in the country."[35]

Now, along with the rejection of the opposition's action, the business community was preparing a strategy to defend their interests in the short and medium term. In the first case, compromising their loyalty to the dictator, a relationship that was expressed in the appointments as ministers of representatives linked to employers' organizations such as Modesto Collados, leader of the construction sector, appointed as Minister of Economy in 1984, and Jorge Prado, leader of SNA, designated as Minister of Agriculture. Therefore, the business community acquired some capacity to influence the interior of the government by strengthening its negotiating role as a better guarantee to obtain benefits and promote a reactivating policy for the economy that would avoid questioning the system as a whole.[36]

In the medium term, the business leadership designed a strategy to defend the model, in which Álvarez and Campero coincide, on a business project that will begin to be implemented from 1986. After a defensive policy, in which business organizations resisted questions about the model and managed to influence the formulation of public policies, they got prepared for the new political situation in which Pinochet would be the most likely candidate in the succession plebiscite of 1988.

The CPC elected as new president the mining entrepreneur Manuel Feliú, who represented the project strategy of entrepreneurs. Feliú was influenced by the leader of the Spanish employer's association CEOE Alfredo de Molinas, a person who visited the country in April 1986, where he held a series of conferences in which he defended the relevance of the private sector in the democratic system. Then, Feliú together with a group of leaders known as the "ideologues" designed a strategy to strengthen the role of the business community as a political actor and improve their image before society.

In this way, the group led by Feliú organized the National Business Meetings (ENADE) where they discussed topics of general interest, along with it; meetings with representatives linked to the opposition were arranged to know the point of view of the parties regarding the freedom of enterprise, property rights, and private initiative. In this regard, in a report published in El Mercurio, the president of SOFOFA, Ernesto Ayala, said that "what we are looking for is to consolidate the private enterprise beyond the policy of the ruling regime,"[37] for which they were willing to talk with economists from the opposition, although discarding that they were doing politics but defending their associations' interests.

Business organizations were considered fundamental actors of national development because they would contribute to generating wealth and therefore greater benefits to the whole society. Thus, it was sought to deliver a more positive vision of the business community by disseminating social content activities in which they were protagonists, to shake their image as actors benefited exclusively by the dictatorship.[38] In this way, the business community was placed on the stage of the "battle of ideas," a vital issue to build a new type of hegemony that would guarantee the conservation of its values within society. In this sense, the businessmen defended a neoliberal vision of society, stating that concepts such as subsidiary state and economic freedom should be the foundations of any government action, placing the emphasis on a long-term vision, in which the defense of private initiative or business pride would constitute the main orientations of business community as a political actor in a future democratic system. Along with this, they raised respect for the rules of the game, a fact that implied avoiding the questioning of the process of privatization of state-owned companies, which had acquired new vigor since 1985 with the sale of stock packages of several large companies belonging to Production Promotion Corporation (CORFO), a process that favored the large national and foreign business groups, allowing the enrichment of the former executives of these companies, in charge of their respective privatization processes such as José Yuraszeck, Julio Ponce Lerou, among other officials of the dictatorship.[39]

This emphasis was contradictory to the practice of business leaders, who joined the campaign in favor of Yes during the period before the plebiscite of October 5, 1988. A business sector participated in the Civic Committees, where the former president of the CPC, Jorge Fontaine, had a central role, while another group, led by Manuel Feliú, from the Entrepreneurs for Development platform, positioned itself in the field of the "battle of ideas" to defend the neoliberal project and the need of its continuity under the ratification of Pinochet's mandate. In this regard, an editorial in the journal *Estrategia* noted that

> Realistically, it has been seen that the way to combat poverty and achieve the integral development of society is to consolidate a reliable system capable of producing wealth . . . that system, we reiterate, is that of free enterprise. In order to establish its bases and achieve its permanence, it must be disseminated so that each member of society internalizes it, freely accepts and enjoys its benefits.[40]

Therefore, the business discourse sought to build a depoliticized vision of the neoliberal model, since the values they defended referring to economic freedom would have to be assimilated by broad layers of the population, omitting the authoritarian-repressive component at the origin of such a policy. In this sense, any reference to human rights violations was not considered to be part of an annoying past, which was better to forget and raise a battle for the future that did not call into question the legitimacy of the neoliberal model. Guillermo Campero points out that "the businessmen did not want to be identified with the dictatorial face of the government but with their modern and successful face. Moreover, they tried to present the business community and the private enterprise as the main exponents of that modern side. They therefore tried to talk about the future and not the past."[41] This "modernization" of the political-business action would be expressed in associating the neoliberal model with the social market economy, as indicated by the president of SOFOFA, Fernando Agüero, who explains the adhesion of entrepreneurs to the Yes because they are giving their support to a system of social market economy in which the preponderant role of private activity is fully recognized, the spaces are open for entrepreneurs to develop all their creativity, it is reiterated that the state must fulfill a subsidiary role in productive matters, and, perhaps, above all, a libertarian economic system is supported, without obstacles to trade or productive activities, open to the outside, and so on.[42]

In other words, business leaders sought to dissociate the repressive aspect of the dictatorship from their "modernizing" work, presenting it as separate compartments, so that in the next transitional period the democratic vocation of the business actor and its country project embodied in the social market economy would not be questioned.

Once the Yes option was defeated in the plebiscite of October 5, 1988, businessmen intensified their policy of defense of the neoliberal model, effectively installing the issues of stability and trust as axes of the action of the new democratic government, which, according to the results of the past plebiscite, would undoubtedly fall to some representative of the opposition. In that sense, Manuel Feliú sought to build bridges with the trade union movement with the objective of building a social agreement that would allow them to obtain guarantees regarding the continuity of the neoliberal model. In this regard, Feliú suggested that the business community must remain alert "to indicate in a timely manner. With firmness, clarity and persuasive efficiency the harmful or negative elements that may exist in the different political proposals."[43] Thus, the business community prepared themselves to participate in the new political stage that would begin with the triumph of Patricio Aylwin in the presidential elections of December 11, 1989, without the burden of the authoritarian past they had defended and with a social validity recognized by the actors that would control the political process in the years of the transition to democracy.[44]

CONCLUSIONS

Through the analysis of the position of business organizations toward the military dictatorship, a clear ideological commitment to the economic-social project defended by it can be observed.

Indeed, business leaders adhered to the regime from the outset, without questioning its repressive policy. This support was consolidated because economic policy responded to business requirements in favor of the free private initiative and a decrease in the role of the state in the economy and the regulation of labor relations.

This aspect leads us to the relationship between dictatorship, neoliberal model, and the business community. This link would have given ideological project content to the Pinochet regime while consolidating the economic power of large business, expressed in the formation of a new correlation of forces, which was benefited from the policies imposed by the "Chicago Boys." In this way, the support of the business associations to the dictatorship had an ideological and also material basis, which allowed them to project themselves as a fundamental political actor in the new structure of power emerged as a legacy of the dictatorship during the new democratic period after the year 1990.

NOTES

1. See Guillermo Campero, *Los gremios empresariales en el periodo 1970–1983: comportamiento sociopolítico y orientaciones ideológicas* (ILET, 1984).
2. *El Mercurio*, September 4, 1973.
3. *El Mercurio,* October 2, 1973.
4. *El Mercurio*, October 17, 1973.
5. Juan Carlos Gómez, *La frontera de la democracia. El derecho de propiedad en Chile 1925–1973* (LOM ediciones, 2004).
6. The issue of corporate involvement in crimes during the dictatorship has not been systematically studied by historiography. In the field of journalism, the work of Javier Rebolledo, *A la sombra de los cuervos. Los cómplices civiles de la dictadura* (Ceibo Ediciones, 2016).
7. An overview of the dictatorship's anti-union policy in Guillermo Campero and José Antonio Valenzuela, *El movimiento sindical en el régimen militar chileno, 1973–1981* (ILET, 1984).
8. A summary of the fundamentals of the privatization process in Rolf Lüders, "El estado empresario en Chile," in Daniel L.Wisecarver (ed.), El Modelo Económico Chileno (Instituto de Economía de la Pontificia Universidad Católica/Centro Internacional para el desarrollo económico, 1992).
9. Fernando Dahse, *El mapa de la extrema riqueza: los grupos económicos y el proceso de concentración de capitales* (Editorial Aconcagua, 1979).
10. On the origin of the "*Chicago Boys*", see Manuel Gárate, *La revolución capitalista en Chile 1973–2003* (Ediciones Universidad Alberto Hurtado, 2012).
11. According to Garate and Huneeus, the military led by Pinochet decided on the Chicago Boys plan, attracted by their discourse on efficiency and criticism of the statist development model as a brake on the modernization of the country. Gárate, *La*

revolución..., 189–93 and Huneeus, *El régimen de Pinochet* (South American, First Edition, 2000), 399–401.

12. Campero, *Los gremios empresariales*, 110.

13. Gárate, *La revolución,* 189–207.

14. *El Mercurio*, April 6, 1976.

15. On the subject of the historical legitimacy and economic efficiency of the dictatorship, see the interesting analysis by Carlos Huneeus, *El régimen de Pinochet* (Editorial Sudamericana, 2000).

16. The concept of the "Chilean miracle" can be questioned based on the analysis of social indicators for the period. Antonio Cassese stated in the final part of a report on international aid to Chile: "The fundamental reason that social progress has not accompanied economic recovery is, in the opinion of the rapporteur, in the chosen economic policy and in the basic attitude of great indifference to civil and political rights. By its very nature, the economic policy adopted by the Government tends to sacrifice the needs and aspirations of the great majority of the population, particularly the less privileged sectors" in Antonio Cassese, Estudio del impacto de la ayuda y asistencia económica extranjera en el respeto de los derechos humanos en Chile, Chapter IV (United Nations, Economic and Social Council, 1978), 6.

17. *El Mercurio*, December 27, 1977.

18. *El Mercurio*, December 17, 1977.

19. Guillermo Campero y José Antonio Valenzuela, *El movimiento sindical chileno en el capitalismo autoritario, 1973–1981* (ILET, 1981).

20. *El Mercurio*, July 5, 1979.

21. *El Mercurio*, August 14, 1980.

22. Ídem.

23. *Hoy* Magazine n° 165, September 1980.

24. Huneeus, ibid., 222.

25. Campero, ibid., 226.

26. See Rebolledo, ibid. Especially chapter on the crimes of the Litter bin.

27. Patricio Meller, *Un siglo de economía política chilena (1890–1990)* (Editorial Andrés Bello, 2007), 198–211.

28. *El Mercurio*, October 1, 1981.

29. A complete analysis of the days of protest in Gonzalo de la Maza and Mario Garcés, *La explosión de las mayorías. Protesta Nacional: 1983–1984* (ECO, 1985).

30. Guillermo Campero, "Los empresarios chilenos en el régimen militar y el post plebiscito," in Paul Drake e Iván Jaksic (ed.), *El difícil retorno a la democracia en Chile* (FLACSO, 1993).

31. Rolando Álvarez, *Gremios empresariales, política y neoliberalismo. Los casos de Chile y Perú (1986–1990)* (LOM ediciones, 2015).

32. *El Mercurio*, September 4, 1986.

33. *El Mercurio*, August 14, 1983.

34. *El Mercurio*, March 30, 1984.

35. *El Mercurio*, November 7, 1984.

36. Carlos Huneeus affirms that the opening cabinet presided over by Interior Minister Sergio Onofre Jarpa put into practice sectorial policies that benefited sectors

that had led to opposition positions, with the objective of deactivating a broad opposition social coalition such as that faced by Salvador Allende in the final period of Popular Unity. See Huneeus, ibid., 513–18.

37. *El Mercurio*, June 14, 1986.

38. The policy change of the business leaders would account for a process of renewal of the business elite and reinforcement of its sources of power, in this regard see Ricardo Nazer, "Renovación de las elites empresariales en Chile," in Ossandón José and Tironi Eugenio (eds), *Adaptación. The Chilean company after Friedman* (Ediciones Universidad Diego Portales, 2013) and Undurraga Tomas, "Transformaciones sociales y fuentes de poder del empresariado chileno (1975–2010)," *Ensayos de Economía* nº 41, July–December 2012.

39. A detailed study of the privatization process of State-owned enterprises in Maria Olivia Monckeberg, *The Looting of Economic Groups from the Chilean State* (Penguin Random House, 4th edition, 2016). See regarding the participation of transnational groups in the privatization process in Patricio Rozas and Gustavo Marín, *1988: el "mapa de la extrema riqueza" 10 años después* (Santiago: CESOC/PRIES/CONO SUR, 1989).

40. *Estrategia*, week of 13–19 June 1988, p. 3.

41. Campero, ibid., 288.

42. *Estrategia*, week of 30 May to 5 June 1988, p. 17.

43. *Estrategia*, week of 31 October to 6 November 1988, p. 26.

44. Cecilia Montero maintains that the business community has remained in a position of strength as a result of its capacity to adapt to the changes generated by the application of the neoliberal model, see Cecilia Montero, "El actor empresarial en transición," Colección de Estudios CIEPLAN nº 37, June 1993.

Chapter 13

The Media during the Dictatorship

Between Economic Benefits and Journalistic Complicity

Carla Moscoso

INTRODUCTION

The media is not only the expression of the myriad of opinions that coexist in any society, but it also has the purpose of safeguarding the people against possible abuses of power and of promoting a far-reaching and democratic public debate. From that premise, it follows that the behavior of the media in authoritarian contexts proves of major importance, if the protection of fundamental human rights, such as the right to life and freedom of expression, is understood to depend greatly on what sort of actions the media takes in the face of abuses carried out by the authorities.

Augusto Pinochet's dictatorship gave rise to a drastic process of political persecution and commodification of the media system, which resulted in a loss of pluralism and a growing market concentration, among others. In this context, the relationship between the media and the civilian–military government proves significant for two reasons: on the one hand, it shows how the cultural industries of the press, radio, and television broadcasting legitimized the military regime, allowing it to embark on its neoliberal transformation project aided by the most outrageous human rights violations. On the other hand, it places the spotlight on how the current media system relies heavily on the economic reforms and deals which were forcefully implemented by the military government, with the help of some media outlets. It is impossible to understand either the current state of the market or the degree of influence that some media outlets possess in the country without revising this part of Chile's history.

This chapter is divided into three sections. The first one deals with the role that the economic and political elites played in the configuration of media systems, and to what degree their influence has been associated with the most powerful groups in Latin America, be it during democratic governments or dictatorships. In the second section, the focus is placed on Chile, and on describing the relationship that, since their origins, the press, radio, and television broadcasting have developed with the state and private sectors regarding their financing and political affiliation. Finally, a recapitulation is provided in regard to the type of relationships that different actors in the media have established with the civilian–military government from a political, cultural, and economic perspective.

THE MEDIA AND ITS DEPENDENCY ON THE POLITICAL AND ECONOMIC ELITES

Since their origins, media systems in Latin America have displayed a trend of predominantly private ownership, and have been used by the ruling national elites to exert political and social control. Therefore, in most countries, the media scene was not the result of a fight for participation and debate, but a product of a business model for the press and the radio based on the precepts of classic liberalism.[1]

In the field of broadcasting services, this model was implemented through privately owned radio and television stations, funded by advertisements, and operated in competitive markets which featured one or more large companies controlling a significant portion of those markets.[2] In the case of written press, this model has been staunchly defended by the tycoons of the sector, who, in the name of free market and freedom of the press, have condemned any type of government intervention in terms of regulations.[3]

One of the main criticisms of this business approach to the media is linked to the inevitable instrumentalization of media outlets by those who run them. This critique highlights that private media outlets operate not only from an economic rationale but are also used for political ends.[4] Latin America is a good example of this, as both in broadcasting and the written press the trend is for the media to be closely linked to local elites, and to be thought of as political companies instead of merely as businesses.[5]

However, the supremacy of the business model has not prevented that the state plays a significant role in media systems in the region.[6] Two elements are key for understanding this seemingly paradoxical idea: first, the blurry line between government and state in political institutions; second, the advantageous relationship that the national elites have established with each government, to acquire guarantees regarding political stability and economic growth.

From a political perspective, the power of the media to shape reality, in combination with the often-antidemocratic nature of regional governments, reveals how determining the political control of the media has been for the ruling elites. From an economic viewpoint, the role played by the state in media systems can be explained mostly by the interaction between a slow development of private capital and its dependence on state intervention.[7] Therefore, if the political influence is crucial for successful businesses, the state's role in the economy is crucial for understanding why media outlets owners are so involved in politics.

To sum up, whether under authoritarian or democratic rule, the relationship between the state and the media in Latin America has been defined by the power of political and economic elites to control or influence the balance between free market and state interventionism. This is why the liberal principle of media "autonomy" has not been successfully implemented;[8] moreover, it shows to what degree media systems are determined by the behavior of national elites in the economic and political spheres.

The characteristics of this phenomenon in Chile will be addressed in the following section, to identify the historical dimension of the nation's media system, from the perspective of its level of commodification and its relationship with the state. This analysis is necessary for any attempt to identify the changes and/or continuing trends that constitute the legacy of the dictatorship in this subject.

THE WRITTEN PRESS, THE RADIO, AND THE TELEVISION IN CHILE

The daily press in Chile emerged at the beginning of the twentieth century and went through the process of becoming a mass medium during the 1950s, taking an active part in the generation of political awareness within the most educated sectors of society. The interdependence of state and media is revealed in this field of communications. Here, the market monopoly has remained for a long time in the hands of two families, who own the two largest media outlets in the country. The first one belongs to the Edwards family, who owns the corporation El Mercurio S.A.P.,[9] which controls the leading regional and national newspapers *El Mercurio, La Segunda*, and *Las Últimas Noticias*. *El Mercurio*, founded in 1900 by Agustín Edwards McClure, is currently the main business of the Edwards family, once one of the most powerful economic groups in Chile. This newspaper's relevance lies in the fact that it has been notably influential throughout the history of the country's press and its politics. A large number of Chile's political and economic conflicts have been discussed in its pages. As a result, its symbolic capital has been accurately labeled as the guardian of the bourgeoisie's historic interests, and as a forum for the discussion of the dominant economic and political sectors' agenda.[10]

The other large media group is Copesa,[11] which was founded in 1950 by the Picó Cañas family and sold toward the end of the dictatorship to a group of investors led by the businessman Álvaro Saieh, who, in conjunction with his family, has held control of the group's shares ever since. Currently, this group owns the national circulation newspapers *La Tercera, La Cuarta, La Hora*—a free newspaper—and the influential magazines *Qué Pasa*, which covers politics, and *Paula*, which focuses on the female audience.[1213] The group's founders, brothers Agustín and Germán Picó Cañas, kept a close relationship with the political and business worlds. In the case of Germán Picó Cañas, his political career led him to become Chile's Minister of Finance during Gabriel González Videla's government (1946–1952), executive vice president of the Corporación de Fomento de la Producción (CORFO), and a member of the Asociación de Industriales Metalúrgicos y Metalmecánicos (ASIMET), among other renowned positions. Its current owner, the businessman Alvaro Saieh, a well-known collaborator of the military government,[14] made his fortune (one of the largest in Chile) by way of business deals related to finances, retail, real estate, hotels, and media outlets. Despite his links with the dictatorship, Saieh has kept a broad network of contacts in the world of politics and business, which through time has allowed Copesa to gain notoriety and influence regarding the definition of the public agenda.[15]

And despite the fact that the newspaper *La Tercera*—Copesa's main exponent—has been associated since its origins to the political right and the middle classes, after the return to democracy, it progressively gained a leading role in the political debate, thus becoming the one setting the agenda for the most liberally oriented elites, against the conservatism of *El Mercurio*. In the case of the *La Cuarta* newspaper, which was created in 1984 and recognized as the second-most important one of the group, it maintained its sensationalistic, popular, and quick-witted tone after the return of democracy.

Regardless of the control gained by the aforementioned media groups, it should be noted that before the military coup of 1973 the structure of the press system displayed a pluralism of ideologies and journalistic styles. This means that most of the parties and political factions had their own popular and illustrated newspaper. However, after the dictatorship seized power, the number of media outlets that were closed, accused of opposing the regime, increased the economic concentration and the ideological and political power of the media in the hands of Mercurio S.A.P. and Copesa.[16]

In the field of radio broadcasting, Chile presented a steady growth since the 1960s, owing to technological development and resources from private advertising. Radio stations were mostly privately owned, they belonged to an individual who managed them and decided what contents the station would include. At the same time, some radio broadcasting networks began to emerge, with larger amounts of capital available to them and better technology for large-scale broadcasting. The owners of these types of radio stations were part of powerful groups linked to mining, agriculture, finance, and the industrial sector. Among these networks, some are to be highlighted, such as the Sociedad Chilena Radiodifusora (owned by Radio Minería), the Compañía Chilena de Comunicaciones, and the Sociedad Nacional de Agricultura, among others.[17] Moreover, during the 1980s, and owing to the technical progress in the fields of quality and power of the signal, the number of Frequency Modulation (FM) radios grew tremendously, as the presence of the FM radio began to rapidly spread throughout the regions and the capital. This fact led to a reordering of the radio broadcasting system, which in combination with increasing competition in the FM radio market, paved the way for the incorporation of foreign capital in the radio broadcasting sector in the coming decades.

Despite the fact that radio broadcasting in Chile is based on the principles of economic liberty and individual freedom, the state is the one who grants the usufruct of the radio waves to a specific competitor. Consequently, the role of the state in terms of regulation has not been to establish a broadcasting monopoly, but to regulate the distribution of the radio frequency spectrum. Nevertheless, because the development of radio broadcasting has been closely linked to the revenue, they make from selling advertising; the appearance of radio broadcasting networks which started taking over smaller, local radio stations is the result of a model that encourages the economic prevalence of the former over the latter. In this scheme, the presence of a political and economic elite with strong ties to the state, and who also owns the most important radios at a regional and national level, exemplifies the already-mentioned tension between the market and a state that is in the hands of the same groups that should regulate this market.

Finally, regarding television, Chile exhibits a singular trait, which is that television stations were born under the wing of universities and the state. The first broadcasts started in 1959 with the Universidad Católica de Valparaíso and Universidad Católica de Santiago's signals. In 1960, the channel of the Universidad de Chile was added to that list, and in 1969, Televisión Nacional de Chile was born. The latter provided national coverage and had the goal of fostering integration in the country from a state perspective. In general terms, the goals of promoting education and culture that were behind the creation of these public-access television channels delayed the arrival of private capital to the television market. Proof of this is the fact that the legitimacy and proper functioning of the university-state television system are rooted in a law passed toward the end of Eduardo Frei Montalva's government (1964–1970), which was amended only after the return of democracy. In contrast, the Television Law of 1989 encourages a business model for T.V. broadcasting, meaning an opening of the system's ownership to the private sector and the prevalence of advertising as a means of financing, as well as the privatization of some university signals.[18]

From what was previously mentioned, it could be understood that the university or state-owned nature of television that existed well into the 1990s contributed to weaken the influence of the national business groups over a television system that did not entirely depend on advertising for its funding. However, the elite's sway over this sector was significant, because both the universities and the state were intervened by the military and officials who were loyal to the regime. Moreover, the close relationship between television and the dictatorship was not only related to economic cooperation, but also an ideological and cultural affinity of a part of the elite to the dictatorship's rhetoric.

COMPLICITY OF THE MEDIA DURING CHILE'S DICTATORSHIP

Despite their historical, economic, political, and cultural differences, most Latin American dictatorships were aware of the central role that the media played in maintaining control of the government. This is why the process of modernization of media systems that took place during the period of dictatorial rule in the region was brought about by the state—ruled by the military—instead of national or international capitals. As was to be expected, instead of promoting and diversifying the role of civil society in the ownership and management of the media, the antidemocratic nature of these governments resulted in state policies that strengthened the growing economic autonomy in national media industries, especially in those linked to the political-economic elites and corrupt and dictatorial governments.[19]

In the case of Chile, the civilian–military dictatorship made use of state institutions to enforce its control over the existing media at the time and to establish an authoritarian communications policy. As a result, the National Direction of Social Communication (Dirección Nacional de Comunicación Social—DINACOS) was created.[20] Its goal was to broadcast propaganda supporting the government, and to provide official news to the media.[21] The official speeches broadcast on television, radio, and published on the written press regarding politics and economics were drafted and provided by this institution, which also had a direct line of communication with top government officials. Therefore, DINACOS' role was instrumental in the implementation of a political and ideological framework for media coverage, which was also reinforced by the collaboration that some media companies offered to the regime's political project.

Consequently, to understand the signs of resistance or complicity shown by the media, the relationship that it established with the dictatorship will be analyzed. The importance of this analysis lies in the fact that complicit media companies during the dictatorship were guilty not only of receiving economic benefits in exchange for defending the political duress and violence displayed by the state but also of helping to spread and enforce a national identity based on the commodification of the social and private spheres of life. The collateral effects of this collaboration have endured until the present day, and have represented a watershed moment in the country in terms of concentration of property, pluralism, and freedom of expression.

The Written Press

During the dictatorship, economic expansion was helmed by the government and benefited mostly privately owned media companies, in exchange for their political subservience and, in some cases, their explicit support for the regime. Two large media cartels—El Mercurio S.A.P. and Copesa—were the chief winners after the elimination of media groups that before the coup had represented both competitors at a market level and an opposing voice in political terms. This mutually beneficial relationship was consolidated during the dictatorship and later gave rise to the economic and cultural predominance of both conglomerates in the country.[22]

El Mercurio

Despite it being a well-known secret that *El Mercurio* used its political leverage to organize the country's right-wing groups to stop the election of Salvador Allende—with the political and economic support of the Central Intelligence Agency of the United States (CIA)—this was only publicly corroborated decades later. The complicity of Agustín Edwards and Richard Helms—CIA's director—came to light thanks to the declassification of secret files related to this period of Chile's history that was held by no other than the White House.[23] These documents provided evidence of the financial assistance that Richard Nixon's administration offered to El Mercurio S.A.P. to subsidize the purchase of paper and hiring journalists and columnists to destabilize Salvador Allende's government and to prepare the ground for a coup d'état.[24]

But this collaboration to assist the military was not exempt of economic benefits for *El Mercurio*. By the start of the 1980s, the owner of El Mercurio S.A.P.—Agustín Edwards Eastman—was the proprietor of the Banco de A. Edwards,[25] and the majority shareholder in the Compañía de Seguros La Chilena Consolidada and the AFP[26] El Libertador, besides owning shares in real estate, farming, and mining investment companies. Edwards' influence, and *El Mercurio* in particular, in the national economy, was the true reflection of the complex relationship between the government and this group's political and economic interests. The fact that the minds behind the dictatorship's economic reform, Fernando Léniz, Álvaro Bardón, and Joaquín Lavín, were part of the government at the same time as they played a leading part in the creation of the Economy and Business section of the newspaper, is a proof of this power.[27] *El Mercurio*'s influence in the discussion of the economic agenda was unparalleled.

Nevertheless, the profitability of this relationship was tested in 1983. El Mercurio S.A.P. was undergoing a deep economic crisis, due to the large investment it had made at the beginning of the decade for the acquisition of new technologies that would allow it to improve its computer systems and lower its printing costs. This modernization was possible thanks to loans granted by national and international institutions which, as a result of the economic recession of 1982,[28] experienced a three-and-a-half fold increase in their debt to equity ratio, which reached nearly US$ 100 million. And although the economic crisis resulted in the state's intervention of banks and companies in every sector, in the form of severe belt-tightening measures, the Edwards group was not affected; moreover, it was given the opportunity to renegotiate its debt to its advantage.[29]

This is how in 1986, and to recover from the difficult economic situation that El Mercurio S.A.P. was enduring; Edwards created the shell company Comercial Canelo S.A. and proceeded to buy assets from El Mercurio S.A.P. and other companies to acquire enough goods to use them as a guarantee to renegotiate the deadline of its credits. Pinochet's government assisted El Mercurio S.A.P. through a loan granted by the Banco del Estado (Bank of the State) in exchange for a percentage of the company's shares. This meant, among other things, that the bank owned 60 percent of the group's debt; that it was able to select one of its five directors of the company; and that it was granted the benefit of auctioning its debts. This, in simple terms, allowed the company to purchase the debt from smaller creditors at a lower value, and therefore to reduce its total amount. This preferential treatment regarding the managing of its debits allowed El Mercurio to cut its debt significantly by the end of the dictatorship, leaving only 30 percent of its assets in the hands of the state.

Despite the privileges granted by the military government, the Edwards economic empire in Chile came to an end after the economic crisis of the

1980s. By the end of 1989, the amount of debt that Comercial Canelo S.A., El Mercurio S.A.P., and even Agustín Edwards owed to the Banco del Estado reached US$ 200 million.[30] Economic difficulties had undermined the family's business structure, forcing an end to its involvement in other sectors of the economy and limiting its activity to the media market (El Mercurio S.A.P., La Sociedad Periodística del Norte S.A., El Mercurio de Valparaíso S.A.P., and La Sociedad Periodística Araucanía S.A.). This situation meant that El Mercurio S.A.P. became the Edwards family's last stronghold, a company that due to its symbolic value and political influence continued to exist to safeguard the right's interests in the context of a process of political democratization.

Copesa

The economic crisis affected Copesa as well—this group controlled the newspapers *La Tercera* and *La Cuarta*—and it was forced to renegotiate the debt it had incurred as a result of the crisis through its representatives Germán and Gonzalo Picó Domínguez; the former a Copesa representative and the latter an agent of Malán Inversiones S.A. —a shell company, the majority shareholder of Copesa, which had been created to buy Copesa's debt. The military government came to Copesa's rescue, as this company's directory comprised renowned regime loyalists. The debt accrued with creditors and the Banco del Estado amounted to a large sum, and after the process of debt restructuring of 1988, the Banco del Estado emerged as the owner of 70 percent of the assets of Malán S.A., which meant that it was Copesa's creditor. As a result, after the bankruptcy of Malán S.A. and Copesa was avoided, 70 percent of *La Tercera* and *La Cuarta* landed in the hands of the state.[31]

In 1989, and before the imminent return of democracy, the Picó Cañas family left the consortium and transferred Malán S.A., and therefore Copesa, to the Sociedad de Inversiones la Fuente on the one hand and to Sociedad Aska Limitada on the other, two paper companies whose investors included Álvaro Saieh, Carlos Abrumohor, Alberto Kassis, Sergio de Castro—former Minister of Finance of Pinochet—and Juan Carlos Latorre among others. The new owners bought Copesa's debt for a third of its original value, a sale which resulted in millions of dollars in losses for the state, and which had the goal of subsidizing the purchase of these companies and, especially, to leave the ownership of these media in the hands of a group who shared the regime's interests.[32] Copesa's property went through a process of fragmentation, which put it in the hands of a group of businesspeople who were not traditionally in the media market, and who were tempted to enter it mostly because of an extremely favorable scenario, generated from the links that many of them had established with the military regime.[33] Throughout the years, Álvaro Saieh remained as the majority shareholder of Copesa, despite the share transfers that occurred between associates. However, it was only after the year 2000 that his influence grew, due to the retirement of shareholders De Castro and Latorre, a situation that allowed Saieh to become the president of the conglomerate and adopt a modern and liberal stamp for its editorial line.

From an economic perspective, the irregular process that encompassed the sale of these two large media companies was evidenced in the swap of the credits that both companies had incurred with the Banco del Estado for credits with other entities, whose financial situation was more precarious and their guarantees of payment weaker. The goal of these maneuvers was to prevent the companies from remaining as debtors to the bank, considering that from that point onward it would be managed by a democratic government. Moreover, the transaction that allowed this tax fraud to be committed happened on the last business day before the new authorities took office. Álvaro Bardón, a regime's official who was the president of the Banco del Estado, authorized the credits of the shell company Comercial Canelo S.A., El Mercurio S.A.P., and even Agustín Edwards Eastman, as well as the ones of Malán S.A., the owner of *La Tercera* and *La Cuarta*, to be swapped for other ones with transfer difficulties. The result of this movement was the loss of US$ 25 million, which amounted to 8 percent of the Banco del Estado's capital and reserves.[34]

From a journalistic perspective, the complicity of El Mercurio S.A.P. and Copesa with the dictatorship was noticeable particularly in the coverage that their most relevant newspapers provided in the field of human rights. A good example of this practice is the news coverage related to the Operación Colombo, a scheme devised by the National Intelligence Direction (Dirección de Inteligencia Nacional—DINA) to convince the public that 119 members of the Movimiento de Izquierda Revolucionaria (MIR), a leftist group, which had been reported as missing, had died as a consequence of internal fighting in armed clashes in Argentina.

The newspaper chain El Mercurio S.A.P. covered this piece of news in a way that was in line with the version that the intelligence services wanted to instill in the public opinion. To achieve this goal, the media scene was prepared by publishing headlines such as this one by the evening paper *La Segunda*: "Two thousand Marxists are being trained in Argentina to carry out a guerrilla war in Chile," followed by statements such as this: "The Argentinian Security Forces have detected the MIR leaders who were supposed to be missing in Chile and who international Marxist organizations had declared to have been murdered, and found them to be training in the country, and even commanding guerrilla groups."[35] Afterward, once the Operación Colombo was finished, *La Segunda* published this headline: "Exterminated like mice, 59 Chilean *miristas* (A/N: members of MIR) have fallen in a military operation in Argentina,"[36] while *El Mercurio* published: "Sixty *miristas* have been identified," with a heading that added: "Executed by their own comrades."[37]

In a less violent tone, and with a more informative headline, *La Tercera* contributed to the creation of this narrative of a supposed armed clash between comrades by stating: "Confirmed: Writs of Amparo had been filed on behalf of the dead *miristas* in Argentina," and also adding that: "the Criminal Tribunal of the Court of Appeal of Santiago has confirmed last night that Writs of Amparo had been filed on behalf of most of the MIR extremists that were killed in the bloody internal clashes of this terrorist group that have been taking place in Argentina, Colombia, Venezuela, Panama, Mexico and France."[38] Thus, *La Tercera* assisted in the propagation of the idea that legal actions filed as a result of the *miristas'* disappearance lacked any purpose because they had died as a result of their internal violence.

The coverage of the Operación Colombo case reveals how the media influence is defined not only by what is said but also by what is omitted at the time of reporting. The way that El Mercurio S.A.P. and Copesa covered deaths and forced disappearances allowed the dictatorship to build a narrative that did not acknowledge any instance of state terrorism, and that placed armed resistance to the regime as a terrorist threat to security and the society. The aforementioned coverage shows how the facts that were presented were not compared with other sources different from the official ones, thus facilitating the process of delivering biased information to the citizens. It was precisely this lack of journalistic ethics that resulted in the undermining of the press' role in the construction of a reliable and truthful public space during the dictatorship.

Radio Broadcasting

The radio broadcasting system in Chile became more market oriented during the decade that followed the coup. This phenomenon brought about a reduction in tariffs, and an increase in the imports of radio receivers, whose number swelled to almost 3 million just between 1974 and 1985.[39] Simultaneously, the number of FM radio stations grew exponentially, most of which were privately owned, or were in the hands of individuals or groups which were considered small-sized companies or independent owners, and depended on private advertising for their funding.

A large number of radio stations in the market created difficulties for any attempt to coordinate any sort of articulated economic cooperation with the regime, and weakened the military's control over the contents of this medium. However, this did not prevent most of the country's radio stations from adopting an ideological and political stance that was supportive of the regime, be it due to obedience or self-censorship. Therefore, one of the main criticisms of the political submissiveness of this sector of the media was that the sheer size and diversity of the radio broadcasting market allowed the stations greater freedom to define their editorial line.[40]

The state-owned radio stations played a more active role in controlling the circulation of information and spreading the regime's political principles. Two such cases are *Radio Colo Colo* and *Radio Nacional*.[41] In the case of independent radio stations, their complicity was limited to omitting any topic related to the abuses carried out by the regime, and focusing simply on harmless subjects such as popular culture. A possible explanation for this phenomenon is that radio broadcasting was associated from its origins with entertainment, and prioritized enjoyment and music in their programming over news coverage.[42] Consequently, the only radio stations which managed to perform the role of counterpoint to the official narrative (Radio Balmaceda, Radio Chilena, Radio Santiago, and Radio Cooperativa, among others) produced news-related content and were close to the Catholic Church or the Partido Demócrata Cristiano (Christian Democratic Party) which was the main opposition party at the time because it was recognized as a valid interlocutor by the government, a characteristic that allowed these stations to stand in a more level playing field when it came to expressing their dissent. This means that their financing depended not on advertising but rather on the funds coming from political parties or NGO's whose goal was to assist the groups that were opposing the dictatorship.

An example of this type of radio station is *Radio Presidente Balmaceda*, owned by the Christian Democratic Party. Despite the fact that it only aired until 1977 due to the constant political pressure and forced closings which pushed it out of the air, its agenda was similar to that of the Catholic Church in the sense that it attempted to avoid polarization and to bring the cases of human rights violations to light.[43] Another example is *Radio Cooperativa*, which was also controlled by Christian democratic militants but remained in the air throughout the dictatorship. It gained a more relevant role as an opposition medium during the demonstrations of 1983 and 1984,[44] where it became a source of nonofficial information among the dictatorship's opponents. In the case of this radio station, part of the cost of maintaining its dissident editorial line was to lose most of its provincial branches, as it only managed to retain a license to operate in the cities of Santiago, Valparaíso, and Temuco. Nevertheless, it continued to offer national coverage due to its retransmission deals with other stations.[45]

Regarding regulations, during the first period of the dictatorship, radio broadcasting fell within the scope of the Decree-Law N° 4 of 1959 or the General Law of Electric Services. Subsequently, it was replaced by the

General Telecommunications Law of 1982, which established a framework that granted radio broadcasting concessions of twenty-five years to the fledgling businesspeople of the sector.[46] This modification resulted in benefits for the large groups that would eventually absorb the local stations which, in addition to breaking the media silence during the dictatorship, were struggling in terms of their income. In conclusion, the regulations that stemmed from the regime promoted the creation and consolidation of a radio broadcasting market which over the years would surpass the national boundaries, and pave the way for the arrival of foreign capitals and the creation of large conglomerates.

Television

The peculiar origins of television are certainly a key element for understanding its behavior during the dictatorship. The General Law passed in 1970, which granted the property of concessions and the management of channels to universities and the state, allowed Augusto Pinochet's government to maintain strict control over the system's institutions. The military government secured its hold over this medium by placing military and public officers in management positions in most channels and universities.

However, it was during the 1980s that the television industry took off, expanding with the help of funding coming from advertisements, and increasing its air time and signal strength. Televisión Nacional de Chile doubled the number of its stations during the decade of 1975–1985 and extended its national coverage. Furthermore, Universidad Católica de Chile's channel expanded its territorial reach to nearly 70 percent of the country. In terms of investment in advertising, the television represented the largest market, over half of the total investment in the country, and produced significant shifts in the economy due to the increase in domestic consumption.[47]

The first signs of opening to private ownership appeared toward the end of the regime. The trailblazer was Agustín Edwards Eastman, who created the cable TV company Intercom,[48] and was granted an indefinite concession of Chile's utility poles and underground utility lines, because of the favorable relationship it had built with the military government.[49] Despite the advantages that Edwards enjoyed while he monopolized this sector, in the mid-1990s he decided to sell 80 percent of the company's shares to the firm Telefónica de España, for US$ 55 million, and to keep only 20 percent of them. From that point onward, the field of television would undergo a progressive process of privatization which even reached the public-access channels. Therefore, the dictatorship's most significant legacy was to open the system to private capital, represented by both national and foreign businesspeople, while at the same time it imposed self-financing and the implementation of market practices similar to those of the private channels to state-owned television channels and to the commonly named university television.[50]

In cultural terms, television broadcasting was characterized by its compliance with the regime's interests, which included to encourage the predominance of a shallow and vapid programming to promote the benefits of the consumer society, and to capture the attention of an audience that was weary of the country's political and economic issues. The television offer was centered on high budget music and game shows, which dazzled the viewers with the idea of life as luxurious as the ones of their international guest stars.[51] The military government invested large sums in the prime time shows of Televisión Nacional de Chile, to present the image of a prosperous country, connected to the reality of the first world. The Viña del Mar Festival of 1981 was proof of this, for it included the presence of many world-renowned artists such as Miguel Bosé, Julio Iglesias, José Luis "Puma" Rodríguez, and KC and the Sunshine Band, among others.

This strategy was implemented even in the field of news reporting, considering that the main newscast of the state channel, called "60 minutos," hired Raquel Argandoña—former Miss Chile and known supporter of the regime—as anchorwoman, so that she would amaze the audience every night with her hair-styles and fashionable outfits. The scenario was similar in the Universidad de Chile's channel, where news anchors had to refer to Pinochet as *president* and to the disappeared detainees as *allegedly* disappeared. At the same time, the Universidad Católicás channel started leaning toward a pro-government bias, against the will of some religious authorities such as the Cardinal Raúl Silva Henríquez who, despite his high rank inside the church, avoided interviews due to his publicly known disagreements with Pinochet's government.[52] The chief result of this strategy was the establishment of a news broadcasting system that was blind to any challenge to the established order and the political violence that a dictatorial context entailed.

The foregoing analysis reveals that television broadcasting cooperated with the dictatorship by introducing market principles in the collective consciousness, as well as by promoting an individualistic national identity. Regarding the market, an economic approach that fostered the predominance of a business system in the television sector gained strength and resulted in the disappearance of the public nature that had been present since this medium's origin. Furthermore, an array of political and ideological principles focused on depoliticization and consumption, enforced by practices of censorship, curtailment of the public debate, and trivialization, were introduced to address a country that seemed to be living in a parallel dimension unrelated to the horrors of authoritarianism.

CONCLUSIONS

During the dictatorship, the media system saw an abrupt decline of several voices representing opposing views to the regime, as well as a deep transformation in terms of its relation to the state and its growing commodification. The double part played by the national elite, both as owners of the most important media groups and as regulating elements of a state which had lost its democratic legitimacy, was crucial.

The aforementioned meant that the cooperation between the large media groups and the political and economic elite that supported the regime resulted in a mutually beneficial relationship, which was determined by the affinity between a restrictive and repressive regulatory framework and a growing commodification of the communications system, which set entrepreneurial freedom and lack of regulation as the founding blocks of the new media system. Thus, both restrictions to the public debate and omissions regarding human rights violations were part of the cost that the national media paid in exchange for direct economic support and/or the guarantee of an increasingly unregulated market in which to compete.

In the case of the written press, this process resulted in the consolidation of a duopoly integrated by two companies which were closely linked to the political and economic elite and the political right. This entailed a rise in the levels of concentration of property, along with restriction of competition and an unchecked influence regarding ideological content. These groups' coverage in the area of human rights is proof of that, as they published headlines which assisted in the creation of a narrative that was supportive of the state violence being perpetrated by the government. As a result, their most evident legacy is related to political homogenization and to the deterioration of the news coverage regarding political events and acts of abuse that marked the country's history.

In radio broadcasting, market growth was regulated by the available funding in the sector of advertising. Despite there not being any record of direct economic benefits being granted to radio stations by the government, it is possible to affirm that the radio broadcasting networks in the hands of economic and political elites which were close to the military government were benefited with twenty-five-year-long broadcasting concessions. This fact did not only weaken market freedom, benefiting a select few, but it also resulted in the takeover of independent radio stations by larger conglomerates. From a cultural perspective, the radio broadcasting sector showed a lack of coverage of political and social conflicts, while distancing itself from news reporting (with a few exceptions) to focus on entertainment, with a programming centered on music and recreation.

As for television broadcasting, cooperation with Pinochet's government took place in a more cultural and political sense. The government's control settled at the heart of the institutions of a system that was managed by the state and the universities, and which remained in place until the return of democracy. And although economic expansion occurred as a result of incoming funds from advertising, the television channels' complicity with the dictatorship revolved mostly around their ideological affinity related to social order and the market society. Therefore, the leading contribution from the television to the dictatorship is the creation of a narrative where the purchase of goods is considered the Chilean people's life goal, and where both lack of political freedom and human rights violations are trivialized and treated simply as disregard for the status quo.

NOTES

1. A business model for the media features a defense of the autonomy of its members regarding the government, and private property, as necessary conditions for the development of a democratic system.
2. Elizabeth Fox y Silvio Waisbord (eds), *Latin Politics, Global Media* (University of Texas Press, 2002), 1.
3. Silvio Waisbord, "Media in South America: Between the Rock of the State and the Hard Place of the Market," in *De-Westernizing Media Studies*, eds. James Curran and Myung-Jin Park (Routledge, 2000), 51.
4. Daniel C Hallin y Stylianos Papathanassopoulos, "Political Clientelism and the Media: Southern Europe and Latin America in Comparative Perspective," *Media, Culture & Society* 24, (2002), 175–95, 177.
5. Fox and Waisbord, op. cit.
6. For more information regarding this argument, see Waisbord, op. cit.; Fox and Waisbord, op. cit.; Hallin y Papathanassopoulos, op. cit.; Jairo Lugo-Ocando, *The Media In Latin America* (Open University Press, 2008); Carolina Matos, *Journalism and Political Democracy in Brazil* (Lexington Books, 2008).
7. This relation acquired strength due to the work of the Alianza para el Progreso (1961–1970), which established economic cooperation ties between the United States and Latin America. This alliance legitimized State investment and planning in the communications sector, which until then had been controlled exclusively by private capital, thus reviving some of the goals of the state during the 1920s and 1930s. For a more in-depth analysis regarding this topic, see Elizabeth Fox, "Media Policies in Latin America: An Overview," in *Media and politics in Latin America: the struggle for democracy*, ed. Elizabeth Fox (Sage, 1988).
8. The principle of autonomy in the media establishes, on the one hand, the necessary independence of the media to discuss and publish content regarding political issues with no state interference, and on the other hand, it affirms that the market is the system where diversity of offers guarantees access to information and freedom of expression regarding the different social ideologies.
9. Sociedad Anónima Periodística (Journalistic Public Limited Company).

10. Eduardo Santa Cruz, *Análisis histórico del periodismo chileno* (Nuestra América Ediciones, 1988).

11. Consorcio Periodístico de Chile (Journalistic Consortium of Chile).

12. Gustavo González, "The Media in Chile: The Restoration of Democracy and the Subsequent Concentration of Media Ownership," in *The Media In Latin America*, ed. Jairo Lugo-Ocando (Open University Press, 2008); Maria Olivia Mönckeberg, *Los magnates de la Prensa: Concentración de los medios de Comunicación en Chile* (Random House Mondadori, 2009).

13. In May 2018 Copesa announced the closure of the magazines *Qué Pasa* and *Paula*. Regarding the latter, despite its whole staff being fired, the name was used in place of the supplement *Revista Mujer*, with a less journalistic approach and more focused on fashion and beauty.

14. During the dictatorship, Álvaro Saieh was part of the board of directors of state companies which were under military control. Moreover, while the University of Chile was intervened by the military, he held the position of head of the Department of Economics, followed by his appointment as vice-rector of the institution.

15. María Olivia Mönckeberg, *El saqueo de los grupos económicos al Estado chileno*(Ediciones B, 2001), 161.

16. González, op. cit.

17. Guillermo Sunkel and Esteban Geoffroy, *Concentración Económica de Los Medios de Comunicación* (LOM ediciones, 2001), 58.

18. Bernarda Labarca y Carolina Matta, *Radiografía al sistema chileno de medios* (Universidad Academia Humanismo Cristiano, 2010), 42.

19. Fox, op. cit., 1988; Elizabeth Fox, "Tres visitas al paradigma de la dependencia cultural," *Chasqui. Revista Latinoamericana de Comunicación* 44 (1993), 80–87.

20. Although it was created after the coup, its powers were established officially on the 31 of December of 1976, by the Decree N° 11, which defined the powers of the Ministry General Secretariat of Government.

21. Paulette Dougnac et al., "Mercurio: más pesado que el plomo", in *El Diario de Agustín: Cinco estudios de casos sobre El Mercurio y los Derechos Humanos, (1973–1990)*, ed. Claudia Lagos (LOM ediciones, 2009), 66.

22. Ken Dermota, *And Well Tied Down: Chile's Press under Democracy* (Praeger, 2003).

23. The secret documents held by the United States' secret service became public during the years 1999 and 2000.

24. Peter Kornbluh, *Estados Unidos y el derrocamiento de Allende: una historia desclasificada* (Ediciones B Chile, 2003).

25. The Banco de A. Edwards was recovered by Agustin Edwards Eastman during the military government after Alvador Allende's administration had nationalized most of the private banks. For more details on this process, see Mönckeberg, op. cit., 2009, cap.5.

26. Pension Fund Administration (Administradora de Fondos de Pensiones—AFP) was a system of individual capitalization established in Chile in 1980 and still

in place, where these administrators manage the workers' retirement, disability and survivors pensions.

27. See "Periodismo en tiempos de excepción," in Claudia Lagos (ed), op. cit., 66.

28. This economic crisis had its origins in the financial crisis that Latin America endured in 1980, which when combined with the Chilean peso's overvaluation (as it was pegged to the American dollar) and the existence of high interest rates, contributed to the markets' collapse and the soaring levels of unemployment.

29. Gonzáles, op. cit.

30. Mönckeberg, op. cit., 2009, 43–55.

31. Ibid., 51.

32. Ibid., 50–63.

33. Osvaldo Corrales J. and Juan Sandoval M., "Concentración Del Mercado de Los Medios, Pluralismo y Libertad de Expresión," ICEI, Universidad de Chile (2005), available at <http://www.comunicacion.uchile.cl/docs/corrales2005.pdf> (last accessed on December 19, 2019).

34. Mönckeberg, op. cit., 2001, 181.

35. *La Segunda* Newspaper, July 12, 1975.

36. *La Segunda* Newspaper, July 24, 1975.

37. Harries, "La prensa sin fe de erratas: El caso de los 119 según El Mercurio," in ed. Claudia Lagos, *El Diario de Agustín* . . . op. cit., 155–61.

38. Marco Herrera, "Operación Colombo: La prensa que se calló con Pinochet," *Chasqui. Revista Latinoamericana de Comunicación* N° 96, (2006), available at <http ://www.revistachasqui.org/index.php/chasqui/article/view/1598/1621> (last access on December 19, 2019).

39. José Joaquín Brunner, Alicia Barrios, and Carlos Catalán, *Chile: Transformaciones culturales y modernidad* (FLACSO, 1989), 128.

40. Rosalind Bresnahan, "Radio and the Democratic Movement in Chile 1973–1990: Independent and Grass Roots Voices During the Pinochet Dictatorship," *Journal of Radio Studies* 9 (2002), 161–81.

41. Karen Donoso, "El "Apagón Cultural" en Chile: políticas culturales y censura en la dictadura de Pinochet 1973–1983," *Outros Tempos 10 – Pesquisa em Foco – História* 127, (2013) available at <http://www.outrostempos.uema.br/OJS/index.php/outros_tempos_uema/article/view/285> (last access on December 19, 2019).

42. Carla Rivera, "La Verdad Está En Los Hechos: Una Tensión Entre Objetividad y Oposición. Radio Cooperativa En Dictadura," *Historia* 41 (2008), 79.

43. Ignacio González Camus, *Radio Balmaceda 1973–76: bajo el asedio de los 'Guatones' y Pinochet* (Grafikacolor, 2016).

44. The economic crisis at the beginning of the 1980s brought about mass demonstrations which took place between May 1983 and October 1984. These demonstrations occurred in the country's most important cities and were characterized by the violent clashed between the police and the demonstrators that ensued.

45. Bresnahan, . . .op. cit., 161.

46. Marcela Amaya, "La 'Ley Pinochet de Telecomunicaciones'. Disputa por el dial," *Chasqui. Revista Latinoamericana de Comunicación* 80 (2002), 46–51.

47. Brunner, Barrios y Catalán, op. cit., 123–26.

48. Intercom was legally owned by the Edwards family, as 80 percent of it belonged to Compañía de Seguros la Chilena Consolidada and the other 20 percent to El Mercurio S.A.P.

49. Mönckeberg, op. cit., 2009.

50. González, op. cit., 2.

51. Donoso, op. cit., 107.

52. Oscar Contardo and Macarena García, *La Era Ochentera* (Ediciones B, 2005), 16–17, available at <https://es.scribd.com/document/352551486/Libros-211548898-Contardo-Miguel-La-Era-Ochentera> (last access on December 19, 2019).

Chapter 14

A Cat with No Bell

The Privatization of the Chilean Pension System during Pinochet's Dictatorship

Mariana Rulli

INTRODUCTION[1]

The broadest social security programs in financial and budgetary terms are pension systems, so it follows that they have a significant impact on economic growth, income redistribution, and especially in the living conditions of the population. In political terms, pension system reforms and projects have been crucial tools to win elections, as shown by the cases of Chile in 2006,[2] Argentina after the 2008 reform and Peru in 2011. Moreover, these kinds of reforms have brought about massive demonstrations on the streets of countries such as France[3] and Greece[4] in 2010,[5] and more recently Argentina in December 2017 and Chile, where over a million people participated in the No+AFP referendum.[6] Furthermore, pension schemes make up the most dynamic sector within social policies, not only because of the number and frequency of reforms but also because of the interest and attention they attract in academic and political debates. During the period 2010–2015, over 105 governments across the world (approximately sixty from developing countries and forty-five from high-income ones) began to debate and implement pension system reforms, such as increasing contribution rates and raising the retirement age, among others.[7]

Pension systems are constitutive pillars of the welfare regime in each state. Whether they are based on universal rights and citizenship or labor rights, they reflect how societies recognize different types of paid or unpaid work, how they redistribute income and risk among different generations and gender, and what role they ascribe to public and private institutions in social protection.[8] This means that studying pension system reforms can provide an understanding of how state, market, and society relate in terms of their relative strength, and who are the real winners and losers within the system.

In 1980, Pinochet's dictatorship carried out a reform of the Chilean pension system. The Decree Law No. 3,500 of 1980 created a new capitalization pillar in the aforementioned system and ruled that pension fund administrators (Administradoras de Fondos de Pensiones—AFP), which were for-profit private companies, were the only ones allowed to control and manage the mandatory 10 percent contributions that salaried workers had to pay into their personal retirement accounts (excepting the armed forces and the police). This system allowed for a captive market, a sort of legal asset-freeze,[9] inasmuch as workers' pension savings were (and still are) held by AFPs, with no chance of them being transferred to a nonprofit administrator.

In 2008, following an extensive debate, the pension system was reformed again,[10] and although changes were introduced to improve coverage and noncontributory pensions, the capitalization pillar remained in place.

In 2015, the Presidential Advisory Commission on the Pension System, known as the *Bravo Commission*, submitted a report analyzing the pension system created by the Decree Law No. 3,500 of 1980 and reformed by Law No.20,255 in 2008. The Bravo Commission was mandated with assessing the system's performance and proposing solutions to the problems or shortcomings they might discover. Among the Commission's recommendations,[11] the categorization of noncontributory benefits for persons made redundant for political reasons as financial compensations instead of pensions, to guarantee access to social security, is to be highlighted.[12]

Recently, in 2017, a heated debate took place regarding the issue of the high pensions received by those convicted of crimes against humanity, as a result of the fact that military and police workers remained under a publicly funded pension scheme. In contrast, the pensions of those who were made redundant for political reasons were minimal. Concerning this issue, the Chilean Command of Politically Dismissed Persons (Comando de Exonerados de Chile) has released a communiqué stating:

> the paradox of torturers, rapists and murderers against humanity receiving millions in pensions while the victims have to manage with miserable ones, meaning that, in practice, there are executioners living a wealthy life while victims barely survive." They point out that "the inmates in Punta Peuco receive $1,727,000 pensions on average and public officers who took their place and "blew the whistle on them" receive $600,000 pensions, however 80% of pensions received by persons who were fired for political reasons reach on average a mere $162,000.[13]

It follows that the case study of the Chilean pension system reform of 1980, the country's economic performance, and the concentration in the AFPs market provide a view of the new economic order put in place after 1973 and the influence of economic elites that benefited from privatizations, elements which persist even after the democratic transition, and to this day. These economic elites not only control a large portion of Chilean wealth but also influence the democratic system and any options there may be of reforming the social security system, by means of financing political allies and several other lobbying mechanisms.[14]

The goal of this chapter is to analyze the social and economic impact of the pension system reform, highlighting its legacy in the present. It will focus especially on how the reform was implemented in a context of authoritarianism, with no chance of social dialogue, political participation, or union involvement for the workforce, and how it strengthened and benefitted a Chilean elite linked to international financial institutions. That is to say, how the mandatory concentration of workers' retirement funds (excepting the armed forces) in the hands of a few companies allowed for economic openness and the attraction of foreign capital associated with Chilean concentrated economic groups. Currently, salaried workers' pension funds are controlled by only six administrators, closely influenced by foreign capital.

This chapter is divided into three sections besides this introduction. The first section contains an analysis of the politics behind the Chilean pension system reform during Pinochet's dictatorship and its impact as a model for other regions worldwide. To this end, a brief description is provided of the characteristics and historical evolution of the system as well as the significance of social dialogue in this type of large-scale reforms. In the second section, the fiscal, economic, and social consequences of the privatization of the pension system are analyzed. To do so, evidence is presented of the fiscal deficit brought about by the reform, the development and market performance of pension funds administrators, and the evolution of coverage rates. The final section offers a conclusion highlighting the fact that the winning and losing sectors of the reform remain unchanged even today.

THE POLITICS BEHIND THE CHILEAN PENSION SYSTEM REFORM IN AN AUTHORITARIAN CONTEXT

Chile, along with Uruguay and Argentina, was one of the pioneering countries in the introduction of a social security system[15] framed in the German model of Bismarckian schemes. Since 1924, after the first occupation-specific social security funds, the system saw an accelerated and disorganized development. Toward the end of the seventies, Chile's pension system was one of the most developed and complex in the region. However, it also presented high costs, fragmentation, and inequality[16]: the system consisted of 35 pension schemes and 150 different regimes based on 600 different regulations.[17] During the governments of Jorge Alessandri (1958–1964), Eduardo Frei Montalva (1964–1970), and Salvador Allende (1970–1973), attempts were made to implement reforms to unify and standardize the multiple regimes that composed the social security system and fix financial issues; however, the necessary consensus to move forward with the desired transformations could not be reached.[18]

Pinochet's coup d'état gives way to a new era of neoliberal structural reforms, in which the privatization of the pension system plays a relevant role. Between 1973 and 1975, the civilian-military dictatorship introduced changes to the pension system to set up single regimes for family allowances, unemployment benefits, bereavement benefits, and noncontributory pensions. In 1979, the most significant inequalities of the public, defined benefit, pay-as-you-go (PAYG) system were countered, and the retirement age and contribution rates were raised and adjusted.

In 1980, after the Decree Law No. 3,500, the former (public) collective funding scheme was replaced by a new pension system of privately administered pension funds based on individual capitalization.[19] Financial management of the new private savings accounts was assigned to the private sector, namely the pension fund administrators, who were overseen by a government agency, the Superintendence of Pension Fund Administrators (Superintendencia de Administradoras de Fondos de Pensiones—SAFP). These mandatory private savings accounts were complemented with a pillar of minimum pension guarantees for people with at least twenty years of contributions and a third pillar of voluntary savings. Furthermore, in 1975, the noncontributory pension program was created. This system granted tax-funded transfers to older people living in poverty and with no coverage. The reform affected the civilian population because the police and the armed forces retained their separate regimes, which included superior benefits and were mostly financed by the state.

The privatization of the Chilean pension system, which at that time was considered an exceptional neoliberal experiment implemented by an authoritarian regime, became the role model for pension reform during the nineties. Under the wing of the Washington Consensus,[20] the *New Pension Orthodoxy*, and recommendations by international financial institutions such as the World Bank,[21] several Latin American countries implemented multi-pillar pension schemes, with a mandatory privately managed system of individual pension accounts, invested in different financial instruments, and transformed into annuities or programmed withdrawals at the time of retirement as the main source old-age income. By 2008, thirteen countries[22] (over half of South and

Central America's total) had implemented reforms on their pension systems. Moreover, the Chilean reform influenced countries far beyond the region's borders and was used as a model by countries in Eastern Europe,[23] Asia, and Sub-Saharan Africa.[24] Supporters of these reforms argued and promised that these would promote private savings, create and bolster capital markets[25] to foster investment and growth, streamline systems, broaden coverage and, in consequence, improve the general quality of life of the population. However, as will be shown in this chapter, several studies have proved that these were empty promises.

On the other hand, the radical transformation that the Chilean privatization entailed did not only set the stage for the rest of the world but was also carried out in an authoritarian context, which meant that there was no room for debates or involvement of any of the affected social or political sectors.[26] This is a significant matter. In fact, in 2001, the International Labour Organization (ILO) underscored the need to meet the required social participation standard for such reforms, because in the region most reforms were implemented disregarding any debate or social participation, which, in turn, caused legitimacy issues.[27]

The main actors pushing these reforms in Latin America[28] were neoliberal economists working in ministries of finance, international financial institutions (IFI), organizations of employers, and the financial sector. Alternatively, the opposing sectors were left-wing political parties, the social security bureaucracy, unions, and pensioner associations.[29] Reformists[30] argued that privatization would increase public savings and foster development in the financial sector and the capital market. The political ability of different actors to promote or discourage reforms depended on preexisting institutional arrangements and political factors such as the degree of parliamentary control held by the executive, the relationship between the government and unions, or the use of mechanisms of semi-direct democracy such as referendums, as was the case in Uruguay.[31] As for the Chilean reform, the interruption of the democratic regime and strong civil and political rights restrictions undermined the political power of parties and unions and their capacity to oppose said reform.[32]

The Chilean pension system reform took place in an economic context marked by the period named "neoliberal economic revolution" (between 1975 and 1981), in which several policies were implemented, such as severe cuts to government spending, mass layoffs, rises in regressive taxes, commercial and financial liberalization, and the privatization of several companies that had been nationalized by Allende's government. However, these measures were not successful in redistributing property and giving rise to a new and stronger middle class. On the contrary, property became increasingly concentrated in a few private hands, and a new powerful elite appeared, with a strong grip on assets, markets, and political influence.[33] The next section will analyze how the industrial development of AFPs resulted in a progressive market concentration in the hands of a few domestic and foreign financial institutions.

FISCAL, ECONOMIC, AND SOCIAL CONSEQUENCES OF THE PRIVATIZATION OF THE CHILEAN PENSION SYSTEM

The Fiscal Cost of the Transition

The privatization of Chile's pension system implied an exceedingly high economic cost for the state.[34] The reason for this is that PAYG systems consider pensioners as creditors of the state based on the contributions they paid during their period of economic activity. To serve this debt, the state borrows from currently active workers in the form of contributions. The replacement of this system with one of individual capitalization produces fiscal consequences, especially during the transition period, due to the financial restrictions and limitations arising from the state having to issue debt, and then repaying it using other sources in the government budget.[35]

To assess the extent of the fiscal effort that this transition to a new pension system entailed for Chile, it should be noted that: (i) the armed forces and the police were not included in the reform and remained in the old state-funded system; (ii) every person entering the workforce as a salaried employee was forced to join the individual capitalization system; (iii) affiliates of the old system could opt to transition to the new one, encouraged by the payment of "recognition bonds" based on their contributions to the previous system; and (iv) these pension schemes became mandatory for salaried workers and voluntary for self-employed workers.

In consideration of those facts, an estimate of the fiscal deficit produced by the privatization of the Chilean pension system during the civilian-military dictatorship has been calculated by adding up the current value of pensions at the time of the reform, the current value of benefits received by those who remained voluntarily within the old system, and the current value of the recognition bonds offered to those who switched to the new system, to compensate them for their contributions to the old one. Moreover, an estimate was made of the deficit created by the armed forces and police retirement scheme, which remained under the PAYG system, as well as that arising from state-guaranteed minimum and noncontributory pensions.[36]

This means that the reform placed the entire financial burden of state guarantees (minimum and noncontributory pensions and the armed forces and police schemes), and the repayment of the resulting social security debt, on the fiscal budget. The transition gave rise to a budget deficit of approximately 2 percent of the GDP for over twenty-five years, which represents an average of roughly 5 percent of the GDP per year between 1981 and 1998.[37] Even as of 2010, the fiscal costs of privatization still reached 4.7 percent of the GDP[38](table 14.1).

On the other hand, the indirect positive effects on the economy that were expected of the reform, such as the development and strengthening of capital markets, and the direct effect of said development on productive investment, were limited.[39]

The AFPs Industry

As previously mentioned, at the end of the seventies, the reformists' main arguments were that privatization would solve the system's fragmentation and deficit issues, increase national savings and stimulate the development of the financial sector and the capital market. Furthermore, the general idea was that a competitive market of different providers would guarantee low costs for affiliates. Nevertheless, those promises were not fulfilled.

The reform gave rise to the industry of AFPs, which as public limited companies were the only ones managing pension funds. They provided benefits and services while collecting their affiliates' mandatory contributions and transferring them to each affiliate's individual account. These resources were afterward invested in different financial instruments, and the returns on those investments financed the pension funds that were used to provide benefits based on defined contributions. In addition, administrators had to ensure their resources, separate from pension funds, and proportional to the number of affiliates. The reform established payment for retirement, disability, or survivor benefits (paid to the affiliate's surviving dependents). In exchange for these services, AFPs charge a commission for administrative costs and premiums for survivors and disability insurance. The amount charged for both commissions and premiums depended on the competition between providers in the market.[40]

Several studies have demonstrated the imperfections of the pension administrators market and its inefficiency in promoting competition. The regulations implemented to protect pension funds have hindered product differentiation between administrators, and high operation costs per contributor have become an obstacle to price reductions.[41]

The low number of companies competing for that 10 percent of salaried workers' contributions, as well as the high market share of the first three AFPs and in whose hands these administrators were, represents a central issue for the analysis of the flow and concentration of riches that the reform entailed. It is important to highlight the strong international openness present

Table 14.1 Public Pension Deficit and Its Components (1981–1999) (% of GDP)

	Transition-Related Deficit					*Others*		*Deficit*
	Direct State Contributions INP (transition)			*Transitional Deficit*		*Direct State Contributions INP Others*		*Social Security*
Years	*Civil*	*Total*	*Recognition Bonds*	*Civil*	*Total*	*Noncont.*	*Min.*	*Total*
1981–1990	2,9	5,5	0,2	3,2	5,7	0,4	0,4	6,1
1990–1999	3,1	4,3	0,7	3,8	5	0,3	0,3	5,3
1981–1999	3	4,9	0,5	3,5	5,3	0,4	0,4	5,7

Source: Uthoff (2001) op. Cit.

in pension funds, as the AFPs ownership structure in the Chilean pension market has been composed mostly of foreign companies even to this day.

Concentration in the AFP Market until the Present Day

The following analysis will show how since the system was created, the number of administrators and the competition between them has remained very low, and currently, there is evidence of greater concentration. Over ten years after the creation of the system of pension funds administrators, three moments can be identified: the establishment of the first administrators, with the participation of financial institutions; the changes in the administrators' ownership structure as a result of the 1982 financial crisis; and the creation of new administrators between the mid-1980s and -1990s (many of whom were created by workers associations' initiatives, see table 14.1). Thus, in 1990, there existed fourteen administrators (see table 14.2), they reached their highest numbers between 1993 and 1994 with twenty-one, and after 1995 a downward trend started until in 2018 there were six (see table 14.3).

In 1981, as the new system was put in place, several domestic and IFI set up AFPs: Provida, was related to the Banco de Santiago; Santa María to the Banco de Chile; Invierta to the Banco de Concepción; San Cristóbal to the BHC; Alameda to the Banco Hipotecario Internacional Financiero (BHIF); and El Libertador to the Banco Edwards.

Table 14.2 AFPs Based on Wealth, Ownership, and Percentage of Affiliates (By December 1990)

AFP	*Wealth (Thousands of US$)*	*Ownership (a)*	*Controlling Shareholder (%)*	*Affiliates (%)*
Provida	37,761	3/4	40	29
Santa María	21,708	3/4	51.2	20.1
Habitat	22,570	2	52.5	17.1
Unión	5,031	3	100	9.1
Summa	9,600	1	25.9	8
Invierta	3,435	1	52	3.9
Concordia	1,150	1	22.7	3.4
Planvital	1,345	1	50	2.6
El Libertador	3,553	1	99.5	2.2
Cuprum	5,867	4	9.6	1.8
Magister	2,597	2	96	1.7
Protección	1,714	2/3	40.4	1
Futuro	598	2	97.5	0.2
Bannuestra	000	4	3.5	0

(a): 1 Few local shareholders; 2 Unions or trade associations; 3 Foreign capitals; 4 Several local shareholders. *Source*: Elaborated by the author based on Acuña e Iglesias (2000) Op.

Table 14.3 AFPs According to Controlling Shareholders, Percentage of Affiliates, and Monthly Fees (January 2018)

AFP	*Controlling Shareholder (1)*	*Affiliates (%) (Jan 18) (2)*	*Monthly Fee (%) (Jan 18) (2)*
Provida	MetLife, Inc.	29.2	1.45
Habitat	Prudential-CChC	19	1.27
Capital	Sura Asset Management	15.9	1.44
Modelo	Navarro Haeussler	15.1	0.77
Planvital	Assicurrazioni Generali SPA	15	0.41
Cuprum	Principal Chile Ltda.	5.8	1.48

Source: Elaborated by the author based on (2) Superintendencia de Pensiones (2018) (1) Fundación Sol based on each AFPs institutional memory in 2016.

In 1982, as a consequence of the collapse of the Chilean financial system,[42] the ownership structure of the AFPs experienced its most relevant change, as several financial institutions were forced to liquidate their assets. Bankers Trust bought shares in Provida, and Aetna and a large number of small shareholders bought shares in Santa María. The Compañía de Aceros del Pacífico bought shares of El Libertador as well. In 1985, Alameda and San Cristóbal merged to create union, with major participation by American International Group. Additionally, between 1985 and 1990, three new AFPs were created by workers of the financial sector: Protección (1986); Futuro and Bannuestra (1990). 41 percent of Protección was bought in 1990 by insurance group Assurances Generales de France.[43]

By the end of the 1990s, the system consisted of fourteen administrators. Table 14.2 shows that almost 60 percent of affiliates were enrolled with administrators owned by foreign capital and domestic shareholders (Provida, Santa María, and Unión). Barely over 18 percent belonged to those owned by unions or worker associations (Habitat and Magíster) and around 20 percent to administrators whose ownership structure was in the hands of a few local shareholders (Summa, Invierta, Concordia, Plan Vital and El Libertador).

By January 2018, the system was concentrated in the hands of only six administrators, who provided services for the 10,461,241 affiliates and 5,460,876 contributors, of which over 97 percent were salaried workers.[44] By March 2017, three U.S. companies (Met Life through Provida, Prudential through Habitat, and Principal Financial Group through Cuprum) controlled 73 percent of the total pension funds' assets, which is equal to 54 percent of Chile's GDP.[45]

Currently, Provida is the most popular administrator choice among Chileans, and over 90 percent of its assets belong to the North American company MetLife Inc. Between the years 2000 and 2013, Provida was owned by the Spanish group Banco Bilbao Vizcaya Argentaria (BBVA) which had started its operations in Chile in 1999 after buying the administrator and the

BHIF bank. In 2015, the Superintendence of Pensions (Superintendencia de Pensiones—SP) allowed the MetLife group to create the AFP Acquisitino Co. SA to merge with Provida, a move that generated a revenue of over 182 billion pesos due to access to tax benefits.[46]

The second AFP in terms of percentage of affiliates was also created at the same time as the system and belongs to Inversiones La Construcción (ILC)[47] and Prudential Chile (the Chilean branch of United States' Prudential).[48] The Chilean Construction Chamber (CChC) owns 67 percent of ILC's shares. It is worth noting that after the coup, in October 1973, the CChC expressed its support for the new government by stating that "*we hope that the Military Junta remains in power for as long as it takes to uproot (the evils) that were sown in the fertile ground . . . of a democracy undermined by demagogy.*"[49]

Capital, the third AFP, belongs since 2011 to the Colombian group SURA, which owns 99.65 percent of its shares and has the Corporación Internacional Financiera, a member of the World Bank Group, as one of its minority shareholders. Previously, Capital was owned by the Dutch group ING (Internationale Nederlanden Group) under the name Santa María.

In 2010, to encourage reductions in administrative costs, the Superintendent of Pensions created a bidding process under which all new contributors over the following two years would be enrolled in the AFP that offered the lowest fees in the market.[50] The winner of the bidding was the AFP Modelo, owned by the association of Inversiones Atlántico Ltda. (55.5 percent), Inversiones Atlántico-A Ltda. (17.4 percent), and Inversiones Atlántico-B Ltda. (13.4 percent), whose main shareholders are members of the influential Navarro Haussler family.[51]

In the case of Plan Vital, an 86 percent of its shares are owned by Asesoría de Inversiones Los Olmos SA, which is controlled by Sociedad de Islas Vírgenes Británicas Atacama Investment Ltd, which, in turn, is owned by Assicurrazioni Generali SPA, one of the largest insurance groups in the world. In 2014 and 2016, PlanVital won the bidding that Modelo had previously obtained and was awarded the new contributors. Last, another AFP created at the time of the system's establishment, Cuprum, is currently controlled by Principal Financial Group, also one of the largest insurance and pension companies in the world, with operations in eighteen countries. Between 1988 and 2012, Cuprum was controlled by Empresas Penta SA,[52] owned by Carlos Eugenio Lavín and Carlos Alberto Délano, two businessmen who were linked to the "*Penta Case.*"

On the other hand, several civilians can be found within the boards of AFPs who supported and contributed to the privatization process and were afterward awarded positions in those companies, such as Máximo Silva (Minister of Labour 1982–1983 and afterward Director of Banmédica, Clinica Santa María and Banco de Chile); Luis Larraín (Minister of ODEPLAN and later AFP director); Alvaro Donoso (Director of ODEPLAN and afterward Provida); and Carlos Alberto Délano (Advisor to the Ministry of Health and owner of the Grupo Penta), among others.[53]

High Commissions for Affiliates, High Profitability for AFPs

As has been previously stated, AFPs charge commissions for "administrative costs" on each affiliate's pensionable earnings, as well as a percentage fee for the payment of pensions (Programmed Withdrawal and Temporary Income) and fees for voluntary savings accounts. The rates of commissions have been high since the beginning of the system: In 1982, they represented 3.57 percent of pensionable income, in 1983 4.87 percent, and have been going down ever since. In 2001, twenty years after the reform, commissions amounted to 2.31 percent of pensionable income.[54] Moreover, those who had contributed to the system for at least fifteen years were estimated to have paid commissions over 4 percent of their pension fund.[55]

As a result of several measures aiming to lower commissions (such as bids and allocation of new affiliates), by April 2017, the average monthly commission had dropped to 1.36 percent[56] (see table 14.4) and by January 2018 it reached 1.16 percent[57] (to see the level of commissions according to each AFP in 2018 go to table 14.3).

The percentage of the AFPs revenue that the commissions paid by contributors represent is substantial: by December 2016, it amounted to 89.4 percent of total revenue, according to the financial statement of the pension system published by the Superintendence of Pensions.[58]

On the other hand, to analyze and assess the number of profits accrued by AFPs a possibility is to observe the return on equities that indicates the company's earnings related to its assets. Figure 14.1 shows the AFPs return

Table 14.4 Commissions Charged by the AFP System (April 2017)

Commissions Charged by the AFP System			
AFP	*Monthly Commission (04/2017) (1)*	*Programmed Withdrawal and Temporary Income commission (2)*	*VA Commission (2)*
Capital	1.44	1.25	0.51
Cuprum	1.48	1.25	0.7
Habitat	1.27	0.95	0.55
Modelo	0.77	1.2	0.5
PlanVital	0.41	1.25	0.47
Provida	1.54	1.25	0.92
Promedio	1.36	–	–

Source: Gálvez (2016) op. cit. (1) Based on Superintendencia de Pensiones (Ficha estadística Nro. 54) (2) Each AFP's web page.

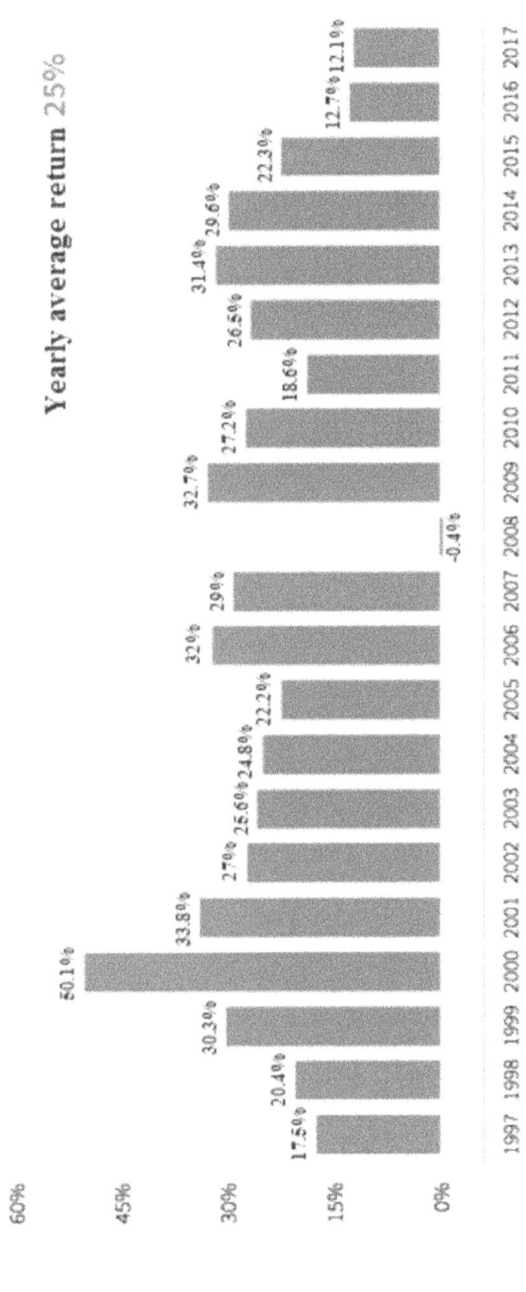

Figure 14.1 Return on Equities of the AFP System (1997–2017). *Source*: Fundación Sol based on data provided by the Superintendencia de Pensiones.

on equities over the past twenty years, with a yearly average of 25.7 percent and spikes of 50 percent during the year 2000. Also, table 14.5 shows the profitability of AFPs (in pesos as of 2017).

Impact on Coverage

Regarding the reform's social impact, the evolution of coverage rates was one of the greatest disappointments, as this indicator never quite reached pre-1981 levels. As can be observed in table 14.6, under the previous PAYG system, coverage had reached 74 percent of the workforce in 1975 and plummeted to 59 percent in 1979, a year before the reform. After 1981, both of the new systems (the AFPs and the Pension Normalization Institute, including the armed forces and the police) saw a drop in occupational coverage during the first year followed by a recovery until it reached 67.7 percent in 1997. In terms of effective coverage, the same trend as before can be observed, with a steeper fall resulting from higher unemployment rates during the deep economic recession in 1982,[59] and a faster recovery in 1997, amounting to coverage levels of 64 percent.[60] In the case of self-employed workers (under voluntary participation schemes), coverage levels have remained dismal; they reached 4.8 percent in 1986 and fell to 3.8 percent in 1998.[61]

Table 14.5 Evolution of AFPs Earnings

Year	*AFPs Earnings (In pesos, as of December 2017)*
1981–1989	85,524,862,944
1990–1999	659,864,674,645
2000	221,777,336,574
2001	166,574,458,411
2002	144,750,429,278
2003	140,045,129,693
2004	144,468,151,645
2005	136,655,675,060
2006	200,137,554,999
2007	193,261,700,930
2008	-3,960,577,673
2009	338,225,851,986
2010	336,404,763,661
2011	245,696,522,870
2012	341,539,191,043
2013	391,979,599,183
2014	371,679,247,528
2015	597,416,929,955
2016	361,195,600,285
2017	347,495,864,000
Total	5,420,732,967,017

Source: Fundación Sol, based on data by Superintendencia de Pensiones

Table 14.6 Occupational and Effective Coverage (1975–1999)

	Occupational Coverage Contributors/Employed Workers			*Effective Coverage Contributors/ Total Workforce*		
Years	*AFP*	*INP*	*Total*	*AFP*	*INP*	*Total*
1975		74.3	74.3		64.7	64.7
1976		68.9	68.9		60.1	60.1
1977		65.4	65.4		57.7	57.7
1978		59.8	59.8		51.2	51.2
1979		59.4	59.4		51.3	51.3
1980		56.4	56.4		50.5	50.5
1981	33.6	21.5	55.1	29.8	19	48.8
1982	36	20	56	29	16.1	45
1983	38.2	18	56.2	33.5	15.8	49.3
1984	40.6	16.7	57.3	35	14.4	49.3
1985	44	15.7	59.7	38.8	13.8	52.6
1986	45.9	14.2	60.1	41.1	12.7	53.9
1987	50.6	13.5	64.1	45.7	12.2	58
1988	50.6	12.2	62.7	46.6	11.2	57.7
1989	50.8	11	61.8	47.2	10.2	57.4
1990	50.6	10.3	60.9	46.8	9.6	56.4
1991	53.7	9.7	63.4	49.9	9	58.9
1992	55.3	8.9	64.2	51.8	8.4	60.2
1993	54.6	8	62.6	51.1	7.5	58.6
1994	56.2	7.6	63.8	51.8	7	58.9
1995	57.2	7.6	64.8	53.5	7.1	60.6
1996	58.9	7	65.9	55.7	6.6	62.3
1997	61.3	6.4	67.7	58	6.1	64.1
1998	58	6.3	64.2	53.8	5.8	59.6
1999	49.8	5.4	55.2	45.4	4.9	50.3

Source: Uthoff (2001) op. cit.

Moreover, because the armed forces and the police were exempted from participating in the new system, different groups of contributors were not treated equally. Furthermore, the reform had a detrimental impact on women, because the system of individual accounts eliminated gender redistribution mechanisms, which deepened biological gender inequalities (such as lower pensions because of higher life expectancy) and labor market inequalities (such as lower pensions due to lower wages and interrupted careers).[62]

As Uthoff reports,[63] before the 2008 reform, only 45 percent of the population was able to fund their pensions with the accumulated savings in their AFP accounts, while only 5 percent had access to a minimum pension guaranteed by the state. The other half of affiliates had no certainty regarding their access to old-age income, and even those with the right to a pension fund had to assume the risks that came with the volatility of the financial and capital markets where their contributions had been invested. Those who were not under any pension scheme or could not fulfill the minimum requirements depended on social assistance pensions (Pensiones de Asistencia Social—PASIS), which covered 2.3 percent of the population, or 358,813 people in 2000–2001. This number grew to almost half a million people at the time of the reform of 2008.[64]

CONCLUSIONS

Pinochet's privatization of the pension system represented, on the one hand, one of his great neoliberal reforms and, on the other, a costly legacy for the Chilean people. Therefore, studying this subject contributes to the explanation of the conditions and characteristics of the current political and economic systems. Structural reforms implemented on social policies, and the resulting commodification of social rights such as education, health, housing, social security —as analyzed in this chapter—and others, have aggravated inequality[65] within the Chilean society.

The evidence analyzed in this chapter shows that the implementation of the pension system, which did not include the necessary social dialogue, has resulted in issues such as fiscal strain arising from the transition period, problems, and inequality in coverage, rising operational costs and high commissions due to an imperfect AFP market. Also, despite there being a semblance of development of a capital market, its effect on productive investment has been limited.[66] Moreover, evidence has been provided for the analysis of how Chilean economic elites and foreign capitals have benefited from the privatized pension system to the detriment of Chilean workers. The reform meant that a large amount of capital was transferred from the workforce to the AFPs, in the form of mandatory contributions and administrative commissions; the very same AFPs that were owned by the most powerful Chilean business groups and by international companies. As a result, the pension system became one of the most profitable and less risky businesses in the country, even after the transition to democracy.

Unlike other Latin American countries, where the neoliberal reforms of the eighties and nineties have been rolled back through the renationalization of pension systems (Argentina in 2008[67] and Peru in 2011), the capitalization pillar remains intact in Chile and the three largest AFPs that concentrate 64 percent of affiliates are owned by foreign groups. The importance of AFPs as political and economic actors and their lobbying power have been crucial to the survival of the private system. In contrast, other countries in the region and in Europe where the influence of powerful groups was not as strong, and public pillars remained in place, were able to undo the privatization reforms.

The continuity of the private system shows that the pro-market, neoliberal legacy forcefully imposed through mass human rights violations by

Pinochet's military government remains in force and constitutes one of the fundamental causes of social and economic inequality in Chile.

NOTES

1. In 1995 José Piñera, former Minister of Labor and Social Security during Pinochet's dictatorship, and architect of the Labor Reform (DL 2756, 2757, and 2758) and the privatization of the pension system (DL No. 3500), published a book titled "Belling the cat" where he discussed the history of the implementation of the Chilean pension system reform of 1980. In the book, he mentions that when the time came to share the news on the creation of the DL No. 3500, someone claimed "We have belled the cat! Long live Chile!" as a metaphor for describing how through the reform all of the historical problems that the system had had, such as funding and fragmentation, would be solved.

2. Bachelet submitted her pension system reform bill in 2006 and created a Commission to debate it. Finally, the reform was implemented in 2008. See Hujo, K. and M. Rulli, "The Political Economy of Pension Re-Reform in Chile and Argentina Toward More Inclusive Protection," (Research Paper 2014–1, UNRISD, April 2014).

3. In 2010, France saw violent and massive demonstrations in response to the pension system reform, which entailed, among others, an increase of two years in the retirement age. By achieving the implementation of the reform, Sarkozy accomplished what Jacques Chirac had not been able to, as in 1995 he had to pull back a similar project after weeks of protests and public transport strikes throughout the country.

4. Several large-scale protests took place in Greece in 2010, against cuts to retirement benefits and the raising of the retirement age to sixty-five years. The reform was implemented by the socialist government of George Papandreou as a requirement to access the rescue package by the European Union and the International Monetary Fund.

5. Hujo and Rulli (2014) op. cit.

6. See http://www.nomasafp.cl/inicio/.

7. Ortíz, I. et al., "The Decade of Adjustment: A Review of Austerity Trends 2010–2020," (ILO: Geneva, 2015).

8. Hujo, K., "Reforming pensions in developing and transition countries: Trends, debates and impacts. Introduction," in *Reforming pensions in developing and transition countries, Social Policy in a Development Context Series*, ed. Hujo, K. (UNRISD-Palgrave, 2014).

9. Solimano, A., *Pensiones a la chilena, la experiencia internacional y el camino a la desprivatización* (Editorial Catalonia, 2017).

10. See Hujo and Rulli (2014) op. cit.

11. On the Bravo Commission and the current state of the Chilean pension system, see also "Informe Anual 2016 'Situación de los Derechos Humanos en Chile'" by the *Instituto Nacional de Derechos Humanos*. Available at http://bibliotecadigital.indh.cl /handle/123456789/998.

12. See *Informe Final de la Comisión Asesora Preseidencial sobre el Sistema de Pensiones* (2015:147) available at http://www.comision-pensiones.cl/Informe_fina l_CP_2015.pdf.

13. See *Comunicado del Comando de Exonerados de Chile* (Santiago, May 29, 2017), available at https://issuu.com/coexchag/docs/comunicado_29-05-2017-y_as__ _tratan.

14. See Ahumada and Solimano, chapter 6 in this book.

15. Mesa-Lago, C., "Social Security in Latin America. Pressure Groups, Stratification, and Inequality" (University of Pittsburgh Press, Pittsburgh, 1978).

16. See Maldonado Valera, Carlos, and Andrea Palma Rocco, "La Construcción de Pactos y Consensos en Materia de Política Social. Origen y Trayectoria de Tres Casos de Política Pública en América Latina: México, Chile y Uruguay. Informe pre-eliminar," (Santiago: CEPAL, 2013); and Mesa-Lago (1978) op. cit.

17. Arenas de Mesa, A., "Cobertura previsional en Chile: Lecciones y desafíos del sistema de pensiones administrado por el sector privado," *Serie Financiamiento del desarrollo* 105, (Santiago: CEPAL, 2000).

18. Arenas de Mesa (2000), op. cit.

19. Arenas de Mesa, A. and Hernandez Sánchez, H., "Analysis, Evolución, y Propuestas de Ampliación de la Cobertura del Sistema Civil de Pensiones en Chile," in *Cobertura Previsional en Argentina, Brasil y Chile*, ed. Fabio Bertranou (Santiago: Oficina Internacional del Trabajo, 2001).

20. Williamson, J., *Latin America Adjustment. How Much has Happened* (Washington, DC: Institute for International Economics, 1990).

21. World Bank, "Averting the Old Age Crisis: Policies to Protect the Old and Promote Growth" (Washington, DC: Oxford University Press, 1994).

22. Chile (1981), Peru (1993) Argentina and Colombia (1994), Uruguay (1996), Bolivia and Mexico (1997), El Salvador (1998), Costa Rica (2001), Nicaragua, Ecuador and the Dominican Republic (2003) and Panama (2008).

23. Müller, Katharina, *Privatising Old-Age Security: Latin America and Eastern Europe Compared* (Cheltenham: Edward Elgar, 2003).

24. See Lewis, C. M. and Lloyd-Sherlock, P., "Social Policy and Economic Development in South America: An Historical Approach to Social Insurance," *Economy and Society* 38: 1 (2009): 109–31; Casey, Bernard H., "Pensions in Nigeria: The Performance of the New System of Personal Accounts," *International Social Security Review* 64(1): 1–14 (January–March, 2011); Fang, Lianquan, "Towards Universal Coverage: A Macro Analysis of China's Public Pension Reform," in *Reforming Pensions in Developing and Transition Countries*, ed. Katja Hujo (Basingstoke: UNRISD and Palgrave, 2014); Orenstein, Mitchell, *Privatizing Pensions: The Transnational Campaign for Social Security Reform* (Princeton: Princeton University Press, 2008); Orszag, Peter, and Joseph E. Stiglitz, "Rethinking Pension Reform: Ten Myths about Social Security Systems," in *New Ideas about Old Age Security: Toward Sustainable Pension Systems in the 21st Century*, ed. Robert Holzmann and Joseph E. Stiglitz, (Washington, DC: World Bank, 2001); Hendricks, Fred, "The Private Affairs of Public Sector Pensions in South Africa: Debt, Development and Corporatization," in *Reforming Pensions in*

Developing and Transition Countries, ed. Katja Hujo (Basingstoke: UNRISD and Palgrave, 2014).

25. For an analysis of the impact in the capital market, see Uthoff (2001) op cit.

26. At the same time as the pension system reform was implemented, there were reforms in the healthcare system that created private healthcare providers which attracted the highest-earning sector of the workforce, competing with a public health sector that was facing several problems and restrictions. (Arenas de Mesa, 2000, op. cit.).

27. Mesa-Lago, C., "Re-reform of Latin American Private Pensions Systems: Argentinian and Chilean Models and Lessons," *The Geneva Papers* 34 (2009): 602–17.

28. For an analysis on the link between the civilians who promoted and facilitated the reforms and privatizations and that were benefited afterward with positions in the companies involved, see González Hernando y Undurraga, Chapter 10 in this book.

29. Mesa-Lago and Müller (2002: 715).

30. For a view from the optic of the proponents of the reform, see Piñera Echenique, J., *El cascabel al gato. La batalla por la reforma previsional* (Santiago: Editorial Zigzag, 1995).

31. See Noya, N. (ed.), *Efectos Económicos y Políticos de la Reforma en la Seguridad social en Uruguay* (Montevideo: Centro de Investigaciones Económicas (CINVE), 1998), available at http://web.idrc.ca/uploads/user-S/11051067461 noya.doc.

32. Mesa-Lago, Carmelo and Katharina Müller, "La Política de la Reforma de Pensiones en América Latina," in *Públicos o Privados? Los Sistemas de Pensiones en América Latina después de Dos Décadas de Reformas*, ed. Katja Hujo, Carmelo Mesa-Lago and Manfred Nitsch (Caracas: Nueva Sociedad, 2004).

33. See Ahumada and Solimano, Chapter 6, p. 72, in this book.

34. Hujo and Rulli (2014) op. cit.

35. Uthoff (2001) op. cit.

36. Ibid.

37. Uthoff, A.,"Reformas al sistema de pensiones chileno," in *Serie financiamiento del desarrollo* 240 (Santiago: CEPA, 2011).

38. Mesa-Lago, C., "Pension Re-Reform in Chile," *Zeitschrift für ausländisches und internationales Arbeits- und Sozialrecht* 26(3) (2012): 197–212.

39. Uthoff (2001) op. cit.

40. Ibid.

41. Uthoff (2001) cit.; and Mastrángelo, J., "Políticas para la reducción de costos en los sistemas de pensiones: el caso de Chile," *Serie de financiamiento del desarrollo* 86 (Santiago: CEPAL, 1999).

42. See Ahumada and Solimano, chapter 6 in this book.

43. Acuña R, and Iglesias A., "La reforma a las pensiones," in *La transformación Económica de Chile*, ed. Larraín, F. and Vergara, R. (Santiago: Centro de Estudios Públicos, 2000).

44. Superintendencia de Pensiones, Ficha estadista previsional Nº 64, (March 2018), available at https://www.spensiones.cl/portal/institucional/594/articles-13169 _recurso_1.pdf.

45. Gálvez, R., "El 'corralito legal': ¿Quién gana cuando las AFP se hacen ricas?" *Centro de Investigaciones Periodísticas* (July 7, 2017), available at http://ciperchile.cl/2017/06/07/el-corralito-legal-quien-gana-cuando-las-afp-se-hacen-ricas/.

46. Godoy Mercado, M., "Los dueños de las AFP explicados con manzanitas," *Economía para Todos* (August 24, 2016), available at https://economiatodos.cl/2016/08/24/los-duenos-de-las-afp-explicados-con-manzanitas/.

47. The ILC also manages other insurance and healthcare providers, such as RedSalud, ISAPRE, Consalud, Confuturo, Corpseguros, as well as several schools across the country. See Godoy Mercado (2016) op. cit.

48. See Gálvez (2016) op. cit.

49. See Araya Gómez, Chapter 11 in this book.

50. Godoy Mercado (2016) op. cit.

51. See Gálvez (2016) op. cit.

52. Besides Cuprum, Grupo Penta SA owned healthcare companies such as Isapre Vida Tres, Empresas Banmédica, Clínica las Condes and Help, as well as real estate businesses and shares in the Banco de Chile, among others.

53. See Gonzalez Hernando y Undurraga, chapter 10 in this book.

54. Uthoff (2001) op. cit.

55. SAFP, January 2001, in Uthoff (2001), op. cit.

56. Superintendencia de Pensiones, Ficha Estadística Nº54 (May 2017), available at https://www.spensiones.cl/portal/.

57. Superintendencia de Pensiones, Ficha Estadística Nº54 (May 2017) , available at https://www.spensiones.cl/portal/.

58. AFPs revenue is calculated by adding up the commissions on mandatory deposits and Voluntary Pension Savings; the commissions on programmed withdrawals and temporary income; and the regular income plus the profitability of their legal reserve. See Gálvez (2016) op. cit.

59. See Ahumada and Solimano, chapter 6, in this book.

60. Uthoff (2001) op. cit. For a more detailed analysis of the evolution of coverage, see Arenas de Mesa, A. (2000) op. cit.

61. Bustamante, J., "El sistema chileno de pensiones, Seminario Internacional Reforma da Providencia Social," (Brasilia: Ministerio de Presidencia e Asistencia Social, December 1998); and Mesa-Lago (2009) op. cit.

62. See Arza, C., "Pension Reforms and Gender Equality in Latin America," (Research Paper No. 2012–2: UNRISD, Geneva, 2012); and Mesa-Lago (2009) op. cit.

63. Uthoff (2001: 5) op. cit.

64. Hujo y Rulli (2014) op. cit.

65. For a detailed analysis of the redistributive consequences of the economic model implemented by the dictatorship, see Weber, chapter 9 in this book.

66. Uthoff (2001: 5) op. cit.

67. Rulli, M., *La política de las reformas previsionales en Argentina (1993–2015)* (Colección Nuevos Horizontes, Editorial Universidad Nacional de Río Negro, Viedma, 2019 (forthcoming)).

Chapter 15

Privatization and Repression

Two Sides of the Same Coin

Sebastián Smart

INTRODUCTION

It is widely known that during Pinochet's dictatorship an unprecedented model of privatization was put in place in the country. This privatization process was established as a clear counterpart to Chile's state-centered governments, which, since the beginning of the twentieth century, had supported an interventionist approach regarding the country's economy through the creation of a significant number of state-owned companies[1] that since 1939 had been underpinned by the CORFO (Corporación de Fomento de la Producción in Spanish; Corporation of Production Promotion in English). This state agency was responsible, along with other social groups, for the creation of companies such as ENDESA (Empresa Nacional de Electricidad Sociedad Anónima in Spanish; National Energy Company in English) (1944), CAP (Compañía de Acero del Pacífico S.A in Spanish; Pacific Steel Company in English) (1947), and IANSA (Industria Azucarera Nacional in Spanish; National Sugar Industry in English) (1953), and as a result, by 1973 the public administration accounted for 39 percent of Chile's GDP.[2]

The historic and progressive creation of state-owned companies and the state's involvement in the economy were interrupted by a dictatorial government that brought about a process of privatization that slashed the number of state-owned companies from 596 in 1973 to a meager 49 in 1989. It will be shown how this model presented tremendous levels of concentration of property and income, two factors that have contributed to the current rates of inequality in the nation.[3] Moreover, this happened against a backdrop of repression and illegality which, supported by an obscure legal framework, resulted in a lack of protection for users and the working class, and caused serious harm not only to the small- and middle-sized businesses of the period but also to the most vulnerable sectors of Chilean society. Thus, this chapter will reveal how the process of privatization greatly reduced public revenue, which would have been used, for example, to fund social projects in areas such as health or education.

To demonstrate the links between privatization, repression, and socioeconomic consequences, this chapter will be divided into four sections, besides this introduction. In the first part, Pinochet's role in the process of privatization will be analyzed, as well as how this was only possible due to the high degree of repression present during the Chilean dictatorship. The second part will analyze the first wave of privatizations carried out during the dictatorship. This process took place between 1974 and 1982 and included a first moment (1974–1975) where the companies that had been intervened or nationalized by Salvador Allende's government were restituted to their private owners, followed by a second moment (1976–1981) where public companies that were managed by CORFO were auctioned. In the third part, the spotlight is placed on the process of privatization that occurred after the 1982 crisis, also known as *popular capitalism*. Hereafter, the model of privatization had the goal of selling the shares from the main state-owned companies to strengthen the capital market; moreover, banks and pension funds that were bankrupt were reprivatized. Finally, the fourth part of this chapter will include an analysis on the most significant consequences of the privatization process, which notably featured enormous losses for the state arising from the sale of companies, real estate, and private lending; increasingly high levels of economic concentration and inequality in the country; and last the creation of an obscure and corrupted model which ended up benefitting mostly those who supported Pinochet's dictatorship.

PRIVATIZATION AND REPRESSION

The worldwide emergence of a wave of privatizations and a tendency to favor the market over the state becomes apparent from 1980 onward. Moreover, after 1990 the region saw a weakening of the "Welfare State" model which had defined Latin American governments in previous years.[4] Inspired by the recipes coming from the World Bank, the International Monetary Fund, and the Washington Consensus, and based on the idea that public companies were obsolete or inefficient, the privatization of state-owned companies became one of the fundamental pillars for market stabilization in the short term, mainly in the "global south."[5] This recipe stemmed from the measures implemented by the Chilean and British governments, which had already shown the world that privatizations were possible in the seventies.[6]

Pinochet's dictatorship pioneered the idea of generating a privatization process supported by repression. This idea was mirrored in countries such as Mexico (1980), Great Britain (1980), Spain (1985), France (1986), and

Table 15.1 Starting Year for Privatization Processes by Country

País	*Año*
Chile	1973
Great Britain	1980
Mexico	1983
Spain	1985
France	1986
Argentina	1989
Poland	1990
Brazil	1991
Panama	1992
Russia	1992
Bangladesh	1993
Colombia	1997
Ecuador	1997
Guatemala	1997
Dominican Republic	1997
Venezuela	1997
Costa Rica	1998
El Salvador	1998
Honduras	1998
Nicaragua	1998
Uruguay	1998
Paraguay	2000

Source: Created by the author based on information by the Chamber of Deputies op. cit.

Argentina (1989), although most privatization experiences, including the ones in former socialist countries, took place during the 1990s (see table 15.1). Therefore, it is possible to consider Chile a regional model in terms of the creation of a mechanism for generalized privatizations. This economic "innovation" could only be implemented in a context of repression and illegality, which would guarantee—as will be shown here—its speed, massiveness, and long reach.[7] In fact, despite there being little comparative literature on the field of privatizations, it is possible to ascertain that the states that were largely involved in the national economy and underwent dictatorial processes tended to resort to privatizations extensively, while those that had a similar economic approach but did not give up their democratic system, such as Costa Rica, were not able to perform large-scale privatizations due to the rejection of the majority of civilians and social organizations.[8]

As has been explained in other chapters of this book, Chile's economy during the times of Pinochet can be divided into three periods, which tried to, at first, reestablish the capitalist model (1973–1975), followed by an attempted neoliberal revolution (1976–1981), until the final process of financial regulation and export promotion (1983–1989).[9] Stemming from these economic conceptions, several different legal frameworks were created to privatize public companies or restore the companies that had been intervened during the administration of Unidad Popular to their previous owners. Hence, during the first period, labeled as "capitalist restoration," the dictatorship's intention was clear regarding its focus on returning the companies that had been nationalized or intervened during Allende's government (1970–1973) to their private owners. Moreover, following the 1981 crisis, and coinciding with the process of financial regulation and export promotion, Pinochet's dictatorship attempted to "reprivatize" several companies—mostly related to financial services—which accounted for 60 percent of the placements of the financial system and around 68 percent of the pension funds connected to the Pension Fund System (Administradoras de Fondos de Pensión—AFP). These two stages of privatization answer to different interests, and lead to different systems, so they will be analyzed separately.

RESTITUTION AND FIRST STAGE OF PRIVATIZATION OF STATE-OWNED COMPANIES

Between 1974 and 1978, approximately 350 companies that had been nationalized or intervened by the Unidad Popular administration were restituted.[10] Most of these restitutions occurred during the period of capitalist restoration, meaning that they happened between 1974 and 1975. In this process, the vice president of CORFO was given the power to revise each company's background information and to order "the restitution of the affected establishments to their owners or legal representatives when the circumstances required it."[11] However, the process did not only include the restitution of companies to their former owners, but it also compelled the state to assist them in the regularization of those companies' financial situation. To achieve that, the companies had their debts with public entities such as the Banco del Estado and autonomous or semi-autonomous state institutions such as CORFO written off.[12]

Under the wing of company restitution, the dictatorship launched a process of restitution of the land that had been seized by the government during the agrarian reform (1965–1973). The surface of the land expropriated during the agrarian reform was 6,783,643 hectares, of which approximately a million had been offered to small-scale farmers—the rest was in the hands of the state—through the Corporation of Agrarian Reform (Corporación de Reforma Agraria—CORA), which had made it possible for the state to own nearly 60 percent of the arable land in the country by 1973.[13] During the "normalization" process that started in Pinochet's dictatorship, some state-owned lands were restituted to their former owners, some were donated to corporations and institutions and some were sold in the market. Of the total amount of land acquired by the state during the agrarian reform, 30 percent was restituted to their former owners, 44 percent was allotted to different private owners (mostly families or cooperatives) or auctioned, and 17.5 percent was transferred to nonprofit organizations.[14] Besides having their land restituted to them, those owners who had been affected by the agrarian reform received monetary compensation. The payment consisted of a transfer of shares from public companies such as ENDESA, COLBÚN, and ENTEL (Empresa Nacional de Telecomunicaciones in Spanish; National Telecom Company in English), among others.[15]

Since 1975, and at the same time as the "neoliberal revolution," the Chilean State broadened its scope regarding privatizations and included the alienation of CORFO's shares in state-owned companies.[16] During this period, CORFO sold its shares in 135 societies and 16 commercial banks, for a total of US$ 547 million.[17] To carry out this alienation, the vice president of CORFO had to authorize it, and determine whether it would be conducted by public auction or public tender. Only exceptional circumstances allowed this process to be carried out by different methods, and it required the favorable vote of four of CORFO's board members. However, despite this requirement, the predominant trading method during this period of privatization and state divestment was one of the direct public offerings where the buyers paid a part in cash and CORFO offered a loan to finance the remaining amount, which caused high levels of concentration and indebtedness.

To ensure broad shareholder participation, individuals were not allowed to buy more than 1.5 percent (3 percent for legal persons) of the capital of financial institutions.[18] However, this rule was easily bypassed. In the words of a former CORFO executive and minister of Frei Montalva and Pinochet, Raúl Sáez, by not demanding consolidated financial statements to buyers,

> economic groups were allowed to use companies or banks that had been previously acquired to buy other firms, possibly also financed by incurring debt, which would make them more indebted when trying acquire a newly tendered company. At the same time, the terms of sale allowed the buyers to incur debt with CORFO, while paying a relatively small percentage in cash. All of this ended in a generalized indebtedness which led to companies finding themselves in a precarious financial situation of high debt to capital ratio.[19]

As a result, the ownership of financial institutions became strongly concentrated, with a large portion of them being controlled by one or two economic groups.[20]

POPULAR AND LABOR CAPITALISM (1982–1990)

After the economic crisis of 1982, the dictatorship found itself in a situation where it had to renationalize and intervene a number of companies and financial institutions. In fact, between 1982 and 1985 fourteen state-owned companies were created, and fifty companies which had been privatized in the first period (1973–1981) and gone bankrupt went back to the hands of the state and were intervened, among which were, for example, banks such as Banco de Chile, Banco de Santiago and Banco de Concepción, the AFP's PROVIDA, Santa María and COPEC (Compañía de Petróleos de Chile in Spanish; Chilean Petroleum Company in English), the forestry company Forestal Arauco, and others such as INFORSA (Industrias Forestales S.A. in Spanish; Forestry Industries in English), CCU (Compañía Cervecerías unidas in Spanish; United Beer Industries in English), Compañía Minera Pudahuel, and CTC (Compañía de Teléfonos de Chile in Spanish; Chilean Telephone Company in English).[21] Moreover, Pinochet's dictatorship understood that the high levels of concentration produced by the first period of privatizations had been one of the causes for the bankruptcy of several financial institutions, and consequently CORFO began a process of splitting up several of its companies into subsidiaries, bringing about a period of "popular capitalism" which aimed for higher market diversification.[22]

From 1985 onward, the country experienced a radical process of privatizations that the dictatorship called "popular capitalism." This process consisted in an attempt to lower the concentration of state-owned companies, by reprivatizing firms that had returned to the hands of the state, and by "distributing the shares of important companies in the country among every sector of the population."[23] The Law N° 18,398 created the so-called "indirect popular capitalism" or labor capitalism, which allowed Pension Fund Administrators (AFPs) to invest their resources in publicly traded companies where the state was the majority shareholder. According to CORFO's official stance, "the investment of workers in their AFPs would be beneficial to them, because AFPs would invest the workers' capital in profitable and reliable instruments, which would increase their funds."[24] To be allowed to invest, the operation had to be previously approved by the Risk Rating Commission, to avoid unnecessarily risky moves. Paradoxically, the aforementioned law established that for it to be possible to invest in state-owned companies these had to be in the process of selling at least 30 percent of their stock, which implied an attempt to capitalize CORFO's subsidiaries.

On the other hand, the Law N° 18,401 of 1985 was passed to soften the blow of the 1982 crisis, which had resulted in the intervention of a large sector of the national banking system. The said law had the goal of regularizing the situation of the financial entities that had been intervened and of reprivatizing their capital. Strictly speaking, re-privatization should be the term used, as after the financial crisis the state was forced to intervene several banks that had been previously privatized in the first period, such as the banks of Talca, Español-Chile, Fomento de Valparaíso, and Regional de Linares. Afterward, in 1982, these banks entered a liquidation process along with the Banco de Fomento del Bío-Bío and the Banco Austral de Chile. As an example, to illustrate the point, during the first term of 1985, the two main banks that had been intervened were sold (Banco de Chile and Banco de Santiago).[25] This law also fostered capital deconcentration, by not allowing CORFO, after it had been reprivatized, to own more than 49 percent of the paid capital, and no person to acquire more than 10 percent of the shares except when the Superintendencia de Valores y Seguros (Superintendence of Securities and Insurance) expressly authorized it.

Last, it is worth highlighting that between 1988 and 1990, that is, after the referendum, several privatization initiatives gathered momentum, and resulted in the sale of important companies that until that time had belonged to the state or in which the state was a majority shareholder. In a desperate attempt to privatize state-owned goods before the return of democracy, Pinochet's dictatorship sold an important part of the companies it controlled, such as Chile Firms, Chilgener, CTC, ENDESA, Entel-Chile, IANSA, INACAP, Laboratorios Chile, LAN, and SOQUIMICH, among others. Those privatizations were conducted at low prices and to the benefit of certain business groups. In fact, the Contraloría General de la República (Comptroller General of the Republic) has pointed out that

> it was determined that CORFO sold during the year of 1989 an important part of the shares it held in its subsidiaries. In updated figures as of December 31 of 1989, the cost of those shares according to their book value was $207,719,513,766 and they were sold for $118,202,736,216. This resulted in a negative balance of $89,516,777,550 at book value, and therefore an asset decrease of 19.6% approximately.[26]

CONSEQUENCES OF THE PRIVATIZATION PROCESS

State Losses

The Comptroller General of the Republic has highlighted several times that a large portion of Chile's state-owned companies were sold at a lower price than their book value, which resulted in a loss of public assets.[27] In fact, the World Bank itself has declared that "in most of the privatizations, the shares were priced below their real economic value."[28] This fact has been accepted by economists both in favor and against the process of privatizations.

A conservative estimate submitted by the Investigative Commission of Privatizations of the Lower Chamber of 1991 concluded that in 32 of the nearly 600 companies sold between 1985 and 1989, the state had lost a net amount of US$ 2,223 million, at exchange rates of 1989.[29] Moreover, CORFO had assumed the liabilities of these companies, increasing its debt by 131 percent.

Mario Marcel has noted that, depending on the method used to calculate the losses of the Chilean State, they vary between 27, 42 and 69 percent of the capital sold in the period 1985–1989.[30] Perhaps one of the clearest examples to illustrate the state's losses is the privatization of CAP. The net amount of losses incurred during the sale of CAP's actives is estimated at US$ 706.44 million, which represents one-third of the total losses incurred by CORFO (out of the thirty-two companies which have been recorded). This was carried out in a completely irregular process, where shares were issued, followed by a reduction in capital and redemption of shares, which allowed for a private group of investors to increase their participation from 16.7 percent to 49 percent with no additional contribution.[31] Similar to the CAP case, there were the ones of ENDESA, which saw losses of US$ 661 million, SOQUIMICH, US$ 260 million, and IANSA with losses of US$180 million.[32]

However, the losses of the state were related not only to the sale of companies and shares but also to a significant number of CORFO's debtors who were unable to fulfill their obligations. According to former CORFO's attorney Guido Machiavello, uncollectable debt amounted to US$ 35,000 million pesos (at 1990 rates), which at a 2017 exchange rates equals US$ 125.1 million.[33] Those loans became uncollectable due to a series of irregularities such as CORFO not being a preferred creditor, the existence of fake information in loan applications, the sale of prescribed shares, and the granting of similar guarantees for different credits, among others.[34] An example of uncollectable debt is Manufactura de Algodón S.A. (MACHASA), a company that was granted a loan for US$ 11 million and that after declaring bankruptcy did not service its debt. Another example is the Sociedad Ganadera Monasterio Ltd., owned by Julio Ponce Lerou, a staff member at CORFO and the son-in-law of Augusto Pinochet, who was granted an irregular loan of nearly US$ 800 million pesos, which was serviced in real estate and cattle, but with no adjustment, and as a result generated losses of approximately 117,244 UF (Unidad de Fomento) for the treasury.[35]

Last, it is worth noting that the state sustained significant losses related to donations that it made to the Armed Forces and to private parties. CORFO donated to the Armed Forces "vehicles, movable property, radio equipment, laboratories and real estate valued at approximately 25 million dollars."[36] Those donations also involved private parties linked to Pinochet's circle. A clear example of this is the land donated by the state to nonprofit organizations such as CEMA Chile, led by Lucía Hiriart, the wife of Augusto Pinochet, whose net worth by 2005 was US$ 3,350 million (92 percent of which consisted in donations of property granted to CEMA by the state between 1973 and 1990).[37] Another noteworthy event is the donation of INACAP and seventy-six other Institutes of Technical and Vocational Education to the Confederation of Production and Trade (Confederación de Producción y Comercio—CPC) by CORFO, and which has been assessed to have resulted in a loss of US$ 4,000 million (at 1988 exchange rates).[38]

Concentration and Inequality

There is no doubt that the first period of privatizations contributed to the concentration of wealth in the hands of a few business groups. After this became evident, and following the crisis of 1982, the dictatorship was forced to implement—since 1985—a popular capitalism scheme with the goal of deconcentrating the state's assets. However, this scheme did not bring about the expected results. During the second period of privatizations, the purchase of state-owned companies required greater solvency and economic power, which added to the levels of concentration of property. Ricardo Ffrench Davis explains this phenomenon highlighting that "the process took place in the middle of an intense recession and skyrocketing internal rates of return. Due to this, few groups within the private sector had the required purchasing power, benefitting those with greater access to foreign credit, which reinforced the privileges of a small minority and increased the concentration of property."[39]

It is possible to observe that between 1985 and 1988 public property landed in the hands of national or international groups and pension funds, who had acquired banks and companies through public tenders or direct purchase to the investors who had purchased said companies previously.[40] Within the national economic groups, the most notable ones were Cruzat Larraín, Vial, Matte, Angelini, and Luksic, who acquired 14.8, 10, 4.8, 3.2, and 3.2 percent of state-owned companies, respectively. Foreign investors, on the other hand, concentrated 14 percent of state-owned companies, holding shares in CTC (25 percent), CAP (44 percent), SOQUIMICH (22 percent), and Laboratorios Chile (41 percent), among others.[41]

The privatization process was one of the elements that contributed to the negative impact on income redistribution. And it is mentioned as one of the elements because it was not the only variable that contributed to the increasingly wide gap between the rich and the poor. One thing is clear, and that is, as explained by Javier Rodríguez Weber in a different chapter of this book, that inequality increased during the dictatorship. Public spending directed to the poorest fifth of the population dropped from 7.6 percent in 1969 to 5.2

percent in 1978 and 4.4 percent in 1988.[42] Another possible conclusion is that the process of privatization had a serious impact on working conditions and on the already analyzed distribution of property, which influenced income redistribution.

This process also brought about mass layoffs and a deterioration of the population's living conditions. If by 1970 the top 20 public companies generated 126,360 jobs, by 1986 that number dropped to 95,683.[43] This was a result of the process of mass layoffs caused by the privatization of state-owned companies. In addition, there were nearly 100,000 public officials who lost their jobs. All of this contributed to a significant nation-wide rise in unemployment, which in 1975 was 15.7 percent and in 1983 grew to 19 percent of the total workforce (740 thousand unemployed).[44] Moreover, the policies implemented to increase companies' productivity led to a reduction in workers' real income. The average salary fell by 8 percent between 1970 and 1989. Last, there existed an anti-state viciousness that became apparent not only in the privatization of companies but also in the privatization of social protection mechanisms such as education and health. Moreover, between 1974 and 1990 social spending (health, education, and housing per inhabitant) was slashed by 10–15 percent and family allowance was cut by 72 percent.[45] As a result, mass layoffs in addition to lower salaries, higher costs of public services,[46] and a lack of adequate social protection by the state all contributed to degradation in the living conditions of the lower quintile of Chile's population.

Transparency and Corruption

The difficulty in establishing the total amount of losses and gains resulting from the privatization process stems from the lack of transparency of the said process. Pinochet's repression, evidenced in the lack of freedom of the press, the absence of a parliament with the power to investigate the alleged irregularities and the nonexistence of regulatory agencies during the dictatorship, collaborated to increase the lack of transparency in the subject. It can be inferred from the previous analysis that some individuals made use of privileged information to access public tenders or sales conducted during the dictatorship. The figure of Julio Ponce Lerou is a clear example of these practices, as in his position of public officer and as the son-in-law of Pinochet, he managed to acquire several properties and to receive credits from CORFO, to gain control of important state-owned companies (such as SOQUIMICH). Despite the fact that the basic principles of transparency and anti-corruption measures tend to inhibit, control, and punish illegal links between money and public office, this was perfectly possible during Pinochet's dictatorship. Besides Ponce Lerou, there exist several other examples of this connection:

on the one hand, the family of Roberto Andraca bought shares in CAP, despite his position as public officer of the company with the power to set these shares' price, and him having been a manager of CORFO in the past; on the other hand, José Yurazeck managed to acquire an important part of the electricity companies that had been privatized during the dictatorship, even though he had been a staff member in ODEPLAN (Oficina de Planificación Nacional in Spanish; National Planification Office in English).[47]

The dictatorship's legislation also did not ban relations between officials in the Armed Forces and their involvement in the privatization of public companies' shares. Other chapters of this book give details on the corruption scandal for which Augusto Pinochet was sentenced, also known as Riggs case.[48] If the highest-ranking officer in the government was involved in corruption cases, it is not hard to imagine that the conduct of his staff members was also stained by illegality or at least irregularities. The Law N° 18,747 was a clear example of this irregular conduct, as it allowed the Armed Forces and Carabineros (the Chilean Special Police) to buy shares in state-owned companies. There are two noteworthy things about this law. First, it appears to be a desperate attempt to benefit the accomplices of the dictatorship over the past years of the regime, and second, within the list of the people that made use of this benefit, high-ranking officers either of the military or CORFO can be found, such as José Toribio Merino, Fernando Matthei, General Héctor Guillermo Letelier (former vice president of CORFO), José Rafael Martínez (military officer and former CORFO executive), Eugenio Enrique Lavín (Colonel and former general manager of CORFO), among others.[49]

CONCLUSIONS

From the evidence shown in this chapter, it is possible to identify two separate periods of privatizations, and despite them having different emphases and goals they both reached the same point: a high degree of economic concentration. As has been analyzed, the first period of privatizations (1974–1982) placed its focus on two different issues. A first moment attempted to reestablish the capitalist model by returning companies and land that had been expropriated during previous governments to their private owners. This process was accompanied by the trend of offering shares in state-owned companies as a form of economic compensation for the harm caused by the said expropriations. The second moment of this first period was marked by the neoliberal revolution, which simply intended to privatize fiscal resources, mainly through the alienation of companies and financial institutions that were controlled by CORFO. However, this privatizing momentum was halted by the 1982 crisis.

From 1982 onward, a new form of privatization was created, called popular capitalism. Having learned from its previous mistakes during the first period, the dictatorship set limits to the levels of concentration and attempted, through the AFPs, to give the ownership of public companies to the workers. In reality, none of those measures was successful, as companies were mainly bought by foreign or national business groups that had the economic solvency to acquire the shares alienated by CORFO. To sum up, it is clear to see that in both periods there was a trend toward economic concentration in the country.

Moreover, this process generated significant social and economic effects. The state incurred massive resource losses. Despite the lack of transparency regarding the processes of privatization, which makes conducting a precise macroeconomic assessment difficult, a conservative estimate shows that the losses related to the sale of only thirty companies total over US$ 15,000 million at current exchange rates. This amount would account for part of the budget cuts in the social protection network made by the Pinochet's government, particularly in the fields of labor rights, health, and education, which persist even to this day, and continue to raise the levels of inequality in the country.

Last, it is worth pointing out that the extent of the privatization process during the dictatorship was only possible because of the context of repression and illegality. This conclusion derives not only from the fact that such a far-reaching model of privatization had not been implemented anywhere in the world before 1974 but also from the fact that every one of these processes, despite the discursive efforts to label them as popular or labor capitalism, tended to benefit an economic and military elite, to the detriment of the working classes and the most vulnerable sectors in the country. Repression, in its many shapes and forms, and privatizations, were two sides of the same coin in Pinochet's dictatorship.

NOTES

1. There are several examples, but some worth mentioning are LAN (1932), ENAP (1950), Banco del Estado (1953), ENAMI (1960), and TVN (1970), among others.

2. Helen Nankani, *Technical Paper Nº 89, Volume II Selected Country Case Studies en Techniques of Privatization of State-Owned Enterprises*, World Bank report (1988).

3. See the chapter by Javier Rodríguez Weber.

4. Public companies played an important role in Latin American economies. Before the crisis of 1982, the added value of state-owned companies as a percentage of the GDP was close to 5 percent in Brazil, 14 percent in Chile, 8 percent in Mexico, and 30 percent in Venezuela. See Devlin, R., "Las Privatizaciones y el Bienestar Social," *CEPAL Magazine* 49 (April, 1993), p. 155.

5. This statement does not only apply to developing countries, as privatization processes could be seen in the Spanish economy (in the 80s), the French economy (from 1986 onwards), or the already-mentioned British economy (where the process starts during the 1970s).

6. Schamis, H., "Conservative Political Economy in Latin America and Western Europe: The Political Sources of Privatization," in *The Right and Democracy in Latin America*, eds. A. A. Borón, D. A. Chalmers y MC de Souza (Westpoint CT).

7. See *Chamber of Deputies of Chile*, "Informe de La Comisión Investigadora Encargada de Analizar Presuntas Irregularidades En Las Privatizaciones de Empresas Del Estado Con anterioridad Al Año 1990" (2006).

8. *Chamber of Deputies*, op. cit., p. 15.

9. See the chapter by Andrés Solimano y José Ahumada.

10. See Raúl Sáez, "La Privatización de Empresas en Chile," CIEPLAN Dcoument Nº 26, 1989. See also Dominique Hachette and Rolf Lüders, "La Privatización en Chile" (Centro Internacional para el Desarrollo Económico, CINDE, 1992).

11. See Decree Law Nº 88 (1973).

12. See Decree Law Nº 333 (1974).

13. See *Departamento de Derechos Humanos y Estudios Indígenas, Universidad Arcis*, "Las Tierras y los Campesinos de la Reforma Agraria Chilena, LEYES ASIGNATARIOS Y DESTINO" (2003) in Chamber of Deputies, op. cit.

14. Chamber of Deputies, op. cit.

15. See Law Nº 18.664.

16. See Decree Law N° 1,068 (1975).

17. See *CORFO* "Privatización de Empresas y Activos 1973–1978," (1980) and *Trabajo de Asesoría Económica al Congreso Nacional*, "Privatización de Empresas Públicas" (June, 1991), in collaboration with ILADES/Georgetown University and USEC, Unión Social de Empresarios y Ejecutivos Cristianos.

18. Chamber of Deputies, op. cit., p. 62.

19. Sáez, op. cit., p. 85.

20. Some noteworthy groups during this period are Grupo Cruzat-Larraín, Grupo BHC (Banco Hipotecario de Chile) and Grupo Claro. See Paredes R., and Sánchez J. M., "Organización Industrial y Grupos Económicos: el caso de Chile," *Departamento de Economía de la Universidad de Chile* (1994), p. 11.

21. Lüders y Hachette, op. cit.

22. Nankani, op. cit.

23. Valenzuela, M., "Reprivatización y Capitalismo en Chile," *Centro de Estudios Públicos* 33 (1989), p. 176.

24. *CORFO, Informative Leaflet* "Filiales CORFO: fundamentos y objetivos de la venta de acciones a las AFP," (1983).

25. The Banco de Chile was capitalized by the emission of shares for an amount of 28,000 million pesos, while the Banco de Santiago was capitalized in shares for 18,012 million, which equaled 141 percent and 96 percent of the capital and reserves of both banks, respectively. See Rosende F. and Reinstein A., "Estudio estado de avance del programa de reprivatización en Chile" (CEP), p. 262.

26. Report on consolidated financial statements as of December 31, 1989, by CORFO, presented for comparative purposes with the ones of 1988.

27. See reports by the Contraloría de desempeño CORFO, in *Cámara de Diputados* op. cit.

28. Nananki, op. cit.

29. It is worth pointing out that the GDP in 1990 was US$ 34.650.520.000. In 2016 numbers, where the GDP reached US$ 247.027.900.000 the asset loss related to the thirty alienated companies would amount to US$ 15.849 million.

30. When comparing them to the book value, capital losses related to privatizations would amount to nearly 69 percent. When comparing them to the market prices of the shares, it would reach 27 percent. When using present values, it would be 42 percent. See Marcel, M., "Privatización y Finanzas Públicas: el caso de Chile, 1985–1988," *Colección Estudios CIEPLAN* 26 (June, 1989).

31. Chamber of Deputies, op. cit.

32. Ibid.

33. Machiavello, G., "¿Quo Vadis, CORFO?" (Santiago: Editorial La Noria, 2003), p. 129.

34. Report by the División Auditoría Administrativa de la Contraloría General de la República Nº238/91, 09.12.91, p. 2.

35. Machaivello, op. cit, p. 117.

36. Ibid., p. 66.

37. Figueroa, J., "Lucía Hiriart sigue vendiendo propiedades que el Estado cedió a CEMA: ingresos suman $6.300 millones," *CIPER-Chile* (November 25, 2015).

38. Chamber of Deputies, op. cit.

39. Ffrench Davis, R. (Fourth edition, updated, and expanded), "Entre el Neoliberalismo y el Crecimiento con Equidad" (LOM Ediciones, 2005), chapter VII, p. 17.

40. Sáez, op. cit., p. 91.

41. See Fernando Dahse, op. cit., p. 147.

42. Ffrench Davis, op. cit., 2005, p. 40.

43. Calculated by the author, using data by Sáez, op. cit., p. 86.

44. Ffrench Davis, R. (Fourth edition, updated and expanded), "Entre el Neoliberalismo y el Crecimiento con Equidad" (LOM Ediciones, 2005), chapter VII, p. 8.

45. Dahse, F., "Mapa de la Extrema Riqueza: los grupos económicos y el proceso de concentración de capitales" (Editorial Aconcagua, Colección Lautaro, 1979), p. 174.

46. During the dictatorship, water, gas, and electricity tariffs went up considerably. See Marcel, op. cit., p. 29.

47. See the declaration by María Olivia Monckeber in Deputies Chamber Commission, op. cit.

48. See the chapter by Juan Pablo Bohoslavsky and Mariana Rulli "Unravelling financial assistance during Pinochet's regime" and the one by Naomi Roht-Arriaza "The delayed centrality of the economic dimension in transitional justice."

49. See Deputies Chamber Commission 2005, op. cit.

Section 4

REPRESSIVE RULES AND PROCEDURES FOR CORPORATIONS

Chapter 16

Union Law

Anti-Unionism as a Neoliberal Victory

Daniela Marzi Muñoz

INTRODUCTION

On December 29, 2014, a bill was presented to reform collective labor law in a bid to foster and strengthen labor unions, thus putting an end to the workplace relations system imposed by the dictatorship[1] through Law-Decrees in 1979. This design, somewhat militaristically labeled "Labor Plan" [Plan Laboral], was authored by José Piñera (minister of labor and social welfare, 1978–1980) and sought to take away power from workers' organizations while fully guaranteeing the right to property. This—fulfilled—objective, as we will see, continues to be the most untouched heritage of the dictatorship, since it has remained present and protected during the democratic governments that followed.

The reason for following the core guidelines of the Labor Plan is rather obvious: collective law is a juridical instrument that is directly connected with the possibility of limiting and rationalizing the right to property. Therefore, its preservation would have been impossible for a dramatic reason: the Chilean political class had undergone a phenomenon that Pasolini had labeled "acculturation,"[2] that is, a group's absorption of another group's values. In this case, it was the so-called center-left—represented by the Nueva Mayoría (New Majority) —that adopted the views of the sector currently known as Chile Vamos (Chile, Let's Go), which represents the right wing. This is not an inconsequential occurrence, given that neoliberalism "operates through culture, and culture 'is produced via changes in life styles, everyday life practices, and behaviors.'"[3]

After the start of the dictatorship,

unions lost the power to protect the living standards and the working conditions of their members. The military purged their leaders and activists, replacing democracy with gerontocracy by banning union elections and naming the most senior workers to take charge of the unions, which were reduced to associations that provided mutual support and funeral assistance, thus reverting not only the enormous increase in power that the workers had achieved during the revolution, but also the "conquests" resulting from decades of struggle.[4]

In this regard, it is necessary to point out that Chile has never normatively respected union autonomy since it has always tended to issue detailed regulations on how relations between workers' organizations and business owners should be conducted. In addition, as early as 1964, the most advanced doctrine held that the main right derived from the rebalancing effect of unions' and employers' bargaining power—the right to strike, ruled by the Labor Code of 1931 and Regulation Set No. 839—was curtailed by a heavy set of rules and excessive legal formalities, with no distinctions existing with respect to the concrete relevance of these legal demands, all of which could limit the juridical validity of the exercise of the right to strike.[5] Unions amassed truly relevant political, economic, and social power within the political context of the Unidad Popular government, during which the workers' cause became identified with the political direction taken by the country.[6] The Agrarian Reform constitutes another whole field of study within this process. This measure, aimed at increasing the dignity of peasants' living conditions, had the main normative effect of incorporating per-branch collective negotiation through Law No. 17.074 of 1968. This wide-ranging and deep impact of the process also explains the dictatorship's brutal retaliations in the countryside, considering that there was no real enemy there in terms of force.[7]

However, the Labor Plan's legal goal of making union freedom unfeasible becomes almost trivial compared to the massacre of union leaders, workers who were turned in to the authorities by their own companies, which have never been punished for taking part in crimes against humanity. This void, which reflects society's moral emptiness, reverberates once in a while; for instance, when it is pointed out that, amid the public outrage due to the toilet paper price fixing in which CMPC engaged in 2015, it is also worth remembering the state's collusion with the CMPC paper company to kill its workers and bury them with the quicklime that they produced (the Laja murders).[8] All these crimes have not only lacked judicial punishment: perhaps more damningly, there has been no social punishment.

The void produced by this purge was never filled.[9] Not only because of what death means in itself but also because the victims of the dictatorship were enclosed in black and white pictures, never remembered as social leaders in land occupations, industrial self-defense groups, and political parties, among other spheres.[10] What came later was a political class that began to share an ideology regarding unions.

THE LABOR PLAN

For some authors, the Labor Plan must be considered in connection with all the Law-Decrees that regulated work and made it precarious during the dictatorship, including those related to individual labor law,[11] mainly Decree-Law No. 2.200. This piece of legislation, for example, in a key field such as dismissal norms, eliminated compensations due to contract termination (except for severance, i.e., dismissal with no stated cause, which obligated employers to pay one month's wages) and introduced a battery of disciplinary reasons for dismissal related to the disturbance of the company's operations (Article 15 of Decree-Law No. 2.200). We differ from authors who consider that the Labor Plan encompasses all the norms leading to the precarization of work and social security because they overlook the words of the creator of the Labor Plan, who was fully aware that the core of a work system is defined by the regulation of collective power. "The other branch of labor law is collective labor law, and that is the area that the Labor Plan sought to cover. The Labor Plan has nothing to do with individual labor law. The Labor Plan is just a union plan; we did not label it so only because we thought those two words did not fit together well. The name 'Labor Plan' was much more beautiful."[12] In Chile, it is necessary to put forward a mass of arguments to explain a fact demonstrated by comparative experience: that unions, together with tax policies and power redistribution in society, are the main instrument of wealth distribution and may even be the most relevant one.[13]

Let us then examine the "four pillars" of the Labor Plan regarding union freedom: collective bargaining at the company level, non-paralyzing strikes, union plurality—allowing several organizations with a limited number of workers to coexist in one company—and union depoliticization.[14] These pillars achieved their goal of "producing the largest deconcentration of economic and social power ever to occur in Chile."[15]

Unions have no power because they have few affiliates who must face their employer directly and are permanently at risk of dismissal; this is not an effective clash of powers as in per-branch or per-industry negotiation, in which delegates of the most representative workers' organizations negotiate minimum goals for their sectors, which must then be applied in each company. Therefore, regardless of union affiliation rates, in countries such as Austria, Denmark, Finland, Germany, or Uruguay, the coverage of collective contracts is above 90 percent,[16] because unions negotiate for all workers who fall under the subjective sphere of applicability of the per-branch collective contract, which produces general effects.

Strikes do not paralyze companies since legal methods were created to make replacement possible, mainly the payment of a bonus for each replacement worker hired, and because strikes are self-tutored actions conducted by the workers of a given company within the context of the negotiation of a company-level contract. The Labor Plan forbids strikes for other reasons that may reflect the workers' freely determined collective interests and their autonomous course of action. In consequence, strikes become actions executed by a few workers within the boundaries of the employer's right to property and with only one recognized purpose: the negotiation of a collective contract as the final phase of a failed bargaining process.

Added to this is union atomization: not only because additional unions may form as long as the legal quorum is met but also because the regulations allow ad hoc groups, called bargaining groups, to negotiate a collective instrument enjoying the same rights and effects as a permanent union. However, once the contract has been signed, bargaining groups have the advantage of disappearing and leaving the employer without a valid interlocutor to defend its fulfillment.

Depoliticization is a logical consequence of the limitation of workers' collective interests: in this context of weakness, unions will barely be able to sign a collective contract addressing salaries and working conditions, being wholly unable to exert an influence at an economic, social, cultural, or political level.

This architecture, devised by José Piñera, was tested by history; therefore, the foundations of the system have remained nearly unchanged since the dictatorship. The reason is that the Labor Plan is not just another reform among the seven Modernizing Measures implemented by the dictatorship[17]: it is the most relevant for neoliberalism since it makes it possible to control power derived from property and free enterprise, while also operating as a wealth redistribution instrument.

Available figures show that the dictatorship's heritage in terms of unions remained stable and even became more entrenched: it should be noted that the highest union affiliation rate (34 percent) was recorded in 1973. In the mid-1980s, the union affiliation rate was comparable to that of the post-dictatorship period (a little over 10 percent). In 1991, the union affiliation rate reached 18.7 percent, with 11.7 percent of workers being covered by a collective contract. This peak was followed by a decline that bottomed out in 2013 when 14.2 percent of workers belonged to a union and 8.4 percent were covered by a collective contract.[18]

The following section covers some of the most significant elements of the new union legislation—Law 20940 of 2016—and several milestones in the discussion of this bill. All these aspects are aimed at blocking collective autonomy as a way of conducting labor relations and "recreate" the pillars of José Piñera's Labor Plan.

ASSIMILATION OF THE LABOR PLAN MODEL AND BACKWARD STEPS RESULTING FROM THE NEW LEGISLATION

The law adopts the deformity of the hyper-regulated Labor Plan. Hundreds of norms were replaced with an equivalent number of new concepts, thus preserving the pathological heteronomy and proceduralization of the Chilean collective relations system, which has drawn criticism from some legal scholars[19] for several years. The huge mass of norms introduced by the reform may lead to the false impression that a major transformation is underway, a common trait of reforms implemented since 1990;[20] however, as we will explain, structural elements are not modified and the exercise of the fundamental rights of union freedom is curtailed.

The Government's Firm Refusal to Discuss Per-Branch Collective Negotiation.

According to Article No. 65 of the Constitution, the president of the Republic has the sole prerogative to initiate a discussion on collective bargaining. The government clung on to this norm to refuse to discuss the nearly one hundred and fifty suggestions presented in the House of Representatives, including one about per-branch bargaining[21] advanced by Representatives Gabriel Boric and Giorgio Jackson, since all had been deemed to be unconstitutional. This assertion of unconstitutionality is a mere defense of the model since the Constitution of 1980 does not prohibit levels of bargaining; rather, it only ensures company-level collective bargaining (Article 19, No. 16). In this context, incorporating the law into other levels was a potential choice for the executive.

The implications of this refusal to discuss per-branch or industry-wide bargaining must be weighed considering what this measure consists in: each productive sector negotiates a contract that will apply to all workers in one field, without exception, because this collective contract does not only affect workers affiliated to a specific union but all those working in the field regulated by it.

To reach this agreement, unions and employers in each branch choose their representatives and set their starting points for bargaining. This results in baselines for each specific area. Thus, collective contracts operate as a per-sector minimum wage law, which grants them the flexibility that such laws lack. For instance, accountants in the mining sector will probably have a higher baseline salary in their collective contracts than those working in the hostelry, since sectors differ in terms of their economic ability to pay salaries or provide other types of working conditions. In Chile, this level of bargaining was regulated by the Peasant Unionization Law of 1967 (Law No. 16.625), as part of a general and novel process aimed at improving the living conditions of countryside workers. This process, focused on granting dignity to peasants, explains the dictatorship's enormous retaliations against peasants, which were more of an attempt to teach them an unforgettable lesson than a way of countering a real enemy force. The union reform of 2016 fails to grant these workers protection against dismissal or the right to strike, nor does it compel employers to negotiate in any way.

Evidently, this system has powerful wealth distribution effects and requires bargaining processes to activate in each negotiating camp to reach common positions.[22] Then, businesses and unions will negotiate with each other based on these previously defined positions. All these are beneficial processes for democracies, given that they indicate that the state allows relevant social agents—such as those who participate in labor relations in capitalist economies—to establish their norms.

A key aspect of per-branch bargaining is that unions can reach all workers since all companies must abide by the baselines established by the contract signed by their sector. This means that the cost of labor becomes a nonfactor in competition among businesses since they must all start from the same baseline.

Beyond this quick list of social benefits of per-branch collective bargaining that our system will continue to leave out even after the 2016 reform, the choice to preserve company-level collective bargaining in the text of the reform contradicts article 4 of ILO Convention No. 98,[23] since it did not modify norms to allow and guarantee social actors to freely determine the level of the collective bargaining that they wish to conduct, which would allow per-branch bargaining and any other approach that all parties deem adequate considering their needs and negotiation capabilities.[24] Instead, in line with the 1979 Labor Plan, the reform kept collective bargaining at the company level—the most irrelevant one since it is where workers have the least power.

The Ideological Debate on Unions in Small Businesses

The labor reform increased the quorums for establishing unions in companies with fifty or fewer workers. Before the reform, a union could be established by eight workers; now, according to the third section of Article No. 227 of the Labor Code, unions with eight members may be created as long as they represent 50 percent of all the workers in a company. This innovation, which makes it more difficult for workers to create company unions, the main organizations in our system, was not part of the original project; rather, it was proposed by a group of "pro-SME" legislators[25] with the stated objective of freeing small companies from unions. This aim is ideologically consistent with the rejection of per-branch negotiation because it is the main instrument that makes it possible for the effects of collective bargaining to reach smaller companies in foreign systems.

However, if one digs a little deeper, it becomes clear that the discourse of freeing small enterprises from unions is ideological in the worst possible way: it is an empty message of pure anti-unionism. This view is supported by the fact that the quorum increase is not a concrete measure for a pervasive problem in Chile: there are very few unions with eight members or fewer in small companies. A look at the data shows that Chilean unions have "88 workers on average, a figure that is common to all union types."[26] This is perfectly reasonable from the perspective of the workers organizing themselves since unions with a handful of members are wholly incapable of acting and therefore pointless. Therefore, this is yet another manifestation of the anti-union discourse employed by pro-SME legislators—representing all political sectors—during the discussion of the reform, which focused on hindering the creation of workers' organizations and only stood for anti-unionism.

A Major Goal, Betrayed: The Absolute Prohibition of Hiring Replacement Workers during Strikes.

Before the text of the reform of collective labor law became known in 2014, there was a belief that worker replacement during strikes would finally be prohibited, after being included in Patricio Aylwin's 1989 presidential platform.[27] If this promise had been fulfilled, it would have emerged as an unquestionable achievement, because unions would have gained the power to exercise their right to strike effectively, thus boosting their ability to defend workers.

However, the project immediately weakened that prohibition by incorporating minimum services to prevent current and irreparable damage to company property (art. 359 of the Labor Code). This creation of Chilean legislators is at odds with the right to strike, which can be defined as "any collective action undertaken by workers aimed at altering the productive process, including the total and planned suspension of the productive process, as well as any behaviors that disrupt this process; in the absence of express normative restrictions, the aims of these measures are free for workers to choose, and can include general economic goals or purely political ones."[28] Importantly, damage as a means of exerting pressure is the central characteristic[29] of the right to strike. This "right to damage," which sounds repulsive, is a strictly logical matter, given that strikes, which operate through a threat of damage, fall apart if this threat disappears.

Article no. 359, added to the Labor Code as part of the 2016 reform, states the following with respect to minimum services: "the union negotiation committee will be required to provide the staff necessary to protect the company's material goods and premises and prevent accidents, while also guaranteeing the purveyance of public utility services, meeting the population's basic needs, including those related to people's life, safety, or health, and preventing environmental or sanitary damages." The main purpose of this norm had always been the creation of minimum services for protecting property, which is at odds with the very point of strikes—which should be able to harm production—however, this time the method involves not external but internal replacement workers, which the striking union is forced to provide through a procedure established by the law. This procedure has enormous potential for judicialization.[30]

To judicialize is "to employ judicial methods to address an issue that could be solved differently, generally through political means."[31] Union relations are meaningful only if they are autonomous and, as pointed out nearly one hundred years ago,

> no one can deny the advantages of autonomy. The State is relieved of their weight. Juridical development becomes more mobile and flexible. The distance between needs and juridical regulation becomes shorter. Now, it is also possible to create norms without the extra step of involving the State. This direct path increases the expressive capabilities of law. It delves deeper into the human-life relationships observed, focusing on their concrete diversity rather than on their abstract forms. Therefore, autonomous labor law must be perfected: it must rank first within the labor legislation of the future.[32]

It is in this context that we speak of the judicialization promoted by legislators, who had promised to modernize and strengthen union relations. Since legislators did not choose autonomy, the increase in court involvement only compounded this pathological proceduralization, heteronomy, and lack of dynamism already mentioned in this chapter (given that judicialization plays a major role within the labor reform).[33] This choice preserved the core objective of the Labor Plan: stripping workers of economic, political, and social power. And in consequence, it countered the original idea: labor law, through collective means, overcame the typical search for instruments capable of solving individual controversies, and created a productive technique for governing social ties, making an effective clash of powers possible.[34] The project was and is decidedly political; as noted by Hugo Sinzheimer, the main German labor law specialist of the early twentieth century, it was about the state delegating the legislative function to workers, who should be free to define the rules that will bind them to their employers.[35]

NEGOTIATING GROUPS: AN OBSESSION WITH AN ANTI-UNION PRACTICE

Constitutional Tribunal (CT) sentence No. 3016 (3026)-16-CPT, issued on May 9, 2016, addressed several aspects reported by several right-wing senators who expected them to be declared unconstitutional. This is a long ruling that touches upon multiple topics, expressed through decision-aligned votes and several dissident votes; therefore, the following observations will only refer to union priority. This is a strange case of a step forward intended neither by the government nor by the senators who requested the CT to issue a ruling; rather, it was an unexpected judicial effect of the CT ruling itself.

Union priority, in the government's original proposal, meant that unions would adopt the collective form that the law recognizes to conduct a collective bargaining process, and that only in the absence of a union would a negotiating group be able to participate in the bargaining process. This element was labeled the "heart" of the project by the government.

Negotiating groups first appeared in 1979, as a result of the Labor Plan. Before the 2016 reform, negotiating groups were lightly regulated, being legally designed bodies with the specific aim of allowing organizations other than unions to exercise one of their most relevant rights: collective bargaining. In Chile, collective bargaining at the company level is practically the only right that unions can exert somewhat effectively since negotiations of this type are the procedure to which the right to strike is expressly linked.

Although the senators' request described the negotiating group as having a constitutional presence, even if we consider the intentions of the writers of the Constitution, it is clear that neither the minutes of the Ortúzar Commission[36] nor the text of the Constitution mention them. These documents only discuss unions, which is the term used in the Constitution.

Nevertheless, the volume of the arguments for and against negotiating groups in the CT ruling suggests that the Constitution is being confused with the Labor Plan. The senators' insistence on giving negotiating groups constitutional presence, which the CT agreed on, in no way means that these groups have some degree of constitutional reach: this is merely an obsession grounded in the fact that this is a legal anti-union practice. This legal willingness to accept manifestations of union freedom in associations other than unions is chiefly because negotiating groups are transient. These groups disappear when the bargaining process is over. This issue is compounded by the fact that the equality between the rights of negotiating groups and those of unions is indicative of competition, which to some degree discourages unionization. We must point out that this is only true to some degree, as recent studies demonstrate that the rate of bargaining processes conducted by negotiating groups is very low in Chile, which in and of itself refutes the notion that this is a major issue in our legislation.[37]

However, the CT deemed unconstitutional all the norms awarding these groups collective bargaining rights in the absence of a union, which resulted in the elimination of the whole set of articles that referred to negotiating groups. It was at this point that full union priority was born. Even the dissident vote of Ministers Carmona, García, Hernández, and Pozo announces this, pointing out the following in bold type: "The sentence, paradoxically, supports a non-existent organization: negotiating groups have already disappeared" (dissident vote c.11), which meant that the government and the opposition were left in an unwanted situation. Since the legislators did not advance a new proposal regarding negotiating groups, this body disappeared due to being absent from all the norms in the new set of regulations.

This absolute union priority—that is, the elimination of the negotiating groups created by José Piñera's Labor Plan through decree-laws during the dictatorship—was so unwanted by the government and the "acculturated" part of the opposition, given their homogeneous aim of keeping workers radically powerless, that it was initially not mentioned by Bachelet's government as one of the advances achieved through the new union law. This attitude only changed after the government became the opposition with Sebastián Piñera's victory and accession in March 2018. After the start of the new government, on July 27, 2018, the Labor Agency issued Ordinary Ruling No. 3839/33, modifying the prior doctrine and acknowledging negotiating groups' right to sign collective contracts, thus encroaching on legislators' competences. It was only at this point that the authors of the union reform decided to defend union priority as a fruit of their work. Their attitude was ambiguous even though the elimination of negotiating groups was only a partial step forward: it is not comparable to per-branch collective bargaining or the effective right to strike.

CONCLUSION

Overcoming the dictatorship's heritage in a key field for the distribution of wealth and political, economic, and social power in a capitalist country necessarily involves going back to the beginning, that is, returning to political thinking that is seriously committed to workers and which can pave the way for a model of union relations aligned with these convictions.

A review of the key elements of the work relations system under the dictatorship (union atomization, non-paralyzing strikes, and depoliticization, all which had the clearly stated aim of reducing workers' power), reveals that it became cherished by the whole political class that emerged after the return to democracy. Its many norms have been modified over and over, but its foundations remain untouched. This is not strange, but reasonable, since the aims that inspired the economic paradigm have not been changed: the political world does not intend to create democratic mechanisms for distributing wealth and power in society.

This was the heritage that the political class gladly accepted from 1990 onward, and which some have attempted to appreciate in isolation from the death of union and social leaders. But this is impossible because the victims were the carriers of a political project in which the subordinate classes were expected to gain an increasingly relevant and effective degree of participation in democracy. That was the reason for its demise. And these ideas play a decisive role in the business world, particularly with respect to workers, since their working conditions—and thus their living conditions—are at stake. In consequence, given these historical facts, the political world must take a stand not only regarding the crimes of the dictatorship but also regarding the current validity of the victims' project.

NOTES

1. Decree-Laws No. 2756 and 2758 (1979).
2. Regarding the meaning of this term as the main victory of capitalism due to the social and cultural homogenization that it has produced among both the left and the right wing alike, see Pier Paolo Pasolini, *Scritti corsari*. Garzanti, 2015.
3. Mary Luz Estupiñán, *El ABC del neoliberalismo*. Communes, 2016.
4. Peter Winn, *La revolución chilena*. LOM ediciones, 2013.
5. Arnoldo Camu, *Estudio crítico de la huelga*. Editorial Jurídica, 1964.
6. To gauge this phenomenon, readers may consult Peter Winn, *Tejedores de la revolución. Los trabajadores de Yarur y la vía chilena al socialismo* (LOM, 2004). The Agrarian Reform constitutes another whole field of study. This measure, aimed at increasing the dignity of peasants' living conditions, had the main normative effect of incorporating per-branch collective negotiation. This wide-ranging and deep impact of the process also explains the dictatorship's brutal retaliations in the countryside, considering that there was no real enemy there in terms of force. Le Monde Diplomatique recently devoted a special number to this whole process: *Reforma Agraria* (Editorial Aún creemos en los sueños, 2017).
7. Le Monde Diplomatique recently devoted a special number to this whole process (*Reforma Agraria*) which contains an article on Law No. 17.074 (1968) by José Luis Ugarte: "Una pequeña y poderosa luz en el camino" (Editorial Aún creemos en los sueños, 2017).

8. See Javier Rebolledo, "Los crímenes de Laja y la Papelera: preguntas para Eliodoro Matte," column published on November 6, 2016, in El Mostrador (electronic newspaper). Shortened web link: <https://bit.ly/2NRE1IM>. This moral deterioration has had several concrete manifestations in the institutional domain. For instance, Rosa Egnem, the same court secretary who concealed the complaint filed by Laja workers, was named minister to the Labor Hall of the Supreme Court in 2009, the same period during which this Hall had been persistently criticized due to its rulings against workers. This situation was only remedied in 2014 when new members were chosen and nearly seventy criteria changed in less than a year. Although concealing a complaint during the dictatorship is understandable though ethically exceptionable human action, criticism has focused on the fact that this official was nevertheless rewarded by elevating her to the top of the judicial system. See Macarena Segovia "Rosa Egnem: la Ministra de la Corte Suprema salpicada por el caso Masacre de Laja que fue nombrada por Bachelet," http://www.elmostrador.cl/noticias/pais/2015/08/20/rosa-egnem-la-ministra-de-la-corte-suprema-salpicada-por-el-caso-masacre-de-laja-que-fue-nombrada-por-bachelet/.

9. This void also translates into figures, as there are no union membership records between 1973 and 1979 because unions were declared illegal (see Patrizio Tonelli, *Modelos de Relaciones Laborales y Reforma Laboral. Reflexiones entre poder sindical e intervención legislativa*. Fundación Sol, 2015).

10. For a more detailed analysis of the situation of workers in Chile before and during the dictatorship, see Peter Winn's chapter in this same volume.

11. Irene Rojas, *El Derecho del Trabajo en Chile. Su formación histórica y el control de la autonomía colectiva* (Legalpublishing, 2016).

12. José Piñera, *La revolución laboral en Chile*. Zigzag, 1990.

13. To establish data-based comparisons, the work carried out by Fundación Sol has been invaluable. In OECD countries such as France, Belgium, and Austria, as well as in Uruguay, 90 percent of workers bargain collectively. In Argentina and Brazil, about 60 percent of workers do so. In Germany, 59 percent of the workforce engage in collective bargaining. Chile displays the lowest rate: 8 percent (only surpassed by Mexico). We chose examples of strong economies in their geographical areas. See Marco Kremerman and Gonzalo Durpan, *Sindicatos y negociación colectiva*. Fundación Sol, 2015.

14. Fundación Sol, *Reforma Laboral. ¿Pone fin al Plan Laboral de la Dictadura o lo consolida?* Fundación Sol, 2016.

15. José Piñera's ideas as cited by Manuel Gárate, *La revolución capitalista de Chile (1973-2003)*. Ediciones Alberto Hurtado, 2012.

16. Patrizio Tonelli, *Modelos de Relaciones Laborales y Reforma Laboral. Reflexiones entre poder sindical e intervención legislativa*. Fundación Sol, 2015.

17. The "restructuring measures" devised by José Piñera in the fields of health care, social security, education, the judicial system, State administration, and union relations. This social transformation plan stands out because it came ten years before the guidelines of the Washington Consensus, thus making Chile a pioneer of neoliberalism. On this subject, readers can consult two Fundación Sol documents produced by Narbona, Karina: *Antecedentes del Modelo de Relaciones Laborales*

Chileno (Fundación Sol, 2015) and *Reforma Laboral. ¿Pone fin al Plan Laboral de la Dictadura o lo consolida?* (Fundación Sol, 2016).

18. See <http://www.fundacionsol.cl/graficos/tasa-de-sindicalizacion-y-negociacion-colectiva-en-chile-1991-2013/>.

19. With regard to this criticism, readers can consult, among other sources, Irene Rojas, "Las reformas laborales al modelo normativo de negociación colectiva del Plan Laboral" (*Revista Ius et Praxis*, Vol. 13, Nº 2, 2007); Sergio Gamonal, *Derecho Colectivo del Trabajo.* LexisNexis, 2007; and Eduardo Caamaño & José Ugarte Cataldo, *Negociación Colectiva y Libertad Sindical. Un enfoque crítico.* Legalpublishing, 2008.

20. Irene Rojas, *El Derecho del Trabajo en Chile. Su formación histórica y el control de la autonomía colectiva.* Legal Publishing, 2016.

21. Analyzed by the Labor Committee on April 14, 2015, and declared unconstitutional by the President of the Committee, Communist Party Representative Lautaro Carmona. See http://www.prosindical.cl/reforma-laboral-ix-analisis-de-libro-iii-anticipa-declaracion-de-inadmisibilidad-de-negociacion-por-rama/.

22. See foreign system data in Patrizio Tonelli, *Modelos de Relaciones Laborales y Reforma Laboral. Reflexiones entre poder sindical e intervención legislativa.* Fundación Sol, 2015.

23. "Art. 4: Measures must be adopted considering the country's situation, whenever necessary, to stimulate and encourage among employers and employers' organizations, as well as among workers' organizations, the full development and use of voluntary bargaining procedures, in order to regulate employment conditions through collective contracts."

24. Sergio Gamonal, *Derecho Colectivo del Trabajo*. LexisNexis, 2007.

25. Representing all political sectors, it comprised Eugenio Tuma (PPD), Andrés Zaldívar (DC), Jorge Pizarro (DC), Ignacio Walker (DC), Andrés Allamand (RN), and Hernán Larraín (UDI).

26. Irene Rojas, El Derecho del Trabajo en Chile. Su formación histórica y el control de la autonomía colectiva. Legalpublishing, 2016.

27. Cited by José Luis Ugarte, "El trabajo en la Constitución chilena," in *La constitución chilena.* LOM, 2015.

28. José Luis Ugarte, *Huelga y Derecho* (Legalpublishing, 2016).

29. José Luis Ugarte, *Huelga y Derecho* (Legalpublishing, 2016).

30. As we explain in Daniela Marzi Muñoz "Observaciones sobre la judicialización de las relaciones colectivas: en las antípodas de la autonomía" (*Revista Laboral y de la Seguridad Social*, Vol. 4, Nº 2, 2016).

31. First definition in the RAE Dictionary.

32. Hugo Sinzheimer, "El perfeccionamiento del Derecho del Trabajo," *Crisis económica y Derecho del Trabajo. Cinco estudios sobre la problemática humana y conceptual del Derecho del Trabajo* (Servicio de Publicaciones Ministerio del Trabajo y Seguridad Social, 1948).

33. In connection with the right to strike, we can mention the following norms: determination of companies excluded from the right to strike (articles 362 and 402 of the Labor Code); lockout or employer-mandated closure (article 354 of the Labor

Code); order to resume production (article 363 of the Labor Code); right to information (article 319 of the Labor Code); and ability to impugn the list of workers with the right to negotiate (article 339 of the Labor Code), which is naturally complemented by the regime of anti-union practices. Regarding the latter, readers are advised to consult the analysis and criticism published by César Toledo, *Reforma al Derecho Colectivo del Trabajo*, "Análisis crítico de la sanción de las prácticas antisindicales en la Ley Nº 20.940" (Legalpublishing, 2016).

34. Luca Nogler, "La scienza giuridica italiana tra il 1901 e il 1960 e Hugo Sinzheimer". *Giornale di diritto del lavoro e di relazioni industriali*, 2001.

35. Hugo Sinzheimer, *La lucha por el nuevo derecho del Trabajo*. Edeval, 2017.

36. Available at: https://www.leychile.cl/Consulta/antecedentes_const_1980.

37. ENCLA 2011 shows that only 9.5 percent of companies with a union have signed a collective contract with a negotiating group and that 0.4 percent of those without a union have signed a collective contract with a negotiating group.

Chapter 17

"The Employers Do What They Want With Us"

Unions and Workers under the Pinochet Dictatorship

Ángela Vergara and Peter Winn

INTRODUCTION

The military coup of September 11, 1973, marked a before and after in the lives of Chile's workers and their labor movement. Between 1964 and 1973, labor rights were expanded considerably, including important advances such as the law permitting agricultural unions. During the Allende government, workers won more power than ever before in Chile. At the local level, blue- and white-collar workers participated in the production committees and administrative councils of the nationalized enterprises. They also created Vigilance Committees in private-sector enterprises to make sure that the owners did not sabotage production. At the national level, the Central Única de Trabajadores (CUT), the dominant labor confederation, represented nearly two-thirds of the unions in 1970, acquired legal recognition, and strengthened the participation of unions in national politics and policies. The legitimacy of the labor movement was also reflected in an increase in unionization, from 24 percent to 35 percent, the highest in Chilean history, in only three years from 1970 to 1973.[1] These advances called into question the bases of the elite's economic and social power and, with the nationalizations, the sanctity of private property as well. In response, the military Junta and Chile's business class used every means they had to repress, dismantle, and depoliticize the labor movement.

This chapter examines the history of the workers and their unions during the civil–military dictatorship (1973–1989). This history demonstrates the intimate relationship between the political repression, the legal restructuring of the labor movement, and the imposition of a new economic model that excluded most Chileans. Between 1973 and 1975, a series of proclamations and decree-laws dismantled even the most basic labor rights, allowing employers to exercise iron control over their workers. The repression and the fear of being fired discouraged union activity, which was reduced to a minimum. Years later, Sergio de Castro, Treasury Minister from 1977 and 1980 and the dictatorship's chief economist, summarized crudely the relationship between increases in productivity, labor discipline, and repression: "With a gun in their backs, everybody works."[2] In the middle of the decade of the 1970s, the regime and its allies delineated the economic model with increased clarity. With regard to unions, they implemented a new "Labor Plan." The economic crisis at the start of the 1980s and the lack of political rights may have motivated a massive social response that even called into question the future of the dictatorship. But the neoliberal model had deeper roots.

THE MILITARY COUP, PROCLAMATIONS, AND DECREE-LAWS: THE INITIAL REPRESSION OF THE LABOR MOVEMENT

The experiences of workers during the coup and its immediate aftermath were varied, reflecting the diversity of political and local trajectories. For most workers, the coup put an end to their way of relating to their work, their coworkers, their unions, and politics. The CUT had asked workers to occupy their workplace in case of a coup. In contrast with the failed coup attempt of June 1973, on September 11 many workers did not have time to even get to their workplace in a city that was fast being occupied by the military. In the case of the textile enterprise Ex-Yarur, located across the street from an army regiment, the Workers Assembly voted to send the workers home to prevent a worse repression. In contrast, in the Sumar textile mill, the workers, together with the residents of the Población La Legua and the military apparatus of Allende's Socialist party, resisted the military attack with some initial success, while a group of miners in the El Salvador copper mine barricaded themselves inside the mine with explosives. Despite these attempts to resist, many of them symbolic, by the end of the day the military junta controlled the country and imposed a state of siege and a curfew.

One of the primary objectives of the governing Junta was to control the centers of production, especially those that had been taken over by their workers and nationalized during the government of Popular Unity. Proclamations (*bandos*) 31 and 36 (September 1973) and Decree-Law 198 (December 1973) authorized firing workers for political reasons. The military established an iron labor discipline and suspended labor rights, including the most fundamental union rights, such as the right to elect union leaders, the right to collective bargaining, and the right to strike. These proclamations and decrees substantially eroded the historic rights of Chilean workers, modifying in practice the 1931 Labor Code.[3] So did the repression. The military occupied all the enterprises that had been nationalized under Allende, interrogating their workers and pressuring them to collaborate. Around 10 percent of the workers in those enterprises were fired for political reasons before those enterprises were reprivatized, usually by returning them to their old owners.

Oral testimonies, human rights reports, and workers' memories tell of the dramatic impact of these measures on the daily lives of workers and their families. They also tell of strategies of survival, adaptation, and resistance that workers developed during the seventeen-year dictatorship. Thousands of workers were detained, tortured, disappeared, or forced into exile, generally with minimal economic resources.[4] The many proclamations and decrees facilitated the firing of union leaders, worker activists, and leftist cadres, many of whom were blacklisted and would never have secure jobs again.[5] The physical repression, the threats, and the constant smearing of the victims by both state agents and private employers created an atmosphere of fear and disorientation among the workers. Within a context of economic crisis and without either labor rights or human rights, working conditions deteriorated rapidly and real wages fell brutally.[6] Many survived on a starvation diet of bread, onions, and tea.

One of the most complex issues was the atomization of the labor movement, including the loss of channels of communication between national and local union leaders and rank-and-file workers, and the destruction of the political networks that historically had supported union demands. Claiming that unions and confederations had been converted into instruments of leftist political parties and the Popular Unity government, the Junta promised to "restore true unionism." Especially tenacious was the persecution of the CUT, including its legal dissolution and the confiscation of its property. The military leaders viewed the CUT as a "palpable demonstration of this revolutionary-political denaturalization in union matters."[7] Although not all the union federations were dissolved or lost their official recognition, all were subject to government intervention, and their activities and resources were strictly limited. For a labor movement that had depended traditionally on its links with political parties, congress, and mayors and the mediation of the state, the new norms changed the power dynamics within the workplace, especially in medium and small enterprises.[8]

The suspension of labor rights facilitated the demobilization of even the most organized sectors of the working class. Between 1973 and 1975, union activity was reduced to a minimum, and although the statistics of union membership do not show a big drop, a large percentage of the unions remained inactive and only maintained the minimal activities required by law.[9] Those who had the nerve to call for a strike were fired, accused of sabotage, and, in many cases, processed by the military courts and war councils. This was the case of the fourteen activists working in the construction of the Santiago Metro, who organized a strike of 195 workers in November, 1973.[10] Despite the fear and the repression, some unions continued to function, adjusting their conduct to the new norms imposed by the dictatorship.[11] Aída Moreno Valenzuela, officer of a union of domestic workers, recalled that "in spite of the limitations of that era, we continued having [union meetings], for which we had to ask the government of Santiago for permission each month, saying what we would discuss."[12] Some workers even went to the state labor inspection offices, although with little success. One electrician at the Pizarreño factory recalled that after being detained in the National Stadium, his employer forced him to resign from his job "voluntarily." Together with other coworkers in the same situation, "we continued to fight . . . at the [State] labor Inspection, but it was all useless."[13]

Beginning in 1975, the goal of the repression of the labor movement emerged more clearly: to support the neoliberal economic reforms. The Plan for Economic Recovery, better known as "shock medicine," was the strategy of the *Chicago Boys*: liberalized economic activity and drastically reduced government expenditures. These shock policies and the lack of labor and political rights worsened the exploitation of the workers, increasing poverty, vulnerability, and inequality. The situation became intolerable, even for sectors that had tried to maintain a dialogue with the dictatorship. In December 1975, centrist labor leaders such as Manuel Bustos, Tucapel Jiménez, and Eduardo Ríos formed the Group of Ten, and in the months that followed, through declarations and published open "letters," they demanded a restoration of labor rights.[14] In the following years, activist workers, local union officers, and national labor leaders articulated a discourse that was increasingly critical of the dictatorship and which denounced not only the entangled legal and institutional complex that restricted union and political activity but also the difficult economic situation that afflicted workers and their families.

THE LABOR PLAN, 1979–1981

At the end of the decade of the 1970s, Chile's businesspeople celebrated the end of the crisis, proclaiming euphorically that neoliberal policies had created "an economic miracle" that would give every Chilean a car and a better future.[15] In this optimistic context, the dictatorship rewrote, between 1979 and 1981, the rules that governed the labor market and labor relations, replacing the Labor Code of 1931 with a new uneven playing field that favored private-sector capitalists over workers and unions. The timing of the Labor Plan was not accidental. It reflected the convergence of multiple factors. In the first place, Chile's businesspeople and their Chicago Boy advisers feared that because the reforms that supported their "economic miracle" had been dictated by a de facto regime, they lacked legitimacy and could be rapidly reversed by a democratic government. For that reason, it was necessary to institutionalize these reforms through a new constitution (1980) and the so-called Seven Modernizations, which included reforms of the pension system as well as reforms of medical care, education, state administration, agriculture, and labor. These neoliberal reforms confirmed the process of economic transformation begun in 1973 that sought to establish the market as the only arbiter of Chile's economy and society and to commercialize what had been social rights.

There was also a more immediate and urgent reason to reform the Labor Code in 1979: growing international pressure threatened to become a nightmare for the dictatorship and its business allies. Pinochet shared the virulent anti-communism of Henry Kissinger and the Richard Nixon and Gerald Ford administrations. But, in 1979, the government of Jimmy Carter represented a turn in U.S. foreign policy and increased pressure on the Chilean Junta, especially with regard to human rights.[16] Moreover, with the fading of the revolutionary threat in Chile and the shift of centrist labor leaders from supporting the dictatorship to opposing it, the AFL-CIO, the biggest U.S. labor confederation, became increasingly impatient with the suppression of labor rights in Chile. In 1978, an AFL-CIO delegation visited Chile and warned Pinochet that he was risking international sanctions if labor rights were not restored. The response of Pinochet was to dissolve and confiscate the property of seven national labor federations, representing some 400 local unions with 113,000 workers, and to call a snap election with only four-days' notice in October 1978.[17] Pinochet's arrogance infuriated the AFL-CIO, and the powerful U.S. labor confederation threatened to call for an international boycott of Chilean exports and imports, a nightmare scenario for Chile's military government and their Chicago Boy advisers.

In this context, on December 26, 1978, the Junta named José Piñera, a Harvard-educated engineer and brother of a future president, as Labor Minister. His mission was to prevent an international boycott of Chilean exports and design and implement a neoliberal labor code. Unlike the 1931 Labor Code, Piñera's Labor Plan was not a unified code. Rather it was a group of laws decreed by the Junta between 1978 and 1981. The new regulations represented a rolling back of the rights won by Chile's workers during the twentieth century and adapted working conditions to the exigencies of a neoliberal economy.

The Labor Plan transformed the two pillars of labor relations: the individual work contract and union organization. In July 1978, Decree-Law 2000 made work contracts and management more flexible and jobs less secure, making it easier, faster, and cheaper to fire workers—with or without cause—or to transfer them from one job to another. Then, in June 1979, Decree-Laws 2756 and 2758 weakened Chile's unions by authorizing the formation of parallel unions, making union membership voluntary, and dividing unions into four categories of unions: enterprise, inter-enterprise, construction workers, and self-employed workers. The new regulations only allowed the enterprise unions to engage in collective bargaining and to strike and prohibited sectoral accords and agreements that could interfere with the power of management to direct the enterprise—a clear response to the history of workers' participation in Allende's Chile.[18]

At the same time, the Labor Plan made it almost impossible to go on strike and to win a strike. Only the enterprise unions could declare a legal strike, but it could be prohibited if in the government's view it threatened Chile's national security. The decrees included obstacles that were alien to Chilean labor law: the enterprise could contract strikebreakers during the length of the conflict, and after the first month of the strike it could hire back enterprise workers who wanted to negotiate an individual contract with the enterprise and end their participation in the strike. Moreover, if the strike continued after fifty-nine days, it was assumed that the workers had all resigned and could be fired without severance pay, which in Chile had been considerable: a month's salary for every year served at the same enterprise, which was now limited to a top severance pay of five months, even for firing without cause.[19]

Equally important was what the Labor Plan left out. The ending of the Labor Courts eliminated a space that had traditionally offered workers a counterweight to the power of business. The reduction in the number of labor inspectors and their deliberately low salaries weakened the other traditional state counterweight. Taken together, the measures of the Labor Plan tilted the labor relations playing field strongly in favor of owners and managers, leaving the workers and their unions vulnerable both to the mysterious mechanisms of the market and the arbitrary decisions of their bosses. Arturo Martínez, a longtime Socialist activist and future president of a new CUT, concluded that the Labor Plan was "made by a businessman for businesspeople."[20]

Although the Labor Plan was conceived behind closed doors, which labor leaders denounced, and against the workers and labor leaders, who were not consulted, it also opened up spaces for unions, restarted union activity, and allowed labor leaders to reconstruct old union networks. If the sudden scheduling in October 1978 of union elections took workers by surprise, the electoral process did enable a renewal of union leaders for the first time since 1973 and the emergence of new leaders opposed to the dictatorship, many of whom would play major roles in the struggle for democracy and the reunification of the labor movement. The new enterprise unions also began to participate in collective bargaining and the calling of legal strikes. During the first two years under the Labor Plan (1979–1980), there were 102 legal strikes, including the emblematic strike at Textil Panal.[21] Nevertheless, the results of collective bargaining were not necessarily favorable to the workers, as one union officer of that era recalled: "We entered those negotiations confronting new laws and the specter of unemployment, and with union members full of fear."[22] Parallel to these new forms of union struggle, workers continued their earlier forms of resistance, from work slowdowns and fasts to dumping trays and banging spoons at lunch in the enterprise cafeteria. These forms of "illegal" resistance were particularly prevalent where unions could not bargain collectively under the new Labor Plan. At the national level, labor leaders continued to look for spaces and strategies for convergence and reunification, while maintaining their criticism of the dictatorship and its Labor Plan in public declarations and their calls for days of national protest starting in 1983.

Toward the end of 1980, a strike in Textil Panal, a large enterprise owned by the Galmes family, which also owned the big Almacenes Paris department store, put the Labor Plan to the test. The strike was successful in its terms and demonstrated the creativity and capacity to organize the workers and their leaders, as well as the solidarity networks that still existed in the union world. When the enterprise rejected the union's demands for an improvement in wages, contracts, and working conditions, the roughly 1500 workers voted to strike legally. The election of a new union leadership in 1980, that was critical of the conciliatory stance of the previous leaders, promoted a more combative attitude.

The conflict lasted the fifty-nine days permitted by the new Labor Plan, and the workers remained united and did not allow themselves to be replaced by strikebreakers. The striking Panal workers received massive support from other workers, unions, and social movements, who recognized the symbolic importance of the Panal struggle, as did emblematic labor leaders such as Clotario Blest, the Catholic Church, and the Communist Party. The solidarity aid was so ample that strikers could maintain their living standards and the conflict came to be known as the "millionaire strike." The strike committees organized by the union functioned well, creating a broad base that transcended party politics and enabled the Panal leaders to resist efforts by political groups, primarily the Communist party and the MIR, to control the conflict for their own political ends.[23]

What the workers did not know was that the Chilean cotton textile industry was in a crisis so deep that Juan Naveillan, the Chicago Boy manager of Panal and adviser to the Textile Committee of the CORFO, the government development agency, deliberately provoked the strike with his intransigence in the collective bargaining and used the strike to restructure the cotton textile industry. When the blue-collar workers returned to the Panal factories heads held high after striking for fifty-nine days, they were all fired and the Panal textile mills were closed down. The strike enabled Naveillan to fire its 1500 workers efficiently and cheaply, two neoliberal values. Later, some of Panal's best technicians and most modern machinery would be sent to Machasa (Manufacturas Chilenas de Algodón), a new textile enterprise from the fusion of the capital and factories of Panal with the two Yarur-owned enterprises, Yarur and Caupolicán—the three dinosaurs—as Naveillan was fond of calling them. As part of the deal, Amador Yarur received a US$ 40 million loan from the State Bank to enable him to modernize Machasa. Nevertheless, when Machasa declared bankruptcy in 1982, no major investments in modernization had taken place and the US$ 40 million had disappeared.

In this way, the mass firings and closing of Panal and the fusion of textile capital made it possible to increase the productivity of an industry that was suffering the neoliberal opening of the Chilean economy and the flood of cheap imports from Asia that was the result. During the years of economic crisis in the 1980s, the industrialists—aided by the Labor Plan and their links to the dictatorship—even benefitted from their enterprises going bankrupt, and it was their workers who paid the costs of the crisis. In these legal and economic circumstances, workers' strikes benefitted their bosses. As one metallurgical union leader attested: "our strikes were encouraged by our boss . . . he told us 'go on strike. I have no money to pay you with.'"[24] In practice, although the Panal strike had demonstrated that Chilean workers were capable of declaring a legal strike and sustaining it for the fifty-nine-day limit under the new Labor Plan, the outcome of that strike and other labor conflicts of the era demonstrated that the workers were victims of a neoliberal economy that they could not control. As Patricia Coñoman—the combative Communist president of the CONTEXTIL union confederation in the 1990s—put it, contrasting her era to the past: "The strike no longer serves the interests of the workers."[25]

THE 1980S: CRISIS, PROTESTS, AND THE TRANSITION TO DEMOCRACY

Panal workers were not the only ones to lose their jobs in the 1980s recession. The financial crisis that put an end to the false Chilean neoliberal miracle set off a deep recession during 1982–1983, during which the economy *shrank* by 14 percent, unemployment reached 30 percent, and the public debt exceeded the GNP. The sectors most affected by this crisis were textiles and heavy industry. The latter never recovered the levels of production and employment that it had before the economic collapse. The labor law "reforms" facilitated firing workers, contracts without job security, and the reduction in real wages (which fell 20 percent during the 1980s). Between 1975 and 1985, 46 percent of the textile enterprises in Chile declared bankruptcy, and the cost of labor in the Chilean textile industry was one of the five lowest in the world, competing with Haiti and South Africa in a race to the bottom.

Chilean workers and their families, who had already paid the price of the false neoliberal "miracle" of the late 1970s now suffered even more from the rigid orthodoxy and errors of the Chicago Boys and the avarice and imprudence of their employers. Fear of long-term unemployment led many workers to accept whatever conditions their bosses imposed on them.

Only a few dared to join a union. The number of unions and their members fell to their lowest level between 1981 and 1986. In 1983, only 8 percent of the workers were union members, and these were concentrated in the biggest enterprises and those like mining that were in strategic sectors of the economy.[26]

The depth of the economic crisis and the absence of spaces for political participation in Pinochet's Chile detonated a massive social response during the days of protest of 1983–1984, which for the first time threatened the stability of the dictatorship. It was the copper miners who issued the call for the first protest. They had mobilized to protest the deterioration in their working and living conditions, the reduction in the size of the labor force, and the lack of worker participation. Then, in April 1983, the officers of the copper miners' union concluded that "The moment had come to stand up and say ENOUGH!" They called for a National Strike, which was replaced by a day of protest—"to protest against the new labor laws and the social and economic policies" of the dictatorship.

The call of the CTC resonated throughout Chile and across many social strata, not just among blue-collar workers. On May 11, 1983, from the residents of the middle-class neighborhoods affected by the crisis to the marginalized impoverished youth of the shantytowns, thousands of Chileans united in the first national protest day. As a result of the success of the first day of protest, days of protest continued to take place monthly until the end of 1984, demonstrating the influence of the labor movement even in its weakened state. The mobilizing power of a labor movement weakened by the new labor laws and the economic crisis had its origin in a convergence of social and political forces. From the late 1970s on, under the umbrella of the Catholic Church and its blue-collar Workers' Pastoral, union leaders were able to reconstruct labor movement networks. In 1978, the Coordinadora Nacional Sindical (CNS), under the leadership of Manuel Bustos, a Christian Democrat textile leader, facilitated the first alliances between leftist and centrist labor leaders. In 1983, labor leaders took a giant step toward unity with the formation of the Comando Nacional de Trabajadores (CNT), which would lead eventually to the reunification of the labor movement in a new CUT (Central Unitaria de Trabajadores) on the eve of the 1988 plebiscite.[27]

This political protagonism of the labor movement unleashed the fury of the dictatorship and its business allies. The social movements in the shantytowns were harshly repressed, and many workers were fired for political reasons and blacklisted like a decade before. Many could not find work in Chile and were forced to emigrate in search of economic opportunities, including countries such as Sweden that were both distant and different than Chile in their language and culture.[28] In 1982, moreover, the assassination of Tucapel Jiménez, the emblematic centrist leader of Asociación Nacional de Empleados Fiscales (ANEF), the most important union of state workers, put the labor movement on notice that the dictatorship would continue to use political violence to silence its opponents. That same year, Manuel Bustos, head of the CNS, was sent into exile. During the years that followed, the dictatorship continued to use the rationale of threats to national security to detain and exile internally or internationally the most emblematic union leaders. Rodolfo Seguel, the Christian Democratic president of the Copper Miners union, the CTC, was jailed for mobilizing the protests and then fired from his job.[29]

The brutal repression put an end to hopes of overthrowing the dictatorship through mass mobilization and protest, creating a political consensus that it was necessary to negotiate a peaceful transition to democracy with the dictatorship. Despite the repression, however, the workers had won new spaces of participation and assembly, fortifying the process of reunification of the labor movement. In 1988, workers formed a new CUT. In its founding congress, the CUT leaders thanked the Catholic Church for its important help. They also referred to the significance of the "heroic" strikes in Panal and Madeco (metallurgical factory) and remembered the many union members and leaders who had been assassinated or disappeared. Looking toward the future, they demanded "the repeal of the Labor Code imposed by the dictatorship and its replacement by laws made with the active participation of the CUT."[30] Their audacity met with repression: in October 1988 (the month of the plebiscite), Manuel Bustos and Arturo Martínez, the president and vice president of the new CUT were sentenced to 541 days in internal exile, in distant Parral in the south and Chañaral in the north.

During the past years of the dictatorship, it adopted more pragmatic economic policies that limited the effects of the extreme neoliberal orthodoxy of the 1970s. As a result, the Chilean economy began to show signs of growth, convincing many in the opposition of the benefits of the neoliberal model. Nevertheless, for most Chileans working conditions continued to be precarious. As a result of the elimination of protective tariffs, Chile became deindustrialized, and the new sources of jobs were in increasingly unstable export sectors such as agriculture, fishing, and forestry, or else in equally unstable services, retail commerce, and the informal economy. In these new sectors, which lacked a union tradition, employers imposed seasonal contracts, managerial flexibility, 12-hour shifts, and required overtime. In agriculture, there was an increase in seasonal labor and a corresponding decrease in permanent workers, as well as a feminization of work in the export packing houses. In the new fruit export industry, it was not unusual to find women "legally" working double shifts of 16 hours that began in the early afternoon and did not end until dawn, this in a rural culture where before women never worked outside the household economy.

In the more traditional industries, there was also a restructuring of production in search of greater efficiency and international competitiveness. Even public sector enterprises such as Codelco, Enami, and Soquimich began to increase the number of workers hired by private subcontractors, who were undermining the working conditions and influence of the permanent workers. In the metallurgical sector, technological and administrative renovation increased the pressure and the demands on the workers.[31] Despite the economic recovery, a 1988 public opinion survey by CEM, CETRA-CEAL, and SUR concluded that "70% of the workers in Santiago believed that 'the employers do what they want with us.'"

The transition to democracy did not restore the historic labor rights of Chile's workers. On the contrary, it maintained the essence of the Labor Plan of the dictatorship. Many of those in the center-left Concertación coalition that took over the government from Pinochet's appointees not only accepted the neoliberal economic model inherited from the dictatorship but also considered managerial flexibility and limits on union power as fundamental to modern labor relations. Moreover, seventeen years of censorship and propaganda of the dictatorship had successfully demonized the old labor movement, labeling its class orientation, political links, and complex ideological debates as an aberration of the past. At the beginning of the 1990s, many saw the new unions, atomized and dispersed, focused on immediate worker demands, as a model of modern unions. The business class not only triumphed economically but above all in the institutionalization of their ideas about how to organize production and treat the workers and their unions.

CONCLUSIONS

In sum, the complex legal and economic framework and the political repression of the labor movement that we have analyzed throughout this chapter, demonstrate the complicity and the interests of the civilians who supported the dictatorship and its efforts to impose a neoliberal model of work and to transform the historic relationship between workers, employers, and the state.

It is significant that in the political as well as the economic and the social, the capitalists and the neoliberal economists were not only complicit with the dictatorship but also the big winners from its policies; while the workers and their unions were the losers who paid its costs.

NOTES

1. Manuel Barrera and J. Samuel Valenzuela, "The Development of Labor Movement Opposition to the Military Regime," in *Military Rule in Chile: Dictatorship and Oppositions*, eds J. Samuel Valenzuela and Arturo Valenzuela (Baltimore: Johns Hopkins University Press, 1986).
2. Cited in Manuel Gárate, *La revolución capitalista de Chile (1973–2003)* (Santiago: Ediciones Universidad Alberto Hurtado, 2012).
3. Jaime Ruiz-Tagle, "El sindicalismo chileno entre 1973 y 1990," in *Libertad sindical y derechos humanos. Análisis de los informes del Comité de Libertad Sindical de la OIT (1973–1990)*, eds Elizabeth Lira and Hugo Rojas (Santiago: Ediciones LOM, DIBAM, and Universidad Academia de Humanismo Cristiano, 2009), 19.
4. Comisión Nacional de Verdad y Reconciliación, Chile, *Informe de la Comisión Nacional de Verdad y Reconciliación* (Santiago: La Nación, Ediciones del Ornitorrinco, 1991); and Comisión Nacional sobre Prisión Política y Tortura, Chile, *Informe de la Comisión Nacional sobre Prisión Política y Tortura* (Santiago: Ministerio del Interior, La Nación, 2005).
5. ILO (International Labor Organization), *The Trade Union Situation in Chile: Report of the Fact-Finding and Conciliation Commission on Freedom of Association* (Geneva: ILO, 1975).
6. René Cortázar, "Políticas de reajuste y salarios en Chile, 1974–1982," *Estudios CIEPLAN* 10 (1983): 45-64.
7. "Minuta del Gobierno de Chile sobre acusaciones en relación con la situación sindical en Chile" (April 16, 1975), in *Libertad sindical y derechos humanos*, eds Lira and Rojas.
8. Guillermo Campero and René Cortázar, "Lógicas de acción sindical en Chile," *Estudios CIEPLAN 18* (1985), 5–37.
9. Paul Drake, "El movimiento obrero en Chile: de la Unidad Popular a la Concertación," *Revista de Ciencia Política* 23 (2003): 148–58.
10. We are grateful to Andra Chastain for sharing her as yet unpublished research on the history of the Metro.
11. Guillermo Campero, "Chile: las tareas del sindicalismo," *Nueva Sociedad* 83 (1986): 134–45.
12. Aída Moreno Valenzuela, *Evidencias de una líder: memorias de una trabajadora de casa particular* (Santiago: LOM Ediciones, 2012), 66.
13. David Benavente, *A medio morir cantando. Rastrojos de la memoria chilena* (Santiago: Catalonia, 2007), 81.

14. Rolando Álvarez, "Represión o integración. La política sindical del régimen militar, 1973–1980," *Historia* 43 (2010): 325–55.

15. Gárate, *La revolución capitalista de Chile.*

16. For a general vision of U.S. foreign policy during this period, see Brian Loveman, *No Higher Law: American Foreign Policy and the Western Hemisphere since 1776* (Chapel Hill, NC: University of North Carolina Press, 2010) and Peter Winn, "The Pinochet Era," in *Victims of the Chilean Miracle: Workers and Neoliberalism in the Pinochet Era, 1973–2003*, ed. Peter Winn (Durham, NC: Duke University Press, 2004), 31–32. See also the chapter in this book by Juan Pablo Bohoslavsky and Mariana Rulli, "Untangling Financial Aid to the Pinochet regime."

17. "Disolución de Federaciones Sindicales: las necesidades del modelo" and "elecciones y nueva institucionalidad laboral," *Solidaridad 58* (September 1978). For a more detailed analysis, see Winn ed., *Victims of the Chilean Miracle*, 32.

18. For a detailed analysis of the Plan Laboral and the subsequent labor law reforms since the return to democracy in 1990, see the chapter by Daniela Marzi Muñoz in this volume.

19. The Plan Laboral also revoked the Law of Agricultural Unionization of 1967, promoted by the Christian Democratic government of Eduardo Frei. The 1967 law had permitted the unionization of rural workers by *comuna* (municipal district) and their participation in provincial and national organizations. By 1973, there were 220,889 rural workers unionized. In 1979, the union by farm replaced the union by *comuna*, facilitating anti-union practices by the landowners, perhaps the most ideological and rigid sector of Chilean capitalists. See Sergio Gómez and Jorge Echeñique, *La agricultura chilena: las dos caras de la modernización* (Santiago: FLACSO, 1988).

20. Cited in Peter Winn, "The Pinochet Era," in *Victims of the Chilean Miracle*, ed. Winn, 33.

21. Manuel Barrera, Helia Henríquez, and Teresita Salamé, *Sindicatos y Estado en el Chile actual*

(Geneva: United Nations Research Institute for Social Development and Centro de Estudios Sociales, 1985), 73.

22. Barrera, Henríquez, and Salamé, *Sindicato y Estado*, 94.

23. Peter Winn, "La huelga contra la historia: La gran huelga de Panal de 1980," Paper presented in the International Seminar on Worlds of Work and Dictatorship in the Southern Cone. Rio de Janeiro, Brazil, October 2015.

24. Barrera, Henríquez y Salamé, *Sindicatos y Estado*, 136.

25. Cited in Peter Winn, "No Miracle for Us: The Textile Industry in the Pinochet Era," in *Victims of the Chilean Miracle*, ed. Winn, 155.

26. Campero and Cortázar, "Lógicas de acción sindical en Chile."

27. Rodrigo Araya, *Organizaciones sindicales en Chile. De la Resistencia a la política de consensos, 1983–1994* (Santiago: Universidad Finis Terrae, 2015).

28. Peter Winn, "Flyktingar och emigranter. Chiles historia och chilenarna i Sverige." *Arbetarhistoria* 134–35 (December 2010): 8–22.

29. Araya, *Organizaciones sindicales.*

30. "Declaración final congreso constituyente Central Unitaria de Trabajadores," in *Movimiento sindical en dictadura. Fuentes para una historia del sindicalismo*

en Chile, 1973–1990, Rodrigo Araya ed. (Santiago: Ediciones Universidad Alberto Hurtado).

31. Joel Stillerman, “Disciplined Workers and Avid Consumers: Neoliberal Policy and the Transformation of Work and Identity among Chilean Metalworkers,” in *Victims of the Chilean Miracle*, ed. Winn, 164–208.

Chapter 18

The Dismantling of the Welfare State and Mass Imprisonment in Chile

Silvio Cuneo Nash

INTRODUCTION

This chapter analyzes the impact that dismantling the welfare state had in Chile on the current levels of imprisonment. This piece does not review the prison situation during the dictatorship in Chile nor the violation of human rights of political prisoners but rather seeks to understand how the economic changes imposed by the dictatorship influence and still affect current levels of imprisonment.

During the dictatorship, the imposition of a neoliberal regime was compensated by a more significant penal state that was not only maintained after the advent of democracy but was even more deeply ingrained in society. This went hand in hand with the politicization of crime, which is also a key factor in determining mass incarceration, while imprisonment, as a means of controlling poverty, soared to unprecedented levels. Possibly, the main cause of the current incarceration figures in Chile may be attributed to punitive populism during democracy. For its part, the dismantling of the welfare state is also responsible for the current levels of imprisonment in Chile, but in no circumstance can it said to be *the* cause. In other words, it would be altogether misleading to lay blame for today's incarceration figures solely at the doorstep of the dictatorship, since the greatest increase in incarceration was generated during the years of democracy. However, the dissembling of the welfare state carried out during the dictatorship constituted the start of a complex process of poverty management through imprisonment, a process for which no end is in sight, while its detrimental upshot in all probability is going to mean an even greater increase in imprisonment for years to come.

This paper is divided into four parts in addition to its introduction and conclusions. The first part analyzes mass imprisonment and its cause both in the United States and worldwide to contextualize the Chilean phenomenon. Subsequently, the second part focuses on mass imprisonment in Chile; the third on the existing relations between neoliberal policies implemented during the dictatorship and the criminal justice system; and the fourth part analyzes economic segregation and the criminalization of poverty in Chile.

MASS IMPRISONMENT AND ITS CAUSES

Mass imprisonment is a global phenomenon. The United States is, however, a paradigm with nearly 700 prisoners per 100,000 people (the world average is estimated at about 140 per 100,000). Prison Numbers in Europe and Latin America, without ever being as high as those of the United States, have risen significantly and in 2012 Chile became the country with the largest number of inmates in South America (298 per 100,000).[1] To understand the current level of imprisonment in Chile, one must refer to what has taken place in the United States. The imposition of hegemonic "models" is fundamental to obtaining a true understanding of how U.S. criminal policies were implemented at various latitudes. The form and extent of the punishment are to be analyzed from a multi-casual perspective. Monocausal explanations fall far short of explaining the current imprisonment figures in the world. Mass imprisonment has immediate and mediate causes. Immediate causes are mainly the sentences that send to prison and the laws on which they are based. For their part, mediate causes have to do with the context that makes the existence of immediate causes possible.

The two main mediate causes of mass imprisonment in the United States and the world are[2] (a) the weakening of the ideal of resocialization and (b) punitive populism. The combination of both factors has increased the number of prisoners in today's societies. If what determines the increase in incarceration is the difference between the higher number of people entering prison and the lower number of inmates leaving prison, these two groups of causes are linked with both flows in that they encourage both a greater in—and a lesser outflow. The weakening of the ideal of rehabilitation features strongly in the closing of the valve that allows an early release of inmates. Populism, for its part, manifests itself in increasingly longer prison sentences.[3]

The weakening of the idea of resocialization must be analyzed in terms of a more general change, meaning the weakening of the welfare state and the glorification of the Penal State. This mutation comes hand in hand with the adoption of neoliberal regimes, meaning that it is common—and not purely coincidental—that social deregulation, the rise in wage uncertainty and labor instability are associated with the growth of the punitive or authoritarian state. The "invisible hand" of the insecure labor market finds its institutional complement in the "iron fist" of the state, which reformulates its operations to suppress the disorders generated by the spread of social uncertainty.[4] Thus, the neoliberal "model" that professes economic deregulation generates penal overregulation. The consequences created by the dismantling of the welfare state, mainly material uncertainty in the lower classes, leads to overinvestment in incarceration as an instrument of oppression and social control. David Garland takes pain to highlight the link between the penal system and other social structures and relations.[5] According to the author, the penal system of the welfare state would be a complex that he called the *penal welfare context*. This social or welfare state does not see in the crime an amorality of the offender, but rather a manifestation of a social problem that would be the result of an industrial, classist, and unequal society. This system of welfarist punishments, rather than condemning the individual action of the crime perpetrator, seeks the correction of the criminal, providing him with the tools to reintegrate himself in society. Garland believes that, according to welfarism, the prime objective of punishment would be the individual correction or resocialization of offenders. The same idea of resocialization encompasses that of treatment, which with the progressing on the twentieth century, acquires greater scientificity and contributes to the development of a penal language. "This is the case of reformatories, correctional institutes and associations, therapies, therapists and prison guards."[6]

The shift from industrial production, based on the principles of Fordism, to more flexible forms of accumulation, brought about a general fall in manufacturing, mass unemployment, and job uncertainty.[7] While Fordism gives rise to exploitation, post-Fordism leads to an increase in unemployment and marginality and, as John A. Powell observers with a touch of irony, "to a certain extent, it's actually better to be exploited than marginalized, since if they exploit you they most likely still need you."[8] These new societies with vast marginalized masses—of education, culture, and value of those within—will strive for the security of the included by controlling, segregating, and enclosing the outsiders. Furthermore, this new state is characterized by increasing labor flexibility, leading to less stability for the workers, and growing privatization in different areas. With this collapse of the welfare state and the loss of labor security, new poverty is born, formed by mass unemployment and vast sectors that oscillate between insecure and illegal work (more often than not leading to crime).

The dismantling of the welfare state and the increase of the punitive system are also linked to the rise of a new crime control industry[9] and the waning of the sovereign state as the exclusive controller of crime. It is in the context of a transition from a society that has established a certain degree of job stability and promoted social welfare policies toward a new culture of social and labor insecurity that the ideal of rehabilitation is lost, giving way to punitive forms that are an expression of a narrative that practically loses all interest in the condemned and focuses all its attention on the safety of non-criminals. With the adoption of neoliberal economic politics, every suggestion of a welfare state disappears, poverty increases and, consequently, the penal state grows. In the same way, the crisis of the welfare state results in the collapse of "social constitutionalism," with the consequent reduction or disappearance of various procedural-criminal guarantees, opening the door wide for a truly devastating-prone penal system, restoring giving sentences traits cruelty.[10]

MASS IMPRISONMENT IN CHILE

The increase in imprisonment in Chile has been a relatively new trend. If we analyze the average imprisonment figures between 1974 and 2012, the following may be observed. Until 1992, various fluctuations are evident. Starting from 1993 the trend steadily grows until 2009, when it falls, while nevertheless remaining high compared with our historic levels and with the other realities in the region. Already in the 1980s, imprisonment increased to 136 prisoners per 100,000 people in 1980, to 189 in the year 1989. Later, it once again upsurges in the 1990s (from 171 in 1990 to 198 in 1999) and even more so in the first decade of the current century (215 in 2000 to 313 in 2009).

The increase in imprisonment figures during the dictatorship (from 142 in 1974 to 189 in 1989) can be linked to the disappearance of the social state. Later, the peak figure during democracy between 1990 (171) and 2012 (275) responds to imbalanced economic policies inherited from the dictatorship together with the punitive populism adopted during democracy. Table18.1 and figure 18.1 show the increase in the incarcerated population.[11]

In Chile, as in the United States, we can distinguish between mediate and immediate causes. Among the mediate causes, two stand out: the imposition of a neoliberal economic regime (implemented in the civic–military dictatorship, which continues to this day), and punitive populism that grew particularly strong with the return of democracy. Neoliberalism has generated an environment of inequality for which the response is greater punishment, further accentuating social and economic differences. In this way, imprisonment in Chile has been transformed into a system of control and management of poverty. Consequently, the punitive populism argument, which gained special strength after the return of democracy, was a determining factor in soaring incarceration numbers. This pro-punitive argument was initially the battle cry of the right-wing parties, opponents to the governments of the *Concertación*;[12] however, this reasoning was later imitated and both political coalitions eventually identified with demagogic-vindictive rants that translated into major agreements and authoritarian laws favoring imprisonment.

Table 18.1 Number of Prisoners per 100,000 Inhabitants in Chile.

1974	142
1975	146
1976	149
1977	143
1978	134
1979	135
1980	136
1981	130
1982	144
1983	158
1984	161
1985	167
1986	173
1987	182
1988	191
1989	189
1990	171
1991	156
1992	148
1993	147
1994	148
1995	153
1996	161
1997	170
1998	179
1999	198
2000	215
2001	216
2002	222
2003	228
2004	226
2005	228
2006	240
2007	263
2008	291
2009	313
2010	308
2011	285
2012	275

Source: Author's own creation

These two causes or groups of medium-term causes have produced immediate causes that are criminal and procedural-criminal laws favoring imprisonment. Furthermore, let us not forget that the construction of new prisons is a necessary condition of mass imprisonment and the justifications that with more prisons it is possible to fight prison overcrowding are most of the time simplistic arguments that do not match reality, given that the increase in

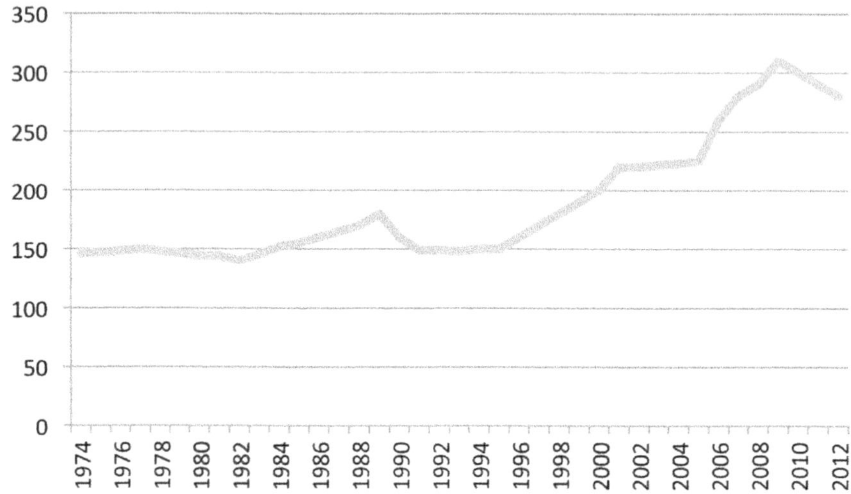

Graph 18.1 Number of Prisoners per 100,000 Inhabitants in Chile. *Source:* Author's own creation

prison space consistently generates an increase in prisoner numbers and not an improvement of their condition. Quite frankly *more prisons do not mean less overcrowding. More prisons mean more prisoners equally overcrowded.*

Although it seems common sense, the idea that an increase in crime causes a rise in imprisonment should be ruled out. This *apparent cause* is not directly connected to imprisonment figures. At least this is what may be inferred from victimization studies that do not account for an increase that may be related to the increase in incarceration. Sebastian Salinero cites a study of twenty-five different countries (Unites States, Canada, Scandinavian countries, of Eastern Europe, of Southern Europe, and so on) that concludes that prison is barely affected by crime levels and trends.[13] The Chilean situation is not very different from the international one and our rise of levels of imprisonment does not match the fluctuating crime rates.

A more questionable and simplistic analysis is that conducted by Jean Pierre Matus and Carolina Peña y Lillo, who believe the increase in imprisonment in Chile is the consequence of the rise of crime rates and not of political-criminal decisions.[14] This type of association, although erroneous, can be found useful and functional to legitimize a greater punitivism and justify the high levels of imprisonment. These authors state that "the shorter the average length of effective convictions, the higher the existing crime rates."[15] Although assertions such as this appear to echo common sentiment, various studies demonstrate that the certainty of being sanctioned and the immediacy of the penalty generate a higher dissuasive effect than the length of the sentence.[16] Matus and Peña y Lillo also state that imprisonment decreases the rate of "future crimes by placing the individual in prison."[17] However, the ingenuity of the authors is unforgivable in believing that no crimes are committed in prison. An analysis such as this either completely ignores what happens in prisons or simply implies contempt for the prisoners.

The Chilean political authorities' response to the issue of poverty and inequality has been to increase punitivism, to criminalize a group of people identified as belonging to the social stereotype of a criminal. It is mainly composed of young men, coming from poor and peripheral districts, with low education, dark skin, indigenous features, wiry hair, and a way of walking and speaking typical of those who live in marginal neighborhoods. With drug control legislation, penal persecution has also been extended to poor foreign migrants and women of humble origins. This response has been promoted by different groups and spurred on by the media. The big mistake of the Chilean punitive response consists in expecting to tackle a problem by almost exclusively focusing on a just part of its effects. The response has been wrong first because with increased penalization, the dignity of many is violated and human rights are violated. Furthermore, this short-sighted analysis fails to bring down crime rates. Thus, the hike in public spending on repression and prisons, promoted by the two ruling coalitions, is inhumane and fails to reduce criminality. Punitivism, *in the American way* that Chile followed, reproduces, on a smaller scale and with fewer resources, several of the mistakes made by the punitive policies adopted in the United States. In both contexts, delinquency and social marginality appear as synonyms. The incomprehensible element is to explain why, if crime is presented as the great problem of our time, its social causes are neglected, and enormous sums are spent on repression and punishments that only make things worse.

Subsequently, we will analyze how Chile's neoliberal regime is the mediate cause of mass imprisonment in Chile. The implementation of this regime by the Chilean dictatorship and, in many respects its refinement by the democratic governments that succeeded it, aggravated inequality, at the same time destroying the vestiges of a so-called welfare state. As previously mentioned, the building of prisons is a necessary condition for a rise in incarcerations. Neither should we forget that in the 1990s, about 60 billion pesos were spent on prison infrastructure, a sum described by the Ministry of Justice itself as "the largest investment in infrastructure in the history of the prison system."[18] As Juan Guzmán and Marcel Ramos point out, "most of this investment takes place under the government of Eduardo Frei, just at a time when overcrowding jumps from six to forty percent."[19]

Neoliberalism in Chile and the Penal System

Generally, on referring to Pinochet's dictatorship (1973–1990), this authoritarian regime is remembered for its mass disappearance of political opponents, the horrifying violations of human rights, censorship, terror, and the impunity of the state's agents. Without neither ignoring nor denying that nothing matters more than human rights, it should also be remembered that these are violated by economic regimes that condemn millions of people to poverty. Both the explicit violation of human rights (e.g., the application of electricity to the genitals of political prisoners) as well as the one less explicit example of the death of a child of pneumonia due to lack of public medical care, are irreconcilable with respect for human dignity. While explicit violations were selective, and not for this reason less reprehensible, economic changes affected the entire population, favoring small groups and harming the majority of Chileans.

The dismemberment of a semi-welfare state with the implementation of a neoliberal economic regime, meant the end of basic social benefits, fostering labor uncertainty and the segregation of the population via the expelling of the poor from the city center, leaving them abandoned in inhospitable sectors on the city outskirts. In these new conditions of spatial segregation, penal response heightened its selectivity with regard to more deprived groups. From these human masses, discarded by the new economic structures, the inhabitants of the prisons are recruited, and the absence of the welfare state is supplemented by more punitivism.

Later, an analysis is undertaken of how the economic transformation in Chile and the implementation of a neoliberal regime worked. It was Milton Friedman himself who advised Pinochet "to impose a series of rapid measures for the economic transformation of the country: reduction of taxes, free market, privatization of services, cut in social spending and general liberalisation and deregulations . . . . It was the most extreme capitalist transformation that has ever taken place anywhere."[20] The changes were immediately carried out as *shock* therapies on two fronts.[21] On the one hand, radical economic changes were implemented, making all vestiges of the social state disappear, impoverishing millions of people and enriching small groups. On the other, armed forces and special police tortured and *massacred* political enemies, terrifying the population, and in this way making a social mobilization against the implemented changes impossible. In the words of Naomi Klein, in Chile, terror was an accomplice to economic change. In a democracy, neoliberal proposals at the most should be measurable reforms, since it is unpopular to dismember the welfare state (for example Reagan and Sarkozy). "To sum up, Friedman's economic model can partially be implemented in democracy. Nonetheless, to achieve its true vision, it requires authoritarian political conditions."[22]

Friedman and the Chicago School believed in a pure market, free from regulations and found interventions uncomfortable, such as Keynesian ideas introduced in the United States, that of the Social Democrats in Europe or developmentalist ideas in the Third World, as well as Socialism in education, state ownership of basic services and all interventions aiming at mitigating the extremes of capitalism. Friedman's ideas sought the elimination of market regulations, the privatization, and the cut or cessation of social programs' funds, meaning, his theory could crudely be summed up in three words: deregulation, privatization, and cuts. With regard to the effects produced by the market without regulations, it is worth remembering that "in such distribution criterion, the market is effectively cruel because it does not take into consideration how much someone needs something, but only whether they have the means to buy it."[23] According to Friedman, economics, as a natural or causal explanatory science, should be approached with the same rigor with which a physicist approaches the phenomena that occur in nature. The problem was the lack of a laboratory where to test his economic theories. No society existed that would let him comprehensively apply his *laissez-faire* theories. It was then, in the 1950s, that the *Chile Project* was born. In the Economics School of Chicago, a *Chile Laboratory* was created, where *Chile's economic problems* were analyzed and scientific recipes for *solving* them were offered. However, after the triumph of Salvador Allende and the Popular Unity in 1970, the *Chile Project* appeared to be a resounding failure. The popular will want to move to the Left, which could come about not only through Allende's triumph. Even the political program of Ramiro Tomic (presidential candidate of the Christian Democratic Party) coincided in several points with that of the Popular Unity. Then, the situation became more complex for the Chicago Boys with the nationalization of the copper mines, which had been until then controlled by United States' companies.

As democracy revealed itself to be so ungrateful to the Chicago Boys, perhaps a dictatorship could offer the academic workshop they longed for. In the heart of the Cold War Nixon, as soon as he found out about Allende's victory, gave Richard Helms (director of the CIA) instructions to "make the economy scream." The United States sabotaged the Chilean economy with various maneuvers, such as the blockade of credits from North American banks and private individuals, the boycott of Chilean products, causing the shortage of dollars in Chile, generating a climate of instability, financing work stoppages, and strikes. However, in 1973, Popular Unity increased its votes compared to the elections of 1970. The Nixon Administration, therefore, began contacting *reliable sources* of the army to carry out a coup. An extreme and radical change was necessary since if the democratic rules were respected, it would be unfeasible to implement the laboratory that Chicago wanted. Thus, the coup in Chile, financed by the CIA, was the result of a collaboration between the army and economists. According to Orlando Letelier, Allende's ambassador in Washington, the Chicago Boys convinced the generals they would be able to complement their brutality with the intellectual assets they lacked.[24]

The coup, although in many ways foreseeable, resulted in brutality no one could have ever imagined. The image of the bombing of the Presidential Palace showed the ferocity with which the military acted. The metaphor of destruction announced the beginning of something completely new.

On September 12, 1973, that is only one day after the coup, a document containing the new economic plan drawn up by the Chicago Boys and known as *El Ladrillo*[25] was distributed among the generals of the army who held important positions in the new *government*.[26] *El Ladrillo* was based on Friedman's ideas of privatization, deregulation, and cuts in social spending. The experiment only benefited foreign companies and small financial groups in Chile. In 1975, Friedman traveled to Chile to try and save the experiment. Friedman met with Pinochet himself where he raised the need for a shock treatment as the only solution, given that gradualism would not solve the serious problems of unemployment and inflation. Pinochet was convinced and left the Ministry of Economy and the Central Bank in the hands of the Chicago Boys. In 1975, the public spending was reduced by 27 percent all at once. Health and public education were the most mistreated sectors (and have still not recovered). Hundreds of state-owned enterprises and banks were privatized. The results were even more dramatic. With the increase of unemployment and the diminishing of the welfare state, the population was condemned to live in poverty. Criticism came from various sectors, but in Chile censorship silenced it. A former disciple of Friedman, who had departed from his ideology, André Gunder Frank, wrote an open letter to Friedman and Harberger, showing how the Chilean patient responded to the shock treatment. In the letter, he pointed out that a Chilean family could barely survive on the minimum wage, having to spend 74 percent of their income on bread, without being able to opt for luxuries such as milk and catching a bus to go to work. In the cuts, they had abolished the distribution of milk in the schools.[26]

Geographical Segregation and Criminalization of Poverty

With the implementation of a neoliberal regime and the reduction of state social benefits, Chile's main cities accentuated their geographical divisions. On one hand, poor people were removed from upper-class neighborhoods and, on the other hand, slums grew in the suburbs of the cities, in areas devoid of paving or sewerage, near landfills, or polluting factories, on underforested lands, making them constant victims of fires and all kinds of catastrophes. This new geographical distribution of social sectors was mainly a consequence of a process of uprooting carried out during the dictatorship. Between 1979 and 1985, thirty-five thousand poor families were expelled from the center of Santiago and abandoned on the outskirts.[27] The process was justified as a mechanism for concentrating poverty to better focus on social investment.

The reasoning does not seem to stand up to any analysis; however, the real reasons were difficult to recognize. Hiding poverty to appear to be a thriving country was a strategy to counteract the high percentages of disapproval of the economic plans promoted under the dictatorship. These measurements did not reduce poverty, but they did disguise it. "Starting from 1979 what was eradicated was not poverty but the presence of the poor in public space . . . Those who lived and worked in the area with the highest income could spend months without seeing any poor than the destitute begging at the exit of the Metro stations. It is therefore not strange that Hernán Briones, former business leader, said in 1993: *they continuously talk about the poor; I have not seen poor people for so long*. At the time the businessman mentioned this, more than 40 percent of the Chilean population was within this social economic classification."[28] The improvised slum population responds to a well-defined profile. These are mostly people who dropped out of college at an early age, without proper jobs, easy victims of drugs, and alcoholism. These people, uneducated and cutoff from the official culture, begin to be perceived as criminals and are criminalized and controlled by the state through the penal system. The physical differences fuel *Lombrosian* prejudices resulting in increasing talk of *criminal-looking* individuals.

Since the 1990s, with the arrival of democracy, despite the hopes that the whole country had placed in the new governments, things did not change, and social inequalities increased. Governments of the social democratic coalition did not want to modify the economic regime implanted during the dictatorship. The most optimistic visions speak, at best, of neoliberalism with a human face.[29] The economic gap remains a central issue, but it is not alone. A further evaluative subdivision helped separate people of similar economic standing into good and bad; decent people and indecent subjects; citizens who could turn to the police and those who could be arrested by them.[30] Criminals could be found anywhere but came from the most vulnerable and unprotected areas. The lack of opportunities, coupled with the stigma that makes young settlers and delinquent synonyms, often ends in a self-fulfilling prophecy. The young settler, labeled a delinquent, ends up delinquent. When a sector of the population rightly feels that it does not have the support of the state, which it only perceives as something that controls and represses, its violent reaction is understandable as a way of defending its legitimate expectations. Living in unpaved roads, suffering from precarious public health, studying in schools with numbers without even dreaming of the possibility of studying at university, not aspiring to a decent job, are some of the causes that violently separate Chileans between being included and excluded. The former call the latter delinquents and have an entire apparatus to segregate them, lock them up and keep them away and controlled. The latter, lacking a good education, defend themselves as they can.

Likewise, the brutal repression of social protests today means that it is not only the lower classes who are aware of the actions of the *Carabineros* (preventive police force), denouncing excessive repression, torture, and death. On May 21, 2015, Rodrigo Avilés, a twenty-eight-year-old student at the Catholic University of Santiago (paradoxically the same university as the Chilean Chicago Boys), nearly lost his life when he fell violently after being hit by a jet from the *Carabineros* water cannon. Several videos show that Avilés was standing passively when the jet of water threw him to the ground causing brain damage. The images show that this was no accident, as the water canon was only a few meters away from the victim. *Carabineros* discharged the officer who operated the water cannon. However, this measure does not change things. This type of situation has been going on for years. Videos show how the *Carabineros* infiltrate masked agents in the protests to delegitimize social demands and justify police repression. The media, on their part, cover the social protests almost exclusively highlighting violent scenes of hooded young people setting up barricades or hurling stones. In this way, they collaborate with the criminalization of protests by sending out a message justifying the actions of the *Carabineros* and surreptitiously asking for more repression and restrictions on citizens' rights. The authorities of the "democratic" Chile, accentuating the economic structures of the dictatorship, defend their *status quo* with the necessary means. Daniel Menco, Matías Catrileo, and Manuel Gutiérrez are three fatal victims in a democracy. They were all shot by *Carabineros*.[31]

In Chile, too, the deregulation of the welfare state—which began under the dictatorship, but survives to the present day—is compensated by more repression and a stronger penal state. However, we do not maintain the economic system to be the sole cause of the tightening of the penal system. As mentioned at the beginning of this analysis, mass imprisonment is a multi-causal phenomenon, which is fostered by the disappearance of the welfare state, while it is also a consequence of other factors, mainly of punitive populism which criminalizes poverty. In this manner, Chilean economic policies have resulted in adverse conditions for integration and a healthy community. These are circumstances that for a large part of the population (the excluded) are inhumane. In this light, Marx and Engels' thinking seems more pertinent than ever: "if man is formed by circumstances, circumstances must be formed humanely."[32]

CONCLUSIONS

The implementation of neoliberal policies by Pinochet's dictatorship led to the disassembling of every trace of the welfare state and, consequently, the introduction of a complementary and germinal penal system that identified in incarceration the ideal tool to control and manage poverty. In Chile, the abusive use of imprisonment of the poor resulted useful and functional to maintain social verticality as a means of control, focusing attention on one kind of delinquency, neglecting the crimes of white-collar workers.[33]

We are all aware of what occurs in prisons and we all seem to accept it without further questioning; however, at the same time, we deny the facts. We cannot imagine that our prisons are only for the poor and purely constitute a system of oppression for people to whom we have denied education, health, and housing. Stanley Cohen created the concept of *State of Denial*,[34] according to which people are aware and at the same time are not aware of a certain phenomenon. Today, we know and do not know that prison is an inhuman space. We are aware that every year a high number of poor people are locked up in prisons and we also know that they can die, be injured, or raped by other inmates or tortured by prison officers. However, as we know that the prisoners are from slums and that they behave in a way that is diametrically opposed to ours, we don't care. Somehow, we believe that they deserve what occurs to them or that they are predestined to it; however, if we question merit in relation to what we have given them and what we demand of them, we know (and do not know) they do not deserve all the injustice they have to live through (hunger, lack of opportunities, lack of decent housing, basic needs, the impossibility of going to university, high probabilities of ending up in prison, and so on). Since we know that imprisonment is essentially unfair as it only punishes the most vulnerable, we have invented constructions that allow us to justify imprisonment. That there are many poor people who do not commit crimes, that the poor are the main victims of crime and, therefore, that the iron fist with crime ends up benefiting the poorest. Thus, we can deduct that the confinement of the most vulnerable is a control system that favors and protects the most vulnerable. False arguments such as these serve to reassure us and hide our functionalism from the current system of oppression. Prison is inhumane, but the denial of prison reality is easy because we know that we will never have to suffer from it.

However, whether intentionally or not, we forget that by imprisoning someone we dehumanize them and to dehumanize a fellow man also means to dehumanize ourselves, and mass dehumanization necessarily means a dehumanization of society. And this is the case, even if we don't know about the pain of the prisoners. Mass imprisonment, as a silent ghost corrodes the freedom of all and ends up taking away the most precious of life itself. On the other hand, the criminal effects produced by prison are also costs that will be paid in the future and that will result in more crimes and higher violence rates, which also generates more prisons, more controls, more police and, furthermore, more criminals. This way, mass imprisonment, as an upward spiral has as its point of arrival the confinement of all. Only a change of direction, a shift toward respect for human dignity, can help us avoid a suicidal policy.[35]

NOTES

1. Data taken from: http://www.prisonstudies.org/world-prison-brief-data.

2. I have covered this more completely in Silvio Cuneo, *El Encarcelamiento Masivo*. Didot, 2017.

3. Loïc Wacquant, *Las Cárceles de la Miseria* (Manantial, 2015) adds as a cause of mass incarceration in the United States the "overlapping and substitution of the penal system with respect to the ghetto as a mechanism of social control." However, I believe that this has more to do with the selectivity with which the penal system operates and could be circumscribed to the two causal groups already mentioned.

4. Loïc Wacquan, *Simbiosi mortale, Neoliberalismo e política penale* (Ombre Corte, 2002), 122. While I essentially share Wacquant's thesis that it is usual for the dismantling of the social state to be compensated by a more penal state, I believe this is only one cause of a more complicated phenomenon. The high rates of imprisonment in countries with a strong Social State such as Cuba, demonstrates that the thesis should be complemented with other factors that analyze detention.

5. David Garland, *Castigo y Sociedad moderna.* XXI Century, 1999.

6. Diego Zysman, *Sociología del castigo* (Didot, 2012), p. 231. Although it appears that Garland is suggesting the opposite, it does not seem to me that before the irruption of neoliberalism, a social state had existed in the United States. At best, one can speak about a semi-social state that slowly disappeared to become a police state that opted to criminalize poverty and lock up, according to social and racial selection criteria, the most vulnerable groups.

7. Roger Mathews, *Pagando tiempo* (Bellaterra, 2003), 312.

8. Cit in Michelle Alexander, *El color de la justícia* (Capitan Swing, 2012), 330.

9. Nils Christie, *La industria del control del delito*. Edtion del Puero, 1993.

10. Iñaki Rivera, *Política criminal y sistema penal* (Anthropos, 2005), 11.

11. Graph and table are a creation of the author with data from the Gendarmerie of Chile.

12. The *Concertación* o *Concertación de Partidos por la Democracia* was a coalition that brought together different political parties opposing Pinochet and that governed Chile from March 11, 1990, to March 11, 2010. Among its main leaders, Patricio Aylwin, Eduardo Freu Ruiz-Tagle, Ricardo Lagos, and Michelle Bachelet, have been presidents of Chile. It is a vast conglomerate that united Christian Democrats, Radicals, Socialists, and other parties.

13. Sebastián Salinero, *¿Por qué aumenta la población penal en Chile?* (*Revista Ius et Praxis*, 2012): 117.

14. The analysis conducted by Jean Pierre Matus and Carolina Peña and Lillo, when linking the levels of crime and imprisonment . . ., seems to ignore a whole literature with empiric basis that concludes that it is not possible to establish positive

relation between those two variables and that mass imprisonment is a result of political-criminal decisions and not of a rise of crime.

15. Jean Pierre Matus y María Peña y Lillo, *Comentario crítico a la investigación de Sebastián Salinero Echeverría. Ius et Praxis*, 2012.

16. See: Tapio Lappi-Seppála, *Confianza, bienestar y economía política. Explicación de las diferencias en materia de política penal.* Dykinson, 2008; Edwin Lemert, *Human deviance, social problems & social control.* Penguin, 1967; Ignacio González, *Aumento de presos y Código penal. Una explicación insuficiente.* RECPC, 2011; Paul Robinson, *Principios distributivos de Derecho penal.* Marcial Pons, 2012; Jesús Silva Sánchez, *Aproximación al Derecho penal contemporáneo* (B de F, 2010), 352; David Lieberman, *Learning, Behavior and Cognition.* Wadsworth, 1993; Nathan Azran, *Fixed Ratio Punishment* (1963); Solomon, Turner y Lessac, *Some Effects of Delay of Punishment on Resistance to Temptation in Dogs* (1968); George Loewenstein, *Out of Control: Visceral Influences of Behaviour* (1996); etc.

17. Jean Pierre Matus y María Peña y Lillo, *Comentario critico a la investigación de Sebastián Salinero Echeverría.* Ius et Praxis, 2012.

18. Ministerial Public Account 1999.

19. Juan Guzmán y Marcela Ramos, *La Guerra y la Paz Ciudadana* (LOM ediciones, 2000), 110.

20. Naomi Klein, *La doctrina del shock* (Paidós Ibérica, 2007), 28.

21. Naomi Klein graphs the implementation of neoliberalism in Chile as a *shock* therapy. Every time we will mention this, we will be following what mentioned by the author in her book *The Doctrine of the Shock.*

22. Naomi Klein, *La doctrina . . .*, 33.

23. Fernando Atria, *Veinte años después. Neoliberalismo con rostro humano* (Catalonia, 2013), 152.

24. Orlando Letelier, *The Chicago Boys in Chile: Economic Freedom's Awful Toll.* The Nation, 1976.

25. Literally translated as "The Brik," the name *El Ladrillo* was given due to the large book's size [TN].

26. Gabriel Valdés, *Pinochet's Economists: The Chicago School in Chile* (Cambridge University Press, 1995), 252.

27. Juan Guzmán and Marcela Ramos, *La Guerra y la . . .*24.

28. Ibid.

29. Fernando Atria, *Veinte años después . . .*

30. Juan Guzmán and Marcela Ramos, *La Guerra . . .*, 19.

31. To those three mentioned fatal victims, we should add the still not finalized list of the repression experienced under the second mandate of Sebastián Piñera. Specifically, in November 2018, the Mapuche community member Camilo Catrillanca was shot dead by Carabineros, and in the social outburst of October 2019 to date, twenty people have died in circumstances that have yet to be determined.

32. Karl Marx y Friedrich Engels, *La Sagrada família, o Crítica de la crítica crítica contra Bruno Bawer y consortes* (Claridad, 1938), 153.

33. Edwin Sutherland, *El delito de cuello blanco.* La piqueta, 1999. It is precisely the low severity with which our criminal law deals with white-collar crimes that

allows us to conclude that imprisonment is not an instrument of crime control, but only one that seeks to control and segregate a type of crime, precisely that perpetrated by the most marginal classes.

34. Stanley Cohen, *States of Denial. Knowing about atrocities and suffering.* Polity, 2015.

35. Silvio Cuneo, *El encarcelamiento* . . . 231.

Chapter 19

Pinochet's Repressive Urbanism

The Violent Neoliberalization of Space in Santiago

José Francisco Vergara-Perucich

INTRODUCTION

According to recent findings compiled by researchers Patricio Bustamante and Ricardo Moyano, the city of Santiago was founded over an Inca settlement, whose layout would coincide with that of Pedro de Valdivia ordering the Alarife Gamboa, following the urban design regulations established in the Laws of the Indies set by the Spanish Crown. Perhaps the main difference between the Inca and Spanish layout is the economic objective that motivated the Valdivian urban design. The fact is that Santiago was founded, then, on two dispossession operations: land privatization and distribution of those plots among the Valdivian hosts to start the productive enterprise, and the crushing and appropriation of the preexisting Inca layout for the development of the colonial installation in Chile.

Crushing and privatizing to produce is what will trigger a long history of spatial violence driven by the pursuit of wealth and class distinction. Since the origins of Chile as we know it, the land has been the object of exploitation and rent on which a large part of the wealth of the elites has been built. In these processes, urbanism (in its archaic colonial forms until its scientific formulation in 1932) has been the instrument to organize the urban space, and with that, has organized the way of relating in society. Chilean urbanism has been subjected to ideological construction, as a representation of the way the elites understand the social space: a source of wealth. Whether following the plans of Pedro de Gamboa, Benjamín Vicuña Mackenna, Karl Brünner, or Arnold Harberger, the urban space of Santiago has been constantly rethought and organized for the benefit of a *rentist* interpretation of the city, optimizing its exchange value, subjugating the use-value and configuring a spatially ordered mechanism for social control. This chapter exposes what the Pinochet government did in the city of Santiago to advance the understanding of the neoliberal dictatorial urbanism that shaped today's metropolis.

City theorist Bernard Tschumi[1] argues that there are no spatial transformations without the exercise of violence, given that the act of changing the forms of the city implies destroying the previously existing ones. For his part, Eyal Weizman states that the urban form can exercise a mode of violence that develops slowly: architecture and the built environment are a type of slow violence. The occupation of an environment was conceived to strangle Palestinian communities, cities, and neighborhoods, to generate unliveable conditions for the people.[2] Weizman uses for his theory the territorial conflicts in Gaza, realizing how effectively urbanism can develop repressive faculties through its practice, separating Israelis from Palestinians, generating areas of destruction and defense, spaces of life and survival. Repressive urbanism, like all urban models, can be objects of design, of social strategies, and consequently, political action.

The forms of violence of the Chilean dictatorship also had their urban representation. Given the neoliberal nature of the Pinochet regime, and the eagerness to repress in favor of carrying forward the free-market revolution, cities such as Santiago are marked by the forensic footprints of repressive urbanism, which is expressed in socio-spatial segregation, metropolitan fragmentation, the gentrification of entire neighborhoods, and the ethical transformation of urban disciplines, which to survive under a neoliberal regime had to abandon their search for the good city—the just city, to finally surrender to the logic of the city as a source of profit.[3] Whether as a neoliberal phenomenon according to Alfredo and Paula Rodriguez[4] or as an exemplary metropolis for Latin America according to Glaeser and Meyer,[5] Santiago had to experience an initial phase of the reorganization of the space to activate the commodification of the urban elements.[6]

This chapter will serve to explain how and why the dictatorship exercised its repressive urbanism in favor of organizing a city like Santiago for profit. In the first section, a brief explanation of the indissoluble dependence of the neoliberal model of urban development is presented, to then expose the way in which in the Chilean case the transformations that allowed the development of the neoliberal city were carried out, pointing out how this urbanism jeopardized the collective conception of the city in favor of an elite centered in the maximization of profits. I was interested in focusing on the violation of article 25 of the Universal Declaration of Human Rights,[7] to take advantage of the audience of this book, as an invitation to understand that our cities, as living beings and representations of the social relationships,[8] have also suffered humiliation and torture, which have not been stopped. These vexations are spatial, expressed in exploited territories that determine the greater or lesser access to the benefits of living in a city, applying the logic of inclusion and exclusion, segregating the inhabitants into communes according to their purchasing power.

It will be important to expose the value of the struggle for the right to the city, a political way to struggle against the repressive urbanism inherited from a fierce dictatorship that continues to be present in the ways of organizing our cities in the present, with obsolete planning instruments that facilitate the transformation of urban products into commodities for financial speculation, following neoliberal land management guidelines and with a tremendous power concentrated in business groups that have understood the city as a source of wealth, crushing the remote possibility of discussing again the social role of the land, and avoiding that urban centers, nowadays, are vital for the development of life in the context of the climate crisis. All this was at the heart of the Pinochet government's urban policies.

A BRIEF EXPLANATION OF THE CITY AS A SOURCE OF WEALTH

Those unfamiliar with terminology and urban theory may have a simpler understanding of the city: a space in which we all live and develop our activities. This is true, although there is also a second layer of information in the city, another way of using it: for capital accumulation through the production of long-term fixed-income assets and, consequently, as a source of wealth fundamental for financial investments to increase its value on time. Post-industrial capitalism has made important advances that are reflected in substantial gains for those who have the resources to invest in certain specific economic factors. Moreover, with the irruption of the global system of information and business flows, what is certain is that this advance has gone very fast and the flows are increasingly efficient. Faced with this vortex, the speed at which capital reproduces itself often crashes against various barriers that hinder its fluid circulation and slow its expansion, which also obstructs the much-desired growth.

What is complex for the expectations of making capital grow is that these barriers have not yet been breached, given the global interdependence of markets between different nations and their internal instabilities, specific geopolitical variables, changes in the supply of labor, and long etcetera on the problems inherent in economic relations in a global society. The problem is that, by taking away the fluidity of circulation, capitalists can face a contradiction by not being able to develop their processes of capital accumulation because of what may be understood as institutional constrains (democratic laws, for instance). Before facing potential stagnation, capital begins to lose profitability. That is the moment when the city and the processes of urbanization come to the rescue of capitalism from its contradictions. As David Harvey explains, in periods when the economy shows excessive growth, capital is withdrawn from other sectors and introduced into everything related to real estate, urbanization, and so on. When other economic sectors are regularized, capitals are reintroduced in other places.[9] It is important to underline that capitalism in its neoliberal form depends not only on the market and the state playing a role as an economic facilitator but also on space, on urbanization processes. With this in mind, when capitalism is reviewed, it is no longer possible to look only to it as a series of abstract relational factors such as financial assets (subject to periodic fluctuations and crises), given that it is in the city where modern capitalism materializes its profits, giving a concrete body to its processes, manifesting itself in physical form, visible, palpable and, of course, tradable.

According to David Harvey,[10] urbanization and military expenditures are the main capital goods available to the capitalist to absorb the surplus of his production, maintaining stable profitability in the long term for the capital they invest. In the particular case of Santiago, this absorption has been developed through the real estate market. Investment in construction generates many jobs (always desirable by governments to reduce unemployment), generates sales for large sums of money, which through credit incorporates the bank in the acquisition of long-term debtors (whether builders or homebuyers), and creates a type of spatial-capital that rarely devalues over time. For example, in Santiago, house prices have been rising steadily since 1984.[11] This implies that investment in the construction and sale of real estate ensures that the return on capital will hardly fail to increase in value over time and will rarely fall below the initial investment. However, for these certainties to occur, both the economic regulations and the urban fabric must comply with certain characteristics. For now, in the business of the city, the most important matter is to ensure that the properties are well-organized and located, near centralities or in exclusive neighborhoods.

The general criterion to determine a prospection of the values of urban products is the centrality of its location, which is explained by the theory of central places. The positivist urban localization theories of the neoclassical urban economy state that the centrality of a real estate defines a large part of its value. By centrality is understood both its proximity to urban spaces where sources of work and services are concentrated, as well as the accessibility that one has to reach those sources of work. For example, access to the Metro, to large avenues, transport corridors, to mention a few examples that increase the value of the real estate business. These principles are based on the theory of the central places of Walter Christaller, who in 1933 proposed that the points where the main services for people are located (work, market, leisure) make up centralities from which a radius of influence can be traced that hierarchizes the value of properties. While prominent econometrists such as Masahisa Fujita, Paul Krugman, and Anthony Venables have relativized that Christaller's criterion is the mantra for the location in the city, the truth is that the evidence indicates that in the case of Santiago the theory well applies to the way in which the dictatorship sought to organize the city for the real estate capital and as a consequence, a transfer is observed from the center of Santiago to central spaces of the high neighborhood of the city (e.g., Barrio El Golf and Nueva Las Condes). This is what I will deepen it in the next paragraphs.

However, in the 1970s, real estate developers would need—as usual—the help of the state to install their capitalist reproduction machinery on the metropolitan space of Santiago. In those years, large plots of urban land close to centralities were occupied by informal settlements whose dwellers were waiting until 1973 for housing solutions. These settlements had arisen due to the very failures of the Chilean capitalist system; and although the governments of Alessandri, Frei, and Allende had advanced in the development of public policies of urban improvement—and in the particular case of Frei and Allende with important levels of materialization of solutions (table 19.1 and figure 19.1), the dictatorship did not hesitate to dismantle the urban planning apparatus and impose ideologically solutions coming from the neoliberal theoretical framework, using public funds to begin to more decisively promote private action through the mechanism of demand subsidies. The slums represented a severe headache for Pinochet, given that since 1957 they arose as an impugnation of the sacrosanct right to private property, a situation that was supported by influential politicians and by the Catholic Church through the Hogar de Cristo[12] and since the promulgation of the 1980 Constitution, this right will be defended by the state with all the necessary physical and institutional force and violence. However, these spaces in seizure were also opportunities to implement the mechanism of subsidy for the acquisition and sale of housing, encouraging the development of private real estate companies. Moreover, given the important social organization required to maintain and manage the slums, for Pinochet these socially active spaces represented an imminent danger of politicization; therefore, it was not only necessary to remove people from these strategic sectors for economic development, but also to divide them and impede the much-feared social engagement of the grassroots (which in any case would follow its course, and with more force). Then, the urban apparatus of repression of the dictatorship will appear, with all its neoliberal creativity and using the armed arm of the state to carry out a true cleansing of the profitable urban land.

Table 19.1 Number of Dwellings Delivered by Sector

Year	*Public Housing*	*Private Housing*
1964	6,938	12,902
1965	37,514	15,054
1966	13,433	14,328
1967	28,285	16,653
1968	32,730	19,683
1969	14,460	23,310
1970	5,914	17,792
1971	76,079	10,893
1972	20,312	13,752
1973	20,877	14,484
1974	3,297	17,084
1975	3,750	12,740
1976	24,022	11,519
1977	14,057	9,455
1978	4,118	17,371
1979	329	33,480
1980	1,846	41,721
1981	589	49,268
1982	436	23,825

Source: Own elaboration based on Kusnetzoff 1987.

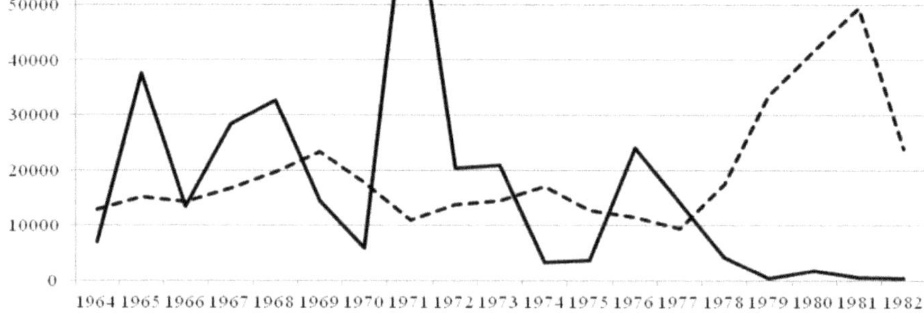

Figure 19.1 Amount of Public Housing Per Year. It is evident that there was a radical change in the fiscal contribution to the housing problem when the neoliberalization of the state began in 1975. *Source*: Own elaboration based on the price of land in Greater Santiago per year built, based on sales publications in El Mercurio newspaper and data from the Ministry of Housing and Urban Development on reference costs of construction price for buildings type D category 1, which corresponds to the highest category for housing.

REPRESSIVE URBANISM AND NEOLIBERALIZATION IN SANTIAGO

An informative poster developed by the Vicariate of Solidarity of 1982 indicated: "Chilean, don't be frightened, let's defend our citizens' rights";[13] and then explain what, in the event of the polices breaking-in a home, should be applied to Articles 4 and 5 of the 1980 Constitution, which stated: "No. 4 Respect for and protection of private and public life and the honour of the individual and his family; No. 5 The inviolability of the home and of all forms of private communication . . .)";[14] together with the invocation of article 12 of the Universal Declaration of Human Rights on the right to protection before the law against arbitrary attacks on persons. The instruction gave an account of the growing process of repression of which the inhabitants were victims after the promulgation of Pinochet's Constitution. However, the repressive urban process began much earlier, with fraternity operations in the late 1970s, as discussed later in this section. For the Chilean case, and in the particular elaboration of this essay, the first approximation to repressive urbanism is developed by Antonio Cassese in 1978.[15] Cassese explains that since the first years of the dictatorship the price of housing increased dramatically, reaching 534 percent in 1974[16] which was problematic for 20 percent of the population who lacked adequate housing. Cassese indicates that between 1978 and 1987, a number of 1,262,735 houses should have been built based on the deficit, a situation that was not fulfilled, and by 1990 the transition to democracy would begin with a deficit of 1,030,828 houses.[17] The dictatorship's response to the deficit will be developed following a neoliberal approach, seeking to maximize the profitability of investments in private hands, and using the opportunity of the enormous deficit as an excuse to invest in projects of public interest.

The urban fabric of Santiago in the first years of the dictatorship was full of conflicts typical of the spatial history of this city (a spatialized class struggle), which during the middle of the twentieth century had developed into a democratic boom and the strengthening of a promising welfare state in the context of Latin America. The configuration of this city did not respond to the new patterns of the state–citizenship relationship imposed by the governing board: Depoliticization of society, elimination of democracy, and militarization of public space. In the face of this distance between the dictatorial project and social reality, the disciplinary form of repressive urbanism emerged. Projecting a theoretical definition, repressive urbanism consists in the exercise of the organization of the functions, spatiality, and administration of the city, starting from a series of imposed measures of transformation which to be implemented required the force of the repressive apparatus of the state; either using police force, military, or, in a less visible manner but more durable, by means of public policies with objectives of social control from the configuration of space. The objective of repressive urbanism will be to discipline the city—both its citizens and its urban order—in favor of fulfilling the expectations of a hegemonic class, without having to face democratic processes, of public impugnation to the measures or simple opposition to the facts in exercise. A clear example of repressive urbanism was Haussmann's remodeling of Paris, where the Parisian authorities removed all the dispossessed classes from the center, placed them in the periphery, and reconfigured a complete city in favor of the embellishment, functionality, and social control of space. Repressive urbanism in Santiago was expressed both institutionally (as public policy and market organization) and spatially (as repressive acts and market operations).

INSTITUTIONALIZED INSTRUMENTS OF SPATIAL REPRESSION: THE DICTATORSHIP'S URBAN DEVELOPMENT POLICIES

In relation to institutional matters, the main tool to maintain the reproduction of repressive urbanism's socio-spatial effects was composed by the national urban development policies of 1979 and then 1985, both tending to monopolize urban development based on market objectives, minimizing the democratic role of the city and leaving the state as a mere facilitator of private initiatives. The National Urban Development Policy of 1979[18] (PNDU 1979) is theoretically justified by an article written by Arnold Harberger, who raises the importance of removing urban boundaries to increase the amount of land available for housing development and thus increase its supply and reduce its price to reduce the housing deficit and improve the prospects of the housing market. Harberger will argue that all major cities had gone through major territorial expansion.[19] However, Harberger will omit that the city of Santiago was not yet dense enough and that existing levels of urban poverty did not make it pertinent to conduct longstanding urban experiments that would tend to hand over all the power of urban development to the market. This will be ignored by the urban advisors of the Pinochet regime and in 1979 the PNDU was formulated. This policy defined that land was not a scarce resource, that urban development must be controlled for its profitability, and that land use must be defined according to market requirements, appealing to the completely flawed interpretation of Adam Smith's invisible hand. The only role attributed to the state will be to protect the common good, without detailing what that common good was.[20] With this policy, 64,000 hectares were added to the urban area of Santiago, which at that time had an area of less than 42,000 hectares.[21] According to Amador Brieva:[22]

> The Policy was approved in March 1979, but its implementation was reduced since although it postulated modifying or replacing the general norms of urbanism and construction, it did not materialise. Where it did find its full materialisation was in the Metropolitan Region, through the issuance of Legislative Decree No. 420 of 1979, which expanded the urban area of Greater Santiago, adding about 64,000 hectares to the urban area. This measure meant lifting the restriction imposed by the urban limit on Santiago's growth, effectively increasing the potential supply of urban land, which facilitated the emergence of new urban areas in the rural area. Although this incorporation of land towards a New Urban Policy in Chile was intended to lower the price of the land. However, the opposite happened and the price increased by 200%.[23]

Criticism of the measure was not long in coming. In 1981, Pablo Trivelli wrote a didactic article explaining the aberrant reality of the results of the 1979 PNDU.[24] Trivelli exposed how complicated it is to generate a regime of land competition when the city and urban development are fundamental to implement public policy programs of general interest to society. Conversely, the 1979 PNDU would simplify the complexities of the urban land market, bringing it to the level of any other type of consumer good, applying a utopian approach to the search for improved land supply. Precisely, while the policy sought to reduce the price of land to make it more accessible to the poorest people, the effect was exactly the opposite. For Trivelli, the annulment of the state as a public planning apparatus will be a serious mistake in the long term: "In a context of rapid economic growth and with a persistent process of concentration of the population in urban areas and, in particular, in the Metropolitan Area of Santiago, these policy decisions added to the liberalization of taxes on urban land . . . and the recovery of construction activity, instead of curbing speculation, have stimulated it."[25] Trivelli emphasizes the clearest evidence of the speculative bias of the 1979 PNDU, the absence of an objective city image. Since the market has controlled urban development in Chile, the spatiality of the city, the urban future we are building, has been almost eliminated by political agendas. Urban design (the art of shaping cities) was replaced by large-scale architecture (large objects over the city) or by pro-business urbanism[26] to generate urban products and not to create a city. For all this, the repressive urbanism in its political form will have a great responsibility.

For its part, the problem of the incipient financing of the housing market was deeply described by Francisco Donoso and Francisco Sabatini in 1980. The results of their research showed that the financial investments had turned to the land market as they ensured high rates of return by incurring low risks. They conclude that "the increase in the sale price of a square meter built at 5.27 U.F. is the result, first, of a greater real estate profit of between 2.97 and 4.43 UF. and, only secondarily, of an increase in costs (between 0.84 and 2.30

UF.)."[27] It would be a turn in the way of managing the soil and with it would appear the power of the owner imposing a speculative model. The authors determine that these new variables in the land market will have a profound effect on the increase in residential segregation, largely because groups with greater purchasing power will have the possibility of concentrating in specific areas of the city (eastern sector) and that the price of land will allow the inhabitants of other classes to be displaced to communes according to their income level.[28] Specifically, Donoso and Sabatini's research will allow us to understand that Pinochet's repressive urbanism tended to create a city model where high-income families will be able to choose where to consolidate their concentration spaces, segmenting the city according to purchasing power and leaving urban spaces of poorer quality (and therefore lower price) for the working classes. However, to carry out these operations of the reorganization of the city, it will be necessary to move masses of low- and middle-income populations embedded in the urban areas desired by the richer classes, so it will be necessary in this a state action to facilitate this transformation.

Faced with these aberrant results, the dictatorship will have to correct its errors and change its policy for the cities, given the overwhelming evidence related to the potential failure of the proposed urban model in the long term, and for its effects contrary to its objectives. As in so many other cases, the dictatorial experiment with Chilean society will fail based on its initial objectives (this urban model can be added to other examples such as the AFP, the privatization of education and health), and Pinochet will try to correct the problems caused by the first national urban development policy, through the PNDU 1985,[29] which will be called the Adjusted Policy, replacing that of 1979. Salvador Valdés, a member of the team that drafted the new policy, will recognize that many of the institutions needed to solve the problem of urban development in Chile could not be included in this new policy since there was no political consensus with the authorities.[30] Nor, admits Valdés, was it possible to incorporate the new aspects discussed in this policy to the General Law of Urbanism and Constructions. Finally, the document operates only as a guide and no legal instrument changed its condition until its repeal in 2000. In this way, although the guidelines will increase the attributions of the state to regulate the land market, in concrete terms, everything will remain in the hands of a self-regulated free-market political economy of the city.

THE PRACTICE OF SPATIAL REPRESSION: THE ERADICATIONS UNDER THE DICTATORSHIP

From the perspective of the urban form, the main action of the dictatorship in Santiago was the processes of eradication of populations of scarce resources and their relocation to the periphery of Santiago. When reviewing this history, it is fundamental to refer to the *Operation of Confraternity*, consisting of the relocation of inhabitants of scarce resources from the communes of Las Condes, Santiago, and La Reina, to communes such as La Granja, San Bernardo, and Puente Alto. Under the excuse of "providing aid to the most dispossessed"[31] and thus move toward "making Chile a country of owners, not of proletarians,"[32] as Pinochet himself promulgated. The main goal of these eradication processes is to restore the right to private property by sanctioning the political action of impugnation composed of the taking of land (common political practice between 1957 and 1973) and cleaning the urban land with good location for the development of real estate projects. For Eduardo Morales and Sergio Rojas, it was possible to carry out a deep cleaning from the communes of the eastern sector, to relocate the population in communes that over the years would consolidate a spatial class bias[33] (see table 19.2). This reorganization of the social fabric of the city, in turn, will shape the application of a market strategy to the organization of urban land:

Table 19.2 Origin and Destination of Eradications under Dictatorship (number of families)

Commune	*Displaced*	*Established*	*Home Income 1990 in UF*	*Home Income 2013 in UF*	*Variation 1990–2013 (%)*
La Granja	1,392	8,519	18.15	27.45	51
Pudahuel	2,435	3,826	19.64	29.89	52
Renca	1,077	3,564	18.85	33.76	79
Puente Alto	326	2,936	25.13	31.83	27
San Bernardo	623	2,065	28.83	29.55	2
Maipú	2,075	2,002	33.84	44.13	30
Ñuñoa	1,771	1,741	67.75	100.50	48
La Cisterna	1,542	1,149	20.53	47.88	133
San Miguel	1,865	1,000	30.18	53.21	76
Quilicura	731	560	20.09	48.84	143
La Florida	2,871	400	31.77	44.37	40
Conchalí	1,544	305	27.62	29.13	5
La Reina	874	120	68.50	101.28	48
Quinta Normal	627	0	22.03	36.50	66
Providencia	205	0	96.00	101.04	5
Las Condes	2,511	0	97.12	117.27	21
Santiago	2,823	0	25.36	61.33	142
Áreas Rurales	3,595	701	17.11	34.62	102
TOTAL	28,887	28,887			

Source: Own elaboration based on Hidalgo 2005 and CASEN 2013.

the segmentation of the land market, creating communes for the rich, middle class and poor, thus facilitating the allocation of urban products, social policies, and control mechanisms.

Between 1976 and 1987, 28,887 families were taken to military trucks and moved out to live in the communes that corresponded to them depending on their purchasing power. In the beginning, in these new lands where they were moved out, the dictatorship promised a decent house, but it never arrived. Instead, the only materialization of this promise was a set of sanitary huts arranged on rural lands, without public transport and services, only precarious constructions. In Santiago alone, more than 100,000 people were displaced. The march of military trucks through the city corresponded to the violent act of territorially displacing people to be relocated in places in accordance with the objectives of a hegemonic class that saw in the land market a fruitful field to sow its seeds of profitability and thus ensure the obtaining of fixed income in the long term. All this was possible mainly due to the protection of private property enshrined in the constitution of 1980 which together with the right to free enterprise will configure a new urban form, individualistic, fragmented, segregated, and permanent. Repressive urbanism will be the action of the state tending to configure the neoliberal urbanism that is solid, enduring, profitable, and builds over the spatial distinction of classes. As table 19.3 indicates, the segmentation of the city allowed to focus the urban development, going from the investment in more central communes or of greater interest for the investors, toward the communes that were near the urban centralities, with the socio-space effects previously mentioned. Today Santiago is the most segregated city among the members of the Organization for Economic Cooperation and Development (OECD), followed by London and Budapest,[34] and of a total of thirty-six nations analyzed, Chile ranks 33rd

Table 19.3 Variations in the Balance between Sales Value and Construction Costs Per Year

Year	*Sale Value*	*Building Cost*	*Sale Value—Costs*	*Return on Investment (Gross)*
Año	*UF/m2*	*UF/m2*	*UF*	*%*
1975	11.44	3.76	7.68	204
1980	14.51	11.65	2.85	24
1985	14.20	12.29	1.91	16
1989	15.30	13.10	2.20	17
1993	17.62	13.73	3.89	28
2000	20.25	14.82	5.43	37
2005	23.80	15.74	8.06	51
2010	33.10	14.97	18.13	121
2016	49.66	15.22	34.44	226

Source: Own elaboration based on the price of land in Greater Santiago per year built.

in quality of housing. While the city has suffered from these phenomena, the real estate business has yielded important returns becoming one of the most profitable ways to produce long-term fixed-income.[35] From this perspective, the city as a financial asset fulfills its mission at the expense of the population.

Based on sales publications in El Mercurio newspaper and data from the Ministry of Housing and Urban Development on reference costs of construction price for buildings type D category 1, which corresponds to the highest category for housing.

In 1982, Santiago's political administration changed from having fifteen to thirty-two communes, one of the largest metropolitan areas in Latin America in terms of the number of adjacent autonomous administrative divisions, without a central authority (mayor) with the powers to carry out comprehensive coordination among the communes. In other words, each commune will operate with high levels of autonomy, obligated to self-finance, and generate its ordinances of territorial regulation embodied in a communal regulatory plan. This model is ideal for reproducing the standards of living in each commune. Under the logic of self-financing and decisional autonomy, rich communes will be able to perpetuate their wealthy standards, protect their lands from the creation of poverty ghettos and generate standards of living that will be highly superior to those of poor communes that, on the other hand, having to self-finance, will be constantly operating with balances close to zero.

With these measures, Pinochet revived the segregated desires of Benjamín Vicuña Mackenna in 1872, who raised the need to separate civilized citizens from barbarism, to make the *lowborn people* be educated based on the example of a superior social class in customs, culture, and abilities.[36] Territorial dominance and the exclusion of the poor from the benefits of urban life have always been a shameful engine of urban development in Chile. The oligarchy has configured public policies to defend its property (source of all wealth in a pure rentier and extractivist Chile), for which it has not hesitated to use the full force of the state and its forceful arms to defend the model. Vicuña Mackenna's repressive proto-urbanism, which was not materialized, revived in the eaves of a ferocious dictatorship whose association with the oligarchy would allow private property order to be restored, strengthen the reproductive possibilities of the oligarchic class, and build an appropriate space to perpetuate this process of spatial subjugation.

CONCLUSIONS

This chapter has sought to highlight the immanent existence of a theory on repressive urbanism in the history of neoliberal spatial transformations in Chile. This, taking as an example the case of Santiago, from the institutional perspective and the actions of the transformation of space based on violence. As a hypothesis, this chapter raises the need to deepen the theorization of repressive urbanism as a bridge for the installation of neoliberal urbanism. In my view, the second could not exist without the first. The accelerated neoliberalization of urban development in Chile could obey a very effective policy of urban violence from the state, repressing potential insurrections against private property using all possible force: A mode of shock therapy in the urban context.

The absolute commodification of land and the neoliberalization of urban disciplines are a vital factor in the struggle to strip today's Chile of its dictatorial legacies, whose hiddenness can only be explained by the participation of diverse political actors in the land market. Without going any further, in the declaration of interests of the congressmen, it can be seen that twenty-one out of thirty-eight senators declare to have investment companies that have participated in the purchase and sale of properties. On the other hand, there is a significant concentration of political and business power in the Chilean Chamber of Construction (CChC). Of the ten most important economic groups in the country, ten participate as active members of the CChC. In addition, it is enough to review the agendas of the ministries of public works and housing to see how systematically the authorities of the CChC have direct access to ministers and undersecretaries, but not associations of residents or groups that seek to transform the neoliberal logics that govern our model of urban development. Furthermore, the CChC has a direct incidence in the design of urban policies, posing the contradiction in which the regulated proposes and validates the rules that will regulate them.

However, a door has opened: the social outburst of October 2019 is reclaiming the city; they demand spatial justice and for doing so, the social movements are organically reorganizing the way we understand the city of Santiago as a whole. The results of these changes are uncertain yet, but the new political scenario is expected to reach a more democratic approach to urban design, in which the community and welfare are more relevant than profitability and the private property. In any case, the outburst may be seen as a demand to put an end to the torture of cities by the market rules and the state as a passive accomplice of the urban atrocities of segregation, displacement, gentrification, and exclusion from urban life.

Finally, a reflection for those who are not accustomed to seeing the city as an object of study, housing is fundamental for the development of life; without housing, it is practically impossible to survive. This is ratified by the Universal Declaration of Human Rights. The fact that housing is only in private hands constitutes a dangerous bet, where the possibilities of configuring monopolies or oligopolies could harm society as a whole. This is the case of Chile, where the CChC oligopolically organizes the market as a gigantic lobby organization for the sake of the real estate business. On the other hand, the state has preferred to leave everything in the hands of the private sector, without assuming its role as an articulating agent of society, as a coordinator of problems in relation to seeking the common good. The passivity of the state has been scandalous so far, even when compared to other neoliberal contexts such as European countries or even in some North American states. The clearest example is that the price of housing in Santiago is not set based on the fierce competition between companies, but is set based on expectations of profit from the investment. This condition originates mainly because housing is basic to the development of life (such as water, health, or education), a population in constant demographic growth assures its demand. Traditionally, the prices of goods and services are set by striking a balance between what companies are willing to pay and what customers are willing to pay. However, in the case of housing, clients (or citizens) cannot stop paying for housing, since there are no assets in addition to their use-value.

Deneoliberalizing the land and housing market is essential to end another of the effects of the Chilean dictatorship, to turn from repressive urbanism to democratic urbanism, once and for all.

NOTES

1. Bernard Tschumi, "Violence of Architecture" [1981] A vol. 20 numb 1, 44–47.
2. Eyal Weizman "The architecture of violence" (Al Jazeera English, 29 June 2014). http://www.aljazeera.com/programmes/rebelarchitecture/2014/06/architecture-violence-2014629113556647744.html. Accessed May 2, 2017.
3. Vergara-Perucich, José Francisco. Urban design under neoliberalism: theorising from Santiago (Routledge, 2019).
4. Rodríguez, Alfredo, and Paula Rodríguez, *Santiago, una ciudad neoliberal* (primera edición, Olacchi, 2009).
5. Glaeser, Edward Ludwig, and John Robert Meyer., *Chile: political economy of urban development* (Harvard University Press, 2002).
6. Henri Lefebvre, "La producción del espacio" (Capitán Swing, 2013).
7. Everyone has the right to a standard of living adequate for the health and well-being of himself and of his family, including food, clothing, housing, and medical care and necessary social services, and the right to security in the event of unemployment, sickness, disability, widowhood, old age or other lack of livelihood in circumstances beyond his control.
8. Lefebvre (n 1).
9. Lefebvre (2013) 221.
10. David Harvey "Rebel Cities" (London: Verso, 2012).

11. Databes of El Mercurio newspaper since 1979, measuring the annual variation of the price of the sale of new apartments in Santiago, using values passed to UF according to evaluated year.

12. Vicente Espinoza. "Para una historia de los pobres en la ciudad" (Ediciones Sur 1988).

13. Vicaría de la Solidaridad. "¿Qué hacer en caso de allanamiento en la población?" (1978, Available at Archivos Nacionales, Biblioteca Nacional de Chile 1982).

14. Vicaría de la solidaridad (1982).

15. Antonio Cassese "Estudio del impacto de la ayuda y asistencia económica extranjera en el respeto de los derechos humanos en Chile" (Consejo Económico y Social de las Naciones Unidas 1978).

16. Cassese (1978) 217.

17. Joan Mac Donald "Aún faltan 888 mil viviendas en el país." (El Mercurio, June 19, 1994).

18. MINVU - Ministerio de Vivienda y Urbanismo "Hacia una nueva política urbana para Chile: Antecedentes históricos" (Ministerio de Vivienda y Urbanismo, Programa de las Naciones Unidas para el Desarrollo, 2013).

19. Arnold Harberger, "Notas sobre los problemas de vivienda y planificación de la ciudad" (AUCA n 37, 1979).

20. In: Gimenez, P., Gazitua, G. (de.) (2012) Hacia una política Nacional de Desarrollo Urbano: Antecedentes Históricos. Volumen 1. Santiago: LOM Ediciones.

21. Database of Ducci y González in Galetovich & Poduje 2006.

22. In Giménez & Gazitúa 2012.

23. Brieva in MINVU 2013, 12–13.

24. Pablo Trivelli, "Reflexiones en torno a la política nacional de desarrollo urbano" (EURE. Revista Latinoamericana de Estudios Urbanos Regionales. Vol 8 Nº 22, 1981).

25. Trivelli, P. 1981, p. 58.

26. López-Morales, Gasic Klett, Meza Corvalán (2012).

27. In Donoso & Sabatini 1980, p. 31.

28.

> This process of residential, commercial and employment segregation of high-income groups—which would have been accentuated from 1974 onwards according to the fourth hypothesis—is, to a large extent, promoted and capitalised by the large development and real estate companies in their projects. Given their income, these groups have the option not only of buying a luxury home, but also the possibility of segregating, with respect to other social groups, their places of residence, services and, to a certain extent, work.
>
> Donoso & Sabatini, op.cit., p. 45

29. MINVU (2013).

30. The constitutionality of Urban Development was an aspect that had to be excluded from the Policy. State action in this area includes numerous ministries, affects dozens of laws, and compromises the attributions of politicians and civil servants who are generally not inclined to cede part of their faculties. Modifying that

substantially exceeded the scope of the Working Group, and there was no political consensus to support administrative changes of this magnitude. Valdés in Giménez & Gazitúa (2012), p. 38

31. In: Jornadas del Presidente de la Republica (1979). p. 13. (full citation).

32. "El Ministerio de Vivienda y Urbanismo a los Pobladores de Campamentos y a la opinión pública en general" [Newspaper insert]. *El Mercurio* (Santiago, July 27, 1980). In: Silva Salinas 2012.

33. Eduardo Morales and Sergio Rojas, "Relocalización socio-espacial de la pobreza: política estatal y presión popular," 1979–1985. (FLACSO 1986).

34. Chile marks a SIGMA of 0.55, while London marks 0.49 and Budapest 0.47. OCDE 2013, p. 58.

35. Vergara-Perucich, José Francisco, Aguirre-Nuñez, Carlos. Inversionistificación en América Latina: problematización del mercado de arriendo para el caso chileno (Habitat y Sociedad. Vol. 1. Num. 12, 2019).

36. Benjamin Vicuña Mackenna, "La transformación de Santiago" (Bookstore Printing of EL Mercurio 1872).

Chapter 20

Autonomy in Times of Economic Complicity

Mining Expansion and Water Practices in Northern Chile

Cristián Olmos Herrera

INTRODUCTION: KICK-OFF[1]

Since pre-Incan times, water has been a culturally central element shaping, distributing, and organizing the Andean landscape of the Atacama Desert.[2] Sophisticated irrigation systems have been utilized for centuries to channel the waters from the high Andean mountain range down to a pattern of canals, which structure towns and settlements in the desert. These canals offer a configuration and a unique model of spatial organization, representing the inseparable connection between the Atacama society and its natural environment[3] which is reflected in collaboration, reciprocity, and autonomy.[4] The characteristics of the territory are inseparable from the society not only in a material sense but also in terms of beliefs, values, and relationships.[5]

The Atacama Desert is the driest desert of the world and further contains the largest deposit of valuable minerals such as copper, nitrate, and lithium.[6] The current Chilean economic system is based on the extraction and export of these natural resources, with many of its regulations having been designed during the dictatorship. It has caused inequalities and constant violations against indigenous communities located near the principal mining production areas,[7] and consequently, threatened the local organizational system and spaces of decision-making of the Atacameño communities.

Currently, many of the communities near the Atacama Salt Lake are put under pressure by the mining sector to exploit their water resources, both superficial and underground, as well as brine and salts reserves,[8] which are fundamental for the lithium extraction process.[9] The power of the mining sector can be traced back to the year 1981, when Chile's Water Code was deeply modified, contributing to the privatization of water resources, where the resource is delivered to the highest bidder under the logic of supply and demand. Hence, the private sector has been immensely supported by a legislative structure, which was created during the Chilean dictatorship and has been maintained by the subsequent democratically elected governments. The legislative structure increased benefits following the economic interests of a specific group and prioritized them over the social interests of the surrounding communities. The framework put water management under the rules of private property and protected it through the Constitution of 1980,[10] causing a fundamental tension between the collective recognition of indigenous peoples' territories on the one hand, and the private water and land market on the other.

Within this legislative and geographical context, this chapter analyzes the repercussions for the communities located near mining centers. It discusses the importance of businesspeople and private companies in the privatization of water management and their impact on Atacameño communities. Also, this chapter reveals the roles of water in this desert communities and illustrates them through the case of the village of Toconao. It analyzes how members of this community, their decision-making power, and cooperative practices, have been affected when dealing with the mining sector putting pressure on the management of their water resources. In the case of Toconao, this pressure comes from the mining company Sociedad Química y Minera (SQM S.A). This company does not only threaten water availability in the Atacama Desert but also productive initiatives in the communities, provoking conflicts at the local level, which affect community practices of solidarity and cooperation.[11]

The chapter will first outline the legislative framework with its origins in the dictatorship. This framework gives rise to the existing extractivist model through policies of water privatization and the privatization of SQM S.A.[12] Second, based on ethnographic work carried out during the years 2014–2015, it will analyze the importance of water in the community of Toconao and how it has been affected by the framework. Finally, this chapter analyzes the expansion of SQM S.A and the privatization of water, which is necessary for the production of lithium. All parts are based on research conducted as part of a PhD thesis titled Hydrosocial territories in the Atacama Desert: An ethnographic analysis of changing water practices in Toconao, Chile.[13]

DRAWING THE DELINEATIONS DURING THE DICTATORSHIP: THE WATER CODE WITHIN THE MINING CONTEXT

The current mining model was created by the dictatorship and had profound consequences for the territory and the distribution of water, mainly due to the distribution of water rights and mining concessions.[14] According to the mining concessions registry of the National Geology and Mining Service, 70 percent of the Antofagasta region is currently granting concessions to mining companies.[15] This demonstrates that the mining sector is not only the primary pillar of the national economy but also the controller of the territory through its expansion.[16] One important characteristic of the economic model established in the dictatorship and consolidated with the Chilean Constitution of 1980[17] was the creation of the Water Code,[18] Law No. 19,253 and the Mining Code[19] of 1983, Law No. 18,248. These legal frameworks provide water rights and mining concessions to private hands by encouraging the commodification of natural resources.[20]

The regional economy rests exclusively on mining, which contributes 9.9 percent to the national GDP and 56.3 percent to the regional GDP.[21] This contribution is due to the substantial foreign investment consolidated by the signing of numerous free trade agreements, which characterize today's extractivist model.[22] This economic development controls the use of the territory, especially the territory that has been claimed for decades by indigenous communities.[23] Therefore, national economic development is contrary to the development of the Atacameño culture, where water and territory are understood as one unity, which is fundamental for their identity.

The mining boom started in the mid-1970s; it was consolidated in the 1980s due to new legislations imposed by the dictatorship and applied in the 1990s by the free trade agreements established in the new democratic era. These three stages have been the cornerstones of a state of injustice and inequality that has accelerated social, cultural, and environmental impacts mainly for local, indigenous communities in the Atacama Desert.[24]

One of the primary mechanisms of this systematic legislative evolution has been to grant rights of access, exploration, and extraction of resources to companies on land regardless of who the land belongs to.[25] Mining companies do not necessarily have to be the owners of the land or water they use for their processes. The Chilean Constitution considers land and water as market goods,[26] which means that the demands on the territory are separated from the claims on its natural resources, such as water and minerals. Therefore, the current Constitution, represents the fundamental nucleus of an institutional framework that pushes the neoliberalization of nature and gives the Chilean State the role of an auditor for mining investments.[27] The neoliberal economic model strengthens the exploitation of natural resources as a mechanism for the integration of the Atacama region into the global economy.[28] Moreover, the Chilean political model establishes administrative mechanisms of decision-making on these matters that exclude local communities in decision-making about the territory they inhabit.[29]

The black areas in figure 20.1 display all concessions for the exploitation or extraction of resources in the territory of the Antofagasta region. The dotted areas are the rights assigned to exploration. The Mining Code,[30] in its article number 14, paragraph 1, states that: "*Everyone has the ability to test and dig in lands of any domain, except those within the limits of a foreign mining concession, in order to find mineral substances.*" Hence, it permits everyone to explore areas to see what minerals exist in that place and to take control of the water that forms part of that particular concession.

Hence, the mechanism of extracting natural resources in Chile takes away community control and autonomy of decision-making over their resources. In consequence, it threatens the practices of communities in relation to water use, which are essential to survive and flourish in this desert.

This legal framework of mining concessions and their protection in the Constitution brings about the need for mining companies to obtain water, which is a fundamental element of copper and lithium mining processes in the Antofagasta region.[31] The Water Code was created in 1981, hence, two years before the Mining Code,[32] under the same understanding of property rights. The Water Code states in article number 5 that water is a public good. However, at the same time, it declares it as an economic good: "*Waters are*

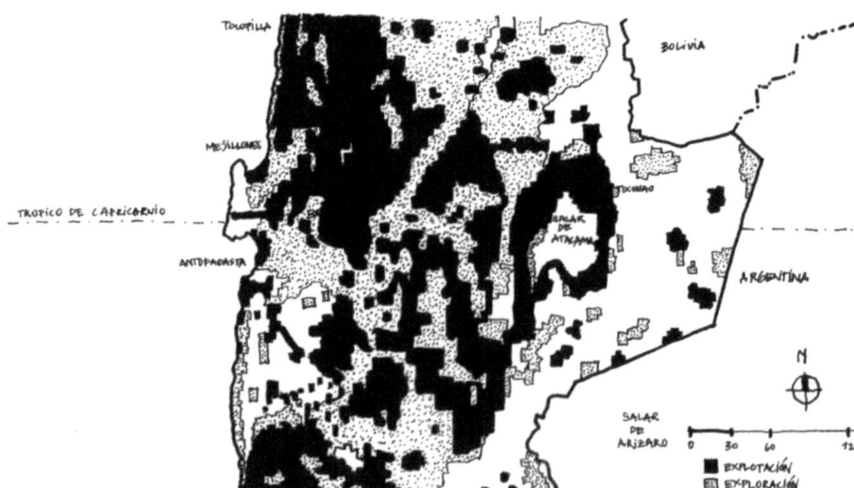

Figure 20.1 Map of Areas for Exploration and Exploitation, Antofagasta Region.
Source: Author based on IDE Chile, 2017

national goods for public use and are granted to private the right to use them."[33] In this way, the separation of ownership of water from the ownership of the land turned water into a commodity, which is free to be marketed under precarious state monitoring.[34]

Water management, from the national legislative perspective, does not consider the geographical, economic, or local cultural specificity and treats all water resources as uniform. There is no connection to water practices corresponding to the desert context, which makes the neoliberal dynamics of the private rights of water and a free market act as independent of the social reality of the territory.[35] Therefore, the free market of water has played a fundamental role in the consolidation of the power structures that underpinned Augusto Pinochet's neoliberal program.[36]

CHILE'S WATER CODE: PLAYING WITHOUT A REFEREE

It is essential for this chapter to understand the protection of privatization through the right to property and how it reflects the transformation of local power relations and their systematic effects on communities.[37] Manuel Cuadra[38] argues that the fundamental cause of the loss of the waters of the Atacameño community has been the lack of legal protection in a context, where mining and the supply of the cities near the productive centers have exponentially increased the demand on water resources. This situation has stripped rural communities of their water, generating severe environmental damage,[39] and increasing migration to urban areas, poverty and inequality.[40] The allocation of water rights to private actors has not only changed the relationship of Andean communities with water but also consolidated the neoliberal market model, whose main beneficiaries were collaborators of the military regime, government technocrats, and the private sector.[41]

At the institutional level, the state agency in charge of managing water is the National Water Directorate (DGA, Ministry of Public Works). This institution grants requests for water rights without any charge, conditional to the physical and legal availability of water.[42] Once the right to use water is constituted, it is governed by private or civil law and not by public or administrative law. Therefore, the rights become subject to the registration of titles of real estate property, which are protected as private property under the Chilean Constitution of 1980.[43] Unfortunately, the DGA has little power and authority over the private use of water, leaving the decisions about water management in the hands of the private sector or associations of irrigators. In the specific case of Toconao, decisions are left to the Irrigators' and Farmers' Association, which independently distributes water rights among its members.[44] Additionally, the DGA cannot cancel or restrict rights once they are granted unless they are amortized due to expropriation. Hence, the DGA does not have decision-making power in conflicts over water, leaving deliberations to the civil courts.[45] As a representative institution of the state, the DGA is subordinated to technical and administrative functions, such as collecting hydrographic data, inspections of hydraulic works, enforcing the regulations governing the irrigation associations, and developing studies or technical recommendations for public policies.[46]

At the local level, farmers and irrigators of the communities adhere to the common property statutes that their respective irrigation associations establish. This local institution emphasizes in its statutes the values of preservation, solidarity, and protection of its waters, thereby ensuring the development of the Atacameño culture.[47] These values share two essential characteristics. First, farmers have control and access to water resources from streams and tributaries located in the association's territory. Second, each farmer can use water based on respecting the welfare of other users through respect and solidarity in the management of existing resources.[48] This can be understood as the moral economy of water;[49] a social order based on the fundamental principles of the right of everyone to have access to water and the responsibility to manage the resource reciprocally.[50]

The National Indigenous Law 19253 was established in 1993 to recognize the existence of eight ethnic groups in the country and to acknowledge indigenous pluralism in Chile. The Law defines the "quality of being indigenous" detached from the roots in indigenous lands and integrates cultural criteria of self-recognition and offspring in the definition.[51] It established measures for the recognition, protection, and development of indigenous lands and created the Fund for Indigenous Lands and Waters, which is managed by the National Development Organization (CONADI). This Law created the legal conditions for the territorial management of specific geographic areas in which indigenous communities can live and build on the particular ways they have established in their cultures to relate to their ecological and social habitat.[52]

Figure 20.2 shows the distribution of different indigenous communities in the Antofagasta region. Through the enactment of Law 19,253 of 1993, the customary and collective right to water of ancestral property of the Atacameño communities is recognized. It allows communities, rather than individuals, to be owners of the waters.[53] However, the use of resources, especially land and water, has been controversial. This is because some leaders of the water associations have taken advantage of the rights that the Indigenous Law gives them. They have signed water supply agreements with the mining sector, changing the ancestral view of water to a perspective that sees the resource as an economic good, protected by the Water Code and the Constitution of 1980.[54]

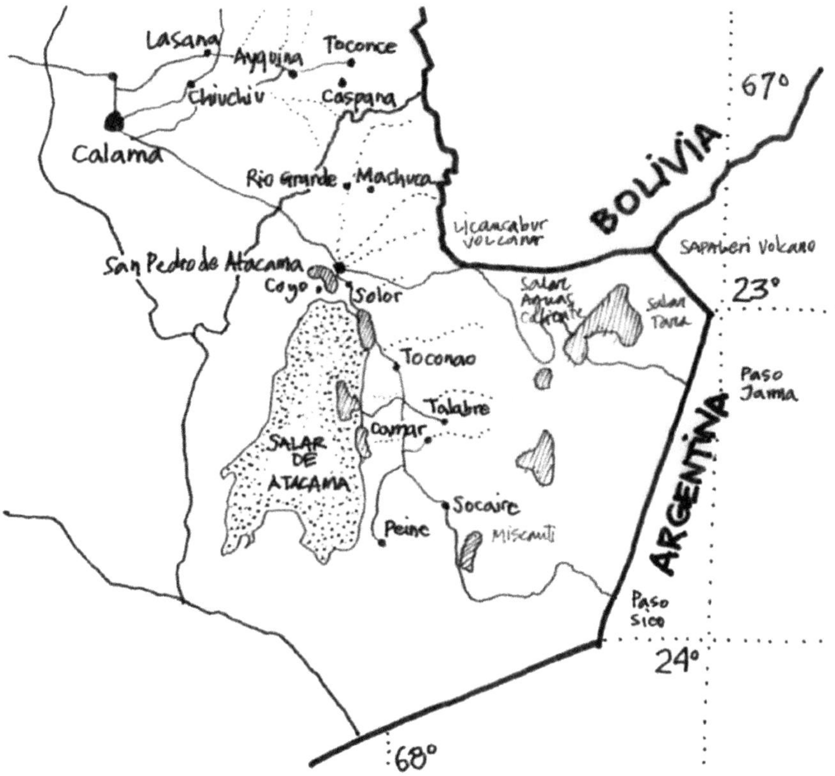

Figure 20.2 Map of Indigenous Communities of the Atacama Desert. *Source*: Author based on Bolados, 2014.

From the institutional point of view, on a national scale, water and territory are understood from the perspective of private property or state ownership through the Ministry of National Assets. Contrary to this state vision of private property is the perspective of indigenous communities on a smaller scale, where resources are commonly used and protected by the statutes of each water committee.[55] However, the evidence gathered in this research shows how communities have changed their discourses when the possibility of obtaining economic benefits for their waters is presented.

In reference to the common resources that the community shares, resources are defined by a local understanding, which responds to the community's respect and practice.[56] However, this can be understood as a skewed view by the private sector, when fighting for their resources against external agents to the community. The pressures from mining companies on community resources ignore the regulations of institutions at the national level.

Tecklin, Bauer, and Prieto[57] argue that Chile is considered successful by the neighboring countries in Latin America for its development toward economic freedom. Throughout Latin America, the concept of development has been linked to discourses of modernization and the degradation of the environment.[58] There is a lack of understanding development from a local point of view and to see the injustices of a given context in their relations with the economic policies of the Chilean State. In the context of the communities located in the Atacama Desert, inhabiting the territory and populating its landscape is a fundamental part of the local control of its resources such as water, land, and soil.[59] That means that the local management of resources as a collective has formal conditions in their management.[60]

THE OWNER OF THE BALL: SOQUIMICH (SQM S.A)

According to the US Geological Survey,[61] SQM S.A is the biggest lithium mining enterprise in Chile and the second largest in the world. The company extracts one-fifth of the worlds' known lithium resources. It is located in the middle of the Atacama Salt Lake, and a direct neighbor of Toconao (figure 20.3). According to SQM's report of the results for the second quarter of 2017, SQM S.A produces 40,000 tons of lithium per year, which represents 42 percent of the national output, followed by the company SCL (Rockwood) with 25 percent.[62] SQM S.A presents profits from the sale of lithium and its derivatives with a total value of US$ 297.4 million during the first six months of 2017. This was an increase of 54.3 percent compared to the US$ 192.8 million recorded in the first half of 2016. According to the projected world demand for lithium, its production will continue to increase.[63]

SQM S.A has developed extractive activities in the area for more than fifty years. According to the National Geology and Mining Service,[64] the company owns most of the mining concessions in the Antofagasta region (1,237,800 hectares) and water rights in the Atacama Salt Lake (344 liters per second).[65] Mönckeberg[66] states that beyond the importance of the company in the production and extraction of natural resources, its role has been fundamental in the privatization of mining in Chile.

SQM S.A was led by Enrique Valenzuela Blanquier during the military coup in 1973. In 1983, it was handed over to Pinochet's son-in-law, Julio Ponce Lerou, who was in charge until 2015 and who built his fortune in the shadow of the dictator.[67] As general manager of the Corporation for the Promotion of Production (CORFO), Ponce Lerou marked his participation in the privatization of SQM S.A with the creation of a sales contract that later made him the owner of the leading company in the extraction of lithium.[68]

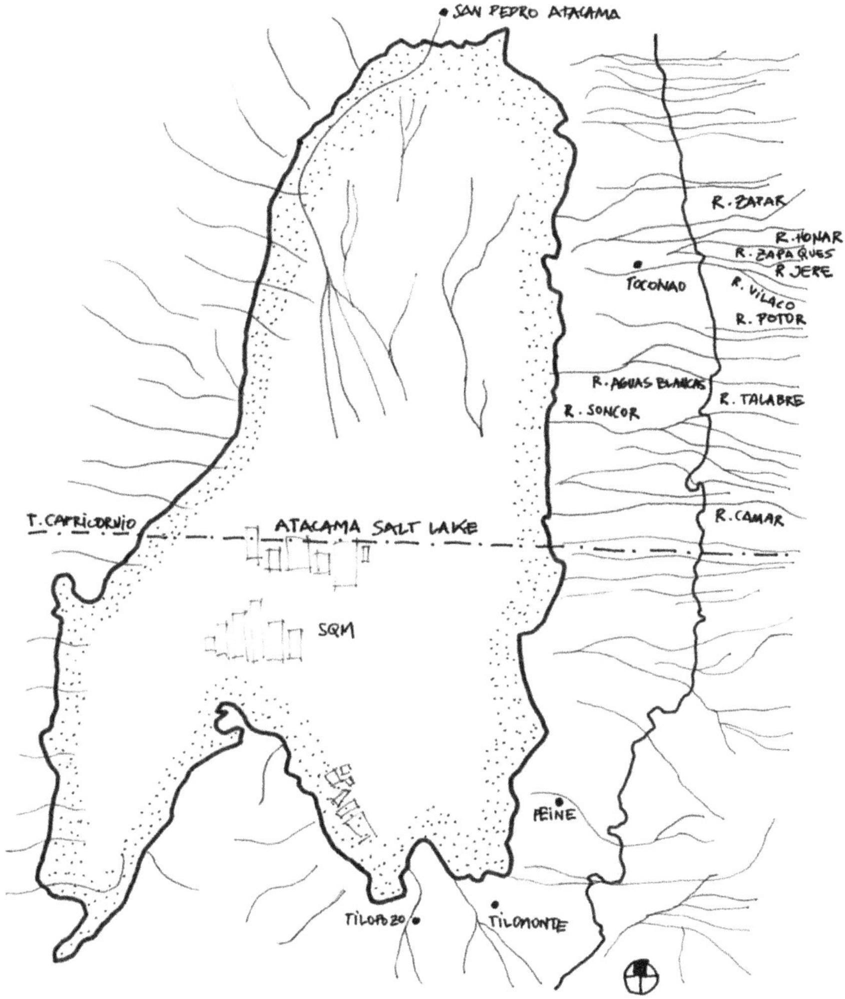

Figure 20.3 Map of the Atacama Salt Lake and its Closeness to Indigenous Communities of Atacama Desert. Source: Author based on Google maps and Games, 2013.

With the support from the army, which included his father, brothers, and friends, who were all protected by Pinochet, he created a framework of action within the government that was later transferred to the privatized SQM S.A, which concentrated its lithium monopoly.[69] Julio Ponce Lerou is considered one of the most powerful characters of the military regime and was not only in charge of the company that produces lithium and fertilizers; he was also leading different institutions that gave him a privileged platform of action to build his empire, including positions as Director of CONAF, President of the

Cellulose Constitution and manager of several state-owned companies. In addition to the economic power that Lerou has generated from managing the iodine and lithium market, he also heavily shaped political alliances in Chile, which have produced and reproduced support for the company to maintain its control and easy access to natural resources.[70]

Additionally, several conflicts have been generated by SQM S.A.'s administration at the community level through its corporate social responsibility (CSR) program. This is because this program has created drastic changes in the traditional and complex systems of water management that the Atacama settlements and most Chilean communities in the Andes have used for centuries. Traditional and sophisticated irrigation systems are the reflections of an intimate connection between the communities and their water resources. Local indigenous communities have seen these connections threatened by SQM S.A.'s CSR programs, especially the one called "Atacama Tierra Fertile" which promotes domestic water use through monoculture techniques.

Indigenous knowledge focuses on the materiality and spirituality of the water cycle, building a strong sense of community identity in relation to rituals and the day-to-day use of water.[71] As a consequence of the CSR program, the ethical practice of water use has been deteriorated through the loss of fundamental values such as solidarity, reciprocity, and autonomy.

PLAYING IN AN UNEVEN SOCCER FIELD: THE VILLAGE OF TOCONAO

Toconao has been subject to constant pressures from the concessions of land to SQM S.A. The community of Toconao is located 33 kilometers south-east of San Pedro de Atacama and was declared as an indigenous community by law on August 12, 1995.[72] Toconao has currently 732 inhabitants, of which 76 percent declare themselves as indigenous and 70 percent are classified as elderly people. About 50 percent of the population lives from agriculture, while the other half works in jobs related to mining, services, tourism, and crafts.[73] The main supply of potable water and water for agricultural purposes is owned by the community and administered by the Committee of Rural Potable Water and the Irrigators' and Farmers' Association of Toconao, respectively.[74] Figure 20.4 shows the main three ravines—"*Zapar*," "*Jere*," and "*Aguas Blancas*"—which geographically divide the area of the Indigenous Community of Toconao. They further represent the three Irrigators' and Farmers' Associations. Toconao's waters come from the streams *Honar, Vilaco, Zapaques, Jere, and Zilapeti*, and their waters are distributed among all members of the association. The irrigation canal system of Toconao covers an area of 92 hectares and has an extension of 17,000 meters,

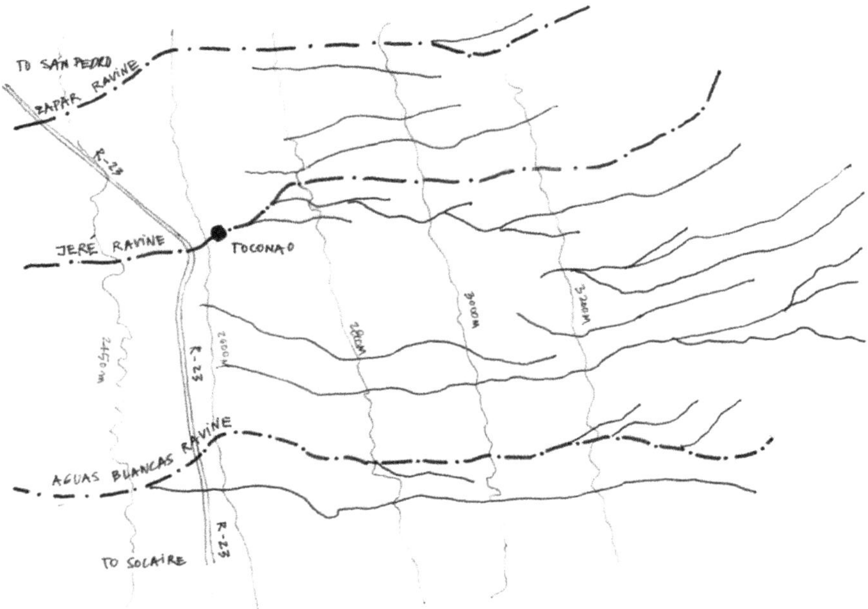

Figure 20.4 Map of Ravines with Potable and Agricultural Water, Toconao Sector.
Source: Author based on Google Maps, 2015

which is considered an adequate capacity to be an independent community regarding water supply. The community is entitled to 581.3 liters per second from the rivers, canals, and springs.[75]

Lautaro Núñez[76] argues that there is a clear relationship between the inhabitants of the town of Toconao and the use of its irrigation canals. This is based on the way of inhabiting this particular space, changing and transforming its territory, molded through daily practices and mobility. He also mentions that the festivities around water and water cycles are activities that best reflect the Atacameño's spirit.[77] Roy Rappaport[78] suggests that these rituals are the medium through which inhabitants communicate themselves with the environment. Through these activities, people create bonds between their work, their ancestors, community members, friends of the community members, between the ancestral and contemporary water infrastructure, and the natural and divine world.

A clear example of this relationship is the annual community festivity of the cleaning of the canals, which reaffirms forms of belonging, identity, and culture in a social space. During this festivity, it is possible to observe negotiations over the control over water and the territory.[79] Beyond the physical and functional need to keep the canals in good condition for agricultural purposes, these activities are a form of celebrating, and being grateful for, water resources.[80] However, in the case of Toconao, one interesting finding is that these practices have been weakened. This results mainly from incentives to work individually and the promotion of monoculture through technical irrigation systems, which are pushed by the CSR program. Additionally, there are constant pressures on the territory for the delivery of concessions of land to mining companies, generating conflicts over the use and distribution of water for community processes.[81]

The concession plan (figure 20.5) shows that Toconao's territory is included in the mining plan and an exploration concession granted to SQM S.A. (Salt flat I2-3). Hence, like many other communities, it has been subject to constant pressures from mining companies to exploit its natural resources and the use of water effluents which facilitates the exploration and later extraction of mineral resources. The rectangles which are adjacent to the community account for the extraction concession (also granted to SQM S.A.), whereas the rectangles shown in dotted line represent the area of exploration.

SQM S.A obtains economic advantages at the expense of the welfare of the communities. Through the privatization of the waters, SQM S.A has generated a scenario of injustice and inequity in this territory.[82] In this area, the mining sector holds 93 percent of groundwater rights and 6.9 percent of surface water.[83]

The dictatorship had a severe impact on Toconao through regulating access to property titles for housing and agricultural plots, as well as through providing assistance to construct infrastructure, roads, and irrigation canals.[84]

Currently, for the majority of the indigenous communities bordering the Atacama Desert, the scarcity of water, the lack of recognition of their communal water rights, the lack of water infrastructure, and the low level of recognition of their voices in the Irrigators' and Farmers' Associations, offers little power in negotiating conflicts over water.[85] Moreover, many farmers adhered to the laws of the market and promoted the sale of their resources to mining companies. For example, the Irrigators' and Farmers' Associations of "*Aguas Blancas*," belonging to the community of Toconao, began to supply water to the company SQM S.A in 2013. According to the water supply contract between the Irrigators' and Farmers' Associations of "*Aguas Blancas*" and the mining company SQM S.A, the association sells, or as its members phrase it, supplies, water to SQM S.A. It transfers 4,752 m³, 55 liters per second, at a value of US $ 1.05 per m³.[86] This contract created fragmentation in the community of Toconao, because many members opposed the sale of water to a mining company since it clashes with the fundamental values of their worldview. Moreover, this situation led to economic conflicts, because the sale provided monetary benefits only for the members of the Irrigators' and Farmers' Associations of "*Aguas Blancas*" and not for the entire population of Toconao.

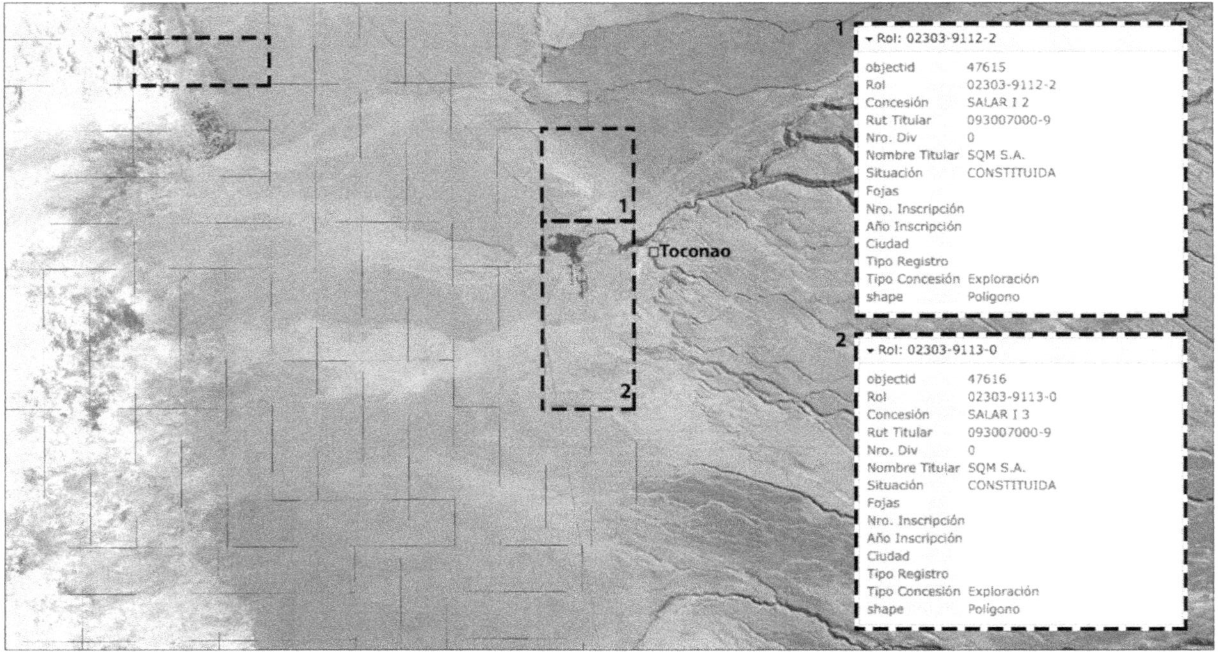

Figure 20.5 Map of Mining Concessions in the Toconao Sector. *Source*: Author based on IDE Chile (Infraestructura de Datos Geoespaciales), Ministry of National Goods, 2017.

These conflicts have generated a complex scenario: First, the water flows have considerably diminished. Second, there has been a change in the water balance and groundwaters, altering the natural water cycle of Atacama's salt flat basin which brings life to this ecological system. In addition, concern arises because of a strong lack of community engagement and a persistent individual interest that has been created by the existing free trade model. Currently, the reduction in water use and availability do not only constitute the principal threat to the community, but also the changes in the hydrological cycle and the access to groundwater being used by mining companies.

PENALTY KICKS: DISCUSSION AND CONCLUSIONS

There is no doubt that mining is one of the most significant contributors to the water crisis in Chile. The current legislation supports the private sector and favors free market economics.[87] Mining companies enter indigenous territories through claiming their water rights and often ignore local rules. Therefore, new patterns of exploration, extraction, and commodification create new territories.[88] The manifestation of the current legislation and the introduction of new modes of agricultural production through new irrigation systems have produced changes in water management as well as changes in the social and power relations around water. Jessica Budds[89] argues that the relationship between water and power is central to understanding the economic actions implicit in Chile.

Since the dictatorship, water was considered a productive element subjected to market logic. Water became a commodity that should be used efficiently.[90] The state and the mining sector have taken this premise of being productive and efficient through technological development. Therefore, new irrigation systems have been promoted by the CSR program as a relationship-building approach, helping local farmers to produce efficiently and reduce the quantity of water in their agricultural production.

At the national scale, the company SQM S.A, led by Julio Ponce Lerou, has taken advantage of the legislative platform created in the dictatorship to dominate the lithium market and the territory through mining concessions and water rights. Understanding the current consequences of mining business models imposed by the dictatorship not only requires analyzing the relationship between the privatization of state enterprises and the privatization of water and natural resources but also demands an understanding of the changes in water practices and relations of solidarity, access, and autonomy in the distribution of resources in the Andean villages.

It is essential to understand the legislative platform generated by the dictatorship, the current Constitution, the Water Code, and the Mining Code, which together have generated an institutional base for protecting the private sector at the expense of the territory of the inhabitants of the Atacama Desert. Moreover, this platform helps to understand the conflicts in the everyday practices of the inhabitants of Toconao. It is causing a constant and systemic violation of human rights, not only through the extraction of mineral resources but also through their massive water demand. This loss of water rights has been the result of granting water rights to third parties through mining concessions.[91]

This chapter highlighted the weakness of the state in protecting indigenous communities, which is reflected in the limited oversight by the DGA. On the other hand, the state is active and agile in its relation to the private sector, especially in the delivery of concessions and water rights. This situation is manifested through changes in the forms or practices related to water, responding to the neoliberal logic established by the power dynamics created in the dictatorship. It ignores a vision of the human scale,[92] which is sustained in the support of fundamental needs such as autonomy, solidarity, cooperation, and local traditions, which are pillars of the Andean culture.[93]

Communities face challenges of being invisible in development models promoted by mining companies, which makes it necessary to visualize the different ways of understanding development and, above all, the various ways to manage water resources. However, as long as the Chilean State continues to provide water rights and mining concessions to private companies, SQM S.A will continue to take advantage of the market model and communities will continue to lose rights when captured by these dynamics. Therefore, a paradigm shift is imperative concerning the distribution of natural resources and the protection of communities close to the production centers.

SQM S.A forged its strength at the hands of a dictatorship and managed to accumulate a tremendous political and economic power in the democratic era. Its strength was reinforced by a strategy of legitimation based on its business success; a model to be followed by many of the community members, who benefit from CSR programs. SQM S.A increasingly emphasizes assisting localities through its agro-productive development plans, whose primary aim is to promote economic development. However, it does not seriously consider the ancestral cultural heritage of local communities. Overall SQM S.A promotes social programs but continues to advance its territorial expansion and search for water resources through mining concessions with an extractivist vision,[94] which commercializes ancestral water practices.

The chapter showed how the current legislation, established during the dictatorship, has not changed over time. However, communities have changed their practices, following the free market laws, generating fragmentation among the inhabitants of the Atacama Desert.

NOTES

1. This text is based on Chapter 4 "Setting up the context" of a PhD research titled "Hydrosocial territories in the Atacama Desert: An ethnographic analysis of changing water practices in Toconao, Chile," which was conducted at The Bartlett Development Planning Unit, University College London. I wish to thank Toconao's council and its members for their constant support during this research as well as Dr. Caroline Newton, Dr. Manuel Prieto, and Dr. Alexandre Apsan Frediani for their supervision, time and interest in discussing issues related to Lickanantay territory. Finally, I thank the editors of this book for their valuable comments on this work.

2. Bente Bittmann, Gustavo Le Paige, and Lautaro Nuñez, *Cultura Atacameña, Serie El Patrimonio Cultural Chileno*, ed. Francisco Olivares, 1st ed. (Santiago de Chile: Gabriela Mistral, 1978).

3. Lautaro Nuñez, *Vida Y Cultura En Los Oasis de San Pedro De Atacama* (Santiago de Chile: Editorial Universitaria, 2007).

4. Marygold Walsh-Dilley, "Negotiating Hybridity in Highland Bolivia: Indigenous Moral Economy and the Expanding Market for Quinoa," *Journal of Peasant Studies* 40, no. 4 (2013): 659–82.

5. Alonso Barros, "Autonomía y Territorio," in *XII Congreso Internacional Derecho Consuetudinario y Pluralismo Legal: Desafios En El Tercer Milenio* (Arica: LOM Ediciones, 2000), 548–54.

6. Jonathan D.A. Clarke, "Antiquity of Aridity in the Chilean Atacama Desert," *Geomorphology* 73, nos. 1–2 (January 2006): 101–14.

7. Rodrigo Mundaca, *La Privatización de Las Aguas En Chile: Causas y Resistencia*, ed. Rodrigo Faúndez, Primera Ed (Santiago de Chile: Editorial America en Movimiento, 2014).

8. Manuel Prieto, "Transando El Agua, Produciendo Territorios e Identidades Indígenas: El Modelo de Aguas Chileno y Los Atacameños de Calama," *Revista de Estudios Sociales (RES)* 55, no. 1 (2016): 88–103.

9. Nancy Yáñez and Raúl Molina, *La Gran Minería y Los Derechos Indígenas En El Norte de Chile*, First edit (Santiago de Chile: LOM Ediciones, 2008).

10. Chile Sustentable, *Conflictos Por El Agua En Chile: Entre Los Derechos Humanos y Las Reglas Del Mercado*, ed. Sara Larrain and Pamela Poo, *Chile Sustentable*, Primera ed (Santiago de Chile: Grafica Andes, 2010).

11. Paul Trawick, "The Moral Economy of Water: Equity and Antiquity in the Andean Commons," *American Anthropologist* 103, no. 2 (2001): 361.

12. Sebastian Smart, "La Política Del Extractivismo: Origen En Dictadura y Continuidad En Democracia," in *Un País Desigual a La Fuerza: Complicidad Económica Con La Dictadura Chilena*, ed. Juan Pablo Bohoslavsky, Karinna Fernández, and Sebastian Smart (Santiago de Chile: LOM Ediciones, 2018), In Press.

13. Cristián Olmos Herrera, "Hydrosocial Territories in the Atacama Desert: An Ethnographic Analysis of Changing Water Practices in Toconao, Chile" (University College London, 2019).

14. Manuel Prieto, "Privatizing Water in the Chilean Andes: The Case of Las Vegas de Chiu-Chiu," *Mountain Research and Development* 35, no. 3 (2015): 220–29.

15. Sernageomin, "Catastro Minero On Line – Sernageomin," 2018, http://catastro.sernageomin.cl/.

16. Patricio Meller, *La Viga Maestra y El Sueldo de Chile: Mirando El Futuro Con Ojos de Cobre* (Santiago de Chile: Editorial Uqbar, 2013).

17. Ministerio del Interior, "Ley N° 19.175 Organica Constitucional Sobre Gobierno y Administracion Regional," 2005, 2005, http://www.leychile.cl/Navegar?idNorma=243771&buscar=19175.

18. Ministerio de Justicia, "Codigo de Aguas" (1981).

19. Ministerio de Minería, "Codigo de Mineria" (1983).

20. Mattias Borg Rasmussen and Christian Lund, "Reconfiguring Frontier Spaces: The Territorialization of Resource Control," *World Development* 101 (2018): 388–99.

21. Banco Central de Chile, "Cuentas Nacionales de Chile 2013–2016" (Santiago de Chile, 2016).

22. Chile Sustentable, *Conflictos Por El Agua En Chile: Entre Los Derechos Humanos y Las Reglas Del Mercado*.

23. Yáñez and Molina, *La Gran Minería y Los Derechos Indígenas En El Norte de Chile*.

24. Alonso Barros, "Pachamama y Desarrollo: Paisajes Conflictivos En El Desierto de Atacama," *Estudios Atacameños* 13, no. 13 (1997): 75–94.

25. Paola Bolados García, "Procesos Transnacionales En El Salar de Atacama-Norte de Chile: Los Impactos de La Minería y El Turismo En Las Comunidades Indígenas Atacameñas," *Intersecciones En Antropología* 15 (2014): 431–43.

26. Carl J. Bauer, "Water Conflicts and Entrenched Governance Problems in Chile's Market Model," *Water Alternatives* 8, no. 2 (2015): 147–72.

27. Paola Bolados García, "Los Conflictos Etnoambientales de 'Pampa Colorada' y 'El Tatio' En El Salar de Atacama, Norte de Chile: Procesos Étnicos En Un Contexto Minero y Turístico Transnacional," *Estudios Atacameños*, no. 48 (2014): 228–48.

28. Beatriz Bustos, Manuel Prieto, and Jonathan Barton, *Ecología Política En Chile: Naturaleza, Propiedad, Conocimiento y Poder* (Santiago de Chile: Editorial Universitaria, 2014).

29. Paola Bolados, "¿Participación o Pacificación Social? La Lógica Neoliberal En El Campo de La Salud Intercultural En Chile: El Caso Atacameño," *Estudios Atacameños*, 2009.

30. Ministerio de Minería, Codigo de Mineria.

31. Yáñez and Molina, *La Gran Minería y Los Derechos Indígenas En El Norte de Chile*.

32. Codigo de Mineria.

33. Ministerio de Justicia, Codigo de Aguas, 71.

34. Bauer, "Water Conflicts and Entrenched Governance Problems in Chile's Market Model."

35. Prieto, "Privatizing Water in the Chilean Andes: The Case of Las Vegas de Chiu-Chiu."

36. Jessica Budds, "Water, Power, and the Production of Neoliberalism in Chile, 1973–2005," *Environment and Planning D: Society and Space* 31, no. 2 (2013): 301–18.

37. Nancy Yáñez and Raúl Molina, *Las Aguas Indígenas En Chile*, First edit (Santiago de Chile: LOM Ediciones, 2011).

38. "Teoría y Práctica de Los Derechos Ancestrales de Agua de Las Comunidades Atacameñas," *Estudios Atacameños* 19 (2000): 93–112.

39. Yáñez and Molina, *La Gran Minería y Los Derechos Indígenas En El Norte de Chile*.

40. Walter Imilan, "Socaireños En Movimiento. Atacameños y Calama," *Estudios Atacameños: Arqueología y Antropología Surandinas* 33 (2007): 105–23.

41. Jessica Budds, "Power, Nature and Neoliberalism: The Political Ecology of Water in Chile," *Singapore Journal of Tropical Geography* 25, no. 3 (2004): 322–42; Jessica Budds, "La Demanda, Evaluación y Asignación Del Agua En El Contexto de Escasez: Un Análisis Del Ciclo Hidrosocial Del Valle Del Río La Ligua, Chile," *Revista de Geografía Norte Grande* 184, no. 52 (2012): 167–84; Budds, "Water, Power, and the Production of Neoliberalism in Chile, 1973–2005."

42. Ministerio de Obras Públicas, "Dirección de General de Aguas," n.d.

43. Cuadra, "Teoría y Práctica de Los Derechos Ancestrales de Agua de Las Comunidades Atacameñas."

44. Carl J. Bauer, "Bringing Water Markets down to Earth: The Political Economy of Water Rights in Chile, 1976–1995," *World Development* 25, no. 5 (1997): 639–56.

45. Yáñez and Molina, *La Gran Minería y Los Derechos Indígenas En El Norte de Chile*.

46. Juan P. Orrego, "El Estado de Las Aguas Terrestres En Chile: Cursos y Aguas Subterráneas" (Santiago de Chile, 2002).

47. Manuel Prieto, "Practicing Costumbres and the Decommodification of Nature: The Chilean Water Markets and the Atacameño People," *Geoforum* 77 (2016): 28–39.

48. Comunidad Atacameña de Toconao, "Estatuto Comunidad Indigena Atacameña de Toconao" (2015).

49. Trawick, "The Moral Economy of Water: Equity and Antiquity in the Andean Commons."

50. Amber Wutich, "The Moral Economy of Water Reexamined: Reciprocity, Water Insecurity, and Urban Survival in Cochabamba, Bolivia," *Journal of Anthropological Research* 67, no. 1 (2011): 5–26.

51. Ministerio de Planificacion y Cooperacion, "Ley Indigena No 19253" (1993).

52. Ministerio de Planificacion y Cooperacion.

53. Manuel Prieto, "El Riego Que El Mercado No Quiere Ver: Historia Del Despojo Hídrico En Las Comunidades de Lasana y Chiu-Chiu (Desierto de Atacama, Chile)," *Journal of Latin American Geography* 16, no. 2 (2017): 69–91.

54. Cuadra, "Teoría y Práctica de Los Derechos Ancestrales de Agua de Las Comunidades Atacameñas."

55. Milka Castro Lucic, "La Tecnología Del Riego En La Cultura de Los Pueblos Andinos," in *Modernización de Riegos y Uso de Tecnologías de Información* (La Paz, 2007), 10.

56. Nicholas Hildyard et al., "Reclaiming the Commons | The Corner House," The corner House, 1995, http://www.thecornerhouse.org.uk/resource/reclaiming-commons.

57. "Making Environmental Law for the Market: The Emergence, Character, and Implications of Chile's Environmental Regime," *Environmental Politics* 20, no. 6 (2011): 879–98.

58. Astrid Ulloa, "Environment and Development: Reflections from Latin America," in *The Routledge Handbook of Political Ecology*, ed. Tom Perreault, Gavin Bridge, and James McCarthy, 1st ed. (London & New York: Routledge, 2015), 320–31.

59. Barros, "Pachamama y Desarrollo: Paisajes Conflictivos En El Desierto de Atacama."

60. Elinor Ostrom, *Governing the Commons: The Evolution of Institutions for Collective Actions*, First Edit (Cambridge: Cambridge University Press, 1990).

61. *Mineral Commodity Summaries 2018, U.S. Geological Survey*, 2018.

62. Comisión Chilena del Cobre, "Mercado Internacional Del Litio Diciembre 2013," 2013.

63. Sociedad Química y Minería, "Informe de Resultados Del Segundo Trimestre de 2017 SQM S.A." (Santiago de Chile, 2017).

64. Sernageomin, "Catastro Minero On Line - Sernageomin."

65. Ministerio de Obras Públicas, "Dirección de General de Aguas."

66. *El Saqueo de Los Grupos Economicos Al Estado Chileno* (Santiago de Chile: DEBOLS!LLO, 2015); *La Máquina Para Defraudar: Los Casos Penta y Soquimich*, Digital Ed (Santiago de Chile: DEBATE, 2015).

67. Mönckeberg, *La Máquina Para Defraudar: Los Casos Penta y Soquimich.*

68. Alberto Arellano and Juan Pablo Figueroa, "El Día En Que El Estado Le Entregó El Control Del Salar de Atacama a Ponce Lerou," CIPER Chile, 2015, http://ciperchile.cl/2015/06/26/el-dia-en-que-el-estado-le-entrego-el-control-del-salar-de-atacama-a-ponce-lerou/.

69. Victor Osorio and Iván Cabezas, *Los Hijos de Pinochet*, Colección Chile--Su Historia Inmediata (Santiago de Chile: Planeta, 1995).

70. Carlos Huneeus, *El Régimen de Pinochet* (Santiago de Chile: Penguin Random House Group Editorial, 2016).

71. Jamie Linton and Jessica Budds, "The Hydrosocial Cycle: Defining and Mobilizing a Relational-Dialectical Approach to Water," in *Seventh International Workshop on Hydro Hegemony* (London, 2014).

72. Gobierno Regional Antofagasta, "Área de Desarrollo Indigena Atacama La Grane: Plan Inicial Integral Comunidad Indigena de Toconao" (Antofagasta, 2009).

73. Gobierno Regional Antofagasta, "Política Regional Para La Integración de Localidades Aisladas: Implementación de Ejes Estratégicos Para La Atención de Los Factores Condicionantes de Aislamiento En La Región de Antofagasta" (Antofagasta, 2012).

74. Dirección General de Aguas, "Derechos de Aprovechamiento de Agua Registradas En DGA, Comuna de San Pedro de Atacama" (Antofagasta, 2017).

75. Dirección General de Aguas.

76. *Cultura y Conflicto En Los Oasis de San Pedro de Atacama*, First (Santiago de Chile: Editorial Universitaria, 1992).

77. Nuñez, *Vida Y Cultura En Los Oasis de San Pedro De Atacama.*

78. *Ritual and Religion in the Making of Humanity (Cambridge Studies in Social and Cultural Anthropology)* (Cambridge: Cambridge University Press, 1999).

79. Paola Bolados and Sally Babidge, "Ritualidad y Extractivismo. La Limpia de Canales y Las Disputas Por El Agua En El Salar de Atacama-Norte de Chile," *Estudios Atacameños*, no. 54 (2017): 201–16.

80. Reinaldo Lagos et al., "La Limpia de Canales y Acequias de Santiago de Rio Grande," *Revista Chungará* 21 (1988): 43–78.

81. Anita Carrasco, "Entre Dos Aguas : Identidad Moral En La Relación Entre Corporaciones Mineras y La Comunidad Indígena de Toconce En El Desierto de Atacama," *Chungara Revista de Antropología Chilena* 46, no. 2 (2014): 247–58; Mundaca, *La Privatización de Las Aguas En Chile: Causas y Resistencia*; Isabel Sepúlveda Rivera et al., "Aguas, Riego y Cultivos: Cambios y Permanencias En Los Ayllus de San Pedro de Atacama," *Estudios Atacameños*, no. 51 (2015): 185–206; Yáñez and Molina, *Las Aguas Indígenas En Chile.*

82. Mundaca, *La Privatización de Las Aguas En Chile: Causas y Resistencia.*

83. Yáñez and Molina, *La Gran Minería y Los Derechos Indígenas En El Norte de Chile.*

84. Cuadra, "Teoría y Práctica de Los Derechos Ancestrales de Agua de Las Comunidades Atacameñas."

85. Manuel Prieto, "Human Rights, Indigenous Peoples and Extractive Industries," Public Political Ecology Lab, 2013, https://www.youtube.com/watch?v=0Qn3BMbSa8I.

86. Sociedad Química y Minería, "Contrato de Suministro de Aguas: Aguas Blancas - SQM 2014" (Calama, 2014).

87. Bauer, "Bringing Water Markets down to Earth: The Political Economy of Water Rights in Chile, 1976–1995."

88. Rasmussen and Lund, "Reconfiguring Frontier Spaces: The Territorialization of Resource Control."

89. "Power, Nature and Neoliberalism: The Political Ecology of Water in Chile"; "Contested H2O: Science, Policy and Politics in Water Resources Management in Chile," *Geoforum* 40, no. 3 (May 2009): 418–30; "La Demanda, Evaluación y Asignación Del Agua En El Contexto de Escasez: Un Análisis Del Ciclo Hidrosocial Del Valle Del Río La Ligua, Chile"; "Water, Power, and the Production of Neoliberalism in Chile, 1973–2005."

90. Daniela Henriquez et al., "Creating Small Farm Entrepreneurs or Doing Away with Peasants? State-Driven Implementation of Drip Irrigation in Chile," in *Drip Irrigation for Agriculture: Untold Stories of Efficiency, Innovation and Development*, ed. Jean-Philippe Venot, Marcel Kuper, and Margreet Zwarteveen (London & New York: Routledge, 2017), 122–33.

91. Yáñez and Molina, *Las Aguas Indígenas En Chile*.

92. Manfred Max-Neef, *Human Scale Development: Conceptions, Application and Further Reflections*, First (New York: The Apex Press, 1991).

93. Alonso Barros, "Pachamama and Development: Conflicting Landscapes in the Atacama Desert" (University of Cambridge, 1997).

94. Eduardo Gudynas, "Extracciones, Extractivismos y Extrahecciones. Un Marco Conceptual Para La Apropiación de Recursos Naturales," *Observatorio Del Desarrollo, Centro de Latinoamericano de Desarrollo Social (CLAES)*, no. 18 (2013): 1–18.

Chapter 21

Corporate Complicity in Human Rights Violations in Chile

The Case of Forestry Companies and the Mapuche People

José Aylwin

INTRODUCTION[1]

With properties that exceed 3 million hectares, most of which are planted with fast-growing exotic species, forestry companies are the largest landowners in Chile. Approximately 2.1 million of these hectares correspond to forest monocultures found in the Bío Bío, Araucanía, Los Ríos, and Los Lagos regions,[2] occupying both the lands traditionally owned by Mapuche people and lands legally recognized to its communities by the Chilean state since its inception.

An important part of these lands was acquired by forestry companies during the period in which the agrarian reform was reversed—also known as the counter-agrarian reform process—promoted in the first years of the Pinochet dictatorship. This is not a coincidence, but rather is the consequence of the firm support and close link that these companies had with the military regime. Moreover, some of these companies were involved in acts of repression committed against their workers who sympathized with the socialist government of Salvador Allende (1970–1973). The support and close connection of these companies and their directors with the dictatorship was fundamental, not only in the process of expansion of their property in the territory traditionally occupied by the Mapuche people but also in their support by the state, through subsidies established in 1974 for exotic forest plantations, support that have made of forestry one of the country's most important economic activities, generating huge profits for forest conglomerates.

This chapter will analyze the history of the forestry industry in Chile, its situation prior and during the government of President Salvador Allende, the close links of this industry with active collaborators of the military coup, as well as its involvement during the dictatorship in repressive activities that resulted in the murder of workers of a private pulp mill. Subsequently, I describe the counter-agrarian reform process promoted by the military dictatorship and its implications for the Mapuche people, as well as the privatization process of public enterprises promoted by the said regime in its early years, which resulted in the irregular acquisition of lands by the forestry conglomerates and allowed the consolidation of the industry.

I also look at Decree Law No. 701 on forest subsidies enacted in 1974, as well as at the manner in which this legislation was used, until recently, to benefit the forestry conglomerates with state resources and tax exemptions. Then I analyze the impacts that the private forest industry has had on the rights of the Mapuche people, among them the dispossession of their lands and territories of traditional occupation, and the social and environmental implications of this industry, including the impoverishment and the impact on the water generated by the monoculture of exotic tree species planted by them. I also analyze the criminalization by the state, in complicity with the forestry companies, of Mapuche people social protest in the past two decades due to the forestry expansion in their ancestral lands and territories. I conclude by reflecting on the lack of truth, justice, and reparation in relation to crimes committed during the dictatorship, as well as in relation to human rights violations of the Mapuche people committed during that period as well as in recent years, in which according to all evidence, these companies have been involved. I also refer to the persistence of public policies that promote the forestry model controlled by large conglomerates, with its adverse implications on the Mapuche people, reflecting on the responsibility both of the Chilean State as well as that of business, and on the need to ensure nonrecurrence of these human rights violations in the future.

BACKGROUND OF THE FOREST INDUSTRY IN CHILE AND THE CONSOLIDATION DURING THE DICTATORSHIP OF THE PRIVATE CONGLOMERATES THAT CONTROL IT TODAY

Large-scale exotic species plantations for paper production in Chile date back to the first half of the twentieth century. These plantations were developed based on the Forestry Law of 1931 and were run by private individuals, particularly by the Compañía Manufacturera de Papeles y Cartones (CMPC), created in 1920 and controlled by the Matte family, as well as by the state, the latter particularly under the governments of Frei Montalva (1964–1970) and Allende (1970–1973). Along with these plantations, the expansion of forestry activity was manifested in the installation of large pulp mills. Initially, these were built by private companies, such as CMPC's Laja Plant, constructed in the 1950s. Later they were built by the state, such as the Celulosa Arauco S.A. plant built in 1967 and the Celulosa Constitución S.A. plant built in 1969, both companies belonging to the Corporación de Fomento de la Producción (CORFO).[3]

The predominance of this industry in Chile until 1970, however, was in the hands of CMPC. By that year the pulp production reached 220,000 tons per year, its paper production amounted to 150,000 tons, and its exports reached nearly US$ 30 million.[4] Allende's triumph in the 1970 presidential election, and the defeat in the same elections of CMPC board member, Jorge Alessandri, led the Matte clan to participate in plans to prevent Allende's assumption as president.[5] Allende's plans to nationalize the CMPC later led the same family clan, which controlled the company at that time, to promote strong opposition to the Popular Unity government, which had the El Mercurio newspaper as its main ally. It should be recalled that the owner of this newspaper, Agustín Edwards, has been syndicated as one of the main instigators of the 1973 coup d'état; this, through his close and documented connections with the Nixon government and the CIA.[6]

Journalistic investigations carried out in recent years indicate that CMPC, through its directors at that time, was involved in the events that resulted in the death of nineteen individuals, a few days after the coup, the majority of whom were workers at the Laja pulp mill and were involved in the political parties of the Popular Unity. According to these investigations, it has been determined that the names of the people murdered by the police were provided by company executives, and then they were transferred from the detention center—where they were tortured and handcuffed with wire—in a bus owned by the company, and later shot on a property also owned by the company. The corpses of the victims were then covered with lime provided by the company on company property. Consequently, and according to all evidence, the company's executives acted as intellectual authors or at least as accomplices to this crime against humanity.[7] The policemen prosecuted for these acts, pursuant to a complaint filed by the Archbishop's office of Concepción, were absolved in 1980 by the military court that investigated the case, a decision that later, in 1981, was ratified by the Supreme Court. The case was reopened in 2012, being then substantiated by the Concepción Court of Appeals, which initially focused on the prosecution of the police officers for their responsibility in these events.[8] In March 2017, however, the same court accepted the complainants' petition to bring CMPC executives to trial.[9]

The close link between this company and the new civic–military dictatorship soon resulted in benefits in its favor. In October 1973, barely a month after September 11, the military regime liberalized the price of the paper that had been regulated under the Allende government, a measure taken for its obvious benefit.[10] In 1974, Julio Ponce Lerou, a forestry engineer, who had worked for CMPC in Concepción, and son-in-law of Pinochet, assumed the leadership of the National Forestry Corporation (CONAF), where, in October of that year, he promoted the Decree Law No. 701 that established subsidies and tax exemptions for forest plantations aimed at large enterprises. Along with this measure, the dictatorship would promote two processes that were key in the expansion and consolidation of private forestry activity in the southern-central part of the country, to the detriment of the interests of all Chileans and, in particular, to the rights of the Mapuche people.

THE COUNTER-AGRARIAN REFORM AND THE CONSOLIDATION OF THE FORESTRY COMPANIES' PROPERTY IN MAPUCHE TERRITORY

The first of these processes was the counter-agrarian reform, through which the dictatorship restored to its former owners a significant part of the lands expropriated between 1967 and 1973 under the governments of Presidents Eduardo Frei and Salvador Allende pursuant to the agrarian reform law (No. 16,640 of 1967). Moreover, the regime transferred to the state, and to the armed forces, a large part of these lands, and ordered the auction of the remaining expropriated lands by the Corporación de Reforma Agraria (CORA). It is estimated that about one-third of the 10 million hectares expropriated during the agrarian reform were sold by the state to private individuals.[11] A still undetermined but significant part of these lands, in the southern-central part of the country, were sold to forestry business consortia. As pointed out by the ILO in relation to this phenomenon, "the lands expropriated from both peasant farmers and Mapuche communities were auctioned off and bought by business sectors, which in turn acquired the patrimony and timber and cellulosic infrastructure liquidated by the State."[12] The irregularities in land sales during the counter-agrarian reform, including the close relationship between the government authorities of that time and the purchasers,[13] and the undervaluation of the amounts paid by those purchasers were highlighted by a Special Inquiry Commission created by the Chamber of Deputies that looked at the impacts of privatizations that had taken place during the military regime on state assets, set up initially in 1991, a year after the end of Pinochet dictatorship, which only finalized its task in 2004–2005.[14]

Such sales were particularly significant in the southern-central part of the country in the territories of traditional Mapuche occupation. Thus, in the provinces of Arauco, Malleco, and Cautín alone, CORA kept hold of 415,053 hectares that had been expropriated during the agrarian reform in favor of peasant farmers and Mapuche people. These lands accounted for 58.4 percent of the total land expropriated in those provinces, proceeding to auction off most of the land to preexisting or emerging forestry conglomerates, who acquired them at very low prices.[15] Associated with the process of counter-agrarian reform that allowed the consolidation of the forest property in this part of the country, to the detriment of the territorial rights of the Mapuche people, a repressive process was verified, which according to the Report by the Historical Truth and New Deal with Indigenous Peoples Commission[16] resulted in the death or disappearance of an estimated total of 136 people of Mapuche origin,[17] most of them linked to the struggle for land restitution during the Popular Unity government. In addition to this are the numerous cases of people of Mapuche origin linked to the struggle for land in the same period, who were victims of political imprisonment and torture, whom to this day remain unaccounted for.[18]

The second of these processes was the privatization of public companies that was promoted in the years after the coup in the framework of the neoliberal transformation policies carried out by the dictatorship. Such privatization would result in the appropriation by the forest conglomerates of the pulp companies created by the state in the 1960s to stimulate the country's forestry economy. Thus, Celulosa Arauco S.A. and Celulosa Constitución S.A., owned by CORFO, were privatized in 1977 and 1979, respectively, being acquired by Celulosa Arauco and Constitución (now Forestal Arauco), a corporation incorporated in September 1979 as a result of the merger of both former public companies.[19] Another of the privatized companies was Industrias Forestales S.A. (INFORSA) of which CORFO held half of its shares. This company, which could produce 60,000 tons of pulp and paper, was sold in the first years of the dictatorship to a bank consortium of the BHC group and, subsequently, after the cessation of payments by this group, was acquired by CMPC, belonging to the Matte group. The acquisition of INFORSA by CMPC was challenged before the Antitrust Commission since, through this purchase, this group came to have total control of paper production in the country. Such complaint, however, was dismissed by this Commission. Through this operation, CMPC acquired the ownership of several forestry companies (Rio Vergara, Maderas Nacimiento, Papeles Sudamerica, Forestal Crecex, Agrícola Monteverde, among others) with a total of approximately 75,000 hectares planted and another 9,000 to be planted.[20]According to the information contained in the Chamber of Deputies Inquiry Commission's report on privatizations, the sale of these companies and other state enterprises during this period meant millions in losses for the Treasury.[21]

STATE SUBSIDIES TO BENEFIT LARGE FORESTRY CONGLOMERATES

In addition to these privatizing and property concentration processes, the dictatorship's forestry project would be delineated in 1974 by the Decree Law (DL) No. 701, which established the policy of monetary and tax incentives for the sector, largely to the benefit of private conglomerates. This legislation promoted forest plantations, providing incentives for afforestation and recovery of apparently degraded soils.[22] In addition, it established subsidies to the afforestation of land equivalent to 75 percent of the costs of the plantation. As if that were not enough, it established the exemption of the territorial tax for the lands declared suitable for forest benefited with the subsidy.

As a result, between 1974 and1994 a total of 807,203 hectares of exotic monoculture plantations were subsidized.[23] Although subsequent laws (Law No. 19,561 of 1998 and Law 20,326 of 2009) extended the subsidy system to plantations of small and medium-sized forestry holdings,[24] throughout the validity of this legislation, state subsidies mostly benefited large forestry conglomerates. Thus, until 2013, the state subsidized forestation of 1.2 million hectares through DL 701, giving large, medium, and small owners a total of US$ 875 million dollars. Out of this amount, US$ 600 million benefited Forestal Arauco and Forestal Mininco (CMPC).[25]

According to CONAF, as a consequence of this policy monoculture plantations cover today an area of approximately 3,084 million hectares. In total, 1.88 million hectares correspond to plantations of radiata pine, 1.02 million hectares correspond to eucalyptus and the rest to other exotic species. The Bío Bío, La Araucanía, Los Ríos, and Los Lagos regions, which correspond to the territory traditionally occupied by Mapuche, until recently covered by dense native forests with great biodiversity, concentrate a total of 2,191million hectares of plantations. With 1,255 million hectares of forest monoculture, the Bío Bío region has the largest plantation area in the country. It is followed by the Araucanía region, with 632,000 hectares of exotic species plantations.[26]

The DL 701 substantially contributed to the consolidation of private forest ownership in the southern-central part of the country. Although there are about fifteen main forestry companies, two of those companies, Forestal Arauco and Forestal Mininco (CMPC), concentrate most of the property and the monoculture tree plantations. The former has 1,116,788 hectares, of which 766,762 are planted with fast-growing species[27] (the latter has approximately 733,923 hectares, of which 483,400 hectares correspond to fast-growing exotic tree plantations.[28] In 2014, Forestal Arauco declared profits of US$ 437 million and sales of US$ 5,329 million to the Superintendence of Securities and Insurance, while CMPC declared profits of US$ 138 million and sales of US$ 4,846 million).[29]

THE IMPACTS OF THE ACTIVITIES OF FORESTRY COMPANIES ON THE MAPUCHE PEOPLE

As verified in a recent report commissioned by the Forestry Stewardship Council (FSC) International,[30] an entity that until 2016 had certified twenty-one forestry companies in Chile with a surface area of approximately 2.2 million hectares, 1.6 million hectares of them with monocultures,[31] a significant part of the lands on which these companies' activities were carried out overlap with the *Lof Mapu* or lands of traditional Mapuche occupation.[32] As this report shows a fairly large part of these plantations is located on lands restored to the Mapuche through the agrarian reform, which were later taken away from them during the dictatorship, ending up in the hands of the forest conglomerates.

Forest plantations of these companies are also located on lands that were part of the more than three thousand *Títulos de Merced* or mercy titles that the Chilean state granted to the Mapuche people in the late nineteenth and early twentieth centuries and then were appropriated by private individuals. This was a consequence of laws enacted in the 1930s, laws that promoted their division in individual parcels and their transfer to nonindigenous people. Of particular importance in this regard were the laws dictated during the dictatorship (Decree Laws No. 2,568 and 2,570 of 1979), which resulted in the forced division of almost all Mapuche communities existing until then. According to this law, of a strong assimilationist nature, the lands resulting from the division would no longer be considered as indigenous, as well as their grantees. As a result of this legislation from 1979 to 1988, 2,918 Mapuche communities were divided, resulting in the creation of 73,444 parcels with a total of 519,257 hectares, with an average surface of 7.07 hectares.[33] Although these laws prohibited the transfer of lands resulting from the division, they resulted in Mapuche dispossession through various mechanisms, including the sale of shares and rights, leases for ninety-nine years, among others.[34] As a result of these processes, the area currently occupied by forestry companies in this territory far exceeds that of Mapuche land. This considering the lands that were recognized by the state as the communal property of the Mapuche after the military occupation of their territory in the nineteenth century, estimated at half a million hectares. Also considering those lands that have been restored to them in recent years through land purchases made by the Indigenous

Lands and Waters Fund of CONADI (National Corporation for Indigenous Development) created by Law No. 19,253 of 1993 on the promotion, protection, and development of indigenous peoples, as well as those fiscal lands transferred to them in recent years in accordance to the same legislation.[35]

Moreover, exotic monoculture plantations that surround Mapuche communities have radically altered the habitat and the flora and fauna to which Mapuche culture is associated, as well as impacted previously abundant water sources, including springs, estuaries, and rivers. Particularly serious is the desiccation of the waters as a consequence of these plantations. This situation, although evidenced by scientific research and the by Mapuche traditional knowledge, is still denied by forestry companies. This situation not only affects the traditional agricultural activities that Mapuche communities have traditionally developed but also increasingly affects access to drinking water and sanitation, which is considered as a human right by the United Nations.[36] Therefore, many communities are currently supplied with water of dubious quality by the municipalities. In the Araucanía region alone, is it estimated that 10.6 percent of the total regional population, that is, 92,461 people, particularly in rural areas where the Mapuche population is predominant, are currently supplied by water trucks.[37]

Despite the serious environmental implications of forest plantations, they have been carried out without any environmental assessment until the present. In fact, according to the General Environmental Law 19,300 of 1994, its subsequent amendments, and its regulation,[38] only forestry development projects defined as of "industrial" dimension, which in this part of the country must reach an area of 500 hectares or more, have to be submitted to the Environmental Impact Assessment System (EIA). Since the majority of forestry development projects are not this big—by the deliberate decision of the companies—they are not subject to EIA.

The environmental impacts are compounded by the serious social impacts caused by the plantations. According to the Ministry of Social Development, the Araucanía, with a third of the Mapuche population, is the region that has the highest percentage of the country's population living in poverty. Thus, the poverty rate measured by income reaches 23.6 percent of the regional population, in contrast to the national average of 11.7 percent. From a multidimensional point of view, through which the shortfalls in areas such as health, work, social security, education, housing, among others, are measured, the poverty rate in this region reaches 29.2 percent of the population, in contrast to the national average of 20.9 percent.[39] The incidence of forestry activities on high poverty rates is evidenced by official surveys. In 2015, the district that led the levels of income-related poverty in the country, with 38.1 percent of its population in a situation of poverty, was Cañete, in the Bío Bío region. That was followed by the districts of Carahue, with 36.3 percent, Cunco, with 33.7 percent, Collipulli with 32.7 percent, and Nueva Imperial with 31.8 percent, all of them in the Araucanía region. The districts with the highest percentages of multidimensional poverty were Nueva Imperial with 45.8 percent, Padre Las Casas with 44.7 percent, Carahue with 43.3 percent, and Lautaro with 41.9 percent, all in the Araucanía. Coincidentally, all of these districts have a high concentration of Mapuche demography. They also have a high density of plantations with a significant percentage of exotic species monocultures.[40]

The link between the development model based on forest monocultures and the persistence and concentration of poverty in Chile has been affirmed by the National Forestry Corporation (CONAF), the government entity is responsible for the administration of DL 701.[41]

As a consequence of this situation, the communities affected by the monoculture forests and Mapuche territorial organizations have carried out social protest actions in the past two decades. Such actions have included innumerable peaceful demonstrations throughout the Mapuche territory aimed at drawing the attention of the authorities on the impacts that the development of forestry activity has had in their communities, as well as at demanding the restitution of their lands of traditional occupation currently in the hands of forestry companies. Roadblocks, burning of plantations and forestry machinery have also taken place in some areas in this context.[42] In addition to the strong police repression to which the communities involved in social protests against the forestry companies have been subject, and which has resulted in the death of at least five Mapuche people and innumerable cases of torture, and cruel, inhuman, and degrading treatment, the leaders of these communities have been prosecuted by the state. Thus in the past two decades, hundreds of Mapuche people have been accused and prosecuted for their participation in acts of social protest that are considered crimes by Chilean legislation. According to Bidegain, only between 2008 and 2014, a total of 212 Mapuche people were subject to imprisonment, both as a result of convictions by tribunals or due to order of preventive detention by the same different.[43]

Police abuses that have resulted in the torture and death of Mapuche people in the context of social protest acts and in the judicial persecution of Mapuche leaders have raised concerns in international human rights organizations.[44] At least a hundred Mapuche people have been prosecuted under the Anti-Terrorist Act (Law No. 18,314 of 1984) that dates back to the military dictatorship. Notwithstanding its reform with the return to democracy, this law considers a broad range of actions to be terrorist crimes, violates the guarantees of due process, and allows keeping defendants in custody for long periods. This is in addition to establishing high penalties based on presumptions of responsibility. The conviction for terrorist offenses of eight Mapuche people in the context of social protest events against forestry and agricultural properties was observed by the Inter-American Court of Human Rights in its ruling in the case of *Norin Catrimán et al. vs. Chile* (2014). In that ruling, the Inter-American HR Court concluded that the application of the Anti-Terrorist Act in these cases, the State of Chile violated, among other rights, the legality and presumption of innocence, judicial guarantees, and personal liberty. In the same ruling, the court found that, according to information from international bodies and experts, the State of Chile "has not effectively resolved the causes that give rise to Mapuche social protest in the Bío Bío and Araucanía Regions,"[45] alluding directly to the usurpation of lands of traditional Mapuche occupation much of which is now in the hands of forestry companies that generate social conflict.

FINAL REFLECTIONS

The expansion since the dictatorship of private forestry enterprises, in particular the large forestry conglomerates—mostly Chilean owned—into the southern-central part of the country, in the traditional territory of the Mapuche people, has resulted in various forms of human rights violations. According to all evidence, agents of one of these companies, CMPC, were involved in the perpetration of crimes against humanity that resulted in the death of its workers in the early days of the dictatorship. Subsequently, under the same dictatorship, they seized lands, in a context of repression and violence, in the territory traditionally occupied by Mapuche people, lands which had been previously recognized and restored to these people and their communities by the state during the agrarian reform under the governments of President Frei and Allende.

Also, and due to the close ties and relationship that these corporations' owners and executives had with the dictatorship, they fraudulently took over companies that belonged to all Chileans through a privatization process characterized by serious irregularities. Moreover, the plantation of monocultures by these private holdings, which were promoted and subsidized by the state, on Mapuche traditional lands and territories, have resulted in the serious deterioration of the environment and the natural and cultural habitat of the Mapuche people. They have also impoverished their communities, which now make up the most deprived socioeconomic sectors of the country. The social protest of the Mapuche people generated by the adverse implications of forestry activity has been strongly suppressed by the Chilean State in the past two decades, which, far from responding to the Mapuche demand for justice, has used all its coercive power to placate this protest, thereby giving strong support to these companies.

Among the rights recognized in international human rights treaties ratified by Chile and declarations to which the state has adhered that have been violated in the context of the development of the forestry industry since dictatorship until today, we identify the right to life, not only in its biological dimension but also in the case of indigenous peoples, to their collective right to a decent life in accordance with their culture;[46] the right of these peoples to own and possess their lands, territories, and natural resources of traditional occupation; the right to the environment; the rights to water, as well as their right to self-determination and to define their priorities in development.[47] This situation has aroused the concern of international human rights organizations and the condemnation of the Inter-American Court of Human Rights. The same concern is shared by the study commissioned by FSC International, which concluded that forestry companies certified by this entity do not meet the basic human rights requirements that are required to obtain such certification.[48]

The ultimate responsibility to ensure the effective implementation of human rights and to protect individuals from their violation lies in the state. In cases of gross human rights violations, such as those described in this chapter—which include not only the murder of CMPC workers in 1973 but also the disappearance, execution, and torture of members of the Mapuche people involved in the struggle for land rights in the context of the agrarian reform—states, in the context of transitional justice processes as the one Chile is living, must ensure not only truth but also justice, reparation, and nonrepetition or recurrence with regard to such human rights violations.[49] There is also an international law consensus that the state is responsible for the protection of individuals not only against human violations committed by its agents but also against acts committed by persons or private entities.[50]

Regrettably, the Chilean state has not adopted the measures that are needed to adequately address those human rights violations committed during the dictatorship which are related to the forestry activity here analyzed. Although truth with regard to the gross human rights violations committed during that period affecting the Mapuche was partially addressed, first in the early 1990s through the Truth and Reconciliation Commission,[51] and later, in 2003, through the Historical Truth and New Deal Commission with Indigenous Peoples, nonofficial reports on human rights violations committed during the dictatorship show that the impact of repression on Mapuche land right defenders during those years was much higher than that identified by such commissions. Moreover, justice in cases of human rights violations here referred to is far from being achieved. There are very few cases in which those involved in the assassination or torture of the Mapuche have been tried or sentenced to prison.[52] The same can be said if we consider those actions in which forestry conglomerates were involved, or were complicit with, which resulted in human rights violations. It has taken almost forty-five years for a court to prosecute CMPC executives, that according to all evidence, were involved in the murder and in attempts to disappear workers of that company that sympathized with the Allende regime. Fraud against the state as a result of the obscure privatization process of public companies acquired by forestry companies that now are among the wealthiest conglomerates of the country, although investigated by the Special Inquiry Commission created by the Chamber of Deputies that looked after the impacts of such process on state assets never resulted in the prosecution the civil or criminal responsibility of such companies or of their legal representatives.

Although some compensation and reparation has been given to those Mapuche that survived torture or prison or to the relatives of those that were killed as a consequence of repression, in equal conditions to compensation received by other victims of gross human rights violations during the dictatorship, such compensation has been minimal.[53] State policy aimed at the restitution of lands of which the Mapuche were dispossessed during that period, on many occasions by forestry conglomerates, could be considered a form of reparation for that dispossession. This policy, however, which operates through state land purchases at high market values, has not addressed Mapuche claim to obtain restitution of their lands of traditional occupation, an important part of which continues to be in the hands of forestry companies.

Finally, the state is far from ensuring nonrepetition or nonrecurrence of the human rights violations committed to the Mapuche. As previously described, members of Mapuche communities have continued under democracy to suffer different forms of violence by state agents, resulting in several deaths, as well as in a high number of victims of torture, inhuman or degrading treatment. They have also have been prosecuted for their participation in acts of social protest in defense of their land rights, under the antiterrorist law, legislation that does not comply with international human rights standards.

In an intervention on June 23, 2017, President Bachelet apologized to the Mapuche people "for the mistakes and horrors that the state has committed or tolerated in its relationship with them or their communities."[54] Through this apology, President Bachelet indirectly alluded to the dispossession of their lands, in many cases by forestry companies, and to the repression by the police forces of community members. However, far from announcing the revision of the forestry model that has generated the Mapuche social protest, which is demanded by the representative organizations of the Mapuche people, Bachelet announced the creation of a Public Forestation Fund for indigenous lands with "forest suitability," as well as an "associativity" program of Mapuche communities with economic actors, clearly aimed at the continuation of forestry expansion in their traditional territory.[55]

More recently, President Piñera, along with announcing the constitutional recognition of indigenous peoples, proposed incentives and tax exemptions to "all investments" in the Araucania region, the heartland of the Mapuche people, in an implicit reference to investments by the forestry industry.[56]

Civil or criminal responsibility of the forestry companies or of their legal representatives for their actions or omissions that resulted in human rights violations, as referred to, have still not been addressed. Moreover, the due diligence processes that business should undertake in its operations, which include the assessment of the potential impact of their activities may cause on human rights, and the reparation of the negative consequences of their activities, or activities directly related to their operations, that according to the UN Guiding Principles on Business and Human Rights[57] corresponds to private economic entities, has never been implemented by the forestry companies analyzed in this article. Indeed, in cases where their properties overlap Mapuche Mercy titles, such companies have limited their policies to the sale to the state of such lands at speculative prices to the state. Also, they have promoted policies of "good neighborliness" based on "corporate social responsibility" criteria, lacking a human rights focus as was evidenced by the report on FSC report here referred to. Consequently, they have not complied with their human rights obligations.

Unless substantial reforms are introduced, the prospect is that forestry activity, controlled by private conglomerates consolidated during the dictatorship, will continue to grow at the expense of Mapuche human rights. Most likely, conflict with the Mapuche people and its communities will also increase in parallel. The challenge of truth and justice to confront not only the past but also the present human rights violations affecting the Mapuche in which forestry companies have been involved, or at least have been complicit with, is still pendant. Reparation of the harms caused to the Mapuche during the dictatorship, and unfortunately, until today, harms in which forestry companies have an important responsibility, as well as the need to ensure that those violations will not be repeated in the future, are probably the biggest challenges for the state and the Chilean society in general. I hope this article contributes to address these challenges.

NOTES

1. This article was initially presented at the conference on "Limits of Transitional Justice: Post-transition disappearances and impunity for business human rights violations" held at Saint Antony's College, University of Oxford on October 27–28, 2017. It has been complemented with the comments of Laura Bernal Bermudez and Gabriel Pereira, to whom the author expresses his gratitude.

2. CONAF (Corporación Nacional Forestal). "Catastro vegetacional" (2017), http://www.conaf.cl/nuestros-bosques/bosques-en-chile/catastro-vegetacional/.

3. Pablo Camus, Ambiente, "Bosques y Gestión Forestal en Chile, 1541–2005," *Revista de Geografía Norte Grande* 36 (2006): 103–5.

4. Wikipedia, "Empresas CMPC," https://es.wikipedia.org/wiki/Empresas_CMPC.

5. Javier Rebolledo, *A la sombra de los cuervos. Los cómplices civiles de la dictadura.* (Santiago: Ceibo Ediciones, 2015).

6. El Mostrador, "Muere Agustín Edwards Eastman, cómplice pasivo número uno." El Mostrador (Santiago, April 24, 2017), www.elmostrador.cl/noticias/pais/2017/04/24/muere-agustin-edwards-eastman-complice-pasivo-numero-uno/.

7. Rebolledo, *A la sombra de los cuervos. . .*

8. Rol 27-2010, Corte de Apelaciones de Concepción.

9. Information provided by Patricio Robles, lawyer of the Human Rights Program of the Under Secretary for Human Rights of the Ministry of Justice and Human Rights, March 2018. According to Robles, there would be three CMPC officials whose responsibility in these crimes is being investigated, one of them of high hierarchy in Laja plant then owned by this company. See also Manuel Cabrera, "Justicia ordena procesamiento de exejecutivos de la CMPC por violación de derechos humanos." *Biobio* (Concepción, March 15, 2018), https://www.biobiochile.cl/noticias/nacional/region-del-bio-bio/2018/03/15/justicia-ordena-procesamiento-de-exejecutivos-de-la-cmpc-por-violacion-de-derechos-humanos.shtml.

10. Cristian Garay and Karin Willicke, "El Mercurio y el 11 de Septiembre del 73," in *Revista Universum* 1, no. 22 (2007): 318–39, http://www.scielo.cl/scielo.php?pid=S0718-23762007000100020&script=sci_arttext.

11. Nicholas Widmyer, "El pueblo aquí está totalmente humillado. La contrareforma agraria en Chile" (2015) http://www.cedocmuseodelamemoria.cl/wp-content/uploads/2015/12/Nicholas-Widmyer.pdf.

12. Organización Internacional del Trabajo, *El trabajo decente en la industria forestal de Chile* (OIT, 2012), 16, http://www.ilo.org/wcmsp5/groups/public/---americas/---ro-lima/---sro-santiago/documents/publication/wcms_206093.pdf. Citation translated by the author.

13. Along with Ponce Lerou, who acted as CMPC employee, and later became CONAF and CORFO executive, Fernando Léniz, who had also been a high ranking executive of CMPC, and later became Pinochet's Minister of Economy (1973–1975), and Patricia Matte Larraín, a member of the Matte clan who assumed relevant positions in the dictatorship, including the Social Development Secretariat, played key roles in the privatization of public forestry sector enterprises and in their acquisition by the emerging forest conglomerates in this period.

14. The investigative efforts undertaken by the first Special Inquiry Commission of the Deputy Chamber in the early years of democracy after 1990, were never released. This according to Deputy Carlos Montes, President of such Commission, was due to direct threats from the Armed Forces to the democratic regime reinstated which took place at that time. However, in 2004–2005 a second Special Inquiry Commission of the same Chamber was set up to look at this issue, confirming the massive fraud to the State committed by private interests, interests which included those of forestry companies. See Cámara de Diputados, "Las privatizaciones. Informe

Comisión Investigadora de la Cámara de Diputados" (Cámara de Diputados, 2004), http://www.carlosmontes.cl/senador/las-privatizaciones-informe-comision-investigadora-de-la-camara-de-diputados/.

15. Raúl Molina, "Comunidades mapuche y empresas forestales: tierras, bosques y conflictos." En Casa de la Mujer Mapuche et al., *Pueblo mapuche: Desarrollo y autogestión. Análisis y perspectivas en una sociedad pluricultural* (Concepción: Escaparate, 2000), 185–97.

16. Comisión de Verdad Histórica y Nuevo Trato con los Pueblos Indígenas. *Informe de la Comisión de Verdad Histórica y Nuevo Trato con los Pueblos Indígenas* (Colorama, 2008).

17. A study undertaken by the Asociación de Investigación y Desarrollo Mapuche recently estimated the number of Mapuche fatal victims during the dictatorship in 171, 154 of whom are considered to have disappeared, while 17 had been executed for political reasons. The study also highlights the impunity in which most of these crimes have remained. See Hernan Curiñir, Pablo Silva and Conrado Zumelzu, *Informe final de trabajo de investigación, de ejecutados y desaparecidos, 1973–1990. Pertenecientes a la Nación Mapuche* (Instituto Nacional de Derechos Humanos, 2016) https://drive.google.com/file/d/0ByN4tK2Vi_rpeFNKSXZtTjN0bmM/view?pref=2&pli=1.

18. Cayuqueo estimates in thousands those Mapuche who suffered political prison or were tortured throughout the dictatorship. See Pedro Cayuqueo, "Los mapuches y la Comisión Valech" (2004) http://www.mapuche-nation.org/espanol/html/noticias/ntcs-192.htm.

19. Arauco, *Memoria Arauco 2016*, https://www.arauco.cl/wp-content/uploads/2017/07/1-Memoria-Anual-2016-1.pdf.

20. Rebolledo, *A la sombra de los cuervos. . .*

21. According to the Special Commission of Inquiry of the Deputy Chamber (2004), dictatorship authorities were not accountable to citizens and therefore did not leave records of the financial resources obtained through privatization of public companies at that time. However, according to information provided by the Office of the General Comptroller of the Republic to the said Commission, it is estimated that only by the sale of 30 companies alienated between 1978 and 1990, the country lost US$ 2,223,163,439.98, an amount corresponding to 6.4 percent of Chile's GDP in 1990.

22. One of the phenomena this legislation generated was the substitution of native forests for forest plantations. According to a WWF study on forestry practices of Forestal Mininco SA (of CMPC), this company, largely subsidized by the State through the DL 701, replaced a total of 17,969 hectares of native forest between the regions of Maule and Los Ríos from 1994 until 2009. See WWF, "Evaluación formal para la certificación de manejo forestal FSC de Forestal Mininco S. A. Informe de comentarios y recomendaciones" (2011), http://awsassets.panda.org/downloads/2011_1_informe_de_wwf_para_auditoria_certificacion_mininco.pdf.

23. Michelle Bachelet, "Mensaje de S.E. la Presidenta de la Republica con el que inicia el proyecto de ley que entiende la bonificación establecida en el Decreto Ley N° 701, de 1974 sobre fomento forestal, cuyo texto fue reemplazado por el artículo

primero del Decreto Ley N°2.565, de 1979," 2015, https://www.camara.cl/pley/pley_detalle.aspx?prmID=10488.

24. The amount of hectares of small land holders that were subsidized through this legislation increased from 5 percent of the total between 1974 and 1997 to 39 percent of the total between 1998 and 2010. See Francisco González, "DL 701: En 40 años 70 percent de aportes fueron a grandes forestales," in *La Tercera.* (July 18, 2015), http://www.latercera.com/noticia/dl-701-en-40-anos-70-de-aportes-fueron-a-grandes-forestales/.

25. Victor Carvajal, "Colusión del papel liquida subsidio que benefició por décadas al Grupo Matte" in *CIPER* (November 10, 2015), http://ciperchile.cl/2015/11/10/colusion-del-papel-liquida-subsidio-que-beneficio-por-decadas-al-grupo-matte/.

26. CONAF, "Catastro vegetacional"

27. Woodmark Soil Association- FSC, "Resumen público de la evaluación del manejo forestal según estándar FSC (STDPL-201205/311209) Forestal Arauco S.A.," (2013), http://archivo.argentina.indymedia.org/uploads/2013/03/2012_ma_resumen_publico_audit_fsc_en_arauco_v2013-02-28_final_espa_ol.pdf.

28. CMPC, "Empresas CMPC" (2017), http://www.cmpccelulosa.cl/CMPCCELULOSA/interior.aspx?cid=126&.

29. Felipe Menares, "Industria forestal: las millonarias utilidades de Arauco y CMPC en los últimos seis años," in *El Ciudadano* (February 3, 2017) http://www.elciudadano.cl/economia/industria-forestal-las-millonarias-utilidades-de-arauco-y-cmpc-en-los-ultimos-seis-anos/02/03/.

30. Rosamel Millamán y Charles Hale (coord.), *Chile's Forestry Industry, FSC Certification and Mapuche Communities* (2016), https://ga2017.fsc.org/wp-content/uploads/2017/10/Chiles-Forestry-Industry-FSC-Certification-and-Mapuche-Communities-FINAL.pdf. This study was commissioned by FSC International in response to a claim made in 2012 by Mapuche people organizations to this entity, which pointed out that forest companies certified by FSC Chile that operated on Mapuche traditional territory did not meet the standards established for these effects, which include the rights of indigenous peoples as recognized in ILO Convention 169 on Indigenous and Tribal Peoples.

31. FSC Chile, "Superficie certificada FSC Chile," No date, https://cl.fsc.org/es-cl/certificacin/superficie-y-empresas-cetificadas-en-chile.

32. According to the International Labour Organization Convention N° 169 on Indigenous and Tribal Peoples, ratified by Chile such lands are considered to belong to indigenous peoples, in this case, the Mapuche (see Article 14.1 of the ILO Convention N° 169).

33. Comisión de Verdad Histórica y Nuevo Trato, *Informe de la Comisión de Verdad. . . .*

34. José Aylwin (coord.), Matías Meza-Lopehandía and Nancy Yáñez *Los pueblos indígenas y el derecho.* (Santiago: Lom, 2013).

35. According to the National Corporation on Indigenous Development (CONADI), between 1994 and 2014, the State transferred to Mapuche people approximately 200,000 hectares. This both as a consequence of the acquisition of lands previously recognized to them by the State, and currently on private hands,

as well as of the transfer of land that the State considers "fiscal" to its communities Many of these land purchases at speculative market prices are made by CONADI to forestry companies . See Instituto Nacional de Derechos Humanos, *Informe Anual 2014. Situación de los derechos humanos en Chile.* (Santiago: INDH, 2014), http://bibliotecadigital.indh.cl/handle/123456789/740. Lands registered in the Indigenous Property Registry of the State in favor of Mapuche individuals or communities, total 863,619 hectares. See Gobierno de Chile "Informes Periódicos 19°, 20° y 20° de la Aplicación de la Convención Internacional sobre la Eliminación de Todas las Formas de Discriminación Racial de conformidad al artículo 9 de la Convención, Chile" (2012).

36. The General Assembly of the United Nations Resolution 64/292 of 2010.

37. Organización Nacional de Emergencia (2016), in Red por la Defensa de las Territorios (2017). "Informe enviado a Relator Especial sobre el derecho humano al agua potable y al saneamiento," Temuco, April 7, 2017.

38. Law N° 19.300 of 1994 on the General Basis of Environment, modified by Law N° 20.417 of 2010, and Supreme Decree N° 40 of 2012 on the Regulation of the Environmental Impact Assessment.

39. Ministerio de Desarrollo Social CASEN 2015, "Diagnostico nacional y principales resultados regionales," (2016), http://observatorio.ministeriodesarrollosocial.gob.cl/casen-multidimensional/casen/docs/CASEN_2015_Presentacion_con_resultados_regionales_Ampliando_la_mirada_sobre_la_pobreza_yla_desigualdad.pdf.

40. Ministerio de Desarrollo Social. CASEN 2015, "Estimaciones de la pobreza por ingreso y multidimensional en comunas con representatividad," (2016), http://observatorio.ministeriodesarrollosocial.gob.cl/casen-multidimensional/casen/docs/estimacion_pobreza_ingreso_multidimensional_comunal.pdf.

41. CONAF (Gerencia forestal), "Plantaciones y pobreza en comunas forestales. Forestación y estilo de desarrollo," (2014), http://www.conaf.cl/wp-content/files_mf/1395859632PlantacionesyPobrezaenComunasForestales.pdf.

42. Some of these actions have been self-attributed by Mapuche organizations, others not. There are several cases of violence against forestry properties in which the existence of self-attacks has been proven.

43. Germán Bidegain, "From Cooperation to Confrontation: The Mapuche Movement and Its Political Impact, 1990–2014," in Sofía Donoso and María von Bullow M. (eds.), *Social Movements in Chile. Organization, Trajectories, and Political Consequences* (New York; Palgrave Macmillan, 2017), 99–129.

44. These organizations' international human rights entities include the Human Rights Council (2009), the Committee Against Torture (2009), the Committee on the Elimination of Racial Discrimination (2013), and the Human Rights Committee (2014), all of them of the United Nations. The State of Chile has also been represented in the reports of various United Nations Special Rapporteurs, including the Special Rapporteur on the Rights of Indigenous Peoples, James Anaya (2009), the Special Rapporteur on Human Rights and Fundamental Freedoms in the Fight Against Terrorism, Ben Emmerson (2014), and the Special Rapporteur on the Rights to Freedom of Peaceful Assembly and of Association, Maina Kiai (2016).

45. Inter-American Court of Human Rights, *Norín Catriman y otros (Lonkos, dirigentes y activistas del pueblo indígena Mapuche) vs. Chile*, 2011, Par.90. Citation translated by the author.

46. The right to life, according to the Inter-American Court on Human Rights does not only include the right of every human being not to be arbitrarily deprived of his life, but also the right that conditions that impede or obstruct access to a decent existence should not be generated. See Inter- American Court of Human Rights, *Sawhoyamaxa Indigenous Community v. Paraguay*. Merits, Reparations, and Costs, 2006, Par. 161.

47. Aside from Convention 169 of the ILO before referred to, Chile adhered to the United Nations Declaration on the Rights of Indigenous Peoples in 2007, as well as to the American Declaration on the Rights of Indigenous Peoples in 2016.

48. Millamán and Hale (coord.), *Chile's Forestry Industry. . .*

49. See Special Rapporteur on the promotion of truth, justice, reparation and guarantees of non-recurrence, Pablo de Greiff "Report of the Special Rapporteur on the promotion of truth, justice, reparation and guarantees of non-recurrence, Pablo de Greiff." United Nations, General Assembly A/HRC/21/46 (2012) https://documents-dds-ny.un.org/doc/UNDOC/GEN/G12/158/58/PDF/G1215858.pdf?OpenElement.

50. Human Rights Committee (United Nations), "General Observation No. 31: The Nature of the General Legal Obligation imposed on the States Parties to the Covenant" (2004), http://www.unhcr.org/4963237716.pdf.

51. Comisión Nacional de Verdad y Reconciliación, *Informe de la Comisión Nacional de Verdad y Reconciliación.* (1991), https://bibliotecadigital.indh.cl/handle/123456789/170.

52. Curiñir, Silva and Zumelzu, *Informe final de trabajo. . .*

53. The insufficiency of such reparation is addressed in Instituto Nacional de Derechos Humanos, *2017 Informe Anual. Situación de los derechos humanos en Chile.* (2017), https://www.indh.cl/destacados-2/informe-anual/.

54. Michelle Bachelet, "Plan de Reconocimiento y Desarrollo de la Araucanía," June 23, 2017.

55. Michelle Bachelet, "Plan de Reconocimiento y Desarrollo de la Araucanía," June 23, 2017.

56. Sebastían Piñera, "Acuerdo Nacional por el desarrollo y la Paz en la Araucanía" (September 24, 2018), https://prensa.presidencia.cl/discurso.aspx?id=82586.

57. United Nations, *Report of the Special Representative of the Secretary-General on human rights and transnational corporations and other enterprises, John Ruggie. Guiding Principles on Business and Human Rights: Implementing the United Nations "Protect, Respect, and Remedy"* Framework.A/HRC/14/27 (2010), https://www.ohchr.org/Documents/Issues/Business/A-HRC-17-31_AEV.pdf.

Section 5

CASE STUDIES

Chapter 22

Pesquera Arauco and Colonia Dignidad Cases

Karinna Fernández and Magdalena Garcés Fuentes

INTRODUCTION

The judicialization of crimes against humanity committed during the dictatorship in Chile stands out on an international level[1] and is the result of a tireless fight led by the victims, family members, and human rights organizations against impunity that has resisted the idea of "justice as far as possible"[2] that transitional governments have sought to impose. Hundreds of those responsible have been brought to the judicial authorities, defeating the current Amnesty Decree Law, the statute of limitations,[3] the absence of an autonomous crime of forced disappearance and even provisions that attempted to put an end to the investigations.[4] However, criminal proceedings have not focused on determining the causes and consequences of the repression, nor has the role of the various actors who contributed and/or benefited from (the perpetration of) the massive atrocities been judicially established. Here, we refer to the landowners, professionals, businessmen, politicians, as well as the corporations or companies that allowed the repressive apparatus to legitimize their criminal actions and develop.

Those responsible should be pursued in terms of criminal accusation such as direct complicity, complicity by benefiting from the dictatorship, or silence[5] is complicity have scarcely been investigated through the Chilean courts, which are used for the investigation of simple criminal contexts and reductionist criminal figures that limits the persecution of those who gave or followed orders. This situation has guaranteed impunity to the incalculable number of officials and collaborators, depriving Chilean transitional justice of one of the most fundamental characteristics of any transitional process, which is to make the context known whereby the crimes were committed to ensure that it does not happen again and that the right to the truth is fulfilled.

This explains why "there are still sectors of Chilean society that do not know the gravity or justify the violations committed during the dictatorship,"[6] since the judicial truth has not presented the full scope of the crimes or their perpetrators.

Judicially, there has been no been clarification in Chile on the network linking the repressive apparatus with the business community, background on how the repression by the opponents of the regime was financed and the benefits obtained by the collaborators remain unknown. The Report by the National Truth and Reconciliation Commission, as early as 1996, confirmed that the employees of the National Intelligence Directorate (DINA)[7] included officials from private companies[8] and the transnational repressive work had support from the Lan Chile airline and Banco del Estado (State Bank).[9]

This chapter analyzes two emblematic cases of businesses that contributed to the perpetration of crimes against humanity and whose members benefited economically from their relationship with the repressive apparatus: The Pesquera Arauco and Colonia Dignidad companies, located in the current V and VII regions, respectively, whose collaboration with the DINA from the beginning of the dictatorship was well known. However, neither were corporate, financial, or accounting structures, nor have their specific links to the repressive apparatus of the dictatorship been the subject of a complete investigation.

First, a brief review of the Pesquera Arauco is given, the background on its collaboration in transferring people kidnapped by the DINA, and the judicial investigations that are currently underway. Next, we will refer to Colonia Dignidad (hereinafter, also The Colony), a well-known sect that settled in the central south of Chile in the sixties under the facade of being a benefactor company, it carried out important commercial activities and from the beginning of the dictatorship actively collaborated in the forced disappearance of people, as well as in the kidnapping and torture of others, providing the means and personnel to execute crimes in concomitance with the de facto authorities. The processes for human rights violations are reviewed showing the participation by said members of the Colony and the economic benefits obtained by this community. The conclusions point to the common elements of both cases, as well as the importance of developing extensive judicial investigations aimed at unveiling and punishing the perpetrators of crimes against humanity and their corporate accomplices.

PESQUERA ARAUCO

The Pesquera Arauco (Limited Company) was set up with financial support from the Corporation for the Promotion of Production (CORFO) during the 1940s, as part of the country's industrial development plan that focused on (the industrialization of) exports with an emphasis on developing the fishing industry, which was seen as a sector that generated employment and benefitted the population with a healthy diet. Subsequently (1967), with 45.77 percent participation from CORFO, Pesquera Arauco became an industrial group, which led to a new cycle of marine resource extraction until 1973.[10] After the coup d'etat, its board of directors was replaced by members of the different branches of the Armed Forces and by businessmen from civil society.[11] On behalf of CORFO, the President of the Directory appointed Colonel Manuel Contreras Sepúlveda, of the DINA, as Director thus making Pesquera's logistical resources available to repression work carried out by the DINA.[12]

From 1973, ex-prisoners and political prisoners from the San Antonio area (V Region), where the Tejas Verdes School of Military Engineers headed by Manuel Contreras was, as well as survivors of kidnappings and torture by the DINA, have stated that during their captivity they were transferred in vans and refrigerated trucks belonging to Pesquera Arauco.[13] The vans and trucks that still had the fishery logos on them had been adapted to carry people, leaving space for DINA agents to monitor, and guard the detainees during transfer. Periodically, from the end of 1973 until the end of August 1974, these vehicles were driven to the entrance of London 38 Street, a secret detention facility located in Santiago, where bandaged and tied prisoners climbed into the back of the vehicles. In many cases, this is the last trace of people who are still missing. DINA agents have admitted that the victims were frequently transferred to the Tejas Verdes Prisoner Camps.[14] Also, there are testimonies from perpetrators, who reported moving bodies that were later thrown into the sea.[15]

Pesquera Arauco had two sites, one in Lo Valledor in Santiago where most of the refrigerated trucks were and where numerous workers were assigned as agents for the DINA. The Pesquera processing plant was in San Antonio Port, where there were furnaces and boning machines, during the coup d'etat this area was heavily guarded by military personnel.[16] Manuel Contreras appointed Mario Jara Seguel as an auditor of the plant who was a member of the DINA to be in command at the Tejas Verdes Regiment where he also tortured victims. He also served from April 1974, as Commander of the DINA Galvarino Regional Intelligence Brigade, with jurisdiction between La Serena and San Fernando cities.[17] There are police and judicial testimonies proving that the processing plant was used to keep the corpses in refrigerators that were later moved and thrown into the sea.[18]

Pesquera Arauco was sold in February 1975 to Empresa Pesquera Chile Ltda. also connected to CORFO, whose board was chaired by Manuel Contreras and made up of various DINA officers and businessmen, including Alberto Silva, Hubert Fuch, and Luis Verdereau. Empresa Pesquera Chile Ltda. was liquidated and became the Sociedad Pesquera Nueva Aurora

Limitada and in 1979 it sold all its rights in the company Nueva Aurora to CORFO and Sociedad Agrícola CORFO Ltda[19] without knowing who benefited from the said transaction.

Until today, despite numerous declarations from surviving victims on the use of Arauco Pesquera vehicles in the disappearance of people,[20] judicial investigations have obtained limited statements from DINA agents who performed or who knew Pesquera workers and that ordered the preparation of police reports on the various deeds of the company. In this sense, investigations are mostly superficial and disjointed, without specifically addressing the role of the company in the disappearance of people,[21] nor has the financial situation of the company and how the profits from its sale were distributed been investigated. The role and responsibilities of those who made up the board of directors, whether from the DINA, the Armed Forces or the business community, have not been established, meanwhile several of the main stakeholders have passed away.

This situation became more controversial when the "Londres 38, Espacio de Memoria"[22] ("London 38, Memory Space") organization as plaintiff in the proceedings Role No. 27-2014 for crimes of kidnapping, homicide, illicit association, and illegal burial and Role No. 202-2015 for burial and illegal exhumation of missing victims requested that structural investigations be carried out on the disappearance of people from the Yucatan Barracks, located in London 38 in downtown Santiago. These actions and the result of the investigations led to London 38 (victims group) filing a complaint against the DINA agents and civilians that formed the board of the Pesquera Arauco S.A. and Empresa Pesquera Chile Ltda. its managers and assistant managers, and against all those responsible, as perpetrators, accomplices, and cover-ups, for crimes of qualified kidnapping, illegal association, and illegal burial of people from the clandestine detention and torture center located on Londres 38 Street on October 3, 2017.

To obtain factual in-depth knowledge a thorough judicial investigation into Pesquera Arauco is needed. With regard to the remaining unknown facts, such as the magnitude of Pesquera's collaboration in the disappearance of people, it is crucial to further research considering macro-criminality patterns and specifically establishing the institutional role of Pesquera in these disappearances to identify the orders that emanated from the board and its implementation as well as its relationship with the repressive forces. It is also essential to obtain expert opinions on the areas that Pesquera controlled.

COLONIA DIGNIDAD

"Colonia Dignidad" was a religious sect, founded by a group of German citizens who came to Chile following Pastor Paul Schäfer Schneider in July

1961. Schäfer had founded the "Private Social Mission" together with Hugo Baar (lay pastor) and Hermann Schmidt (former German Air Force officer) having separated themselves from the Baptist Church in Germany. Around 1960, the Prosecutor's Office in Bonn began an investigation against Schafer into the sexual abuse of children, leading the three to flee to Chile, where they bought a farm in the town of Catillo, Parral, in the Seventh Region which they named "Colonia Dignidad."[23] Through Supreme Decree No. 3,949 on September 21, 1961, they became a legal society under the name "Sociedad Benefactora y Educacional Dignidad" (Benefactor and Educational Dignity Society).

On June 26, 1961, the Foundation Act and Statutes of the Private Law Corporation "Sociedad Benefactora y Educacional Dignidad "became a public deed, at the request of Hermann Schmidt Georgi. In making the act, Schmidt Georgi pointed out that after the Second War they, together with a group of friends, had founded" and maintained a home in Germany for youth reeducation and help to whose motto was "The Youth Help the Youth" and that the work of the organization "was no longer needed" in Germany due to the country's boom. On the other hand, in Chile, there was a lot of scope to do fruitful work in this regard, especially after the 1960 earthquakes. These events had led them to form "a similar home as in Germany, for which they have the consent of a group of collaborators from the German Home who are willing to donate funds and goods to establish a both homely and educational institution" in Chile.[24]

A school, a hospital, and a cemetery were built inside the community.[25] A group from the Private Social Mission remained in Germany to manage the business there.[26] As Chilean justice would later establish,[27] in Colonia Dignidad "a hierarchical structure was organized that planned and executed multiple crimes, made up of people who were members and collaborators of that corporation, an activity that began from at least 1970 onward."[28] The Supreme Court established that there was active collaboration between the leaders of the Colonia Dignidad and the activities carried out by the DINA, which involved the use of the facilities of the aforementioned German colony to kidnap and disappear civilians who were led there and kept in that condition inside.[29]

In 1998, a complaint for crimes of genocide, illicit association, and others against Augusto Pinochet Ugarte was extended to the "top leaders of the 'Former Sociedad Benefactora y Educacional," which gave rise to Case 2182-98 "Villa Baviera," to investigate the numerous violations of human rights committed within the community.[30] In practice, the case resulted in an investigation into the kidnapping and disappearance of Álvaro Vallejos Villagrán, a university student and militant from the Revolutionary Left Movement (MIR) who had been detained by DINA agents on May 2, 1974, and held in captivity in the DINA centers in London 38 and Cuatro Alamos Prison, and later led to Colonia Dignidad, the place from hence his whereabouts were lost.[31]

Human Rights Violations and the Judicial Investigations

More cases related to forced disappearance victims where information about Colonia Dignidad appeared were left in the hands of various ministers and the investigation of sexual abuse against children was left to the Minister Hernán González during a visit to the Talca Court of Appeals. A series of judicial proceedings had already been initiated for crimes committed on these premises in the 1990s. Paul Schäfer never appeared in the subpoenas and in 1997, to evade the judicial siege, he once again began his escape. He was found in Argentina seven years later on March 10, 2005. Finally, he was expelled from the trans-Andean country due to his illegal entry, which avoided an extradition trial and was deported to Chile, where he was arrested and placed under prosecution for his participation in the disappearance of Alvaro Vallejos.[32]

Following Schäfer's capture, to be more efficient and speed up the investigations the Supreme Court Plenary[33] appointed Minister Jorge Zepeda as Extraordinary Visitor, for his knowledge of the processes related to Colonia Dignidad, except for the case of sexual abuse against children that was maintained by Minister Hernán González. When carrying out his investigations, Minister Zepeda kept notes on the procedures in separate notebooks. For the missing victims, the cases were added by "Illicit Association," after the filing of a complaint by the Ministry of Interior and the State Defense Council; further cases were added of arms trafficking due to the arsenals that were found buried inside the estate, as well as cases for kidnappings and torture of former prisoners and political prisoners; homicide by the former DINA agent Miguel Becerra; use of drugs and narcotics and injuries of settlers, and so on. The illegal burials and exhumations[34] inside the premise and other proceedings related to the forced disappearance of people in Colonia Dignidad were included in the file on the kidnapping of Juan Maino, Elizabeth Rekas, and Antonio Elizondo, all arrested by the DINA and subsequently disappeared.[35] Despite the numerous complaints and background history accumulated in the proceedings, the cases for slave labor to which men, women, and children were subjected, were closed with dismissal dictated by Minister Zepeda.

In accordance to the condemnatory sentence by illicit association, "under the 'Benefit and Educational Dignity Society' a hierarchical structure was organized that planned and executed multiple crimes carried out by people who were members and collaborators of that corporation, an activity that began at least from 1970 onward, as evidenced in the documentation found during 2005 inside the former estate "El Lavadero," formerly "Colonia

Dignidad," currently known as rural property "Villa Baviera," a structure that continued to be organized after the dissolution arranged by the competent administrative authority, precisely because of "deviation from its object."[36] The judgment adds:

> the said perfectly organized structure, in order to act illegally, had a superior or responsible command that was also very well informed of the system created for that purpose, and although it did not imply formally constituting a traditional military organization, it had, regarding the application of rules, experiences and training typical of an activity of that nature, thus counting on enough capacity to carry out military operations.[37]

The same ruling indicates that, at least since September 11, 1973, the members of Colonia Dignidad "armed themselves" and actively collaborated with the security agencies of the dictatorship, especially the DINA. The judicial investigation concludes that there was a close collaboration between the DINA and Colonia Dignidad, as the DINA hierarchy agreed with the hierarchy of the Colony, kidnapped civilians for political reasons, which were kept inside the "Villa Baviera" property where the security agency used the resources of the Colony for its purposes. In addition, the ruling indicates that the whereabouts of Álvaro Modesto Vallejos Villagrán were accredited to Villa Baviera "at that time it functioned as a detention and torture center for people persecuted by the military regime established in the country, at which time the said victim was found to be missing."[38] In this case, Manuel Contreras Sepúlveda as well as DINA officers, Pedro Espinoza Bravo, and Fernando Gómez Segovia were sentenced to four years in prison. The former sect leaders, Kurt Schnellemkamp Nelaimischkies, Gerd Seewald Lefevre, Gerhard Mücke Koschitzke, and Karl Van Den Berg Schuurman all authors by illicit association were also sentenced to the same sentence.[39] The Supreme Court increased the sentences to five years and one day in prison for the convicted.[40]

It is important to show that throughout the various investigations into missing persons, whose fate was linked to Colonia Dignidad, to date only one member of the sect has been sentenced for their participation in the crimes: Gerhard Mücke Koschitzke was sentenced to three years and one day in prison, as an accomplice to the kidnapping of Álvaro Vallejos in the first instance, a sentence confirmed by the Court of Appeals of Santiago, with appeals pending before the Supreme Court.[41]

Paul Schafer was not convicted and was definitively dismissed in several proceedings following his death in 2010. In the case of the kidnappings of Juan Maino, Elizabeth Rekas, and Antonio Elizondo, Dr. Harmuth Hopp Miottel was accused as an accomplice to the kidnappings but was temporarily dismissed after his escape to Germany. Hopp currently lives in Krefeld, where several former settlers were welcomed by the pastor Ewald Frank of the Free People's Mission Church.[42] In the same case, Gerhard Wolfgang Mücke Koschitzke and Johann Van Den Berg Schuurmann were sentenced to five years and one day in prison as accomplices to the kidnappings.[43] However, this sentence was revoked by the Court of Appeals of Santiago, which considered that it was not possible to prove the route of the victims through Colonia Dignidad,[44] which was also confirmed by the Supreme Court.[45]

With respect to people who were kidnapped and tortured in Colonia Dignidad, two sentences have condemned former members of the community, those that received prison benefits because of the low value of penalties.[46] The first sentence was executed (for the kidnapping of Adriana Bórquez) and against the second sentence, the Supreme Court ruling is pending for the kidnapping of fifty people in Parral and Talca committed between April and June 1975.[47]

As for the accomplices to the sexual abuse of children committed by Paul Schäfer, six Colony members were sentenced to five years and one day in prison, a sentence they are currently serving, except for Dr. Hopp, who, as we noted earlier, fled to Germany. Chile requested his extradition, which was rejected since Germany does not extradite nationals. Gerd Seewald died in prison.

Economic Gains

Colonia Dignidad exploited various tax and customs benefits, a product of its organization as a charity, without prejudice to subsidies to the school and hospital. During the dictatorship, it enjoyed open protection. In fact, until 1990, the Chilean authorities did not control the community. This allowed members to be forced to work without pay or basic working conditions; that electroshock be performed on hospital patients, it did not comply with sanitary regulations; that the children did not attend school periodically and were forced to work and the illegal appropriation of Chilean children, among other illicit ones.

Following multiple allegations of irregularities, child abuse, and human rights violations, President Patricio Aylwin canceled the legality of the Benefactor Society in 1991. The decree ordered that the assets of the Corporation be transferred to the Methodist Church; however, before this, all the assets had been transferred to various commercial societies, made up of some members of the Colony. Among these were Abratec S.A., formed by four partners of Sociedad Benefactora in 1988, Sociedad Inmobiliaria e Inversiones Cerro Florido Ltda., whose board included directors from other companies formed by former settlers, such as AGRIPALMA S.A. (closed corporation); BARDANA S.A. (closed corporation), and CINOGLOSA S.A. (closed corporation). The Cerro Florido Society acquired the land on which Colonia was located, which allowed them to continue operating under the name of Villa Baviera.

A judgment for tax crimes of 2003 established that the former Benefactor Society had been established as a private law corporation, "in order to provide assistance to children and youths in need;"[48] and that to achieve its mission, "it executed multiple activities of an agricultural, commercial and industrial nature, which became its own business, all encumbered by the Law of Income, such as exploitation of agricultural real estate, exploitation of a plant crusher and exploitation of freight and family cafeteria."[49] The company obtained benefits from its activity that was not entirely intended for charity.

The ruling adds that the former Benefactor Society did not have internal accounting (balance sheets) and that "the data that was obtained through the accounting practices a reflection of the total income, while not all the values of the expenses were included. Therefore, it was not possible to reliably determine the amount that was allocated to its commendable statutory purposes, an issue that distorted its social purpose and created a detriment in the fiscal funds to access improper benefits by that means."[50]

The former Benefactor Society did not meet the Internal Revenue Service requirements, so it did not prove that the income obtained in commercial activities "was invested in the charitable purposes among which health and education can be mentioned, a source of financing that together with the statutory objectives led the authorities to exempt it from the payment of the First Category income tax, pursuant to Supreme Decree 4250 of the Ministry of Finance."[51] This decree had benefited the Colony since 1962. In addition, it was noted that the former Colonia Dignidad had not done its annual income declarations, an obligation from which it was not exempt.

The ruling mentions that the former Colonia Dignidad had made investments in mutual funds, when rescued were reinvested, but it was not possible to verify their use in their operational work and once the accounting system was standardized (as of 1990) they were no longer accounted for. Concluding that the workings of the Colony had caused property damage to the Chilean treasury, represented by the tax that the Colony had not declared or paid on surpluses and profits not intended for charity; damage that the ruling established at US$ 141,728,739 (one hundred and forty-one million, seven hundred and twenty–eight thousand, seven hundred and thirty-nine in three years) between 1986 and 1989.[52]

The Chamber of Deputies in 1997 reported that although the government canceled the legal status of Colonia Dignidad due to "various irregularities that were detected during approximately thirty years of its existence, in 'Villa Baviera' there is a de facto association that continues its activities," with some of its members under investigation for their responsibility in various crimes, which would affect legal assets such as life, liberty, child protection, and the inviolability of the family. [53]

After Schäfer was arrested, Colonia Dignidad the Chilean State intervened, which appointed the trustee Herman Chadwick as the administrator of the companies owned by the sect. Germany contributed to the financing therapies for the colony members that were still living in Villa Baviera and for the development of productive businesses. Many settlers/members emigrated to Germany, some tried to settle in various areas of Chile and others remained within the Colony. However, the conditions in the Colony were not comprehensively faced by the states. To date, many victims that received forced medication or slave labor by the Colony have not been compensated and remain in precarious economic conditions, some in Chile and others in Germany.

Villa Baviera is currently controlled by three limited liability companies (Agripalma, Bardana, and Cerro Florido), which, in turn, have another series of companies, some of a productive nature (such as Agrícola Valle Florido Limitada) and many other real estate companies (among them is Bamberg Real Estate Limited).[54] The fate of much of the capital accumulated by the former hierarchs of the Colony is unknown.

On the other hand, judicial investigations for human rights violations were incomplete. During the visit by Minister Zepeda, important records were kept secret and work on locating graves and sites where bodies were burnt were paralyzed. To date, except for the case of Álvaro Vallejos, it is not yet known with certainty who and how many people were killed and disappeared in Colonia Dignidad, as well as the responsibility in the respective crimes that corresponded to the settlers. Cases of slave labor and kidnapping of some former political prisoners were dismissed, despite the existence of numerous records in the respective files.

Relatives of the victims, survivors (Chilean and German), human rights defenders and organizations have continued to propel the task of achieving truth, justice, and reparation for the crimes committed in the German enclave, as well as recovering the memory of what happened. In recent years, new complaints have been filed for crimes within the enclave and recently forensic work has resumed on the premises, by order of Minister Mario Carroza.[55]

In Berlin on July 12, 2017, Chile and Germany agreed on the creation of a "Chilean-German Joint Commission to address the historical memory of 'Colonia Dignidad' and the integration of victims into society,"[56] whose purpose is the recovery of the historical memory of the place, through "the creation of a place of memory for the victims of human rights violations as a result of the collaboration between the hierarchs of 'Colonia Dignidad' and the dictatorship"; the cooperation for the conservation of the archives and remains of the crimes committed in the Colony enclave and "the support in the processes of preservation of historical memory and diagnosis of the assets, societies and companies arising from 'Villa Baviera' 'Colonia Dignidad.'"[57] The creation of the Commission originated in a parliamentary motion in Germany.

CONCLUSIONS

Pesquera Arauco was a successful state company, which after being chosen by the DINA openly carried out its repressive work, in 1975 it was sold and this process we may presume economically benefitted its directors. Colonia Dignidad was a private corporation that actively collaborated with the dictatorship in the perpetration of crimes against humanity and that received various benefits for its connections with the repressive apparatus, which allowed its leader, for example, to exercise sexual crimes against children with impunity. Also, the leaders of the sect benefitted from the slave labor of those who were held captive in the Colony. Subsequently, the Colony managed to violate action by the Chilean State through the constitution of commercial companies. Clearly, weak and fragmented judicial action has not yet fully established the truth of the events that took place inside the Colony or the fate of the money that was illegally obtained.

The two cases presented in this chapter show five common elements: (a) the casuistic richness of business complicity with crimes against humanity; (b) the effective contribution of corporate resources in the commission of crimes against humanity; (c) the interest and economic enrichment for the executives of the complicit companies; (d) the lack of political will to move forward with research on economic accomplices; and (e) in the cases in which there were weak advances in the investigations, it has become clear that the research and interpretation methodology are too narrow because they fail to capture the complex relationship plots of criminals and their corporate accomplices.

The existence of economic benefits for the members of these corporations, who participated in the execution of crimes against humanity affirms the need for an investigation into them through judicial processes that contribute to establishing the integral truth of what took place, not only with respect to the fate of those who are still missing but also of the complicit relations between the repressive forces and corporate structures.

The judicial investigations, together with other initiatives such as historical investigation and the recovery of memory from the victims, should fill the multiple existing gaps regarding the role of companies and their members in repressive politics, which would allow to provide a full account of what happened, narrow impunity gaps, generating concrete safeguards of nonrepetition in the economic and corporate sphere.

NOTES

1. Thomas C. Wright, Impunity, Human Rights, and Democracy: Chile and Argentina, 1990–2005 (Austin, University of Texas Press, 2014), 2–3.
2. Ibid, 60.
3. Here we are referring to the different types of prescription included in Chilean legislation, criminal action, punishment, civil action and gradual prescription of the penalty, which only exists in Chile and Austria.
4. The Supreme Court, on January 25, 2005, had 6 months to close the investigations. On May 6, 2005, the resolution was reversed.
5. Sabine Michalowski and Juan Pablo Cardona, "Corporate Responsibility and Transitional Justice" (2015) 11 Yearbook of Human Rights, 173.
6. Report by the Working Group on Enforced or Involuntary Disappearances, Chile, January 29, 2013, A / HRC / 22/45 / Add.1, para 55.
7. The DINA was created by Decree Law No. 521 of June 14, 1974. However, the DINA began to organize itself from the moment of the coup d'etat (as the DINA Commission).
8. Report by the National Truth and Reconciliation Commission (CNVR), Andros Impresores, 1996, Volume 2, 722-7.
9. Ibid.
10. Ricardo Nazer Ahumada, History of CORFO, 1939–2009 (Santiago, CORFO, 2009), 128–35.
11. For example, Huber Fuechs A, Mauricio Celis, Luis Verdereau, Luis Arrieta Echegaray, Carlos Penaglia Rojas.
12. Londres 38, Background for the investigation on criminal patterns used in the disappearance of persons from the clandestine detention facility located in Londres 38 (September 2016), 13 and 16. Available at: http://www.londres38.cl/1934/w3-article-98405.html.
13. CNVR Report (n8) Volume 1, 100; Rol 2182-98, Episode "Colombo Case," Qualified kidnapping of María Angélica Andreoli Bravo, judgment April 10, 2015; Rol 2182-1998, Episode "Conference 1," kidnapping and qualified homicide of Marta Ugarte Román, judgment May 30, 2016.
14. The Tejas Verde prisoners' camp operated on the land of the Tejas Verde Military Engineers Regiment until April 1974 and was also known as Barracks 2. However, they later continued to transfer detainees to the site, which could correspond to cases of missing detainees.
15. Criminal Complaint filed by "Londres 38, Espacio de memoria" against executives of Pesquera Arauco S.A and Pesquera Chile Ltda, dated October 3, 2017, Rol 201-2015, substantiated by the Minister on Extraordinary Visit Mario Carroza.

16. Londres 38 (n12) 16.

17. According to convictions for kidnappings, torture, homicides, and disappearance of persons responsible by the said agency (Cause Role 2182-98 "Carlos Cuevas and others;" Cause Role 2182-98 Bautista van Schouwen and other). In the provinces, the organization of Brigades is not uniform over time. There are several judicial declarations that allow us to presume that the Galvarino Brigade, under the command of Mario Jara Seguel, was structured and independent of the Regiment School of Military Engineers of Tejas Verde, at the closing of the detainee camp of said regiment, in April 1974.

18. Criminal Complaint, Rol 201-2015 (n15).

19. Police Report No. 389, August 23, 2001, in Case Role 2182-98 Episode Operation Colombo-Aedo et al., Judgment of May 30, 2017.

20. As an example; judicial statement by Anatolio Zarate Oyarzún, former official of the Compañía Pesquera Arauco S.A and survivor of torture in cause Role 2182-98 Episode Operation Colombo-Aedo and others.

21. Londres 38 (n12) 17.

22. Londres 38, Memory Space, is constituted as a Functional Community Organization (FCO), whose mission is to recover the historical and political memory linked to Londres 38, former clandestine detention and torture enclosure of the DINA called Yucatán Barracks. Among other actions, Londres 38 conducts studies and legal actions that contribute to the search for truth and justice for the victims of the compound. According to their records, 98 people who passed through the compound were disappeared or killed, www.londres38.cl

23. Over time, the properties of the Colony would increase, such as the Casino de Bulnes, the house on Campo de Deportes street in Santiago, or the Parral house, which was used as Barracks for the South Central Brigade of the DINA, commanded by Fernando Gómez Segovia.

24. Minister Jorge Zepeda, Judgment Rol 2182-98-Illegal Association, of April 9, 2014, Third Consideration letter f.

25. The Privado de Villa Baviera Cementery was authorized by Resolution N° 1524 of 1964, by the Sanitaria Zonal authority at the time, in favour of the "Sociedad Benefactora y Educacional Dignidad."

26. Friedrich Paul Heller, Pantalones de cuero, moños y metralletas. El trasfondo de Colonia Dignidad. (Ediciones Chile América, CESOC, Santiago, 2006) 25.

27. There are numerous sentences that account for the operation of the DINA, for example: Minister Leopoldo Llanos, Rol 2182-98 Villa Grimaldi, on 27 June 2014 and Rol 2182-98 Episode Villa Grimaldi-Cristina Chacaltana and others, on 12 January 2015.

28. Minister Jorge Zepeda, Sentence Rol 2182-98 Episode "Illicit Association–ex Colonia Dignidad," of April 9, 2014.

29. Supreme Court, Role 14.312-2016, sentence 29 December 2016.

30. In the early 1990s, several cases against Colonia were initiated that failed. For one of them, the amnesty of the acts by the military justice was declared for the kidnapping of Vallejos Villagrán. Cause Rol No. 76.542-11, of the 7th Criminal Court.

31. Minister Jorge Zepeda, Sentence Role Nº 2.182 - 98, Episode Álvaro Vallejos Villagrán, May 7, 2015.

32. Paul Schafer died in prison in 2010, he was convicted of sexual abuse against German and Chilean children, as well as serious human rights violations in complicity with the military dictatorship, especially with the DINA.

33. Administrative Orders AD 211-2005, of April 8, 2005. Considering Third.

34. In Colonia Dignidad there are bodies of people that were murdered and buried, which to date have not been identified. In 1978, as part of the "Operation Withdrawal of Televisions," as in all the regiments of the country, the clandestinely buried bodies were exhumed and made to disappear again. In the case of Colonia Dignidad, the bodies were burned and the ashes thrown into the Perquilauquén River. See Causes: Rol 2182-98 Juan Maino Canales and others and Rol 2182-98 Episode Illegal Association, both substantiated by Minister Jorge Zepeda.

35. Cause Rol 2182-98, Episode Illegal Association, Ibid.

36. Minister Jorge Zepeda, Role 2182-98, Episode Illegal Association, judgment of April 9, 2014, Considering Third, "Established facts, A. Characteristics of the organization."

37. Ibid.

38. Ibid.

39. Judgment Cause Rol 2182-98 (n35). Confirmed by the Court of Appeals of Santiago, Rol 923-2014, December 31, 2015.

40. Supreme Court, Judgment Rol 14. 312-2016, of December 29, 2016. Before the Supreme Court ruling, Manuel Contreras Sepúlveda and Gerd Seewald Lefevre died.

41. Cause Role 2182-98 (n30) and Sentence Court of Appeals Santiago, Role 1051-2015 of April 10, 2017.

42. See note "La Tercera," edition of December 4, 2011. Available online at http://diario.latercera.com/edicionimpresa/la-nueva-vida-de-hopp-en-alemania/. In 2014 Ewald Frank filed an appeal against the exempt Resolution No. 5020 of October 17, 2005, which prevented him from entering the national territory. He requested a report from the Head of the Department of Foreigners and Migration of the Ministry of Interior and Public Security, who indicated that his prohibition to enter the country had been arranged, because the Chilean Investigative Police had a history of repeated entries and exits from Chile between 1998 and 2005 and that he had h visited Colonia Dignidad and his presence was presumed to be related to the departure of members from the country and that his evangelical work had not been proven. The appeal for protection was accepted; however, the pastor did not visit Chile again. Judgment Court of Appeals of Santiago Rol 2209-2014 of December 12, 2014 and Supreme Court, Judgment Rol 32.430-14, of December 29, 2014.

43. Minister Jorge Zepeda, Judgment Rol 2182-98, Episode Juan Maino and others, January 23, 2012.

44. Santiago Court of Appeals, Judgment Rol 1.254-2012 of December 30, 2013.

45. Supreme Court, Replacement Judgment Rol 2.931-14, of November 13, 2014.

46. Minister Jorge Zepeda, Judgment Rol 10- 2004, Episode Adriana Bórquez Adriazola, of April 15, 2013 and, Rol 49 - 2004 (attached to Role No. 2182-98), of

October 15, 2015, confirmed by the Court of Appeals of Santiago (Rol 953-2013 and Rol 1843-2015).

47. Supreme Court, Rol: 21.614-2017. The case was seen by the Supreme Court in a hearing on September 7, 2017, it is pending notification on the verdict.

48. Judgment Rol 96.447 of April 21, 2003. Considering Ninth, Obtained in Cause Rol 2182-98 Episode Illicit association, pages 249 et seq.

49. Ibid.

50. Ibid.

51. Ibid.

52. Ibid. Kurt Herbert Schnellemkamp Nelaimischkies was sentenced to three years in prison and received a fine for the defrauded amount, granting him the benefit of conditional remission of the penalty.

53. Draft Agreement No. 506 approved by the Chamber of Deputies in session No. 63 of April 29, 1997.

54. See CIPER Chile, 26 March 2009, http://ciperchile.cl/2009/03/26/los-secretos-del-codigo-moral-que-se-desplomo-en-colonia-dignidad/.

55. The complaints were accumulated in Cause Role 683-2017, substantiated by Minister Mario Carroza. In the same case, a separate notebook was created for fieldwork.

56. Memorandum of understanding between the Government of the Republic of Chile and the Government of the German Federal Republic, Berlin, July 12, 2017.

57. Ibid.

Chapter 23

The Edwards

The Power of a Newspaper

Nancy Guzmán

INTRODUCTION

In 1973, Margarita Paillal declared,

> We know that it is the reactionaries who try to scare us and lie on the radio, in the newspapers, because they are theirs, because nobody has taken them away, because nobody has scared them like the fascist military scares us. Everything is theirs! The laws were made by them! We know that, even if we are farmers. They believe we are dumb and ignorant. We have little education, yes, but we are not ignorant, nor are we fools either, our ears are wide open. And what I want is that when my children grow up, they will be something else, and not what I have been: exploited with no education.[1]

The words of Margarita Paillal were the expression of rebellion in the face of the terror that the campesinos in the Mapuche area of Nehuentue on the coast of Temuco lived on August 30, 1973, when combined military forces in search of a supposed guerrilla camp enforced a barricad by land and air that was granted by the Weapons Control Law.

Several towns in the area suffered from the plans for the counterinsurgent war. There were raids, house burnings, and the sound of shouting and the sound of bullets from rifles. The campesinos were held on one site, and the agricultural settlements' union leaders were taken to the patrons' houses to be cruelly tortured with electricity, were hung, suffered genital burns, dumped in the sea hanging from a helicopter, wounded by blades, deprived of food, and their families frightened and humiliated for four days.

The calculated plan, before its final execution, had valuable collaboration from the El Mercurio S.A.P newspaper chain, which used its pages to deliver false information between September 1 and 11,[2] thanks to the fact that "its journalists were the only ones who could enter the area."[3]

Las Ultimas Noticias cited that the rumor was true that was being spread by the Christian Democratic leader Rodolfo Riquelme Montecino of a suspicious ship supposedly loaded with weapons that was moored off the Tirua pier.[4]

For the plan led by Commander Pablo Iturriaga Marchese,[5] head of the Cautín Military Garrison, helicopters and military logistics were used. The objective was to weaken the campesino's organization by dividing them with terror. Then the communities blamed their leaders for the hardship they had endured. They had been abandoned, trapped in their world, and once again endured violence from the landowners. Many had agreed to inform on young university students and professionals who worked farming their worn-out lands, in health and education for them and their children, while others decided to flee the area.[6]

For the trial nothing was missing. El Mercurio newspaper was in charge of showing the poor campesinos as dangerous extremists to the country. They claimed they had an arsenal of weapons and that the population in the area was terrified. They covered up the torture, suffering, and abuse that the communities had always lived through.[7]

Eleven days later, the country would live an unprecedented repression, known only in advance by the Nehueltue campesinos. The results would be seventeen years of dictatorship, the social, political, economic, and moral breakdown of the country with 3,140 detained, disappeared, and executed people, more than 30,000 people tortured, more than 500,000 people forced into exile, 5000 dismissed from their jobs after being accused of subversion, campesinos expelled from their lands, the ruin of public education, public health, social housing, and the privatization of state enterprises all at an evil price, which would be the basis of the new wealth.

THE EDWARDS AND THEIR POWER

Not just any Edwards is powerful in Chile. You have to be male and be called Agustine. This is according to the story of a family that has influenced the political life in Chile since 1804.[8]

Agustín Edwards Eastman knew well when he assumed direction of El Mercurio newspaper; he only had to take after the dynasty's founder, José Agustín de Dios Edwards Ossandón (1815–1878), the sixth son of the English barber George Edwards Brown and Isabel Ossandón an heiress of the Peñuelas farm.

El Mercurio was founded in 1827 by Pedro Félix Vicuña in Valparaíso and was known as the oldest Spanish-speaking newspaper; it was then passed on to José Santos Tornero, who gave it a European style transforming it into a reference for his social class, which the nineteenth-century oligarchy welcomed with joy. In 1875, the owner was Agustín Edwards Ross and it became a symbol of the family, as well as influencing a nascent Chilean bourgeoisie. In 1900, Agustín Edwards McClure founded *El Mercurio* de Santiago.

Agustin Edwards Eastman, the fifth Agustin in the line of succession, was born in Paris on November 24, 1927, the second child and the first son of Agustin Edwards Budge and Isabel Eastman Beéche.

He studied until the third year of Law at the University of Chile; then he left to study a bachelor's degree in International Relations at Princeton University leaving before finishing.

On the death of his father, in 1956, he became responsible for administering the inheritance, like all Augustinians who had preceded him, becoming the owner of El Mercurio, the Edwards Bank, President of the Federico Santa María Foundation, and in charge of the Edwards holding companies.

Like his father and grandfather before him, he was a furious anti-communist and from the pages of his newspaper would promote the Cold War ideology. "The editorials of El Mercurio became the multiplier effect of campaigns against the Left, they were read on important radio programs and were commented on in the political and academic spheres, becoming a vehicle for CIA ideas reaching an audience of more than 5 million people in 1970."[9]

The first protests began in 1967, as overnight a student rebellion manifested in a takeover of the Technical University Federico Santa María defending that the university foundation had been created by the inheritance of the sugar magnate Federico Santa María who on his death had stopped executing the testament to his grandfather Agustin Edwards McClure and Carlos van Buren.

The students demanded that the Edwards leave the foundation and the University. They wanted answers to the abuse that had been done to the will as Federico Santa María had left this to the children of the workers. They knew that the Edwards had transferred it over to the capital of the Edwards family by way of investments to their companies.

This was possible as when Edwards McClure had tried to legalize the will, since there was no executor in the Chilean legislature justice determined that he was granted the status of modal heir, so granting him full rights to make use of the inheritance[10] and to administer it he created the Federico Santa María Foundation.

The socialist senator Tomás Chadwick upon learning that the university money was invested in companies that the Edwards were presiding over the directories declared that the Edwards had transformed "the foundation of Federico Santa María charity into a true holding of companies, to move capital, control societies and set up an economic empire."[11]

The Deputy Luis Maira and part of the Congress asked the General Controller of the Republic to investigate the financial management of the Federico Santa María Foundation.[12] Politics and society followed a complex course and the transfer of assets from the Foundation to the Edwards family was never completed.

On August 16 of that year, El Mercurio reacted to the takeover of the Pontifical Catholic University, calling it a dark "plan drawn up and disseminated by Communists." The indignant Federico Santa María Technical University responded by putting up a canvas on the front of the Central House, in the middle of Alameda Avenue, that read: "Chileans: El Mercurio lies!"

This was a brutal blow to his ego as not only was he accused of appropriating money from a university but also his most precious asset was under attack. It was a sign that indicated that the pendulum of history did not swing this way.

Six days later, Edwards would create the Cofradía Náutica del Pacífico Austral (The Southern Pacific Nautical Guild).[13] By means of the innocent appearance of a sports organization, he would gather his closest group to prevent Salvador Allende from winning the 1970 presidential elections. Two key men would participate in the foundation: Roberto Kelly and Hernán Cubillos. The aim was to establish contacts with the Armed Forces through the Navy, and influence high ranking officials.[14] Edwards, in the presence of Vice Admirals Patricio Carvajal and Arturo Troncoso is self-designated Commodore and José Toribio Merino second-class Commodore.

THE CONSPIRACY

Documents from the International Telephone and Telegraph (ITT) show that to avoid the rise of Salvador Allende coordinated activities were carried out, financed, and directed from the United States to provoke political chaos where Agustín Edwards and his company El Mercurio S.A.P. played a fundamental role.

One of the cables says that a measure to prevent Allende from assuming the presidency was "that we and other American firms in Chile inject news into El Mercurio."[15]

"Through it [El Mercurio], undercover actions by the CIA were developed, which included 'dark' propaganda, false information presented as true,"[16] to prevent Salvador Allende going to La Moneda and then to destabilize the constitutional government.

The Committee of 40[17] gave Edwards US$ 700,000 for that purpose; he also received unquantified monies from the International Telegraph and

Telephon (ITT).[18] Edwards used El Mercurio S.A.P. to generate the conditions to justify a coup d'etat as a way of transforming the economy and the political system that had been in crisis since the 1950s.

Roberto Kelly was appointed to recruit the group of economists who had traveled on an exchange program to the University of Chicago. The first was Emilio Sanfuente, an Edwards employee at the Center for Social and Economic Studies (CESEC). He was a Sociologist recently graduated from his postgraduate degree in Economics at the University of Chicago. Roberto Pulido, Fernando Bravo, Guillermo Chadwick, Alfredo Dusaillant, Sergio de Castro, Pablo Barahona, Adilio Pipino, Sergio de la Cuadra, Juan Carlos Méndez, and Sergio Undurraga worked together with him.

His first task was to write the economic program for Jorge Alessandri R. When his advisors read it they dismissed it because they thought it was too radical and impossible to carry it out. Sanfuentes suggested that Edwards create an economic section in El Mercurio to influence and propagate Friedman's ideas to the business community that still believed that the state should have some productive functions.

Carlos Urenda, his lawyer and right hand, organized meetings with the Confederation of Production to measure the feeling in that sector and attract them to liberal ideas.

Meanwhile Kelly was in charge of the work toward the Armed Forces and of convincing the businessmen of the restlessness that reigned down on them through low wages and the indolence of the government of Eduardo Frei Montalva. Its purpose was to create the perception of instability, chaos, disorder, and inefficiency of the economic welfare system and liberal democracy.

THE ELECTION OF SALVADOR ALLENDE

On September 4, Edwards looked waited for the election results. As the results appeared, so did his worst nightmare.

At El Mercurio his unconditional staff: René Silva Espejo, a man of confidence, specialist in media campaigns with networks in embassies and the Christian Democracy Party; Roberto Kelly, Hernán Cubillos, Jorge Ross, Carlos Urenda, Arturo Fontaine, and Edmundo Eluchans were waiting for his orders.

Edwards contacted his friend Donald Kendall to ask him to arrange a meeting with Richard Nixon. Kendall proposed a position on the board of Pepsi Cola and promised to make the appointment with Nixon.[19]

On September 9, Edwards left for Buenos Aires, bound for New York. Before he met with his most loyal servants to give them his latest orders and ask them to take care of his interests.[20]

FUBELT[21]

Nixon had not stopped making threats against Allende, as evidenced by telephone conversation recordings with Kissinger, where the latter informs him that "Edwards has escaped and will be arriving here next Monday."[22]

On September 14, 1970, Nixon and the CIA director Richard Helms met with Edwards. Edwards described a terrifying picture of Chile.[23] It was so convincing, that "Late on Tuesday night (Sept. 15) Ambassador Edwards Korry finally received a message from the State Department giving him the green light to act on behalf of President Nixon. The message gave him maximum authority to do everything possible—less an action type [invasion] The Dominican Republic—to prevent Allende from taking power."[24] They should not leave any traces in the FUBELT operation, which would end the life of General René Schneider.

Salvador Allende assumed command in mourning the death of General René Schneider, who was killed by the same hands that three years later would encircle La Moneda Palace and start the bloodbath ending in his own death.

The ITT[25] was the best supporter of El Mercurio. "The El Mercurio newspapers are another key factor. It is extraordinarily important to keep them alive and publishing . . . They are the only frankly anti-communist voice left in Chile . . . This may be the Achilles heel of the Allende people."[26] In 1971, the CIA Station "judged that El Mercurio, the most important opposition publication, could not survive Allende's pressure."[27]

Declassified documents have revealed the resources given to Edwards to destroy the country economically, socially, and politically: "US$1,665,000 from 1971/1972 were delivered [to El Mercurio S.A.P] for press paper and the withdrawal of government advertising."[28]The Committee of forty authorized US$ 700,000 on September 9, 1971, and added US$ 965,000 on April 11, 1972. The amounts were so high that a memo sent to Kissinger by William J. Jorden of the Council National Security on April 10, 1972, said: "It seems that we receive a large bill every few months to keep El Mercurio afloat."[29]

For this reason, the CIA was ordered to verify "some diversion of the funds towards other Edwards companies."[30] A declassified document says that at a meeting between representatives of the State Department and the Agency held on February 23, 1972, James R. Gadner asked whether Edwards would not be using El Mercurio as a pretext to get funds from the United States, destining not only to save his newspaper but some of his other businesses, stating that "the amounts are unusually bulky."[31]

It is estimated at that time that only between 1971 and 1972 the CIA sent US$ 2,000,000 to Edwards to cover-up factious actions, destroy the economy, feed hatred, and generate uncertainty through El Mercurio,[32] to induce the Armed Forces and part of the society to tolerate the coup d'etat and human rights violations. Although Edwards denied this to Minister Carroza:

> What is not evidence of what is said (referring to the statements and documents). I reiterate that I had a meeting in Washington with Kissinger and Helms. In addition, this meeting was held days after the election of Salvador Allende, an opportunity of the circumstances of having a communist president in a democratic country were discussed, but in no case was a coup d'etat or something similar, let alone of financing of El Mercurio newspaper.[33]

Unfortunately, the U.S Nixon government left its fingerprints on the intervention and the coup d'etat in Chile.

In the days before the coup, El Mercurio published exasperating calls to overthrow the government. Terms such as "disqualification" or "waiver of the exercise of command" and threats that if not, "we will need to knock on the doors of the barracks,"[34] filled its pages.

In those crucial days, the *Chicago Boys* had almost finished El Ladrillo, the name they would give to the document that would transform the country's economy. As they had planned, Chile would be the first country that would apply Milton Friedman's theories and the coup d'etat would generate the ideal conditions for this: a totalitarian government that kept the population unarmed under the coercion of terror, preventing the existence of the most minimum social or political organization to resist the creation of the normative framework in the workplace that discourages union organization, allowing for low wages, precarious working conditions, and instability, together with an aggressive privatization of state-owned companies and the transnationalization of the economy.

COMPLICITY

On the morning of September 11, while the machine guns rattled through the streets of Santiago, Sergio de Castro finished printing volumes of El Ladrillo, which would be delivered to the four members of the Military Junta Government.

Edwards, from Barcelona, would follow the events through Hernán Cubillos and directly with Admiral José Toribio Merino.

In Santiago, the fires from the bombing were still blazing, when Army General Javier Palacios went to El Mercurio to look for the photo editor, Juan Enrique Lira, to take photos of the body of President Salvador Allende, leaving the last ever photos of the president in his archive.

At that time, No. 15 Bando of the Military Junta was in progress: As a precautionary measure, on September 12, 1973, the issuance of the following newspapers was authorized: "El Mercurio" and "La Tercera de la Hora."[35]

From that moment "The reports, chronicles and informative notes emphasized the ruthless nature of those arrested; narrating the facts with excessive adjectives in an almost childish style in order to cause rejection from the people who are persecuted and provide a Manichaean vision of what is happening to the population."[36]

The front page of El Mercurio on September 12 read: "Military Junta Controls the Country" and in smaller letters "Allende is dead." Below this "Complacency of the Judiciary Power." This is the advance of the new country.

The incitement to delation appears in the inner pages. The best-known title was: "Locate and Detain the following people" followed by photos and the names of: Carlos Altamirano, Oscar Guillermo Garretón, Miguel Enriquez, Eugenio Lira Massi, Alejandro Villalobos, Miria Contreras, Luis Maira, Luis Corvalán, Mario Palestro, Luis Espinoza, Pedro Vuskovic, Víctor Toro, and Luis Joel Bouquert.[37] El Mercurio S.A.P. does not hide its complicity with the genocidal policy of the dictatorship. One of the most brutal examples was the headline "Exterminate like Rats," which appeared on the cover of the evening edition of La Segunda on July 24, 1975. Operation Colombo was an intelligence maneuver to cover up the crime and the disappearance of 119 Chileans, detained by the National Intelligence Directorate (DINA) between May 27, 1974, and February 20, 1975, who had been seen in different torture centers in poor physical condition as a result of cruel and inhumane treatment. The last time they were seen alive was when they were taken out of the torture areas by DINA agents. Then two foreign publications, which had only one edition, made them appear outside national territory dead.

Operation Colombo was "like many others used by the military dictatorship inspired by psychological war manuals used by the United States military forces."[38]

They were two lists with names of militants of Movimiento de Izquierda Revolucionaria (Movement of the Revolutionary Left) (MIR) killed in alleged power struggles or guerrilla clashes that occurred outside national territory. One list appeared in the Novo O'Dia de Curitiva newspaper on June 25, 1975, and included fifty-nine names of MIR militants killed in a confrontation in Salta, Argentina. In the LEA Magazine in Buenos Aires on July 23 of that year, the following list appeared "60 Chilean extremists have been killed in the last three months by their own fighting companions in a vast and ruthless revenge and political cleansing program."[39]

On the same day, Las Últimas Noticias newspaper reprinted the information with the headline "Executive Payroll" and the title below read "Bloody struggle in the MIR." On July 24, the afternoon edition of La Segunda publishes the same brutal headline in large red letters and adds "The MIR has murdered 60 of its men." "Chilean extremists kill each other" publishes El Mercurio on July 19 in the international section. In an affirmative tone, it says that "the executions were dictated by the people's courts." They add that "59 names, supposedly eliminated in this internal struggle, is highlighted by the paper, include Lira Massi whose body was found in the apartment he occupied in Paris."[40]

At the end of the operation, on November 13, 1975, La Segunda headline "The Dead that You Killed Are in Good Health" ensured that the people who were on the list were alive and out of the country when their relatives accused the dictatorship; despite the fact that on August 9, 1975, El Mercurio had printed an investigation by LATIN that claimed that "the 119 left-wing militants supposedly killed in this country (Argentina) and other Latin Americans were never in Argentine territory."[41]

Years later, it was learned that for this operation the DINA had coordinated with the Brazilian dictatorship[42] and the head of the Triple A in Argentina, José López Rega, through the agents featured in the embassies, officials of LAN Chile, and Enrique Arancibia Clavel.

This operation was followed by a cover-up of the crimes against Marta Ugarte, a communist militant who was arrested by the DINA on August 9, 1976; whose body was found on the La Ballena beach on September 16, 1976.

Its pages covered up the detainees dumped into the sea by making Marta's case look like a passionate murder, even though she still had the wire with which she had been hanged before putting her on the helicopter that threw her body into the sea. El Mercurio and Las Últimas Noticias sent their best reporters: Beatriz Undurraga and Pablo Honorato with instructions to write crime report. Las Últimas Noticias ran the headline "Beautiful Young Woman Strangled." For ten days, the pages were filled with details about her death at the hands of "her husband, lover or psychopath" after being raped and beaten.

Her family would only discover on September 27, 1976, that this lacerated body was that of Marta Ugarte. The two reporters who had been given free rein responded to the courts that they had carried out orders from the directors of their newspapers.[43]

The last operation by El Mercurio was a setup with the CNI, which was the torture of Enrique Barra Stuckraht and Jorge Ernesto Jaña Obregón, two young people kidnapped by the repressive body so that they could be blamed for the serious events that occurred ten days earlier at the homily of Pope John Paul II in O'Higgins Park.

El Mercurio published the photo of the two young people on the cover under the headline: "Identified violent CP (Communist Party) in the Park."[44]

The complaint by the Vicaria de la Solidaridad made Agustín Edwards spend two hours in the Capuchino Prison annex and remain under court order for twelve months by Judge Carlos Bottacci Latrille in the 23rd Criminal Court establishing that "Edwards Eastman had obtained the information the day before [to the arrests] through his direct relationship with the CNI and its General Directors."

The National Court of Ethics and Discipline (TRINED) of the College of Journalists conducted an ethical trial in 2015 and based on this court case rescinded Agustín Edwards Eastman's the possibility of remaining a member of the College.[45]

THE TRANSITION

In the late 1980s, Edwards and El Mercurio were in ruins.[46] Applying the same tactics he used with Nixon, he told Pinochet that El Mercurio would be his only insurance in the transition. In December 1989, two months after the change of command, Pinochet commissioned Álvaro Bardón, President of the State Bank, to look for a way to save Edwards and El Mercurio. With the help of Emilio Sanfuentes and Johnny Kulka, they devised a system of debt swaps that would make any subsequent attempt to reverse transactions impossible, for which the State Bank suffered a capital loss of UF 1,200,000.[47]Although there was a trial by the Treasury for fraud against Álvaro Bardón and he was convicted in the first instance, the same did not happen at the Supreme Court as the decision by the Fourth Chamber exempted him from all charges.[48]

Edwards began the transition to democracy with his capital sanitized by the State of Chile and as the owner of the most feared newspaper by the democratic authorities. In May 2000, the Socialist president Ricardo Lagos was invited to honor the change of format for the 100 years anniversary of El Mercurio. On this occasion, the president said, it would be "impossible to understand the history of Chile without El Mercurio."

CONCLUSIONS

More than forty-five years after the coup d'état that destroyed democracy and the legal norms that protected the citizens and their rights giving way to massive violations of human rights and given the information available today, it is impossible not to qualify that the company El Mercurio S.A.P. and its owner, the journalist Agustín Edwards Eastman, as instigators of the democratic bankruptcy, concealment of massive and serious human rights violations as complicit and contributing to the impunity of these same crimes through a planned campaign with information, misinformation, and manipulation, as well as being economic beneficiaries of the dictatorial government.

The political conditions were never verified as to make Edwards feel threatened, in so much he stated before Judge Carroza, "I must point out that the Military Government saved my life."[49]

NOTES

1. Faride Zerán Ch., Revista Chile Hoy, September 7, 1973.
2. *Breve Historia de la Unidad Popular. La Caída de Allende*, Document from El Mercurio, Chapter 52, page. 412, Edited by El Mercurio S.A.P.
3. Interview with journalist Juan Jorge Faundes Merino, who had traveled to cover facts for the Austral de Temuco newspaper of the SOPESUR chain, he was arrested for questioning and taken to a house where the combined forces operated. After they had confirmed his credentials he was released but was prohibited from approaching the area.
4. *Las Últimas Noticias*, "En cárcel de Temuco los 20 guerrilleros" "20 guerrillas in the Temuco prison," September 4, 1973, back page.
5. Miguel González Pino, Arturo Fontaine Talavera; *The Thousand Days of Allende* (Center for Public Studies, Volume II, 1st Edition 1997), 822. Colonel Iturriaga Marchese was prosecuted by Italian justice for the execution of the Italian citizen, former religious man and professor at the Catholic University of Temuco, Omar Roberto Venturelli Leonelli, which occurred on September 25, 1973, within the framework of the Caravana de la Muerte.
6. Rubén Morales Jara, Professor of mathematics, leader of the MIR, was arrested on September 6, 1973, at his home by order of the military prosecutor of Cautín being accused of violating the Arms Control Law. He was last seen days after the coup in the Temuco Prison in a very bad physical condition. His name is on the list of missing detainees. See Report of the National Truth and Reconciliation Commission, Volume 3, pp. 262–63.
7. El Mercurio, "Foco guerrillero en Nehuentúe. Miristas aterrorizan a campesino" September 3, 1973.
8. Nancy Guzmán J., Los Agustines y la conspiración permanente (Ceibo Ediciones, 2015), 36.
9. Covert Action in Chile: 1963–1973, *Staff Report on the Select Commitee to Study Gobernamental Operation*, page 22.
10. Inheritance petition trial of the Santa María Foundation. Report on the right of French writers and professors Henry Capitant, Georges Ripert, and René Demogert. Printing and Lithographic Society Universo1929.
11. Senate of the Republic of Chile, 59th Session, Thursday, February 8, 1968, p. 2189f.
12. http://w.w.w.bcn.cl/laborparlamentaria/wsgi/consulta/verDiariosDeSesion.py?id=595975.
13. http://www.cofradianautica.cl/quienes-somos/acta-de-fundacion.

14. Jorge Magasich A., Those who said “No.” History of the anti-coup Seaman’s movement of 1973, Volume I, p. 315, Editorial LOM.

15. ITT Secret Documents, Quimantú National Publishing Company, p. 16.

16. *Covert Action in Chile*: 1963–1973, op.cit, page 22.

17. It was chaired by the President for National Security Affairs and was made up of the Deputy Secretary of Defense, the Joint Chief of Staff, the Director of the CIA, and the Assistant Secretary of State for Political Affairs.

18. *Covert Action in Chile*: 1963–1973, op.cit, page 16.

19. Ibid., 111.

20. Patricia Arancibia Clavel, *Chile Un Milagro. Roberto Kelly. Un Padre Fundador*, Editorial Autoedición, 2005.

21. Cryptogram created by the CIA for the undercover operation against Salvador Allende. FU, meant Chile and BELT.

22. Declassified Document Nº 82, September 12, 1970, published in Volume XXI of the series «Foreign Relations of the United States, 1969–1976, available at <http:/ /history.state.gov/historicaldocuments/frus1969- 76v21>.

23. *Foreign Relations of the United States, 1969–1976, Volume XXI, Chile, 1969–1973)*, <http://static.history.state.gov/frus/frus1969-76v21/pdf/frus1969-76v21.pdf>.

24. *Secret ITT Document*. Empresa Editora Quimantú LTDA, 1972, 10.

25. The second ITT man, John MacCone was director of the CIA between 1961 and 1965, recognized that the United States Senate maintained contacts with Richard Helms to overthrow the Government of Salvador Allende.

26. Ibíd., 10.

27. *Foreign Relations of the United States*, 1969–1976, Volume XXI, Chile, 1969–1973.

28. *Covert Action in Chile 1962–1973*, 8. It is estimated that the US$ 1,665,000 today corresponds to more than US$ 10 million.

29. *Foreign Relations of the United States*, 1969–1976, Volume XXI, Chile, 1969–1973.

30. Ibíd.

31. Declassified document N° 259, September 13, 1972.

32. *National Archives, Nixon Presidential Materials, NSC Files, Box 775, Country Files, Latin America, Chile, Vol. V.*

33. Instigators of the coup d'état, October 3, 2013.

34. El Mercurio, September 9, 1973.

35. Manuel Antonio Garretón, Roberto Garretón y Carmen Garretón, *Por la fuerza sin la razón. Análisis de los textos y bandos de la dictadura militar.* LOM editions (1998), 68–69.

36. Nancy Guzmán Jasmen, Role of the Press during the dictatorship, Judgment by the Ethics Court Metropolitan Council Journalist College. Case lists of 119, 10.

37. Ibíd., 64–65.

38. Judgment by the Court of Ethics Metropolitan Council of the College of Journalists of Chile. Case Operation Colombo, 3.

39. Ibíd., 5.

40. El Mercurio, July 19, page. 7.

41. El Mercurio, August 9, 1975.

42. Ver: <http://politica.estadao.com.br/noticias/eleicoes,jornal-deu-nova-versao-para-mortes-no-chile-imp-,1165490>.

43. Cause role 2182-1998, pages 390 and following, pages 624. Statement by Pablo Honorato.

44. El Mercurio, April 9, 1987.

45. http://www.colegiodeperiodistas.cl/p/fallos.html.

46. El Mercurio newspaper had a debt of US$ 80,000,000.

47. Santiago Fifth Criminal Court, Rol 133.228–6, Expert report requested by Judge Alejandro Solís.

48. Rol 133.228-6 was requested from the Judicial Archive, answering "only the folder without documents is found."

49. Rol 2442-2012. Inquiry statement made on September 26, 2013, by Judge Mario Carroza, in the case of Instigators of the Coup d'etat. The complaint filed on December 17, 2012, by the Association of Relatives of Disappeared Detainees and the Association of Relatives of Political Executives investigates the responsibility of civilians in the management of the coup.

Section 6

LEGAL ELEMENTS OF ECONOMIC COMPLICITY

Chapter 24

Corporate Responsibility for Complicity in International and Comparative Law

Juan Pablo Bohoslavsky

INTRODUCTION

Over the past decades, companies have shown an increasing amount of power to influence the different economic, social, and political events on both a domestic and global scale.[1] Consequently, it is not surprising that corporate responsibility, including responsibility for complicity, has evolved significantly in the past ten years in an attempt to adapt to this trend.

This evolution has taken several forms, such as the passing of codes of conduct for companies (some of which already existed before the Chilean dictatorship),[2] several United Nations (UN) guidelines regarding companies and human rights,[3] studies by nongovernmental organizations, a growing body of academic research, and a series of legal actions in national courts.[4]

This trend was synthesized and documented in a report on corporate complicity and legal responsibility elaborated by the International Commission of Jurists (ICJ) in 2008.[5] This report highlights the accountability of companies that support gross human rights violations by *enabling, facilitating, or exacerbating* the commission of such crimes.

Due to companies' involvement in the Pinochet's dictatorship, accounted for in several chapters of this book, it is important to explore which the answer provided by international law is for cases of corporate complicity with serious human rights violations. Section 2 will study whether from an international law perspective, economically contributing to a regime perpetrating systematic gross human rights violations entails illegal conduct. Section 3 will attempt to answer the same question from a comparative law perspective. Section 4 presents the circumstances required for there to be a case of civil responsibility for corporate complicity, analyzing the causal link, the subjective element, and what harm may have come from those actions. Finally, section 5 provides the conclusions of the chapter.

INTERNATIONAL LAW

International human rights conventions expressly penalize complicity in a general sense,[6] that is, in the way of enabling or contributing to the commission of crimes against human rights. This approach has been adopted by a growing body of regulatory and administrative frameworks both at the international and national levels, crystalizing customary international law on the subject, which consolidates the idea that it is unlawful to contribute to human rights violations.

When these contributions are expressed in the form of corporate inputs (goods or services), are they still unlawful? The aforementioned conventions do not differentiate natural and legal persons when it comes to prohibiting complicity in human rights violations, regardless of the principal crime being committed by the state or by non-state subjects. Neither are contributions consisting of specific goods or services exempted. Excluding the provision of commodities from the general prohibition of contributing to human rights violations is not an option that stems either explicitly or implicitly from these conventions.

Moreover, the Charter of the Nuremberg International Military Tribunal already penalized cooperation in the commission of major crimes, as well as providing for the possibility of considering as *criminal organizations* the groups to which natural persons involved in those crimes belonged.[7] The *Industrial Cases* heard by that military tribunal, in which several businesspeople were convicted on the charges of contributing to the Nazi extermination campaign, confirmed the principle that companies and businesspeople can be found to have breached international law even when their directors were the ones criminally convicted, although the *death penalty* was rarely applied to a company.[8] Among other businesspeople, in these proceedings—which were founded on international customary law—several individuals who had contributed commercially (Bruno Tesch, by supplying gas to the Auschwitz concentration camp) and financially (Friedrich Flick, the German industrialist who used slave work and donated money to the SS command) to the commission of genocide perpetrated by the Nazi regime were convicted.[9]

Non-state actors may, technically, breach international human rights laws; consequently, the different considerations regarding states or non-state subjects are, effectively, a less and less relevant issue in legal theory and practice. In fact, corporations are increasingly regulated by international law (e.g., bilateral investment treaties), so that the scope of their rights and obligations becomes the result of political decisions rather than of deductions based on their subjectivity in international law.

In that way, corporations, as natural persons and states, are not exempt from the duty of respecting the fundamental human rights that, depending on the case, concern them. This is the general spirit behind the Guiding Principles on Business and Human Rights adopted by the UN Human Rights Council in 2011,[10] as well as the work of the Intergovernmental Working Group, whose mandate is to elaborate a binding instrument to regulate the activities of corporations in human rights law—adopted by vote in 2014 by the Human Rights Council[11]—and the General comment No. 24 of the Committee on Economic, Social and Cultural Rights, passed in 2017, on human rights and business obligations.[12]

This new understanding of the link between human rights and corporations is the result of two concurring phenomena. The first is a humanist approach in international law, which has been explicitly adopted by the International Criminal Tribunal for the former Yugoslavia:

> A state-sovereign-oriented approach has been gradually supplanted by a human-being-oriented approach. Gradually, the maximum of Roman law *hominum causa omne jus constitutum* (all law is created for the benefit of human beings) has gained a firm foothold in the international community as well.[13]

The second is an integral and horizontal view of human rights, which—with few exceptions in which the state's presence is essential—govern not only the relations between states and individuals but also those among the latter. This responds to the definition established by the Universal Declaration of Human Rights itself in its preamble, which applies to every person and organ of society, including corporations. Whether it is an international tribunal or a national court who should demand that that duty be met is a jurisdictional matter.

Despite the fact that that legal persons, according to the current state of international law, do not fall under the jurisdiction of international criminal courts, they are not exempted from having to abide by the principle that prohibits contributing to the commission of serious human rights violations, especially when *jus cogens* norms are compromised.[14] Admitting that option would mean accepting that corporations can be used as a useful tool to break the law and profiting by facilitating serious crimes, which is unacceptable for the international system of human rights protection. Moreover, it would place corporations in a position of absolute immunity in relation to peremptory norms, a position to which states, as legal persons, could not aspire.

COMPARATIVE LAW

Due to the fact that international responsibility does not entail jurisdiction or a working mechanism for its implementation, domestic legal systems[15] are the ones ultimately in charge of incorporating, recognizing, translating, and defining the concrete implications derived from certain general principles stemming from public international law. Of interest here is the principle that recognizes the responsibility of non-state accomplices that contribute to the commission of serious human rights abuses; as a result, the comparative analysis of this subject becomes particularly relevant (for an analysis of Chile's legal system, *see* the chapter by Sferrazza and Bustos).

The basic international postulates in the subject of responsibility for complicity are reflected, for the most part, in each domestic system of law, which are the ones that specifically regulate and provide concrete answers to the debate on corporate responsibility for damages produced within the territory of a particular state.

While only a few systems have recognized the criminal responsibility of legal persons, the majority of them—both in the common and civil law traditions—admit their civil responsibility in cases of damages derived from their complicity, particularly in cases of human rights abuses.[16] Several institutions have adopted comprehensive systems of human rights protection, including against harmful behavior of the state, natural, and legal persons. The same reasoning is applied in numerous branches of the law, namely in labor law, environmental law, child protection law, and native people's law, all of which somehow crystallize the protection and remedies demanded by certain international principles. In Argentina, Australia, Brazil, Canada, France, India, Japan, the United Kingdom, and the United States, both international and domestic laws have been applied in civil actions for complicity in human rights violations. These solutions are consistent with the international principle that penalizes the contribution to violations of *jus cogens* norms.

Given that over the past fifteen years, United States' courts have been the most active in the subject of corporate complicity lawsuits, significantly influencing the development of global standards in that area, it proves useful to closely observe this country's legal system and jurisprudence.[17] The U.S. Restatement (Second) of Torts § 876 (1979) establishes civil responsibility for complicity. Recovered in modern times in 1980, the Alien Tort Claims Act (ATCA) has been frequently used by that country's courts to bring civil actions against natural persons and corporations for facilitating and contributing to serious human rights violations abroad.[18] These civil responsibility actions advanced because it is accepted that *jus cogens* norms have to be respected by both state and non-state actors, even in civil cases for damages.

The confusion regarding whether international or national law, or both, is to be applied arose basically from the influence of the ATCA debate. First, due to its reference to the *law of nations*, which is linked with the particular criterion adopted by U.S. jurisprudence when it must decide how international law is related to its own domestic law. And second, because of the jurisdictional (extraterritorial) implications of the implementation of the ATCA. In any case, actions brought in the United States under the ATCA pursue, to a certain extent, the same aims as the civil actions available in different domestic law systems, which can be brought in cases of human rights violations, even when they are as diversely categorized as effectively punishing the abuses committed, deterring similar behavior in the future or granting reparation to victims.

Although there are significant regressions in U.S. jurisprudence when it comes to the resolution of cases of corporate responsibility for complicity (e.g., when the extraterritorial application of the ATCA is restricted, as decided by the Supreme Court in 2013 in the famous *Kiobel* case),[19] there is currently a growing judicial consensus on the fact that companies must follow certain minimum standards of conduct when carrying out business with state subjects that are publicly known for perpetrating human rights abuses. Unfortunately, this trend has not resulted in a *justice cascade*—to use the term coined by Kathryn Sikkink—to protect the victims of human rights abuses from businesses.

CIVIL RESPONSIBILITY REQUIREMENTS

For reasons of space, it is not possible to expand on the criteria for the applicability of both criminal[20] and civil responsibility for complicity. I will focus on the latter because it is the least developed one in jurisprudence and legal theory, and also because, unlike criminal responsibility, it applies to both natural persons (acting in a personal capacity or as company directors or representatives) and to legal persons. Moreover, another chapter of this book (*see* Fernández & Garcés) already covers the criminal criteria applied in trials investigating the conduct of businesspeople and military officials who agreed to perpetrate—technically—premeditated crimes against those opposing the dictatorial regime. As explained before, given that international law establishes minimum standards in the subject, the criteria for the applicability of responsibility will be examined in light of international and comparative law.

Corporate Contributions and the Causal Link. The Relevance of Context

Corporate assistance to a criminal regime can consist of the supply of several types of goods and/or services (transportation, logistics, provision of goods, computer services, money, personnel, and so on). The company must have been in a situation of *proximity* with the principal perpetrator of the crime, in terms of the nature of the connection, commercial transactions, and duration and frequency of the relationship. The closer the company and its contribution are to the commission of crimes, the higher the chance that it had the "power, influence or opportunity necessary for its conduct to have a sufficient impact in the conduct of the principal perpetrator."[21] The key is to determine whether, without that factor, the causal chain would have been interrupted, or if, alternatively, it had a significant effect on the development of the criminal activity in question.

The following factors, among others, should be considered when determining if there existed a significant contribution from the collaborator: the nature of the activity supported or financed; the extent of the collaboration provided; if they were present at the time when the harm was caused; their relationship with the principal perpetrator of the harm; their knowledge of the facts and the duration of the assistance provided.

At the time of performing an analysis of the causal link, the aim is to encapsulate the contribution that, far from benefiting the population in terms of their human rights, harmed it, which could have been foreseen by the company had it carried out a careful assessment of the probable use of the goods and services it was providing. Therefore, the intention lies in foreseeing how this collaboration will substantially contribute to the production of harmful effects, and prioritizing the profits derived from that commercial activity, thus accepting the high probability that such harmful consequences occur.

What the vast majority of legal systems require to recognize the legal implications of the causal link in civil responsibility is for the action attributed to have been efficient with respect to the harm caused. This means that the reproached result would usually occur as a foreseeable consequence of that action. Then, the issue at hand is to determine in each case whether it is valid to expect that a commodity provided to a criminal regime will substantially influence, facilitate, or give continuity to criminal practices.

The courts of the United States have been very active when discussing this particular subject. The final ruling issued in "*Re* South Africa Apartheid Litigation"—the trial in which thousands of victims of the South African *apartheid* system brought charges against the companies that provided support for the segregationist regime[22]—does not appear to share the criterion of foreseeable use of commodities. To determine if there was a substantial effect, the court addresses the *inherent quality* of the product or service provided by the author of the crime. Without carrying out even a basic empirical analysis of the concrete effects of the loans at hand (in this resolution the banks that funded the *apartheid* were tried), the judgment establishes that money can never be sufficiently linked to crimes because it is not a *lethal commodity*.

This differentiation criterion, which rests on the intrinsic qualities of the good or service provided—instead of considering its real usage and impact—not only ignores the advancement of international law in the field of responsibility for corporate complicity, it is also challenged by the judgment itself, which accepted that the computers supplied by IBM to the *apartheid* regime, to implement the denationalization policy against black South Africans, were inherently risky and sufficiently connected to the crimes, while at the same time recognizing that lethal gas could be used for legitimate purposes.[23]

Denying a priori and categorically that a commodity which is not *intrinsically lethal* may, in fact, contribute, facilitate, or increase the effectiveness of a campaign of human rights abuses indicates a lack of knowledge of the way in which authoritarian governments make rational decisions based on the resources available to them, as well as of the importance of those same resources in terms of consolidation, operation, and legitimation of those governments, as has been explained in this book's introduction.

Analyzing the causal role of complicity played by Chilean corporations demands focusing on the political, social, and economic factors that allowed Pinochet's government to stage the coup, make progress, consolidate itself, and survive while it executed its plan. A strictly legal analysis must be complemented by an interpretation of the structures, the processes, and dynamics of the authoritarian regime, to understand the context of the causal mechanism of complicit behavior. The theory of rational choice can be of assistance in identifying the structural reasons why the regime and its economic accomplices behaved in a specific way, and how this behavior impacted the operations of the regime and its repressive apparatus.

Thus, when observing how the domestic product was redistributed during the dictatorship, and the evolution of its military budget, it becomes clear, on the one hand, why several businesspeople and the chambers that represented them publicly declared their support to the regime; and, on the other hand, how economic assistance provided to the state facilitated an effective repressive budgetary policy. This information regarding the context is useful to complement the evaluation of complicity's micro-relations, which can range from openly requesting to kidnap workers or participating in company theft operations and other forms of economic crimes, to condescending media policies, funding of the regime, intellectual contributions,[24] and so on.

Finally, it should be pointed out that contributions can be previous, simultaneous, or subsequent to the principal crime. An example of the latter is how a mass media company may manipulate information to guarantee their impunity from earlier crimes.

The Subjective Element

On the international level, there is controversy around the subject of whether the accomplice should be required to have known that their actions would facilitate the commission of crimes, or if they should be required to have harbored the intention to facilitate the crimes as well. Most international statues and jurisprudence have required knowledge of the crime, even if the main objective is not the commission of the principal crime. This was the conclusion reached by several rulings of the British Military Tribunal and the Military Tribunal at Nuremberg, the Draft Code of Crimes against the Peace and Security of Mankind prepared by the International Law Commission in 1996, and the interpretations of the International Criminal Tribunal for the Former Yugoslavia and the International Criminal Tribunal for Rwanda.

The Rome Statute of the International Criminal Court, on the other hand, requires that an intent to facilitate the crimes must exist (art. 25.3), but it states that such purpose may be secondary or nonexclusive, in the sense that another previous goal (such as profit) could have been sought. In other words, "*One who knowingly sells gas to the gas chamber operator for the primary purpose of profit may be inferred to have a secondary purpose of killing people, so that he can keep selling more gas to kill more people.*"[25] This theory seems to be supported by the fact that art. 25.3.d of the Rome Statute establishes that a member of a group shall be criminally responsible for its contributions if that individual is merely aware of the criminal purpose of the group, not only if these contributions were made to perpetrate a crime.

Alternatively, the previously mentioned report of the ICJ demands knowledge—and acceptance—of the consequences of corporate contributions or concurrence with the criminal intent of the main perpetrator. Although the company and the perpetrator of the crime may not share the same criminal intent, knowledge by the company of the essential character of its contribution for the commission of abuses and, thus, of the increased probability that these abuses will happen as a result of those contributions, entails an acceptance of that course of action:

> Even where a company does not actively wish to participate in gross human rights abuses, it may still be legally responsible if it knew or should have known that its conduct was likely to help cause such abuses.[26]

Gross negligence may serve as an indication to prove the knowledge of the collaborator about the consequences of its contributions.

Considering that domestic legal systems must incorporate, at least, the fundamental standards of international law on human rights in the field of civil responsibility, if those domestic systems are even more protective of the victims of human rights abuses than international law, that is a valid—and, in fact, recommendable—legislative option. This means that the subjective element in civil responsibility may consist of either the intention or the negligence of the accomplice, who knew or should have known the foreseeable consequences of its collaboration with the regime.

To establish whether a company knew or should have known the consequences of its contributions, it becomes necessary to analyze the information that was reasonably available at that time. Large companies are characterized by a high degree of professional diligence, which requires them to meet rigorous obligations regarding their means (i.e., their duty is to always act with prudence and not to ensure any particular result) for determining the implicit risk of their operations. In this way, if a company is aware of the harm that may result from its conduct and, even if it acts in the hope that this harm will not occur, still prioritizes the profits derived from the transaction, then it consents to the harm by moving forward with its actions: it acts with *dolus eventualis*. Knowledge can be attributed directly or indirectly, by inferring it from objective facts, as has been established by specialized jurisprudence.[27] Similarly, the facilitator can be judged based on what is presumed that it knew or should have known. If the facilitator acted with negligence—by failing to carry out due diligence obligations—at the time of assessing the foreseeable consequences of its actions, then it may be held accountable as well.

Compensable Damages

Pursuant to international law, civil responsibility is activated when there is a contribution to the violation of fundamental human rights. In this case, recoverable personal damages have to be connected with the crimes that violated human rights. This repertoire of crimes includes, among others, genocide, slavery, torture, and other crimes against humanity, all of which were present during the Pinochet's dictatorship.

As specified under UN General Assembly Resolution 60/147 of 2006,[28] reparations for victims of gross human rights violations have to cover any economically measurable damage caused, and those compensations have to be proportional to the gravity of the violation and the circumstances of each case. The "individual circumstances" of each victim must be considered. At the same time, the resolution calls for reparation in the form of "satisfaction," which implies that the facts related to human rights abuses perpetrated, including complicity, should be found out and revealed. Moreover, the Statute of the International Criminal Court stipulates that reparation shall not "be interpreted as prejudicing the rights of victims under national or international law" (art. 75.6).

When the compensations granted by the very state that committed the crimes are limited and appraised, as a result of standardization of reparations to adjust them to budgetary restrictions, the responsibility of accomplices may remain a pending issue.

Despite the fact that requests to establish this form of corporate responsibility demand a casuistic analysis of the damages caused, the U.S. experience related to this subject has shown that such requests may be harmonized with the practicality of the administrative approach of compensation programs that follow authoritarian periods: the reparation funds for victims of the Holocaust are managed outside the tribunals, although they operate under their supervision.

As regards statutory limitations for civil actions for complicity, the Statute of the International Criminal Court stipulates that the crimes within the jurisdiction of the Court are not subject to any statute of limitations, and it establishes that reparations to victims fall under its jurisdiction (articles 29 and 75). This formula is consistent with the Basic Principles and Guidelines on the Right to a Remedy and Reparation for Victims of Gross Violations of International Human Rights Law and Serious Violations to International Humanitarian Law, adopted in 2005 by the UN General Assembly.[29] Article 7 of this instrument establishes:

> Domestic statutes of limitations for other types of violations that do not constitute crimes under international law, including those time limitations applicable to civil claims and other procedures, should not be unduly restrictive.

The Inter-American Court of Human Rights suggests that there exists a very close link between the obligation to investigate and the obligation to provide reparation for the damage caused. In its jurisprudence, none of these duties can be ignored by invoking domestic regulations.[30]

Truth, justice, and reparation are complementary aspirations rather than alternative responses to gross human rights violations.[31]

CONCLUSIONS

As the crimes committed during the Pinochet's dictatorship have been placed in the legal category of maximum severity (violation of *jus cogens*), an attempt to analyze the conduct of businesspeople who collaborated with that same regime in the light of international standards is not merely an exercise of historical narrative, but a technical and legal assessment to provide an adequate legal answer to the victims. The implications of this attempt are further strengthened when considering the arguments that propose the non-applicability of statutory limitations to this kind of action.

Both international and comparative law clearly prohibit contributing to the perpetration of human rights violations. The law offers a wide array of resources to deal with the varied economic conducts that can be considered complicit, be it by criminal punishment or civil remedies. The challenge is purely judicial: to define how to apply the rules and criteria for establishing responsibility in the face of concrete cases that have entailed different degrees and types of cooperation.

An adequate criterion for assessing complex scenarios such as the one presented by economic complicity is to observe the foreseeable consequences of the usage of commodities rather than their intrinsic nature. This is the criterion adopted for the most part in U.S. jurisprudence to determine whether those providing financial assistance to terrorist groups can be considered accomplices of these groups' actions.[32] Contextual information is necessary to ascribe economic and political meaning to the specific conducts being judged and to understand the complexity of the causal mechanism operating between corporate contributions, the regime's performance and the perpetration of the crimes.

It should be noted that the responsibility for complicity is independent of the conviction of the principal perpetrator of the crime, which means that companies have to offer reparation even is the author of a crime does not or insufficiently does so.[33]

Another issue to be dealt with is to what degree parent companies can be held accountable for the complicit behavior of their subsidiaries. In principle, if the complicit company was merely a tool to break the law, disrupt the public order, act in bad faith, or to damage the rights of others, the associates or controllers who made that possible will be indicted, and they will have to answer jointly and unlimitedly for the damages caused. The answer to this question must account for the duty of reparation demanded by international law: the rules regarding the operations of economic conglomerates should not guarantee these conglomerates impunity when they are involved in acts of economic complicity.[34]

NOTES

1. This chapter expands and updates the text published by the author in Horacio Verbitsky and Juan Pablo Bohoslavsky (eds), *Outstanding Debts to Settle: The Economic Accomplices of the Dictatorship in Argentina* (Cambridge University Press, 2015), 130–42.

2. United Nations, *Declaration on the Establishment of a New International Economic Order*, G.A. Res. 3201, UN GAOR, 6ª special session, Sup. (No. 1), at 527/8, UN Doc. A/9559 (1974); E.S.C. Res. 1913, UN ESCOR, 57th session, Sup. (No. 1), U.N. Doc. 5570/Add 1 (1975).

3. See available information in http://www.ohchr.org/EN/Issues/Business/Pages/WGHRandtransnationalcorporationsandotherbusiness.aspx.

4. For an extensive list of cases in Latin America, Canada, and the United States, see C. Hutto y A. Jenkins, "Report on Corporate Complicity Litigation in the Americas: Leading Doctrines, Relevant Cases, and Analysis of Trends," in *Human Rights Clinic* (Austin: University of Texas, 2010).

5. IJC, *Corporate Complicity, and Legal Accountability. Report of the International Commission of Jurists Expert Legal Panel on Corporate Complicity in International Crimes*, vols. 1, 2, 3 (Geneva: ICJ, 2008).

6. Convention against Torture and Other Cruel, Inhuman or Degrading Treatment or Punishment (Art. 4); International Convention on the Suppression and Punishment of the Crime of Apartheid (Art. 3 (b)); Supplementary Convention on the Abolition of Slavery; the Slave Trade, and Institutions and Practices Similar to Slavery (Art. 6); Convention on the Prevention and Punishment of the Crime of Genocide (Art. 3 (e)); Convention on Combating Bribery of Foreign Public Officials in International Business Transactions (Art. 1 (2)); United Nations Convention against Transnational Organized Crime (Art. 5 (1)(b)); International Convention for the Suppression of the Financing of Terrorism (Art. 2 (5)(a)): International Convention for the Suppression of Terrorist Bombings (Art. 2 (3)(a)); Protocol against the Smuggling of Migrants (Art. 5 (1)(b)); Statute of the International Criminal Court (Art 25 (3)); and Statutes of the International Tribunal for Rwanda (Art. 6); and for the Former Yugoslavia (Art. 7).

7. *Charter of the International Military Tribunal*, Art. 9, August 8, 1945, 59 Stat. 1544, 82 UNTS, 279.

8. On the dissolution of IG Farben ordered precisely because of its implication in serious violations of international law during World War II, see Control Council Law, nº 10, *Punishment of Persons Guilty of War Crimes*, December 20, 1945, in *I Enactments and Approved Papers of the Control Council and Coordinating Committee*, p. 306.

9. "*In re* Tesch (The Zyklon B case)," 13 Ann. Dig 250 (Brit. Mil. Ct. 1946), reprinted in 1 United Nations War Crimes Comm'n, *Law Reports of Trials of War Criminals*, 93, 1947; "United States v. Flick (The Flick case)," December 22, 1947, in *Trials of War Criminals Before the Nuremberg Military Tribunals Under Control Council Law*, no. 10, 1, 1952.

10. Resolution No. 17/4.

11. Resolution No. 26/9.

12. E/C.12/GC/24.

13. ITFY, *Prosecutor v. Tadic*, October 2, 1995, para. 97.

14. According to Art. 53 of the Vienna Convention on the Law of Treaties (1969) *jus cogens* involves "peremptory norms," which mean: "*a norm accepted and recognized by the international community of States as a whole as a norm from which no derogation is permitted and which can be modified only by a subsequent norm of general international law having the same character*," Janis, Mark, *An Introduction to International Law* (Aspen Publishers, 2003), 62–63. *Jus cogens* prohibits, for example, genocide, slavery, torture, and other crimes against humanity.

15. UN Council, "Business and Human Rights: Further Steps Toward the Operationalization of the 'Protect, Respect and Remedy' Framework," *Report of the*

Special Representative of the Secretary-General on the issue of human rights and transnational corporations and other business enterprises, John Ruggie, UN Doc. A/HRC/14/27, 2010.

16. A. Ramasastry y R. Thompson, *Commerce, Crime and Conflict: Legal Remedies for Private Sector Liability for Grave Breaches of International Law. A Survey of 16 Countries* (Oslo, FAFO, Institute of Applied International Studies, 2006).

17. For a list of these lawsuits, see Human Rights Council, "Promotion and Protection of All Human Rights, Civil, Political, Economic and Cultural Rights, Including the Right to Development. Clarifying the Concepts of 'Sphere of Influence' and 'Complicity'," *Report of the Special Representative of the Secretary-General on the issue of human rights and transnational corporations and other business enterprises*, John Ruggie, 2008.

18. R. Faulk, "The Expanding Role of the Alien Tort Claims Act in International Human Rights Enforcement," in *Class Action Litigation Report* 10 (2009), p. 304, available at <http://works.bepress.com/richard_faulk/24> (accessed February 8, 2010).

19. *Kiobel v. Royal Dutch Petroleum Co.*, No. 10-1491, April 17, 2013.

20. See International Commission of Jurists, op. cit. No. 4, Vol 2; the *Special Issue* of the Journal of International Criminal Justice, No. 3, Vol. 8 (2010), on the subject of corporate accountability; and Danielle, Olson, *Corporate Complicity In Human Rights Violations Under International Criminal Law*, International Human Rights Law Journal, No. 1, Vol. 1 (2015), 1.-13. On how and why criminal trials could and should be used not only to denounce and judge violent crimes of the past but also to shed light on how present social and economic injustice may be linked to that violent past; Hannah Franzki, "Criminal Trials, Economic Dimensions of State Crime, and the Politics of Time in International Criminal Law. A German-Argentine Constellation," (Doctoral thesis, University of London, Birkbeck, December 2016), available at http://bbktheses.da.ulcc.ac.uk/304/.

21. ICJ, op. cit. No. 4, vol. 1, p. 24.

22. *South African Apartheid Litigation*, SDNY, April 8, 2009.

23. S. Michalowski y J. P. Bohoslavsky, "*Ius Cogens*, Transitional Justice and other Trends of the Debate on Odious Debts. A Response to the World Bank Discussion Paper on Odious Debts," *Columbia Journal of Transnational Law*, (2010), vol. 48, p. 95.

24. On the legal responsibility of intellectuals in the commission of criminal acts, see Nuremberg International Military Tribunal, *United States of America v Josef Altstoetter et al.* (Justice Case), 1947, 3 T.W.C. 1 (1948), 6 L.R.T.W.C. 1 (1948), 14 Ann. Dig. 278 (1948); and the amicus brief submitted by the European Center for Constitutional and Human Rights in the criminal trial against U.S. officials who authorized the use of torture in interrogations, Audiencia Nacional de Madrid, case 134/2009, September 2012.

25. Cassel, Doug, "Corporate Aiding and Abetting of Human Rights Violations: Confusion in the Courts," *Northwestern University Journal of International Human Rights* (2008), vol. 6, p. 315.

26. ICJ, op. cit. No. 4, vol. 1, p. 20.

27. *United States v. Carl Krauch et al (The Farben Case), Trials of War Criminals*, Vol. VIII, p. 1187; *Trial of the Major War Criminal Before the International Military Tribunal* (1947), Vol. 1, Judgment,. 305–6; *Tadic*, ITFY, May 7, 1997, para. 675–76, 689; *Akayesu*, ICTR, Septemeber 2, 1998, para. 548; *Aleksovski*, ICTY, June 25, 1999, para. 65.

28. "Basic Principles and Guidelines on the Right to a Remedy and Reparation for Victims of Gross Violations of International Human Rights Law and Serious Violations of International Humanitarian Law," para. 20.

29. Resolution 60/147, December 16, 2005.

30. See for example the cases *Rodríguez Vera et al. (Desaparecidos del Palacio de Justicia) vs. Colombia* (2014) and *Gomez Lund at al. (Guerrilha do Araguaia) vs. Brazil* (2010).

31. *Office of the United Nations High Commissioner for Human Rights*, "Rule of Law Tools for Post-Conflict States: Amnesties," UN Doc. HR/PUB/09/1 (Geneva, 2009).

32. Michalowski, Sabine, "No Complicity Liability for Funding Gross Human Rights Violations?," *Berkeley Journal of International Law*, vol. 30, No. 2 (2012), 451–524.

33. For an extended debate on this issue see Carrillo Santarelli, Nicolás, "La responsabilidad internacional de las empresas por complicidad en violaciones graves de derechos humanos," in *El negocio del terrorismo de Estado. Los cómplices económicos de la dictadura uruguaya*, ed. Bohoslavsky, Juan Pablo (Montevideo: Penguim Random House—Debate, 2016), 233–61.

34. Amnesty International, "Injustice Incorporated: Corporate Abuses and the Human Rights to Remedy" (London: Amnesty International, 2014).

Chapter 25

Economic Complicity under Chilean Law

Pietro Sferrazza Taibi and Francisco Bustos Bustos

INTRODUCTION[1]

Chile's coup d'état and the subsequent dictatorial regime were by no means the exclusive responsibility of the armed forces. Civilian political and economic actors were also involved and we will accordingly prefer the term "civil-military dictatorship," here and throughout.[2] These additional actors include so-called "economic accomplices,"[3] who instigated military insurrection, supported and covered up the regime's crimes, looted state businesses, and achieved the imposition of the economic regime that is still in place in Chile today.[4]

The importance of these contributions cannot be overstated. Some accounts suggest that a network calling itself the "Nautical Brotherhood of the South Pacific" (Cofradía Naútica del Pacífico Sur) had embarked upon a major political operation to "construct a new social and economic project for Chile."[5] Members, it is claimed, included businessmen such as Agustín Edwards and serving and retired naval officers (José Toribio Merino and Roberto Kelly, respectively). Numerous CIA documents declassified by the U.S. government show that the actions of civilians were similarly decisive in ensuring and channeling support from the United States. The "Church Report," meanwhile, describes how the United States supported business associations and communications media, making particular mention of influential broadsheet *El Mercurio*.[6] Henry Kissinger, in his memoirs, details how Agustín Edwards, *El Mercurio*'s proprietor, implored then-U.S. President Richard Nixon to take action, and how this conversation was decisive in leading to the infamous order, given by Nixon on September 15, 1970, to "make the [Chilean] economy scream."[7]

During the early period of transition to democracy (from 1990), with few exceptions, a blanket of impunity prevented the investigation of even the most serious regime crimes. Although a few guilty verdicts were brought at the beginning of the 1990s, it was not until after the year 2000 that crimes such as extrajudicial execution and enforced disappearance were investigated more seriously. The investigation of torture and sexual violence took even longer to achieve.[8] Moreover, almost all of these cases have pursued the responsibility of state agents, rather than "economic accomplices." This chapter, therefore, aims to ask whether, and how, the responsibilities of those accomplices could be pursued under Chilean law. We consider whether or not they could be held criminally responsible and/or civilly liable for crimes against humanity. This requires exploration of the relevant statutes of limitation and the grounds on which these could be held to be inapplicable in cases brought against those who benefited from the regime. We close with conclusions and recommendations.

CRIMINAL RESPONSIBILITY

Authorship is attributed to the person or persons who carry out a crime, while participation may be ascribed to those who collaborate in bringing about the intended outcome, without themselves directly carrying out the conduct described in the applicable criminal law.[9] Whatever position is taken with respect to the question of the systematic location of authorship, it must be borne in mind that Chilean law adopts a broad conceptualization of both authorship and coauthorship.[10] The discussion thereby turns on the Special Part of the Criminal Code and the content of article 15 of its General Part. This article lists a range of hypotheses of participation or co-participation, setting out who is "to be considered an author." The correct interpretation of this article remains a subject of legal debate.[11] We will proceed by reviewing the distinct categories of authorship, with a view to evaluate which of them might be said to be applicable to the part played by economic actors in the commission of the dictatorship's crimes.[12]

Direct or material authorship, as the most evident form of authorship, presents few conceptual difficulties.[13] A person or persons who themselves carry out all or part of a particular criminal offense, without making use of intermediaries, would be considered an author.[14] This corresponds to the hypothesis set out in article 15 no. 1 of the Criminal Code, considering as authors or coauthors "those who take part in the execution of the fact, immediately and directly." This figure would not generally apply to those who were instigators, financiers, or civilian participants in the regime's crimes, the few exceptions being cases of businesspeople who directly committed crimes. One example in existing jurisprudence is the criminal case known as "Paine, Collipeumo episode," in which the first instance Special Investigative Magistrate Judge Marianela Cifuentes found landowner Francisco Luzoro Montenegro guilty of the aggravated homicide of six peasant leaders.[15] The verdict was ratified by the Supreme Court, making Luzoro the first civilian to be convicted of crimes against humanity in Chile.[16] This case has however been an exception to a general rule of extreme reticence in prosecuting civilians, even those who did directly participate in crimes.[17]

A second approach to authorship is to consider induction (or instigation), as set down in article 15 no. 2 of the Criminal Code. As a form of participation, induction consists in directly generating in another the decision to take part in a crime or "knowingly inducing another to commit a criminal act."[18] Consequently, the subject who is induced to act is the one who has control over the act and is fully aware of its criminality. To consider whether this category might be applicable to economic complicity, it is useful to spell out its requisites: [induction must] (a) act upon a subject who has sufficient autonomy to decide whether or not to commit the crime; (b) be positive, although not necessarily explicit (it may be tacit); (c) be direct (induction at one remove is excluded); (d) be concrete; and (e) be efficacious.

José Luis Guzmán, in his commentary on the Letelier case,[19] indicates that "a significant number of experts in criminal law consider that we are in the presence of induction, not only when the person(s) induced are fully free, but also when the inductee acted under orders from the instigator, intimidated by the instigator, for the sake of discipline, or in thrall to schemes and artifice on the part of the instigator."[20] We can therefore identify one direct author (Translator's note: The inductee) who is fully responsible and whose actions include all the necessary elements of the crime.[21] National jurisprudence tends to come down on the side of categorizing the crimes committed during the dictatorship under the hypothesis of coauthorship by induction, as set down in article 15 no. 2 of the Criminal Code.[22]

For our part, the present authors are of the view that the actions of dictatorship-era intelligence agencies are best understood as cases of perpetration-by-means,[23] via control over the will of another, in organized structures of power.[24] Perpetration-by-means, as the term suggests, basically consists of the commission of a crime by way of another, whose conduct is instrumentalized.[25] As Guzmán indicates, the legal position occupied by person(s) with responsibility for perpetration-by-means is a particularly delicate or complex one.[26] Doctrine admits a range of hypotheses around this situation,[27] not all of which take the view that the instrument (i.e., the means) does not have or share responsibility: there may be held to be an "author behind the author."[28]

This latter fact—the existence of a second author—is self-evident in cases of massive and/or systematic violations of human rights in which organized structures (the armed forces, police and security services, or other armed groups) commit crimes against a civilian population. In such cases, material authors will receive orders to carry out actions that have been planned by persons who are located at one remove from the scene of the crime. According to Olasolo,

> in such cases the principal protagonists are those who, directing the action, plan the commission of the crime, instruct the organised power structures which they control to carry it out, supervise mid-level superiors in creating a detailed blueprint for the plan orchestrated by [the principal protagonists], and monitor the ways in which lower ranks of the organisation carry out the plan, materially enacting the objective elements of the crime.[29]

While error or coercion of the instrument is not an essential component, fungibility is. Control over the act inheres both in the person(s) with command responsibility (the perpetrators-by-means), and in those who materially carry out the crime, although of course it is expressed differently in one and in the other case.[30]

Chilean legal doctrine is however reluctant to accept this form of authorship,[31] generally preferring to affirm the concepts of induction or coauthorship in the senses already discussed. Another, eminently practical, problem arises because the legal grounds for establishing criminal participation are generally extremely synthetically treated in judicial decisions. There is a tendency to subsume the participation of higher ranks of repressive apparatuses under article 15 no. 2 of the Criminal Code—reserved, as we have seen, for cases of perpetration-by-means via coercion or induction[32]—without acknowledging that this hypothesis requires it to be accredited that the direct authors have acted coerced by "irresistible force or overwhelming fear" (*fuerza irresistible o miedo insuperable*), under the terms of article 10 no. 9 of the Criminal Code.[33]

An alternative approach to participation is the responsibility by reason of command position or "responsibility of the superior," which presupposes the existence of an effective command relationship between a hierarchical superior and his or her subordinates. The superior must be aware that the subordinates commit, or are about to commit, crimes—even when these have not been ordered by the superior—and must also have neglected to take the measures necessary to avoid such crimes or punish them.[34] Although the de facto existence of hierarchical relations of the type described is given where the Chilean dictatorship is concerned, this figure has only recently been incorporated into domestic law.[35] This explains its relatively low jurisprudential take-up to date, which would otherwise be surprising, as in this instance crimes were clearly ordered and encouraged, not simply tolerated, by superiors.[36]

The application of the figure to economic accomplices is more improbable, as it would require attributing particular duties of prevention which are not proper to private actors, except in the case of any duty to act as the position of guarantor that may proceed from one's position or profession.[37]

Yet another alternative could be coauthorship, by which is meant functional control or co-control of the act, the consummation of which is decided jointly by the coauthors and where there is a functional contribution to the outcome of the project.[38] Coauthorship is considered to be covered by no. 1, no. 2 (section 1) and—insofar as the contribution is functional—no. 3 of article 15 of the Criminal Code.

Last, we must discuss complicity. In our legal system, article 15 no. 3 of the Criminal Code contemplates cases of complicity which are treated identically to authorship to determine penalties. The sphere of application of article 16 is reserved for residual cases of nonessential cooperation occurring before or alongside the act.[39] While the broad nature of this provision means it could in theory apply to many cases involving civilians, it would probably not reach to those whose participation was greater, or who benefited most from the dictatorship, even if we call them economic, passive, or civilian accomplices. The larger contribution made by these actors ought rather to place them under the ambit of article 15 no. 3.

The criminal prosecution of economic actors would proceed from their participation in crimes against humanity. Here, crimes such as aggravated homicide, aggravated kidnap (enforced disappearance), torture, and sexual violence do not present any particular difficulties, as they are acts spelt out in the Criminal Code and are also sanctioned by international law. However, the crime of criminal association (*asociación ilícita*), contained in article 292 of the Criminal Code, is of particular interest. This is a formal criminal figure: the mere constitution of the organization is sufficient to trigger the existence of the crime, without the need for any particular material result to follow.[40] The association must be permanent or must enjoy a certain level of temporal stability; it must be made up of several subjects; it must possess a hierarchy, organization, and internal rules; and it must be motivated by the pursuit of an objective that runs counter to social order.[41] The intermediate group which above all others fits the definition of a dictatorship-era criminal association is Colonia Dignidad. This was a sect that functioned with a permanent, rigid, highly stratified structure, led by Paul Schäfer and mid-level operatives. It enjoyed ample control of territory and was organized to commit crimes using material means, including military weapons, the possession of which was facilitated by both the passive toleration and active collaboration of the civil–military dictatorship. There were strong links between the DINA secret police and the Colonia in numerous cases of enforced disappearance.[42] The concept may also apply to entities such as the Nautical Brotherhood, professional associations, news media or businesses, and businessmen who contributed to the financing of DINA operations,[43] as in the case of Ricardo Claro.[44]

CIVIL LIABILITY

The Applicable Legal Regime

One of the principal problems that has arisen in establishing the administrative responsibility of the state for dictatorship-era crimes has been defining the applicable juridical statute. While this is a perennial problem, which has given rise to a range of tendencies in jurisprudence, it has particular ramifications in relation to these specific crimes. If we first examine, the general tendencies—setting aside, for a moment, the issue of crimes against humanity—two broad phases can be observed. In the first, the thesis under which the responsibility of the state was considered an objective responsibility, normatively derived from the Constitution, prevailed. Accordingly, state responsibility was considered to be an issue of public law, grounded in art. 38, section 2 of the Constitution. This section enshrines the principle that all harm occasioned by the administration should be subject to reparation, where a causal relationship can be shown to exist between the behavior of the administrative organ and the harm. This first thesis prevailed from the 1970s until the end of the 1990s.[45]

A later, second, phase of jurisprudence instead maintained that the responsibility of the state was subjective, and was grounded in administrative law, rather than in the Constitution. Specifically, it was considered to be grounded in arts. 4 and 44 of Law 18.575, General Bases for the Administration of the State.[46] The aforementioned articles establish responsibility for the failure of service on the part of the administrative organ. Under this thesis, it is possible to apply Civil Code norms regarding civil liability—including the one which establishes statutes of limitation—in a subsidiary fashion. This is the tendency that came to the fore after the year 2000, when Judge Urbano Marín was named to the Supreme Court.[47]

In regard to dictatorship crimes committed by state agents, we believe that this jurisprudential debate between subscribers to the objective[48] or the subjective[49] theories, is relevant to the issue of the applicability or inapplicability of statutes of limitation. This is particularly so if one inclines toward the thesis that the Civil Code is the correct source.[50] The question of which legal regime should be applicable to cases of economic complicity in the context of the dictatorship must however be considered. The application of constitutional or administrative legal norms regarding the responsibility of the state seems to be ruled out *a priori* since economic actors are not entities that form part of the administration (except for firms that have some state holdings or participation).[51] The applicable legal statute would, therefore, be tort liability, as set down in the Civil Code but complemented with international law. The national model of tort liability is one of responsibility based on culpability. Its elements are the offense or transgression itself; blame; harm, and causality. The offense has a material dimension, consisting of an action or omission, and a subjective dimension, which consists of the voluntary nature of the behavior and the requirement that it be carried out by a person considered to be capable (art. 2319 of the Civil Code).[52]

Blame implies that the act is committed either with intent, in the sense of an intention to inflict harm (art. 44 of the Civil Code), or with negligence, understood as a failure to carry out a duty of care. In extra-contractual responsibility, blame is assessed by reference to a normative rather than a subjective standard, since what has to be evaluated is whether a person failed in a duty of care when their conduct is compared to that which could have been expected from a reasonably diligent person.[53] The determination of the duty of care is usually made by means of law, for example, by codifying a criminal offense.[54] Where no positive norm exists, the judge may identify the standard of diligence that could have been expected in the case at hand, by considering the likely conduct of an ideal-type of a reasonably diligent person.[55] The standard of proof required for the subjective element is less exacting in tort liability when compared with criminal law, as in the former, only a failure of the duty of care is required. The Civil Code even contains a presumption of ipso facto culpability in regard to particularly risky activities (art. 2329).[56] In the matter of presumptions for the acts of another (vicarious liability), the Civil Code regulates presumptions of culpability of a business person for the acts of an employee. These are applied if the employee commits a tortious act in the course of their employment (arts. 2320, section 4 and 2322).[57] These types of presumptions may pave the way for proving liability of "economic accomplices," in particular where we are faced with organizational culpability in which it is difficult to identify individual material authors.

While we do not have sufficient scope here to consider in detail the matter of harms requiring compensation, it should be said that tort liability comprises both pecuniary harm (damages and loss of earnings) and non-pecuniary harm (moral damages).[58] It is our view that the analysis of harm must adopt a human rights perspective, taking into consideration the principle of integral restitution. This in turn requires consideration of the jurisprudential standards on reparations of the Inter-American Court of Human Rights, standards that are applicable to Chile under the control of conventionality doctrine[59].

Last, evaluating the causal relationship between the act and the harm requires a twofold analysis. First, according to the standard of equivalence of conditions, an act may be considered a necessary cause of harm if the harmful result would not have occurred in the absence of the act. Second, in line with the criterion of adequate cause, one must determine whether the harm is objectively attributable to the author, by evaluating whether the harm can plausibly be traced back to the act, in the normal course of events.[60]

Existing jurisprudence on the dictatorship's crimes shows that compensation claims are generally acceded to, even in the absence of comprehensive analysis of the presence of the elements of responsibility.[61] There are almost no extant examples of sentences finding civil liability against economic accomplices, but if criminal cases against such actors should take place, we can anticipate that these defendants will attempt to disclaim civil liability alleging the absence or insufficiency of these same elements. Accordingly, legal strategies adopted by claimants would be well advised to offer a rigorous grounding of the requisites of tort liability, combining the institutions laid down in the Civil Code with international standards on reparations. In this regard, a first instance sentence in the Vallejos Villagrán case is worthy of note, even though the case is ongoing. The sentence ordered the Chilean State to construct a Memory Museum in the environs of Colonia Dignidad, basing itself on the right of victims to integral reparations. The verdict was revoked by the respective appeals court, and the final decision before the Supreme Court was to uphold that verdict.[62]

The Inapplicability of the Statute of Limitations to Civil Claims

We might speculate that one of the principal obstacles to realizing civil liability for economic complicity would be the invocation of the statute of limitation for civil actions. In existing jurisprudence over dictatorial crimes, civil claims tend to arise in association with criminal prosecutions, which are pursued under the old (inquisitorial) criminal justice procedure. These civil claims may be made against the state or the direct authors of harm and they aim to produce a payment in compensation for loss or harm. It is usual for the Treasury or perpetrators' defense lawyers, to argue against claims by invoking the statute of limitation.

We can observe two distinct phases of jurisprudence on this point. In the first, the constitutional bench of the Supreme Court applied the statute of limitation to civil claims.[63] A second phase began in 2014 when the Supreme Court decided to modify its internal distribution of cases to its specialized benches. As a product of the reorganization, all criminal, taxation, and civil matters arising from cases seen under the old criminal procedure would be seen, at the Supreme Court level, by the criminal bench.[64] The criminal bench had already adopted the position that statute of limitation did not apply to criminal investigation and sanction of the dictatorship's crimes. It now extended this principle to civil claims, based on the principle of coherence and norms drawn from international law.[65]

It is useful at this point to consider the principal arguments that are advanced in favor of, and against, the applicability of statutes of limitation to civil claims. The institution of the statute of limitations is traditionally defended on the grounds that it seeks to protect legal certainty. This argument cannot however be sustained in the face of international crimes, which by their very nature are considered an offense against the very notion of humanity. It follows that legal certainty is only safeguarded if the legal order does not place obstacles in the way of pursuing the responsibilities of perpetrators, including their civil responsibility.[66] In such cases, the language of creditor and debtor is not applicable: we are talking, after all, about the authors of atrocious crimes. They inflicted immeasurable harm on their victims, harm which is not remedied by the passage of time. The positive value of justice must, therefore prevail over the positive value of preserving predictability in juridical relations.

In this regard, Zaffaroni has argued that:

> the statute of limitation on civil claims is invoked claiming that security of business and property is at stake. But the property whose security is at issue is often itself part of the proceeds of crimes committed many centuries earlier. Invoking simple civil statutes of limitation in cases of crimes against humanity committed in previous centuries is not merely a problem of neutralising a claim, it is a true juridical scandal . . . because it implies affirming that the only legality matters is the one bounded by those who committed a crime against humanity, taking advantage of the power relationships that resulted from that crime. That is to say, the mere passage of time is allowed to convert something that is a crime against humanity, no less, into a legitimate title against which the rights of victims cannot be counterpoised.[67]

Another argument holds that the principle of coherence requires the application of the same standards to similar situations. If criminal actions over dictatorship-era crimes are not subject to statutes of limitation, logic would suggest that the civil claims arising from the same crimes should share this same quality.[68] An additional problem may however arise in attempting to pursue the responsibilities of economic actors for crimes that do not constitute a crime against humanity. By way of example, in a case brought against Pinochet for misappropriation of public funds, a first instance concluded that the offense was a continuing crime and applied the ordinary rules of statute of limitation to the civil dimension.[69]

A third problem arises in regard to the juridical nature of civil claim making. The line of jurisprudence that favors the application of statutes of limitation views civil claim-making as essentially patrimonial in nature, when compensation is the objective.[70] On this basis, it has been argued that the four-year statute of limitation that the Civil Code lays down for tort liability is the one that should be applied (see arts. 2497 and 2332 of the Civil Code).[71] Fortunately, the jurisprudence that finds statutes of limitation to be inapplicable has clarified that civil claim making where international crimes have been committed does not have a merely patrimonial character. Rather, it has a humanitarian and reparatory purpose, and should, therefore, be regulated according to international human rights law.[72]

Finally, as regards the legal regime that should be used, jurisprudence in favor of respecting statutes of limitation argued that its inapplicability to civil claims would require an express norm, in the absence of which, regular civil law norms should be applied. The observation was often added that international law does not contain an express norm about the inapplicability of statutes of limitation to civil claim making.[73] However, the jurisprudence that favors the inapplicability of statutes of limitation has reached into international law for normative foundations, although with a certain amount of confusion as regard identification of the applicable sources of law.[74] While there is not enough space here to fully develop this point, we believe that it is possible to argue that rules of customary international law do exist in the matter of the inapplicability of statutes of limitation to actions proceeding from crimes against humanity.

CONCLUSIONS

On the basis of the discussion above, we believe that there are possible grounds for criminal prosecution of economic actors for crimes against humanity, including homicide, kidnap, torture, and criminal association. Thus, the mere condition of being civilian does not exempt such individuals from prosecution. The levels of participation attributable to civilians would include direct authorship and coauthorship, under art. 15 no. 1 of the Criminal Code, for those who took part in the commission of crimes. Instigation, as defined under art 15 no. 2 of the Code, would be reserved for those who fomented the coup. A form of joint command responsibility might also be argued for in the case of the latter, given their levels of influence.[75] Similar conclusions about instigation or induction could be reached in cases where trade union leaders were reported or handed over to the new authorities, or over the killing of workers from the CMPC paper mill in Laja.[76] In the latter case, the killings were incited by the firm, which provided a list of names, vehicles, and alcohol to the police officers involved.[77] A case might be made for the applicability of forms of coauthorship[78] such as those contemplated in art. 15 no. 3 of the Criminal Code.

As regards civil action, it is evident that the same consequences that proceed from the inapplicability of the statute of limitation to criminal prosecution should apply. Pursuit civil responsibility, moreover, has various advantages, including the fact that it can proceed against both natural and legal persons.[79] In the subjective dimension, culpability only requires proof of a failure of a duty of care. Some possible disadvantages must however be borne in mind. For example, post-coup modifications in the legal personhood status of a business might derail successful present-day claim making. The pursuit of civil responsibility also often translates into a demand for compensation, undoubtedly insufficient when compared to the notion of integral reparation required by human rights principles. While creative interpretations should not be ruled out, demands for reparations in any form other than compensation ought to be based on arguments that combine elements of civil law dogma with international human rights law.

NOTES

1. Translation by Cath Collins. All quotes from secondary literature are original translations (or retranslations) from the Spanish-language versions or editions cited in the chapter's original version, with the sole exception of UN documents, citations of which have been amended to reference the official English language versions.

2. Javier Rebolledo. *A la sombra de los cuervos. Los cómplices civiles de la dictadura* (Santiago: Ceibo, 2015), 9-11 and 129-134.

3. Horacio Verbitsky and Juan Pablo Bohoslavsky. *Cuentas pendientes. Los cómplices económicos de la dictadura* (Buenos Aires: Siglo XXI, 2014).

4. María Olivia Mönckeberg. *El saqueo de los grupos económicos al estado chileno* (Santiago: Debolsillo, 2016).

5. Luis Ortega. "Las operaciones ideológicas y políticas en la construcción de un nuevo proyecto económico (y social) para Chile, 1950-1970" 11 *Espacio Regional* (2015). See Special Investigative Magistrate (Ministro en Visita Extraordinaria) Mario Carroza, *Golpe de Estado*, Rol 12-2013.

6. The United States Senate Select Committee to Study Governmental Operations with Respect to Intelligence Activities, better known as the "Church Committee," after its president, US Senator Frank Church, published various reports. These included the eponymous "Church Report," whose official title is "Covert action in Chile 1963–1973. Staff Report of the Select Committee to Study Governmental Operations with respect to Intelligence Activities," Washington, December 18, 1975.

7. Henry Kissinger. *Mis Memorias* (Buenos Aires: Atlántida, 1979), 468.

8. José Luis Guzmán Dalbora. "Chile," in *Jurisprudencia latinoamericana sobre derecho penal internacional*, eds. Kai Ambos and Ezequiel Malarino (Montivideo: Konrad Adenauer, 2008), 133-141; Karinna Fernández Neira. "Breve análisis de la jurisprudencia chilena, en relación a las graves violaciones a los derechos

humanos cometidos durante la dictadura militar," *Estudios Constitucionales* 8-1 (2010): 467–88.

9. Claus Roxin. *Autoría y dominio del hecho en el derecho penal*, trans. Joaquín Cuello and José Luis Serrano (Madrid: Marcial Pons, 2016), 52.

10. The view that grounds for individual authorship are found in the typifications set out in the Special Part of Code is held by: Juan Bustos. *Manual de Derecho penal. Parte general.* 3rd. ed. (Barcelona: Ariel, 1989), 285; Eduardo Novoa Monreal. *Curso de Derecho penal.* 3rd ed. (Santiago: Editorial Jurídica, 2005), vol. II, 183; Sergio Yáñez, "Problemas básicos de la autoría y de la participación en el Código Penal chileno," *Revista de Ciencias Penales* 34, no. 1 (1975), 56; Sergio Politoff et al. *Lecciones de Derecho penal chileno. Parte General.* 2nd ed. (Santiago: Editorial Jurídica, 2004), 400. A different reading can be made, proceeding from article 15 no. 1 of the Criminal Code, for which see Héctor Hernández, "Artículo 15," in Jaime Couso and Héctor Hernández (eds.), *Código Penal comentado* (Santiago: Legal Publishing, 2011), 388.

11. Jaime Winter. "Esquema general de la diferenciación coautoría y complicidad en el Código Penal chileno," *Doctrina y jurisprudencia penal* 17 (2014): 40.

12. We do not deal with concealment here, as it is not strictly a form of criminal participation. On deliberate misinformation and cover-ups by and in the communications media, see Claudia Lagos (ed.). *El Diario de Agustín. Cinco estudios de casos sobre El Mercurio y los derechos humanos* (Santiago: LOM, 2009), 152-ff.

13. Sergio Yáñez. "Problemas básicos de la autoría y de la participación en el código penal chileno," *Revista de Ciencias Penales* 34, no. 1 (1975): 52 and see Juan Pablo Mañalich, "La estructura de la autoría mediata," *Revista de Derecho* 34 (2010): 390.

14. Alfredo Etcheberry. *Derecho Penal. Parte General.* 3rd ed. (Santiago: Editorial Jurídica, 1998), vol. II, 97–98.

15. Special Investigative Magistrate Marianela Cifuentes, *Paine-Episodio Collipeumo*, Rol 4-2002(b), March 31, 2016, 19, and the resolutive section. This sentence was ratified by the San Miguel Appeals Court under case reference Rol 58-2016, December 20, 2016, and reviewed before the Supreme Court as Rol 1.568-2017, November 16, 2017. On the facts of the matter, see the Chilevision TV documentary "En la Mira-La Caravana de Paine Chapter 10 June (Part 1)" <https://www.youtube.com/watch?v=r3LeBfuH-vk> Last accessed December 10, 2019. During the process of notifying the final sentence, Luzoro was granted bail by a majority ruling of the San Miguel Appeals Court, who discounted the possibility of a flight risk despite the well-publicized sentence. In the end, Luzoro was successfully notified of the verdict on November 24, and began serving his sentence in a module of the high-security Colina I prison, which has been specially set aside for perpetrators imprisoned for dictatorship-era human rights violations.

16. Some contend that this dubious honor goes instead to Miguel Estay Reyno, alias "El Fanta," a former Communist party activist-turned-double-agent, imprisoned in 1995 after being found guilty of the kidnap and murder of Manuel Guerrero, Jose Manuel Parada and Santiago Nattino, a particularly notorious case in which the three victims had their throats slit (Supreme Court verdict, Rol 31.030-94, October 27,

1995). Luzoro is however the first civilian to be jailed who was not recruited by and working for a repressive intelligence agency.

17. A case in point is the investigation known as *Episodio Mulchén*, Rol 30-2007, overseen by Special Investigative Magistrate Carlos Aldana and currently at the deliberation and sentencing stage. The case is over the killings of 18 peasant farmers, and the participation of civilians has been alleged publicly ever since a dictatorship-era news magazine, *Revista Cauce*, produced an entire edition, edition no. 51, entitled "The Mulchén massacre" (Masacre en Mulchén). <http://saladehistoria.com/Revistas/Cauce/pdf/Cauce051.pdf> Last accessed June 13, 2017.

18. Bustos, *Derecho penal*, 293.

19. Supreme Court Rol 30.174-1994, May 30, 1995, 20–22. Special Investigative Magistrate Mario Carroza recently opened an investigation into the killing of Ronni Moffitt, Rol 910-2011.

20. José Luis Guzmán Dalbora, "El Caso Chileno," in *Imputación de crímenes de los subordinados al dirigente. Un estudio comparado*, ed. Kai Ambos (Bogotá: Nomos, 2010), 80.

21. Juan Pablo Delgado, "¿Aborda la jurisprudencia chilena una construcción de autoría mediata por dominio de voluntad en aparato organizado de poder en causas por violaciones a los derechos humanos?," *Perspectiva Penal Actual* 4 (2016): 75-ff.

22. Delgado, "¿Aborda la jurispudencia?," 107. See Juan Pablo Mañalich, "Organización delictiva. Bases para su elaboración dogmática en el derecho penal chileno," *Revista Chilena de Derecho* 38 (2011): 288, on the applicability of article 15 no. 3 of the Criminal Code to military organizations.

23. *Autoría mediata*, sometimes also translated as "command responsibility" (Translator's Note).

24. Welzel's theory as redefined by Roxin, *Autoría y dominio*, 237-ff., which gave it its now universal standing.

25. Hernández, "Artículo 15," 389.

26. Guzmán Dalbora, "El caso chileno," 80.

27. For example, producing or taking advantage of error; coercion; taking advantage of someone who is exempt from responsibility, or taking advantage of some instrument that removes the anti-juridical nature of the act 389–99.

28. Miguel Díaz y García Conlledo. "Autoría y participación," REJ 10 (2008): 22.

29. Héctor Olasolo. *Tratado de autoría y participación en el Derecho penal internacional* (Valencia: Tirant lo Blanch, 2013), 189. On the anti- or non-juridical nature of the organisation per se, see Kai Ambos, *La parte general del Derecho Penal Internacional. Bases para una elaboración dogmática.* 2nd ed. (Montevideo: Konrad Adenauer, 2004), 234–39. Ambos considers this to be a superfluous requirement.

30. Delgado, "¿Aborda la jurisprudencia chilena?" 70.

31. For a favorable view, see Politoff et al. *Lecciones de Derecho*, 390; Yáñez, "Problemas básicos," 62.

32. Delgado, "¿Aborda la jurisprudencia chilena," 107–8.

33. Ibid., 87.

34. Ambos, *La parte general*, 296-ff. and, in Chilean doctrine, Jaime Winter. *La responsabilidad por el mando en el Derecho Penal Internacional*. Undergraduate thesis (Memoria de grado), Licenciatura en Ciencias Jurídicas y Sociales, Universidad de Chile, 2009. 17-ff.

35. Law 20.357, Typification of Crimes Against Humanity, Genocide and War Crimes, July 18, 2009, article 35.

36. Although they do not refer the exact point at issue here, see the following cases: Santiago Appeals Court, Rol 1253-2016, on the aggravated kidnap of Pedro Vergara Inostroza, pending before the Appeals Court at the time of writing; Special Investigative Magistrate Mario Carroza, Case verdict Rol 673-2011, December 12, 2015, 11-16, on the aggravated kidnap of Segundo Sandoval, ratified by the Supreme Court, Rol 14.284-2015, January 13, 2016. In this latter case, the victim was taken to the military headquarters of the Buin Regiment, which was under the command of lieutenant Patricio Román. Román was convicted as author based on article 15 no. 1 of the Criminal Code, on the grounds that despite the obligations placed on him by his role as base commander, he did nothing to impede the crime.

37. Exceptionally, in one of the follow-up cases to the Nuremberg trials known as the "Medical Trial," vs. Brandt et al., in cases over human experimentation, Karl Brandt was found guilty of having failed in his duty to prevent or investigate the alleged crimes, a duty considered to have been incumbent on him owing to his position. See Cherif Bassiouni, *Crimes Against Humanity* (Cambridge: Cambridge University Press, 2011), 540, and Gerhard Werle, *Tratado de Derecho Penal Internacional*, trans. Claudia Cárdenas Aravena et al. 2nd ed. (Valencia: Tirant lo Blanch, 2011), 54-55. At the time of writing, no confirmed sentences had been passed against medical personnel, but see Special Investigative Magistrate Mario Carroza, verdict in the extrajudicial execution of Federico Álvarez Santibáñez, Rol 77-2010, February 15, 2016, 26–29, currently before the Appeals Court. In this case, doctors Manfredo Jurgensen Caesar and Luis Lozada Fuenzalida were convicted, at first instance stage, as accomplice (article 16 of the Criminal Code) and as an accessory after the fact (article 17 of the Criminal Code), respectively. Notably, the verdict refers to their knowledge of the procedures of the secret or political police (the CNI), to their professional duty, and to a professional failure to act.

38. Enrique Cury. *Derecho Penal. Parte General*. 8th ed. (Santiago: Ediciones de la Universidad Católica, 2005), 613-ff.

39. For this reason, we hold that the participation of the medics who were found guilty in the case of Federico Álvarez Santibáñez would have been more appropriately covered by article 15 no. 3 of the Criminal Code.

40. Francisco Grisolía. "Delito de asociación ilícita," *Revista Chilena de Derecho* 31, no. 1 (2003): 80.

41. It is not necessary that the group should have come into being with illicit purposes as its raison d'être, nor that it should cease to (also) have licit objectives. See for instance the already cited case of Nattino, Parada, and Guerrero, *Caso Degollados*.

42. Supreme Court Rol 14.312-2016, December 29, 2016, 13.

43. Javier Rebolledo. *La danza de los cuervos. El destino final de los detenidos desaparecidos*. 4th ed. (Santiago: Ceibo, 2014), 151-ff.

44. Translator's Note: Claro was a wealthy businessman and ultraconservative Catholic, latterly owner of an influential cable TV channel, who died in 2008. Closely linked to the dictatorship, he is alleged to have directly financed the DINA secret police.

45. Luis Cordero Vega, *Lecciones de Derecho Administrativo* (Santiago de Chile: Thomson Reuters, 2015), 679–87.

46. Cfr. Cordero Vega, *Lecciones de Derecho Administrativo*, 695-ff.; Jorge Bermúdez Soto, *Derecho administrativo general* (Santiago: Thomson Reuters, 2011), 505-ff.

47. Cordero Vega, *Lecciones de Derecho Administrativo*, 687–95, signals that the naming of Marín to the court was decisive to this change in jurisprudence. By way of example, the Supreme Court took this position in the case *Domic Bezic con Fisco*, May 15, 2002, Rol 4753-2001, over the death of Jorge Jordán Dimic Bezic in a military installation in the city of La Serena [Translator's note: 'con Fisco' denotes a claim brought against the Treasury].

48. Santiago Appeals Court Rol 270-2006, June 1, 2009, 10.

49. Supreme Court Rol 428-2003, cassation verdict, August 16, 2004, 15.

50. Supreme Court Rol 4771-2007, replacement sentence, August 16, 2004, 3–8.

51. We do not consider here the issue of the administrative, or potentially even international, responsibility of the state for not having practiced due diligence to avoid the harm caused by economic accomplices.

52. Enrique Barros Bourie, *Tratado de Responsabilidad Extracontractual* (Santiago de Chile: Editorial Jurídica, 2006), 63-ff.

53. Ibid., 80-ff.

54. Ibid., 94–95.

55. Ibid., 105-ff.

56. Ibid., 147-ff.

57. Ibid., 176–77 and 180-ff.

58. For an exhaustive analysis of this requirement, see Barros Bourie, *Tratado de Responsabilidad Extracontractual*, 215-ff.

59. See Claudio Nash Rojas, *Las Reparaciones ante la Corte Interamericana de Derechos Humanos* (Santiago: Universidad de Chile, 2009); Cristian Correa, "Artículo 63," in *Convención Americana sobre Derechos Humanos*, eds. Christian Steiner and Patricia Uribe (Bogotá: Konrad Adenauer Stiftung, 2014), 817-888.

60. Barros Bourie, *Tratado de Responsabilidad Extracontractual*, 391-ff.

61. Supreme Court, Rol 4662-2007, cit., 29-50; Supreme Court, Rol 6308-2007, September 8, 2008, 13–27; Supreme Court, Rol 62211-2016, January 23, 2017, 8–15; Supreme Court, Rol 2962-2016, May 25, 2016, 10–18.

62. Special Investigative Magistrate Jorge Zepeda, Rol 2182-98 (Villa Baviera-kidnap of Álvaro Modesto Vallejos Villagrán), 95–101.

63. For example, Supreme Court, *Chadwick con Fisco*, Rol 2797-2007, January 13, 2009, 6; Supreme Court, *Retamales con Fisco*, Rol 5600-2007, August 27, 2009, 5-ff. Exceptionally, an occasional verdict would accept the inapplicability thesis: Supreme Court, *Episodio Liquiñe*, Rol 4662-2007, September 25, 2008, 48.

64. Supreme Court. *Auto acordado que distribuye las materias de que conocen las salas especializadas de la Corte Suprema durante el funcionamiento ordinario y extraordinario*, December 26, 2014, acuerdo primero, B, 1°.

65. See Supreme Court Rol 20506-2016, August 31, 2016, 7; Supreme Court Rol 28637-16, October 6, 2016, 20–23.

66. Gonzalo Aguilar Cavallo, "Crímenes internacionales y la imprescriptibilidad de la acción penal y civil: referencia al caso chileno," *Ius et Praxis* 14, no. 2 (2008): 179.

67. Eugenio Zaffaroni, *En torno a la cuestión penal* (Buenos Aires: BdeF, 2005), 263–64.

68. For example, Santiago Appeals Court, Rol 270-2006, cit., 7. See Aguilar Cavallo, "Crímenes internacionales" 182; Guzmán Dalbora, "Chile," 154; Mario Campos Poblete, "La prescripción de las acciones reparatorias civiles emanadas de los crímenes de lesa humanidad," *Derecho y humanidades* 18 (2011): 157; Carlos Céspedes Muñoz, "Imprescriptibilidad de la acción civil derivada de la comisión de crímenes de lesa humanidad. Sentencia Excma. CS de 08 de abril de 2010," *Revista de Derecho y Ciencias Penales* 16 (2011): 144. For soft law texts originating in the UN system, see UN Commission on Human Rights, *Report of the independent expert to update the Set of principles to combat impunity*, E/CN.4/2005/102/Add.1, February 8, 2005, 23; UN General Assembly. *Basic Principles and Guidelines on the Right to a Remedy and Reparation for Victims of Gross Violations of International Human Rights Law and Serious Violations of International Humanitarian Law*, UN Res. 60/147, December 16, 2005, 6.

69. Special Investigative Magistrate Manuel Valderrama, *Caso Riggs*, Rol 1649-2004, sentence of May 7, 2015, 20–21, whose criminal aspect was later revoked by the Santiago Appeals Court (CA de Santiago, Rol 999-2015, sentence of June 21, 2017). The case was pending before the Supreme Court at the time of writing.

70. Supreme Court, *Carrasco con Fisco*, Rol 4771-2007, replacement sentence, June 10, 2009, 2.

71. Supreme Court, *Carrasco con Fisco*, Rol 4771-2007, cit., 3–5.

72. See Aguilar Cavallo, "Crímenes internacionales" 178, 183, 184 and 189; Céspedes Muñoz, "Imprescriptibilidad," 146.

73. Santiago Appeals Court, Rol 12811-2006, June 20, 2007, 12.

74. Supreme Court, *Episodio San Javier*, Rol 4723-2007, replacement sentence, October 15, 2008, 13; Supreme Court, Rol 2080-2008, April 8, 2010, 10-11.

75. This could apply to the civilian figures with most influence over the regime, such as Agustín Edwards, and others who conspired with Navy officers and figures within the US government to produce a military coup. It is interesting to note that the first invocation of the theory of control over the act by organized structures of power came in the investigation of the [pre-coup] killing of General Rene Schneider Chereau, and defended its applicability even though the act was committed by private individuals and 'rogue' State agents, including the right-wing extremist Roberto Viaux. See, for all: Sergio Politoff, "Intervención del abogado de la familia

Schneider Sr. Sergio Politoff L." in *El caso Schneider. Operación Alfa* (Santiago: Quimantú, 1972), 87-ff.

76. Supreme Court, Rol 41.122-2016, December 29, 2016, 4, aggravated homicide of Luis Herrera González and Mario Parra Guzmán.

77. Special Investigative Magistrate Carlos Aldana, Rol 27-2010, judicial testimony of Mr. Eduardo Cucvas, March 12, 2012.

78. Supreme Court, *Episodio Guillermo Vallejo Ferdinand*, Rol 34.447-2016, December 1, 2016, a minority opinion emitted by judge Milton Juica favoured convicting Bernardo Trewick Slomka as "instigating author," for having drawn up lists of suggested victims to be handed to police personnel.

79. Tort liability of legal persons is deduced from the interplay between arts. 550 and art. 2284 of the Civil Code, because in expressing will through their organs, they are responsible for the harm that may arise from the commission of a crime.

Section 7

CONCLUSIONS AND PROSPECTS

Chapter 26

Present-Day Chile

Genealogy of a Business Paradise

Julio Pinto Vallejos

INTRODUCTION[1]

Previous chapters of this book have covered, in thorough and nuanced detail, the many and persistent economic complicities both with the 1973 coup d'état and with the military dictatorship that followed it, which substantially subsist up to this very date. Based on such solid foundations, this chapter essays to tread that same course on a more general (and therefore more "interpretive") plane, informed by a deliberately historiographic perspective. For such purpose, the text is structured along a sequence of three successive "moments," corresponding to the progressive buildup of the symbiosis between the entrepreneurial caste and the civilian–military dictatorship. In the first section, titled "The Fears," I address the founding moment of that relationship, when the threat of the Popular Unity government gave the business community a leading role in the political opposition and an explicit connivance in President Allende's overthrow. The second section, titled "The Payoffs," reviews the many and diverse ways, already separately dealt with throughout this volume, in which these actors profited, both directly and indirectly, from dictatorial rule. Finally, a third section, titled "The Legacy," projects this connivance (which perhaps by now should rather be considered an "acquired patrimony"), onto the post-dictatorial years, with clear sequels and echoes up to our own days, still so deeply molded by the dictatorial agenda.

THE FEARS

Throughout its history, Chile's business community had never faced so serious a threat as that posed by the Popular Unity. Although social clashes, and even the idea of superseding capitalism, had been experienced before, never had such notions come so close to fulfillment. It is true that Salvador Allende's program did not envisage the socialization of the economy as a whole, holding such designs only for the country's basic resources and the biggest, or as they were then called, "strategic," enterprises. Beyond those vital nodes, it was stressed time and again, the government intended to respect the vast panoply of small- and middle-sized firms, and even a few larger ones that were not considered monopolistic or strategic. The idea was to secure the support of social strata deemed essential for the success of the Popular Unity's institutional road to socialism. Another plan was to shore up joint public-private enterprises, with all their implications about the feasibility, even the attractiveness, of collaboration between the state and the private sector. But none of those guarantees, repeated over and over again during Allende's thousand days, could evade the fact that the horizon toward which the country was moving was indeed socialism, that is to say, the replacement of capitalism as the basis of the social and economic organization of the country. Faced with that perspective, the entire business community, large, medium, or small, reacted with almost unanimous hostility.

What was that hostility founded on? According to their rhetoric, before and after the military coup, what was at stake was nothing less than "freedom of enterprise," the undisputed underlying principle of their entrepreneurial condition. But what they were fighting for behind that line of defense, they assured, was the entire sweep of democratic liberties, in their view hopelessly compromised by a "totalitarian" ideology such as socialism. It did not matter at all, in this respect, that Allende's government never really jeopardized the exercise of those liberties (of speech, opinion, association, and so on), even when they were instrumentalized in favor of the plots and conspiracies that would finally lead to its overthrow. In the entrepreneurial imaginary and discourse, this respect was no more than a sham intended to pave the way, which they deemed inescapable, to the dictatorship of the proletariat. And even if this were not so, even if every other public liberty remained intact, free enterprise was for them the capstone of the entire democratic edifice. In agreement with the leading ideological inspirator of Chile's capitalist reconstruction, Milton Friedman, the preservation of economic freedoms was so fundamental it could even justify the suspension of every other freedom. In what could perhaps be construed as the Pinochet regime's prime ideological contradiction, supported by the leading figures of global neoliberalism, the defense of those liberties could justify even the bloodiest of dictatorships.

In actual fact, neither the Popular Unity's program nor its concrete political actions espoused a doctrinal rejection of free enterprise. As said before, its agenda allowed for the continuity of private ownership in diverse economic sectors, especially those most intimately associated with small and medium enterprises. In that context, it could be said that the business community's response was out of proportion, especially for those (and they were not few) who never faced any real threats of expropriation. However, it was the possibility of expropriation itself that raised their most primal fears. The mere thought of property rights being infringed, whether programmatically by the state, or worse still, spontaneously by the workers (and it should be acknowledged that the latter did happen, with growing intensity, during the Popular Unity government), was something the entrepreneurial genetic map was not formatted to endure. Any expropriation, even if justified (as the period's language put it) for reasons of "public utility," was not only an (obvious) attempt on their immediate material interests, but an attack on the "rule of law" at large, because, in their view, property rights and free enterprise were the foundations of the entire social edifice, and should thus be upheld at whatever cost. Property, as Chilean historian and political scientist Juan Carlos Gómez has written, was for the business community, and for the political right, the "frontier of democracy."[2]

In that context, and to the extent that both the Popular Unity's program and the social dynamics triggered by its government undoubtedly undermined the principle of private property and their immediate material interests, the entrepreneurial reaction was predictable, even, I insist, among those who were not directly threatened by expropriations. What was at stake for them, in the short or the long run, was not one firm more or less, but the very essence of that principle, and of the entire mode of production and social interaction that emanated therefrom. Most revealing of this impulse was the almost universal alignment of small and medium businesses (retail trade, transport, small industry) alongside the big corporations' defense of capitalism. On this matter, neither the assurances coming from the government, nor the discussion in Congress of a bill regulating (and therefore guaranteeing) three differentiated "areas" of property (public, private, and mixed), proved to any avail. When the decisive moment came, these actors saw themselves more as property owners than as part of low-income communities (as could very well be in the case of shopkeepers in popular districts or proprietors of an individual bus or truck), turning them into very effective "shock troops" in the fight against Allende's government. In the final analysis, and in what proved one of the more momentous failures for a project that needed to sustain stable electoral majorities, entrepreneurial fears swept over a much wider social spectrum than the Popular Unity strategists had envisioned.

It was that fear that rallied the business community, regardless of power or size, around the uncompromising will to bring down Allende's government, resorting, in an ironic turn of a phrase originally coined by the revolutionary Left, to "all forms of struggle."[3] These included passive and active sabotage of economic production, hoarding of goods, street protests, and climaxed in the massive entrepreneurial strikes of October 1972 and July–August 1973, all of which paved the way to the military coup of September 11. They also included a relentless ideological struggle (mainly through control of the major media), as well as active complicity in all kinds of conspiracies, such as that amply covered in this book of press magnate Agustín Edwards with the Nixon Administration, or that of corporate leaders Orlando Sáenz (industry) and Benjamín Matte (agriculture) in support of the military officers who finally ousted the socialist president. The unconditionality of that support, which held firm after the coup despite considerable economic losses (as when the implementation of the neoliberal project devastated domestic industry), was directly proportional to the extent of their fears, and the magnitude of the threat. For Chilean business, the war declared by the armed forces against the Allende government was definitely their own war, and their rendering of the latter as the "saviors of the Nation" was no mere metaphor.

That having been said, can it justify entrepreneurial attitudes regarding the coup d'état and the seventeen subsequent years of military rule? On a strictly "instrumental" level, the answer might be yes, insofar as the prospect of a socialist transition was an objective threat to their interests, which could not fail to elicit defensive reflexes. But on a more ethical plane, it might be asked if that justifies the unflinching and sustained support of the manner in which Allende was overthrown, and of the regime that was constructed upon its debris. The systematic abuse of human rights, the long-term violation of those very rights and freedoms that business claimed to uphold (discounting, of course, those regarding property), were not inevitable outcomes of their hostility to the Popular Unity, or their loyalty toward those who rescued them from that threat. In that context, their overwhelming (because there was some, very meager, minority dissidence) propensity to defend the dictatorship at whatever cost, to play down or justify its atrocities, to endorse its actions without the slightest trace of a doubt, was an ethical and political choice that can hardly be said to be unthinking.

There was also, on a more doctrinaire level, a clear inclination to give priority to the defense of capitalism over that of democracy, upon which business rhetorically sustained its assault on the Allende government. As the governmental performance of the Pinochet dictatorship amply corroborated, what triumphed on September 11, 1973, was not the salvation of democracy, but the will to preserve, and even accentuate, a model of social interplay rooted on individualism, unfettered competition, profit as the leading impulse of human action, and the commercialization of every aspect of social life. It might be said that these outcomes were not so explicit at first when the basic goal was to get rid of the socialist government. But they certainly became so as the months and years of dictatorial rule transpired, and the priorities of its "mission" became sharper, without the business community recoiling one inch—all the contrary—from its allegiance. Looking back, and in the final analysis, what motivated and invigorated Chilean entrepreneurs, before and after Allende's fall, was its defense of capitalism, and anything that might be necessary to make it stronger and more deeply rooted. In that, their symbiosis with the Pinochet regime was inherent, foundational, and long-lasting.

THE PAYOFFS

What business expected from the military coup, and from the regime it inaugurated, was the restitution of a favorable atmosphere for what has always been and still is its fundamental goal: the maximization of profits. As José Miguel Ahumada and Andrés Solimano's chapter has argued, this initially meant the full restoration of a capitalist order endangered by the Popular Unity government, and the intense social mobilization that came with it. Social discipline was reinstated through blood and fire, property rights recovered their status as the mainstay of the social edifice (which meant the immediate return of many expropriated or occupied firms and landed estates), the market came back as the primary regulator of economic action (with the very significant exception of the price of labor, held down by military repression and the ban on all union activity), and the state began a quick and sustained retreat from its condition as a significant economic actor (but not from its role as social and political custodian). Economic stabilization, one of the two chief goals initially taken up by the military government (the other was the "war on communism"), basically translated into the full liberalization of productive, commercial and financial activity, bolstered by harsh control over the workforce and the prohibition of all social and political dissent. In other words, the political blueprint deployed by the dictatorship allocated a very significant (though at first not exclusive, as many officers still harbored "developmentalist" feelings) role for entrepreneurs and the free market, guaranteeing extremely "friendly" conditions for business.[4] The "New Chile" proclaimed by the military would be an unconditionally capitalist and entrepreneurial country.

Before long (by 1975), it became obvious that the economic crisis would not subside by a mere "restoration" of the preexisting incarnation of capitalism. Proof of this were the unabated inflation rate, unemployment figures that would have been unsustainable under normal democratic conditions, and a productive performance that, regardless of very favorable institutional conditions, was not reaching even moderately acceptable growth rates. In that context, a government that was progressively falling under the personal control of Pinochet resolved to drop its remaining "statist" proclivities (impersonated by Air Force Commander-in-Chief Gustavo Leigh and a handful of Army officers who were quickly displaced), and launched a foundational adventure chaperoned by a group of economists who quickly came to be known as the "Chicago Boys."[5] It was a genuine "capitalist revolution" of neoliberal cast, whose main features are well-known and have been examined in several chapters of this book, and which served as a harbinger, virtually a "dress rehearsal," of an economic blueprint that would be subsequently implanted on a global scale.[6]

For what matters here, the crucial point is that this "new" capitalism was even more beneficial for private interests than the mere initial "restoration" of property rights and free trade, leaving all economic decisions to the untrammeled entrepreneurial initiative, and relegating the state to a watchdog function reminiscent of the nineteenth century, only now more intransigent and doctrinaire. Illustrative of this was the steadfastness with which the dictatorial government stood by them, even when, as happened in the deep depression that unfolded between 1982 and 1985, that meant rescuing with public funds (that is, money belonging to society at large) those private firms that had gone bankrupt, only to hand them back, admittedly below their market prices (see chapter 13 in this book), once things returned to normalcy. In the final stages of the Pinochet regime, this "privatizing fever" even swept over productive units that had been born and raised under state ownership, such as the major public firms in the energy sector (electricity and petroleum), or the mining companies that had been nationalized before 1973, with ample (and in the case of copper, unanimous) political support. In this as in many other matters, the military regime's loyalty to its entrepreneurial allies proved as consistent as it was unwavering.

To be fair, this judgment could merit some qualifications. In some focalized sectors, the imposition of the neoliberal model did affect some segments of the entrepreneurial class, especially those linked to manufacturing or the domestic market. It also affected an undetermined number of small- and medium-sized firms hurt by the sustained contraction of domestic demand, the indiscriminate opening to foreign goods, and the loss of all state protections. It soon became clear that the "neoliberal revolution" was most favorable to the large corporations related to the financial sector or foreign trade, as well as those who proved able to redirect their capital toward the export activities which eventually gave its stamp (clearly "extractivistic") to the economic structure with which Chile emerged from dictatorial rule. Even so, these "collateral costs" did not dampen entrepreneurial attachment to a regime they never ceased to see as their basic bulwark, or even more than that, the underwriter of a paradigm that raised capitalism to a higher phase of purity and zeal, in which "private initiative" took on unprecedented centrality. The conclusive defeat of the socialist enemy and the reshaping of the country along entrepreneurial lines were well worth some temporary or limited sacrifices.

One area in which those privileges acquired particular sharpness was that of labor relations, redefined by the dictatorship on terms most favorable to employers. As demonstrated in the chapters by Daniela Manzi, Rodrigo Araya, and Ángela Vergara with Peter Winn, union action was seriously hampered by repressive terror, and later, after 1979, by a new labor legislation that drastically undercut their capacity for negotiating work conditions with even a semblance of parity. The Labor Code devised by Minister José Piñera (current President Sebastián Piñera's brother), with the assistance of massive unemployment and the growing labor precariousness set in by the restructuring of the economy, fragmented and undermined the union movement, stripped the right to strike of most of its efficacy, and sought to delegitimize any intimation of worker militancy, stigmatizing it under the forbidden and dangerous label of "politization." In such conditions, it is not surprising that union membership sunk by the 1980s to a meager 10 percent of the labor force (from a peak of 37 percent in 1973), or that average wages, as shown by Sebastián Smart in his chapter on privatizations, fell by a real 8 percent between 1970 and 1989. The mix between an entrepreneurial stratum allowed to conduct labor relations practically at will, and an economic model that automatically undermined wages and employment, gave shape to a scenario that was optimal for business and private initiative. As Daniela Marzi Muñoz has said in this book, the 1979 Labor Code was not "just another reform" within the dictatorial program, but a strategic pillar both for the consolidation of market economics and for their prolongation beyond the chronological limits of that regime. Or as Ángela Vergara and Peter Winn put it much more crudely, it was proof that under the new rules of the economic game "the employers do what they please."

But the "dividends" collected by the business community as a result of Pinochet's policies were not restricted to the restoration of labor discipline, the extensive privatization of the economy, the shrinkage of the state, the enshrinement of the "laws" of the market, or the sacralization of all those changes in its 1980 Constitution. The retreat of the state and the expansion of market relations to the totality of social interaction were also transferred to most (if not all) services that were previously seen as public goods, or rather fundamental social rights (which as such should be managed and guaranteed by the state), and which now became so many additional "commodities."

This happened in such socially sensitive areas as education, health, or pensions, all of them privatized by dictatorial fiat, and rapidly turned into some of the most profitable ventures of Chile's post-dictatorial period. Special mention merits in this context the retirement system established by the Pinochet government in 1980, which not only exempted employers from contributing to a fund designed to guarantee the survival of those who had completed their labor cycle (as had been the case before in Chile, and as still happens today in most countries of the world) but also endowed the private sector with a mass of capital forcibly extracted from the future pensioners (because in this context the "freedom" to manage one's savings is not respected, as everyone is legally compelled to contribute to private pension funds), and which has become, as a massive investment pool, one of the mainstays of the national economy. This is probably the one area in which the Pinochet legacy's pro-business bias is made most transparently clear, as the compulsory savings of the entire social body are handed over to powerful corporations, national and foreign, to feed undertakings over which the real owners of those funds (the future pensioners) have no control, and for which, on top of it all, they must pay "fees" to those who manage them with no risk to their patrimony. When even public goods and social savings are placed at the disposal of private capital, it is clear that the very concept of "society" tends to splinter into a welter of private decisions activated by the profit impulse, turning all collective creation and interaction into mere "commodities." There is probably a no better description of what a business paradise would look like.

THE LEGACY

It was precisely that paradise that the business community sought to prolong, at least in its essential traits, beyond the chronological limits of the Pinochet dictatorship. It became increasingly clear, as the 1980s wore on, that the most flagrantly repressive and authoritarian facets of the military government could not last forever, both because of the international disrepute they caused (with all its negative connotations for the enticement of foreign investment), and of the growing domestic tensions, ever more difficult to contain. What was required, consequently, was to negotiate a political transition that could "whitewash" the worst stigmas associated with the dictatorship, but preserving the economic-political design that was deemed (and this has not changed) non-negotiable. In this way, and sidelining a military "partner" who was now becoming somewhat awkward, business sought to step away from the "excesses" of the recent past (lowering their profile precisely as mere "excesses," and as part of a contentious past that should be left behind for the sake of "national reconciliation"), the better to defend a "legacy" that had it as its main beneficiary. It was that legacy, however, as Silvio Cuneo makes clear in his chapter in this book, that had impacted society at large, not just those who had been directly hit by political persecution. It was the most strategic gain obtained from military rule and for that very reason the most worthy of defense.

For that operation, the business community's main asset was precisely the power it had accumulated during the long dictatorial years, from which it was emerging in a position that had been unimaginable in the dire (for them) days of the Popular Unity. It was no less than a prominent right-wing politician, Andrés Allamand, who coined in the early 1990s a metaphor ("factual powers") that proved most appropriate to portray this "recharged" entrepreneurial caste that annoyed post-dictatorial authorities and held hostage the newly recovered democracy. As stated in the chapter by Naomi Roht-Arriaza, "the new administrations were wary to antagonize the business community, asking uncomfortable questions about their role in supporting dictatorial repression, or demanding reparations and reforms that could scare off foreign investment." In effect, liberated of the "embarrassment" of doing business with a regime stained by the violation of fundamental human rights, the "Chilean model" now received the blessing of the main global economic actors (including the governments of the leading capitalist powers), touching off a growth cycle that at a certain moment was even dubbed "miraculous," and that turned into yet another entrepreneurial argument in its defense. The current bonanza, however ill-distributed it may have been, was for them reason enough to engage in an exercise of amnesia regarding the recent past, most definitely functional for the perpetuation of the dictatorship's economic legacy.[7]

This is indeed what happened, both regarding the basic workings of the economy (primacy of the market and the private sector, economic withdrawal of the state, unlimited trade opening, a basically extractivist model), and the institutional trappings that rendered them operational, such as the tax system, the privatization of public goods, and the Labor Code. Every time the transitional administrations have tried to intervene these mainsprings of business prosperity, even if only very slightly and not touching the heart of the model, the reaction has been immediate and acerbic. The privatizations have not only not been turned back, but have been amplified (the case of mining resources), or extrapolated to other public goods, such as the management of highways and the access to water. Attempts at tax reform, meant to restore at least a fraction of the state's capacity to respond to social demands, have been resisted, protracted, and when finally implemented, openly sabotaged through "investment strikes" or bad publicity before international regulatory bodies, such as recently happened with the World Bank.[8] The same has happened with efforts at labor reforms aimed at restoring even minimal bargaining equilibrium between employers and workers: as a result of entrepreneurial and right-wing intransigence, union fragmentation and the obstruction of the right to strike subsist to this day as safeguards for a "healthy" business climate. Likewise, obstacles in the way of preventing for-profit ventures in education (nominally forbidden by law) are well-known, while even the slightest hints at modifying the existing pensions system in a more solidary direction, even though backed by a massive social movement, have triggered immediate alarm signals among the business community. Also, a recent attempt to legislate in favor of consumers' rights, challenged by Chile's Chamber of Commerce, was finally blocked by the Constitutional Tribunal,[9] another entity inherited from the dictatorship that has served once and again for right-wing parties and business associations to protect their interests, as has happened with labor reform and attempts at eradicating profit-making in education. On the opposite side, entrepreneurial transgressions, such as collusion for price-fixing, tax evasion, and blatant corruption of public officials for the attainment of favors or perks, have remained mostly unpunished. Apparently, capital is not forced to abide even by the most sacred market laws.

As a result of this correlation of "factual" forces, post-dictatorial Chile has experienced quantitatively remarkable economic growth (compared to other periods in the country's history), but one that is highly concentrated in the wealthiest sectors of society. Poverty rates, which at the end of the dictatorship encompassed 40 percent of the population, have been effectively reduced, but Chile remains, as proved by Javier Rodríguez's chapter, among the twenty most unequal countries in the world, and displays the worst income distribution among countries of high human development. Likewise, in a labor market wholly subjected to the employers' writ, work is both precarious and unstable, which leads to exhausting workdays and a generalized feeling of anxiety, reinforced by decreased social security (what exists is mostly financed by the workers themselves), with remaining state subsidies rather meager or focalized on the most impoverished populations. Post-dictatorial Chile may be more affluent, but it is also much more socially polarized, with very uncertain living conditions, and certainly not very altruistic.

However, the strongest legacy of the entrepreneurial dictatorship may not lie so much in the realm of the economy's workings, as in the psychological and widespread naturalization of the principles of social intercourse that prop up the model: untrammeled individualism, competition as the fundamental manner of human interplay, the commodification of all social relations, and money as the chief indicator of individual fulfillment and social standing. Beyond profit rates, beyond uncontested hegemony over the economy, beyond the power to impinge almost at will on political decisions, the key to the "business paradise" inherited from the Pinochet regime lies in the construction of a neoliberal "common sense" throughout the social body (what Gramsci would call "hegemony"), only sporadically challenged (though increasingly so) in specific areas, such as indigenous or gender rights, education, or the pensions system.[10] That said, what should be asked when trying to assess economic complicities with the dictatorship, and how they survive in present-day Chile (as this book does), is whether we really want, whether it is even minimally consistent with fundamental human rights, to go on living under the parameters listed above: individualism, commodification of life, and so on. It seems an appropriate question when the country has elected, for the second time in less than a decade, an administration conducted by some of the most prominent exemplars (and beneficiaries) of the entrepreneurial paradise. Is that really the country we want to live in? The "social explosion" of October 2019 may provide a dramatic preliminary answer.

NOTES

1. This title is inspired by Tomás Moulian's classic *Chile actual: anatomía de un mito* (Santiago, LOM, 1997). Thanks to the author for permission to borrow his idea.
2. Juan Carlos Gómez, *La frontera de la democracia: el derecho de propiedad en Chile, 1925-1973.* Santiago, LOM Ediciones, 2008.
3. See on this Verónica Valdivia, *Nacionales y gremialistas. El "parto" de la nueva derecha política chilena, 1964–1973.* Santiago, LOM ediciones, 2008.
4. Guillermo Campero, *Los gremios empresariales en el periodo 1970–1983: comportamiento sociopolítico y orientaciones ideológicas*, Santiago, ILET, 1984.
5. Verónica Valdivia, *El golpe después del golpe. Leigh vs. Pinochet, 1960–1980.* Santiago: LOM ediciones, 2003.
6. For an overview of this "revolution," see Eduardo Silva, *The State and Capital in Chile: Business Elites, Technocrats, and Market Economics.* Boulder, Westview Press, 1996.
7. On this, see Mario Garcés et al., *Memorias para un nuevo siglo. Chile, miradas a la segunda mitad del siglo XX.* Santiago, LOM ediciones, 2000.
8. In January 2018, the chief economist at the World Bank admitted that Chile's ranking in their competitiveness index had been "contaminated," to the detriment of Michelle Bachelet's government, by the political inclinations of that organization's staff.
9. Through a sentence of January 18, 2018, Chile's Constitutional Tribunal objected several points in a bill aimed at the revision of the Law for the Protection of Consumers' Rights, in the sense of giving more legal powers, including penalties and fines, to the fiscal department entrusted with the defense of those rights. As a result of this, consumers aggrieved by improper business practices have no other recourse than the regular judicial system, with all the delays and annoyances that implies.
10. This statement must certainly be revised in light of the massive social protests that erupted all over Chile in October 2019, at the very time this article was being translated. What lies ahead is still uncertain, but the hold of neoliberal "values" on social attitudes has been questioned.

Index

About the Editors and Contributors

EDITORS

Juan Pablo Bohoslavsky has a PhD in Law and has studied and conducted research at universities in Argentina, the United States and Europe. Between 2014 and 2020 he was Independent Expert on Debt and Human Rights at the United Nations; he worked for UNCTAD, ECLAC, the Argentine State, and private companies. He is the author of books and articles on finance and human rights.

Karinna Fernández holds a law degree from Valparaíso University, a Master's in International Public Law from the University of Chile, and an LLM in International Human Rights at the University of Essex. She has wide-ranging experience in litigating human rights cases at the national and international levels. She has served as an advisor on matters of international penal cooperation and extradition to Chile's Public Prosecutor's Office and as a legal advisor to the Interior Ministry. She has worked as a consultant with the Inter-American Commission on Human Rights (IACHR).

Sebastián Smart has a degree in Law from the Catholic University of Chile, a Master in Human Rights from the University College of London, and a PhD in sociology at the same university. Currently, he is the regional director for the Chilean Human Rights Institute. He has worked in various NGOs in Chile, Haiti, and the United Kingdom and has published several articles on human rights. He is also coeditor of the book *Chile and the Inter-American Human Rights System.*

CONTRIBUTORS

José Miguel Ahumada is an academic of the Department of Political Science and International Relations, Universidad Alberto Hurtado, PhD in Development Studies, University of Cambridge, MSc in Development Studies, London School of Economics, Master in International Economics and Development, Complutense University of Madrid, Political Scientist, Diego Portales University. He is the author of *The Political Economy of Peripheral Development: Chile in the Global Economy* (2018).

Rodrigo Araya Gómez has a PhD in History from the Autonomous University of Barcelona. He works as a full professor at the School of History of the University Academy of Christian Humanism. He is the author of articles on recent history of Chile and the books *Movimiento sindical en dictadura. Fuentes para una historia del sindicalismo en Chile* and *Organizaciones sindicales en Chile. De la resistencia a la política de los acuerdos 1983–1994.*

José Aylwin is a lawyer, Master in Law at the University of British Columbia, Canada. He is coordinator of Globalization and Human Rights Program of the Observatorio Ciudadano, a human rights promotion entity based in Temuco, Chile. His work deals with human rights, indigenous peoples, the environment, citizenship, among others. He is a professor of Indigenous Rights at the Universidad Austral de Chile, Valdivia. He is also a former member of the board of the National Institute of Human Rights.

Laura Bernal-Bermúdez is an assistant professor at the Faculty of Law of Pontificia Universidad Javeriana in Bogotá, Colombia, and affiliated researcher and research consultant at the Latin American Centre of the University of Oxford, UK.

Francisco Bustos Bustos is a lawyer, Bachelor of Law and Social Sciences, University of Chile, and holds a Master's Degree in Law, from the same University. He integrates the Legal Team of Agrupación de Familiares de Ejecutados Políticos and the Desclasificación Popular collective. Lawyer of the Nelson Caucoto Law Firm. Associate Collaborator of the Observatory of Transitional Justice of the Diego Portales University, and serves as professor (teacher aide) of Legal Clinic at the Faculty of Law, University of Chile, and professor of Criminal Law at Andrés Bello National University".

Silvio Cuneo Nash has a PhD degree in Law from the Universitat Pompeu Fabra and the Università degli Studi di Trento. He has been a Public Criminal Defender in Chile and is currently a professor of Criminal Law at the

Universidad Central de Chile. He has published several articles and books on criminal legal matters, criminal policy, and film. He is the author of the books *Cine y Derecho penal* (2019), *Cárceles y Pobreza. Distorsiones del populismo penal* (2018), *El encarcelamiento masivo* (2017), *La cárcel Moderna. Una crítica necesaria* (2017), and *Las influencias de Cesare Zavattini en el cine chileno* (2010).

Elvira Domínguez-Redondo (LLB, Dip. Business Management, MPhil, PhD) is an associate professor of International Law at Middlesex University, London (UK). She has held visiting positions at Columbia University (United States) and University Alcalá de Henares (Spain). In the past, Dr. Domínguez-Redondo held different academic positions, at the Transitional Justice Institute (University of Ulster, UK); the Irish Centre for Human Rights (NUI, Ireland); the University of Alcalá de Henares (Spain); and University of Carlos III de Madrid (Spain). She has worked as a consultant with the Special Rapporteur on Torture at the Office of the High Commissioner for Human Rights (Switzerland). She is the author of a wide range of publications on international law and human rights topics, including three monographs: *In Defense of Politicization of Human Rights*, *Minority Rights in Asia* (coauthored with J. Castellino) and *Procedimientos Especiales de la Comisión de Derechos Humanos*.

Magdalena Garcés Fuentes has a degree in Legal and Social Sciences from the University of Chile and a PhD from the University of Salamanca. She is a lawyer for former political prisoners and relatives of missing and executed victims during the military dictatorship. Together with other lawyers, she has presented cases to the Inter-American Human Rights System. She also collaborates with Londres 38, memory space.

Marcos González Hernando has a PhD in sociology at the University of Cambridge, where he is an affiliated researcher. His work focuses on the sociology of intellectuals and knowledge, particularly around the potential role of think tanks and public policy experts during economic and political crises. He is currently a researcher at TASC (Ireland), where he carries out a research project on the discourse on inequality of economic elites in several European countries.

Nancy Guzmán is a journalist and has a Diploma in History. She wrote reports and interviews for the no longer existing newspaper *La Nación*. She has published seven books: *Un grito desde el silencio* (1988); *Romo, confesiones de un torturador*, Prize Planeta on Investigative Journalism 2000; I*Ingrid Olderock, la mujer de los perros* (2014); *Los Agustines. El clan*

Edwards y la conspiración permanente (2015); *El Fanta, historia de una traición* (2016). She has coauthored *Historia para no olvidar* (2004) and *Los crímenes que estremecieron a Chile* (2013).

Daniela Marzi Muñoz is a professor at the Department of Labor Law of the University of Valparaíso, Chile. She completed her undergraduate studies at the same house of studies, obtained her Master's Degree in Labor Law from the University of Bologna, Italy, and a PhD in Law from the Autonomous University of Madrid. She is an Italian translator and author of several articles on Labor Law. She is currently the Director of the Equality and Diversity Unit of the University of Valparaíso.

Juan E. Méndez is the professor of Human Rights Law in Residence, commissioner, International Commission of Jurists, Former UN Special Rapporteur on Torture (2010–2016); he was a member of the Inter-American Commission on Human Rights of the Organization of American States (2000–2003), and served as its president in 2002, Washington College of Law, American University.

Carla Moscoso is a sociologist and master in political communication from the University of Chile. MPhil in Modern Societies and Global Transformations at the University of Cambridge, where she is currently pursuing a PhD in sociology. Her academic specialization has led her to study the social impact of the media and its effects on democracy and citizenship in developing countries, with a special focus on Latin America.

Cristián Olmos Herrera is an architect and urban designer with a PhD in Development Planning and MSc in Building & Urban Design in Development from The Bartlett Development Planning Unit, University College London. His research has focused on hydrosocial territories and indigenous communities in the context of territorial fragmentation due to mining expansion in northern Chile. Through the use of visual methods, Cristian has examined and visualised narratives of everyday water practices to reveal spatial networks of people, institutions, and technology and to make visible the political economy of water and issues of unequal access. Currently, Cristian is a Post Doc researcher at the University of Amsterdam on the T2SGS project: Transformations to Groundwater Sustainability, where he is comparing grassroots initiatives of groundwater governance, focusing on local practices of knowing, accessing and sharing water.

Leigh A. Payne is a professor of sociology and Latin American Studies, University of Oxford, UK. She is the recipient of British Academy, ESRC,

AHRC, NSF, Open Society, and other awards, and the author of books, articles, and book chapters on transitional justice.

Gabriel Pereira is a professor of human rights at the University of Tucuman, Argentina; and Researcher at the Consejo Nacional de Investigaciones Científicas y Técnicas, Argentina, and affiliated researcher at the Latin American Centre of the University of Oxford, UK.

Julio Pinto Vallejos, PhD in History from Yale University (1991) and full professor of the Department of History of the University of Santiago de Chile. His lines of research include the sociopolitical history of the popular sectors in Chile during the nineteenth century and the transition to the twentieth century, and the social construction of the state in the countries of South America. He has published *Contemporary History of Chile* in five volumes, coauthored with Gabriel Salazar (1999–2002), and several monographic studies on the saltpeter cycle in Chile, the revolutionary left in dictatorship, and the social construction of the state in Chile, Argentina, and Peru.

Naomi Roht-Arriaza is a distinguished professor at Hastings College of Law. She is the author of *The Pinochet Effect: Transnational Justice in the Age of Human Rights* (2005) and *Impunity and Human Rights in International Law and Practice* (1995), and coeditor of *Transitional Justice in the Twenty-First Century: Beyond Truth versus Justice*. She is a coauthor of *The International Legal System: Cases and Materials* (7th Ed.) with Mary Ellen O'Connell, Dick Scott, and Daniel Bradlow (2015). She continues to write on accountability, both state and corporate, for human rights violations as well as on other human rights, international criminal law, and global environmental issues. In 2011, she was a Democracy Fellow at the U.S. Agency for International Development, and in 2012 she was a Senior Fulbright Scholar in Botswana.

Javier Rodríguez Weber is PhD in Economic History from the Universidad de la Republica and professor of the Program of Economic and Social History based in the said Institution. He is the author of the book *Development and Inequality in Chile (1850–2009). History of Its Political Economy* (Santiago: DIBAM, 2017; LOM, 2018). His work has been awarded by the economic history associations of Spain and Chile.

Mariana Rulli is a political scientist (UBA), with a PhD in Social Sciences from FLACSO, a Master's Degree in Social Policies from the Latin American Faculty of Social Sciences (FLACSO) and a Master's Degree in Gender and Family Diversity from the University of Barcelona. She has worked as a teacher at the UBA and is currently a professor and researcher in the area of political science, CIEDIS-National University of Río Negro (UNRN). Her main research topics are gender, social security, business, and human rights on which he has made numerous publications in Latin America and Europe.

Pietro Sferrazza Taibi holds a PhD in Advanced Studies in Human Rights, Carlos III University of Madrid, and a Master's Degree in Advanced Studies in Human Rights, from the same University. He is a lawyer from the University of Valparaíso. He currently serves as professor of Public International Law and Constitutional Law of the Universidad Andrés Bello and professor of Public International Law of the University of Valparaíso. His lines of research are related to international human rights law and transitional justice.

Magdalena Sepúlveda Carmona is the executive director of the Global Initiative for Economic, Social, and Cultural Rights. She is also a member of the Independent Commission for the Reform of International Corporate Taxation (ICRICT). From 2008 to 2014, she was the United Nations Special Rapporteur on Extreme Poverty and Human Rights. Magdalena holds a PhD in International Law from Utrecht University in the Netherlands, an LLM in human rights law from the University of Essex in the United Kingdom.

Andrés Solimano holds a PhD in Economics from the Massachusetts Institute of Technology (MIT), Economist, and Master in Economics from the Catholic University of Chile. He is the founder and president of the International Center for Globalization and Development (CIGLOB). He has been Director of World Bank countries, executive director of the Inter-American Development Bank, regional advisor of ECLAC, and director of FLACSO-Chile. He is a regular guest on economic issues on TV, radio, and national and international media.

Tomás Undurraga is a professor in the Department of Sociology at Alberto Hurtado University and an honorary member of the Science and Technology Studies Department, University College London. Doctor in Sociology from the University of Cambridge, his research intersects economic sociology, sociology of culture, and the role of the media in the public sphere. He is the author of *Divergences: Paths of neoliberalism in Argentina and Chile* (2014) and several articles in journals such as *Cultural Sociology*, *The Sociological Review*, *Journalism Studies*, and *Cultural Economy*.

Ángela Vergara is a professor in the History Department of California State University Los Angeles. She completed her undergraduate studies at the Catholic University of Chile in Santiago (1994), and obtained her PhD from the University of California, San Diego (2002). She is the author of *Copper Workers, International Business, and Domestic Politics in Cold War Chile* (2008) and coeditor of *Company Towns in the Americas* (2011) and the special issue of *Radical History Review The Other September 11th-Chile, 1973* (2016).

José Francisco Vergara-Perucich is an architect at Universidad Central de Chile, Master in Architecture by Pontificia Universidad Católica de Chile, Master in Sciences in Building and Urban Design in Development by The Bartlett Development Planning Unit and Doctor in Planning Development by University College London, chief researcher of *FONDECYT 11180569: Towards a Theory of Informal Urbanisms*, and current director of Centro Producción del Espacio at Universidad de Las Américas, Santiago de Chile.

Peter Winn is a professor of Latin American history at Tufts University in the USA and editor of the *International Labor and Working Class History* (ILWCH). He is the author of the book *Tejedores de la Revolución. Los trabajadores de Yarur y la vía chilena al socialismo* (2004), and coauthor and editor of the book *Victims of the Chilean Miracle: Workers and Neoliberalism in the Pinochet Era, 1973–2002* (2004).

www.ingramcontent.com/pod-product-compliance
Ingram Content Group UK Ltd.
Pitfield, Milton Keynes, MK11 3LW, UK
UKHW021032041026
15470UKWH00014B/1413

9 781793 616494